MW00630419

Teachings of the Rebbe on Chinuch

Project of Anash Chinuch

First Edition *Iyar* 5777
Second Edition *Tammuz* 5777

Comments and corrections can be forwarded to:
info@anashchinuch.com

ISBN: 978-0-692-77724-4

Cover Design by Shoshana Bendelman

Photo on cover by Algeimer Journal/Lubavitch Archives

Visit our website www.AnashChinuch.com for a collection of chinuch resources.

OFFICE OF EDUCATION משרד החנוך

A Division of

Merkos L'Inyonei Chinuch

CENTRAL ORGANIZATION FOR JEWISH EDUCATION

784 EASTERN PARKWAY, BROOKLYN, NEW YORK 11213,SUITE 304 • P: 718-774-4000•
www.chinuchoffice.org

Rabbi Nochem Kaplan, Director
rabbi@chinuchoffice.org

What would the Rebbe advise? The Rebbes writings, his maamarim-Chassidic discourses, his sichos-public talks and his letters fill more than 100 volumes; how is one to find his teachings on a particular issue? Of course there are indices but even they are volumes and too many people find it inhibiting to even begin a search. ***Teachings of The Rebbe on Chinuch*** gathers a great many of the Rebbe's ideas and advice on chinuch-education into one eminently readable volume and in the process it gifts to thousands of his followers, a wealth of his instruction and guidance on this subject in the language they best understand.

Teachings of The Rebbe on Chinuch is a long overdue work. It is the product of a tremendous amount of work and the coming to fruition of Mrs. Keren Gordon's dream. It is thoughtfully organized, user friendly, with the readers' needs given uppermost consideration so that they can easily find what they are looking for. Everyone who leafs through these pages owes her a debt of gratitude.

The Rebbe's teachings and advice are at the same time broad and general in nature, while they may practically be dealing with a very specific issue. He delves into the very core of an idea while discussing something apparently tangential. That is the nature of Torah in general and the Rebbe's approach in particular; his words cannot be read superficially if one is to benefit from their profundity.

It is therefore to the credit of the translators and editors that they labored hard to be true to the original words of the Rebbe. They did not read their own interpretation into his words, even to make it easier for the reader to understand. The product of this labor of love is not a volume about the Rebbe's views on chinuch issues, it is a volume <u>of his views</u> on chinuch. I pray that readers will study and learn from it appropriately.

A word of caution might be in order. The Rebbe's words need to be studied very carefully before forming any kind of opinion about his view on any particular chinuch theme.

The Rebbe said on many occasions that one should not literally apply his words, advice and responses, to every situation. It is not always appropriate to extrapolate a response to a given dilemma from something the Rebbe said in a similar situation. People and places are different, circumstances vary and what the Rebbe advised an individual or group in one place may not necessarily apply to different people in another place.

The Alter Rebbe writes in his preface to his magnum opus, the Tanya, (loosely translated) "if one finds himself unable to find the advice he seeks from the words in this volume, he should discuss his issue with the elders within his community who will be able to help him understand how to apply the words of Tanya to his own dilemma." I believe that is the approach readers of this work must use as they look for answers to issues they face in their own lives.

On the eve of 3 Tammuz 5776

Nochem Kaplan

Departments: ASSOCIATION OF CHABAD PROFESSIONAL EDUCATIONAL LEADERS • NATIONAL ACCREDITATION BOARD • MERKOS INTERNATIONAL BOARD OF LICENSE * DEPARTMENT OF SCHOOL SERVICES * EDUCATIONAL PUBLICATIONS DEPT * WWW.CHINUCHWORKS.COM

Table of Contents

Acknowledgments

First and foremost, we are grateful to our dear Rebbe, whose teachings continue to provide fresh and relevant guidance, tools, and inspiration in every aspect of life. In particular, the teachings presented here on *chinuch* are nothing short of life-changing. They infuse infinite meaning and purpose into life as a parent and educator. The Rebbe placed a revolutionary and awe-inspiring emphasis on *chinuch*, particularly of the smallest children, which provides for them spiritually from the first moments of life.

This project would not have been possible without the countless hours Shoshana Bendelman wholeheartedly devoted. She has been my partner in this *shlichus* and has contributed more than I can list in this small space.

Rabbi Yehoishophot Oliver, Rabbi Levi Goldstein, Mrs. Beila Goldstein and Rabbi Yosaif Yarmush provided vital tutelage and guidance. Rabbis Oliver and Yarmush helped me understand the Rebbe's words when I was stuck; Rabbi Goldstein helped me find sources, and Mrs. Goldstein has served as our mashpiah.

Rabbis Yehoishophot Oliver, Yaakov Goldstein, and Yakov Yosef Raskin for reviewing the accuracy of the translations and developing the text. Rabbi Oliver did the vast majority of reviewing the text in comparison with the source material, as well as translating many excerpts himself.

Mrs. Rivkah Chaya Gordon, Mrs. Rus Devorah Wallen, Mrs. Devorah Shor for proofreading, Mrs. Chana Shloush for preliminary editing, and Ms. Esther Rochel Elkaim for editing the final draft.

Rabbi S.B. Schapiro for allowing us to republish sources from *Nissan Mindel Publications, The Letter and the Spirit - Letters by the Lubavitcher Rebbe,* as well as Rabbi Shimon Hellinger, director of *Merkaz Anash,* and Rabbi Avrohom Bergstein, compiler of *The Rebbe's Holy Care* for sharing many translated sources with us.

Chabad.org for allowing us to use their glossary terms, which comprise the majority of our glossary.

Mrs. Gani Goodman for technical help with printing.

Finally, all those who took part in our campaign raising money for this sefer to be prepared for publication.

May the great merit of disseminating these teachings draw down an abundance of material and spiritual blessings to you all.

Mrs. Keren Gordon
Director of Anash Chinuch

Editors' Foreword

The well-known saying of our Sages, "There are three partners in making man: his father, his mother, and *Hakadosh Baruch Hu,*" is worthy of closer study. The partnership is divided so that the spiritual matters of the child (his *chinuch*) are the responsibility of the father and mother. Hashem invested with parents His most precious deposit – a חלק אלוקה ממעל ממש (A [child whose *neshamah* is a] G-dly portion from above, literally!) – with the hope and expectation that they will care for the *neshamah* of the child in such a way that it will be recognizable that we are, to Him, a "kingdom of priests and a holy nation." The physical and material matters of the child, including feeding him, providing his *parnassah*, caring for his health and the like, are the responsibility of *Hakadosh Baruch Hu*. (*Hisvaaduyos* 5743, vol. 3, p. 1482)

As parents and educators we must always remember that every child is a child of *Hakadosh Baruch Hu* (our Father in Heaven). We are only the *shluchim* of *Hakadosh Baruch Hu*, having been given the great merit and privilege to give birth to the child and to raise and educate him.

In this *sefer* we wish to provide guidance to parents and educators as to how to nurture the *neshamos* of our precious *kinderlach* in the best way possible by making the beautiful teachings of the Rebbe on *chinuch* available and accessible in English. The sources have been translated with special care in order to stay as true to the Rebbe's *lashon* as possible, so that one can get a feel for the Rebbe's intention without needing to worry that the meaning has been lost or altered in the translation.

Sources in this sefer in the Courier font are sources which were originally in English.

The importance of gathering and translating such material is evident from the Rebbe's words in a letter: "I was pleased by the suggestion that material that is spread out in *sichos* on the topic of *chinuch* will be gathered. If only this would be approached with the fitting enthusiasm. It is understood that it needs to be in the spoken language... though it should be kept as close to the original as possible.

The Rebbe has given us *chinuch* directives appropriate for the unique characteristics, challenges and mission of our generation, the generation that will usher in the *geulah*. As we stand at the threshold of the times of *Moshiach* it is necessary to take steps toward living a more *geulahdik* life. The Rebbe has provided us with clear and, most importantly, practical and achievable instructions for immersing ourselves in *kedusha* and ridding our lives of *tumah*, in preparation for a time when Hashem will remove all of the *tumah* from the world. By learning and living with the Rebbe's *chinuch hora'os* we can ready ourselves, our families, and the world at large for a life of *Moshiach*.

We hope that this *sefer* will deepen the bonds of parents with their children, teachers with their students, and *klal Yisrael* with *Hakadosh Baruch Hu* and with our *Nasi*, the Rebbe.

Through providing the children of this generation with the proper *chinuch*, we will establish *Tzivos Hashem* that will leave this *galus* through our righteous redeemer. May we merit to go speedily before *Melech HaMoshiach* and say, "*Re'u Gidulim Shegidalti.*" – "Look at what I have raised!"

CHAPTER 1

Introduction

"You are children to the Lord your G-d"

Devarim, 14:1

The Mitzvah of Chinuch

Raising the child of *Hakadosh Baruch Hu*

Every[1] child is a child of *Hakadosh Baruch Hu* (our Father in Heaven). The physical father and mother are only the *shluchim* of *Hakadosh Baruch Hu* who were given the merit to give birth to the child, raise, and educate him.

Chinuch is more than a preparation

The[2] Torah learning of children is not only a preparation for their fulfillment of Torah and *mitzvos* when they get older; it is also inherently important. In certain matters, the fulfillment of Torah and *mitzvos* of children is higher than the fulfillment of Torah and *mitzvos* of adults, as we find[3] some *midrashei Chazal* that explain the great advantage of הבל תינוקות של בית רבן ("learning [literally: breath] of little children") [4].

A life of perfection religiously, morally, and ethically

The[5] purpose of Chinuch (Jewish education) is to bring up the Jewish child, boy or girl, to a life of the utmost possible degree of perfection, religiously as well as morally and ethically.

Chinuch begins from the most tender age

The[6] *mitzvah* of *chinuch* – guiding and accustoming [a child] to perform *mitzvos* – begins at the most tender age of a *Yid's* life. The greatness of *chinuch* is that not only is it a preparation for the age [at which one becomes obligated in] *mitzvos, bar mitzvah* or *bas mitzvah*; rather, it lays the foundation for one's entire life. As the wisest person who ever lived [King Shlomo] stated, "Educate

---

1 *Hisvaaduyos* 5747, vol. 2, p. 650.
2 *Hisvaaduyos* 5748, vol. 4, p. 229.
3 E.g., *Shabbos* 119b.
4 *Shabbos* 119b; *Hilchos Talmud Torah Admur HaZakein* 1:10.
5 *Letters from the Rebbe*, vol. 2, p. 44.
6 *Likkutei Sichos*, vol. 11, p. 285.

the lad according to his way, and even when he ages he will not depart from it."[7] It is understood that although the *pasuk* refers to a "lad," it applies to girls as well, as is true regarding various *pesukim* in Torah.

The age of *chinuch*

["The[8] age of *chinuch*"] refers to the age of six.[9] However, more specifically, the age of *chinuch* for positive *mitzvos* depends on the child's ability to grasp the information and his level of knowledge in each particular area.[10]

Chinuch is "above the realm of a *mitzvah*"

In[11] the matter of *chinuch,* we find something shocking: The ability to fulfill *mitzvos* when a *Yid* becomes obligated to do so depends on the knowledge and *chinuch* he received as a child. Yet the Torah does not contain an explicit command to educate one's sons and daughters in *mitzvos.* How is this possible?

[The answer:] The child's fulfillment of Torah and *mitzvos* is "above" the realm of a *mitzvah.* The main purpose of *chinuch* is to accustom Jewish children to have *kabbalas ol* – to accept that they should fulfill Hashem's commands. This is comparable to the principle that *kabbalas ol* is not counted as one of the 613 *mitzvos*, yet it is clear that until a person accepts upon himself the yoke of the King, the commands of the King have no bearing upon him.

Every effort is worthwhile

Regarding[12] *chinuch* during childhood and adolescence, even a small change for the good, or the opposite *chas ve'shalom,* can cause the greatest and most significant results throughout the lifetime of the student. From this it follows that every single effort to improve the situation is worthwhile.

---

7 *Mishlei,* 22:6.

8 *Hisvaaduyos* 5751, vol. 1, p. 315, fn. 66.

9 *Kesubos,* 50a.

10 *Alter Rebbe's Shulchan Aruch, Orach Chaim* 343:3.

11 *Hisvaaduyos* 5748, vol. 4, p. 229.

12 *Igros Kodesh*, vol. 14, p. 451.

Every effort is justified

When[13] the tree is young, especially when it is still in the stage of a seedling, every good care given to it in that early stage, however insignificant it may seem, is an investment which in due course amplifies itself many times, and the full effects become evident in the mature, fruit-bearing tree.

Likewise is the minute attention given to a child, even where the benefit for the moment appears to be quite small, so much so that one may wonder if it is worth the effort. For even a "small" benefit may in time turn out to be of a lasting quality and extraordinary proportions, reaching into the daily conduct according to the Torah and Mitzvoth; and as our Sages of blessed memory expressed it: "What are real fruits?—the Mitzvoth." Therefore every effort is justified in the field of *Chinuch*, for what is at stake is the whole future of the student and his life-long benefit.

Chinuch should be carried out with enthusiasm

As[14] has often been mentioned before, every activity in *Chinuch* should be carried out with particular enthusiasm, inasmuch as it is like planting a seed, or taking care of a seedling, where every additional effort, however small, will eventually be translated into extraordinary benefits when the said seed or seedling becomes a mature fruit-bearing tree. The same is true of the care taken to shield the seed or seedling from harmful effects.

By the same token, it will be realized that, although Mitzvos and good deeds should be done without thought for reward, nevertheless the reward for every activity in *Chinuch* is greater than the reward for any other Mitzvah, inasmuch as the effects are lasting and cumulative and reproduced from generation to generation.

---

13 Letter of the Rebbe from the 4th of Shevat 5725, reprinted with permission from chabad.org.

14 *Letters from the Rebbe*, vol. 2, p. 88.

Accustoming a child to have *kabbalas ol*

This[15] is the main purpose of *chinuch:* to accustom Jewish children to obey the command of *Hakadosh Baruch Hu* in His Torah. This accomplishes that the children express in a revealed fashion the *kabbalas ol malchus Shamayim* that every Jew possesses innately.

The foundation of *chinuch*: *Yiras* Hashem and *ahavas* Hashem

... [*Chinuch*[16] begins with] the general principle of ראשית חכמה יראת ה׳ ("The beginning of wisdom is fear of Hashem"),[17] which includes *ahavas Hashem.* These are the foundations for the fulfillment of all areas of Torah and *mitzvos.* As is written at length elsewhere, although the *mitzvah* of *chinuch* does not have the status of an obligation, nor is it a *mitzvah* from the [written] Torah, it is nevertheless of the utmost necessity according to Torah, like a הכשר מצוה (preparation for a *mitzvah*), which is simple to understand and obvious.

Accustoming a child to *kedusha*

The[18] true purpose of *chinuch* is not only for the child to learn. The purpose of *chinuch* is to accustom the child to *kedusha*, which connects his soul with *kedusha* and with *Hakadosh Baruch Hu.*

Chinuch has no limits

Every[19] *mitzvah* has a limitation, even donning *tefillin.* In contrast, the influence of *chinuch* has no limitations: It remains in full force for that child, his family, and his grandchildren for all generations.

---

15 *Hisvaaduyos* 5748, vol. 4, p. 229.

16 *Hisvaaduyos* 5749, vol. 3, p. 75.

17 *Tehillim,* 111:10.

18 *Likkutei Sichos*, vol. 35, p. 12.

19 *Mikdash Melech,* Vol. 2, p. 427.

Changing one's habits

The[20] entire purpose of *chinuch* is to change the nature of one's habits. By nature, a child does whatever he feels like, with no inhibitions. As the *pasuk* puts it, יצר לב האדם רע מנעוריו ("the imagination of man's heart is evil from his youth")[21] [This attests to this fact regarding human nature.] Therefore one must educate him, in order to limit and change one's nature, until the mind rules over the heart. This also applies to the *chinuch* of adults: The objective is also to change one's nature and reach a higher level.

The salvation of the Jewish people

At[22] a time that Yaakov [the Jewish people] are in distress, one of the main [sources] of salvation for the entire Jewish nation lies in the *chinuch* of Jewish boys – and girls – in the spirit of Torah and *Yiddishkeit*, and the implanting of the hope of *geulah*, so that people do not despair, *chas ve'shalom*.

---

20 *Sefer HaSichos*, 5747, vol. 1, p. 74.

21 *Bereishis*, 8:21.

22 *Igros Kodesh*, vol. 1, p. 94.

CHAPTER 2

Before Birth

"For this child I prayed"

Shmuel, 1:27

Chinuch begins before birth

The parent's oath

The[23] Alter Rebbe begins the *Sefer HaTanya* by quoting the following dictum of our Sages: "They have him swear that he will be righteous and not be wicked[24]."

Here, the famous question is posed: Who is the one who swears? – At that point, the soul is in a state of being in which there is a candle shining over his head and he is being taught the whole Torah, etc. … such that the need for a warning not to be a *rasha* when the whole concept of *avodas* Hashem down here in a body, with all the difficulties involved, is something that has not yet come into existence!

My saintly father-in-law, the [previous] Rebbe, once explained the above dictum alludes to the fact that this vow is actually elicited (also) from the parents of each and every child, obligating them to assure that their child will be "righteous" and not "wicked." That is, the parents must conduct themselves in a manner such that they can be confident that their offspring will be "righteous."

True, a child ultimately grows up, gains independence, and is granted the freedom to choose between right and wrong. However, our Sages tell us, *Chanoch lan'ar al pi darko gam ki yazkin lo yasur mimenah* – "Teach the child in his unique manner, so that when he grows old he will not deviate from it." That is to say, the responsibility of setting the child on the righteous path is placed upon the parents, so that when the child eventually grows old, he will continue to live in this spirit.

Yet, in addition to the child's upbringing after its birth, there is also the influence that the parents have on the child before the birth through keeping *taharas hamishpachah* which ensures that the birth is in a state of purity. Similarly, the *Tanya* teaches that an integral component of the child's makeup, namely one's *levushim* – "garments" (i.e., the intrinsic nature of one's thought, speech, and deed) – are determined by the measure of sanctity practiced by the parents at the time of the child's conception.

---

23 *Sichah*, Kislev 19 5721, The Rebbe's Holy Care, Issue 3

24 *Niddah,* 30b.

This is true similarly concerning their general mode of conduct: A parent is responsible to assure that the *le'umas zeh* (impure influence) has absolutely no domination or influence upon their own private quarters. Indeed, herein lies the responsibility of raising children in a manner that ensures that the child will be "righteous" and not "wicked."

My saintly father-in-law, the [previous] Rebbe, once proclaimed, "*Kol hakodosh b'Yisrael*" – the responsibility of all that is holy and sanctified to the Jewish nation – "*nimserah l'hanoshim b'Yisael*" – the Torah has conveyed to the care of Jewish women.

Taharas hamishpachah and *kashrus*

The[25] truth is that the *chinuch* of a child starts even before the child emerges into the world. It begins during the nine months of pregnancy. Even before this, the preparations [for *chinuch*] consist of being careful about *taharas hamishpachah* (Family Purity), the *kashrus* of the food and beverages consumed by the father and mother – for the flesh and blood of the parents is created from their food and drink[26] – and in the kindling of the holy *Shabbos* and *Yom Tov* candles. All these matters were entrusted to Jewish women.

The[27] Torah tells us that a child's *chinuch* begins before he is born. This is completely dependent upon the mother, and it begins nine months before the child is born. If parents want a child to be both materially and spiritually healthy, they must ensure that all matters [of the home] are *tahor* (pure), kosher, and *kadosh* (holy), as Hashem wants. Not only should the child be "kosher," but also holy and pure in body and soul. The preparation for this begins nine months before, when the soul enters the body. ...

This matter was entirely entrusted to the wife. If she wants, she can fulfill this by observing *taharas hamishpachah* and *kashrus* in every minute detail. ... She must know that this will affect the child and its children for all generations.

---

25 *Hisvaaduyos* 5744, vol. 2, p. 1319.

26 Cf. *Likkutei Amarim, Tanya* ch. 8.

27 *Sichos Kodesh* 5729, vol. 1, pp. 161, 163.

Deficiency in *taharas hamishpachah* causes bad *middos* in children

All[28] the current challenges one might have when dealing with children are caused by the parents' prior conduct. When my father-in-law, the [Freirdiker] Rebbe was asked, "How is it possible that such things never occurred in past generations?" in reference to the problems that Jewish communists instigated for *Yidden*, he responded that in the past, people kept *taharas hamishpachah;* however, when it is not kept, this fact is recognizable in the children.

In *Maseches Kallah*[29] it is written regarding a defiant person, that he was born to a woman who was not *tehorah*. When there is a deficiency in *taharah,* a son rises up against his father, a daughter against her mother, a daughter-in-law against her mother-in-law, etc.

...It seems that one can ask: The *chinuch* [or deficiency in *taharas hamishpachah*] already took place, and that was many years ago. What can be done now?

Regarding this, it is said that *teshuvah* is the *baal habayis* (has mastery) over the past. A person must also make positive resolutions for the future, with a determination that from now on the *chinuch* of his children will be as it is supposed to be. But this is only to prove that the regret is sincere, and then the *teshuvah* is accepted.

Even when the parent did not give the child a proper *chinuch,* once the parent does *teshuvah,* the child is aroused from Above to have thoughts of *teshuvah.* Even if there was a deficiency during the nine gestational months, the situation can still be corrected.

Taharas hamishpachah affects future generations

Surely[30] it is unnecessary to elaborate on the great importance of the matter of *taharas hamishpachah.* In addition to its being one of the primary *mitzvos* in our holy Torah, *taharas hamishpachah* and all matters related to it are one of the main pillars which, through, and in whose merit, *Yisrael* has the ability

---

28 *Sichos Kodesh* 5729, vol. 1, pp. 161-162.

29 *Cf. Kallah Rabasi* 1:16.

30 *Igros Kodesh*, vol. 6, p. 10.

to withstand all obstacles and the yoke of *galus*, to be healthy physically and spiritually. This is so particularly because fulfilling this *mitzvah* not only affects those fulfilling the *mitzvah* alone – the husband and wife – but rather, it affects their children and the children born to their children for all generations. When parents keep the laws of *taharas hamishpachah,* their children are kosher. If *chas ve'shalom* the parents are not careful in this area, this blemishes the souls and bodies of the children and their children's children and so forth.

This is not a private matter which affects only the parents and the children, but it affects all of *klal Yisrael*, as is explained in teachings of our Sages of blessed memory, that through *taharah* the *Shechinah* dwells on *Yisrael.*

Intentions during intimacy

As for what is written in the *Zohar* and in *Zohar Chadash* that the essential factor is that one conducts himself in a holy manner during marital relations...

This is because there is no *nefesh, ru'ach*, or *neshamah* that does not receive its [spiritual] garment as it stems from the essence of the father and mother. All the *mitzvos* that a person does are influenced by that garment, etc. Even regarding the *shefa* (flow of blessing) that a person is given from the Heavens, it all comes about through that garment.

If a person sanctifies himself, he will draw down a holy garment for the *neshamah* of his child.

(End of *Likkutei Amarim, Tanya*, ch. 2)

Conduct of pregnant woman affects fetus

The[31] conduct of a woman while pregnant influences the fetus. Therefore, the custom of righteous women is to be extra cautious and adopt more *hiddurim* in Torah and *mitzvos*, performing them (in a beautified manner), for the good

31 *Hisvaaduyos*, 5747, vol. 2, p. 37, fn. 6.

of the fetus.[32] Even before this, it is customary for women to be careful at the time of leaving the *mikvah* house.[33]

Making great efforts to see only that which is pure and holy

It[34] is customary for righteous women to take care to [avoid looking at impure things, looking only at creatures and objects which are *tahor* and *kadosh]*. This conscientiousness begins even before the child is born – during the time of pregnancy, as is the known custom of Jewish women that during the time of pregnancy they are very careful not to glance at things that are not *tahor*, and [to only look at] things that are *tahor* and holy.

The[35] following *halacha* appears in *Shulchan Aruch:* "After immersion in a *mikvah,* women should be careful ... that the first thing they encounter should not be an impure creature such as a dog or donkey ... If she encounters such things, a G-d-fearing woman will return and reimmerse herself." ... The reason for this is that seeing impure things has a negative impact on the fetus, while seeing holy things while leaving the *mikvah* has a positive impact on the fetus.

***Tznius* during pregnancy**

Even[36] the conduct of parents during the nine months before the child is born has a noticeable impact on the baby. It is related in the *Gemara:*[37] "Kimchis had seven sons, and each one served as *Kohen Gadol. Chachomim* asked her, 'What did you do to merit this?' She responded, 'The walls of my home never saw my hair.'"

That is to say, Kimchis conducted herself with the ultimate *tznius* – to such an extent that even when she was in her home alone, when no one was with her, she did not expose her hair even to the walls of her home. [In this way,] her influence on her sons was so far-reaching that through it they all merited to be *Kohanim Gedolim.* This means that the way she conducted herself

32 Cf. sources cited in *Otzar Habris, Yerushalayim* 5746, sec. 4.

33 Cf. *Shulchan Aruch, Yoreh Dei'ah,* 188 end, *Remo.*

34 *Hisvaaduyos* 5750, vol. 3, p. 180.

35 *Hisvaaduyos* 5744, vol. 1, p. 487.

36 *Hisvaaduyos* 5742, vol. 4, pp. 2191-2192.

37 *Yoma,* 47a.

had an influence many years later, when her sons were beyond *bar mitzvah* age – twenty years old – at the point when they were fit to assume the position of *Kohen Gadol.* Her conduct also impacted their children and grandchildren, since the position of *Kohen Gadol* is passed down from father to son.

Since this information is transmitted to us by the Oral Torah, it is understood that this story is not merely discussing a past event... Rather, it is a teaching and "instruction for life" for every Jewish woman and girl. She should know how important it is to be careful in *tznius*, even when no one is home, and so on. The reason is that "habits become one's nature." If she is not careful with *tznius* when she is at home alone, she may also forget to be careful when someone else is at home. Clearly, *tzniusdik* conduct at the highest level has an influence on sons and grandsons.

Not to publicize pregnancy

There[38] is a known directive from my father-in-law, the Rebbe, that until she enters the fifth month of pregnancy, she should not publicize it.

Telling people one is very close to is not considered publicizing

She[39] surely knows the directive of my father-in-law, the Rebbe, that "until she enters the fifth month [of pregnancy], she should not publicize it." It is self-understood that this is in regard to publicizing. However, telling people one is very close to, and not in a public fashion [is permissible].

Immersing during the ninth month

Regarding[40] his question concerning the custom of his wife's family that after entering the ninth month [of pregnancy], the woman immerses in a *mikvah*: Although I have not heard of this being done amongst *Chabad chassidim*, on the other hand, since this is the custom of his wife's family, it is understood that there is no need to prevent her from following this custom; of course, [she should do so] with the doctor's permission.

---

38 *Likkutei Sichos*, vol. 12, p. 178.

39 *Likkutei Sichos*, ibid.

40 *Likkutei Sichos*, ibid.

Checking *mezuzos*

They[41] should check all the *mezuzos* in their home and replace any that are not kosher with kosher ones.

Additional *tzedakah* to the *Rabbi Meir Baal Ha'nes* Fund, 18 pennies

She[42] should increase the amount of *tzedakah* she has given until now before candle lighting to the fund of *Rabbi Meir Baal Ha'nes,* and she should give an additional 18 pennies each time.

Adding in *tzedakah*

[The[43] pregnant woman should] donate a few coins to *tzedakah* each weekday morning, in addition to what she surely customarily gives before lighting *Shabbos* and *Yom Tov* candles.

Tehillim of the day

Her[44] husband, the *Rav,* should strengthen himself in keeping the *shiur* of *Tehillim* each day (as it is divided into the days of the month), at the very least until after she gives birth, at a good and auspicious hour.

Chapter 20 before bedtime *Shema*

Without[45] making an oath to do so, every night before *kriyas Shema,* [the husband of the pregnant woman] should recite [*kapitel* 20 of *Tehillim*] למנצח יענך. Once he has completed the entire *kapitel*, he should repeat the *pasuk* למנצח יענך and have in mind while he is reciting it that Hashem should consider it as if he had contemplated all the *kavanos* that are appropriate at that time.

---

41 *Igros Kodesh,* vol. 6, p. 105.

42 *Igros Kodesh,1* vol. 5, p. 327. Cf. ibid.

43 *Igros Kodesh,* vol. 7, p. 303.

44 *Igros Kodesh,* vol. 6, p. 105.

45 *Igros Kodesh,* vol. 4, p. 454.

Opening the *aron kodesh* when the Torah is read

If[46] it is possible to do so without being conspicuous, he should make an effort to open the *aron* [*kodesh*] during days that the Torah is read, until after the birth, [may it be in a] good and auspicious time[47].

Childbirth

Childbirth – *Shir Hamaalos*

A[48] custom of the Jewish people that has been practiced since days of old, and מנהג ישראל תורה היא ("Jewish customs have the status of Torah"),[49] is to hang up sheets of paper with divine names and *pesukim*, such as *Shir Hamaalos* and the like in the home of the woman giving birth as a *segulah* for the protection of the mother and baby. This helps for the birth itself, that it should be easy and without complications, and also for the days following the birth. The practice also elicits blessings for a good and long life.

Furthermore, this is vital for the newborn baby, so that as soon as he emerges into the air of the world, he will be surrounded with matters of *kedusha*. It is known that things that even a one-day-old baby sees and hears have an impact even when he grows older. This fact has been revealed in recent generations to scientific researchers as well, and even with regard to the period of pregnancy. Therefore, when a child is surrounded with matters of *kedusha*, this adds *bracha* and *hatzlacha* so that the parents will merit to raise the child to "Torah, *chuppah*, and *ma'asim tovim*."

---

46 *Igros Kodesh*, vol. 7, p. 108.

47 This directive of the Rebbe has a few stipulations:

1. It is a private directive in a private letter to an individual, and is not a directive for the public. The Rebbe erased it from the *Koveitz Minhagim* of pregnancy.
2. This custom is for the 9th month of pregnancy.
3. It is to be done inconspicuously.

48 *Hisvaaduyos*, 5747, vol. 2, pp. 37-39.

49 *Menachos* 20b, *Tosafos*, s.v. *nifsal*. *Maharil*, cited in *Rema* on *Yoreh Dei'ah*, 376:4. See *Likkutei Sichos*, vol. 22, p. 56.

It is important to bring this matter to the attention of the Jewish people, since it is something that in our days requires correction, as will be explained.

In previous generations, women would give birth in their homes (with the help of a midwife), and all were careful with the abovementioned custom at the time of birth (beginning with preparations for the birth).

However, in our times, for medical reasons, women give birth in hospitals, and they are not careful to keep this *minhag* until the woman and baby come home from the hospital, which is already several days after birth. Yet this custom is, of course, even more necessary at the time of the birth and the time immediately following the birth, when the mother and infant are still in the hospital.

Therefore, it is a *mitzvah* to bring this custom to people's attention in each and every place where Jews live. Even when the woman and baby are in the hospital, they should make efforts to hang the *Shir Hamaalos* just as they are accustomed to doing at home, in the room of the birthing mother and of the newborn baby (or on the bed or the like), at the time of and following the birth, since this is when it is most important.

A *rav* should be consulted as to whether it needs a double covering, and the like.

As to receiving permission from the hospital: With the most minimal efforts, permission will surely be granted without opposition. ...

When the doctor and staff at the hospital are given the explanation that the *Shir Hamaalos* hanging in the room of the birthing woman calms her and lifts her spirits (because she truly believes in the protection it draws down, etc.), then surely there will be no opposition. They will gladly agree to give permission in order to do as she pleases so that she will be calm and at peace...

Efforts should be made to fulfill this *minhag* immediately at the time the woman reaches the hospital, at the time of preparing for birth, and how much more so during the birth itself, as well as after the birth.

...All that was said applies not only in a large city with many Jews that has hospitals where many Jewish women give birth, but even in small towns, in hospitals where there is only one Jewish woman giving birth. There, too, doing this is necessary and possible.

Handwritten letter of Rebbetzin Chaya Mushka*

Translation:

1) May it be in a good, auspicious time
2) It is desirable that she should do as many are accustomed to do – those who go to the hospital- that they bring with them a *tzedakah* box and several nickels and dimes. Every day in the morning and afternoon, the patient [should] with her own hand, put some [coins] into the *tzedakah* box.

*Note:
[There is a similar source from the Rebbe regarding someone who was in the hospital for a heart attack (see handwritten note on the following page). It seems the Rebbe encouraged this practice for people going to a hospital: "They should bring a *tzedakah pushka* for him to the hospital, and twice a day, during week-days (before *Shacharis and Mincha*) he

should donate a coin into the *pushka*... It would be very great if he would also encourage others there [including non-Jews] to do the same. The merit from this will help him in all of the above. I will mention him at the *Tziyun*."]

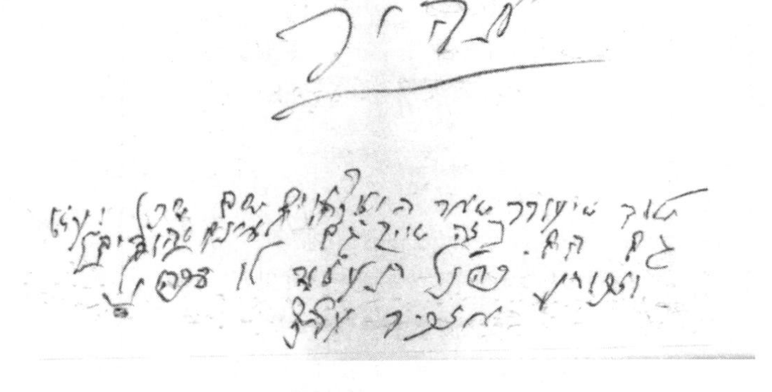

Husband should not be in delivery room

It[50] is clear that the *rav shlita* is correct in his ruling that the husband should not be present [in the delivery room during the time of birth].

It is shocking that this question is even asked.

Saying *Tehillim* during labor

[During the birth of the Rebbe Maharash, the Tzemach Tzedek instructed his sons to say] Chapters 1, 2, 3, 4, 20, 21, 22, 23, 24, 33, 47, 72, 86, 90, 91, 92, 93, 104, 112, 113 until the end [of the entire *Tehillim*].

(*Sefer Hatoldos Admor HaMaharash*, p. 5.)

50 *Shaarei Halacha U'Minhag*, vol. 4, p. 39.

Having children hastens the *geulah*

A[51] birth is a time of *simchah*. First of all, it is a *simchah* for the parents who gave birth to a son or daughter, so much so that the father and mother have an obligation to make a *bracha* on this *simchah*.[52] It is also a *simchah* for *klal Yisrael*, for another *Yid* has been added to *klal Yisrael*.

Through the birth of each child, the *geulah* is hastened. Our Sages say, "The son of David will not arrive until all *neshamos* come down into bodies."[53] "There is a treasure-house of souls, and its name is 'body'; from the beginning, all the *neshamos* that were to be created were placed there."

"Conquering the world" through *pru u'revu*

...By[54] fulfilling the first *mitzvah* in the Torah, פרו ורבו ומלאו את הארץ ("be fruitful, multiply, and fill up the earth"),[55] in a manner of כבשוה ("conquest") – conquering the entire world, rendering it in the state that is befitting of its title. This is all accomplished through *chinuch* of sons, who will conquer the world outside the home, for כל כבודה בת מלך פנימה ("all the glory of the King's daughter is within")[56] and through the *chinuch* of daughters, helping each one in her role as *akeres habayis*, so that they may prepare themselves to build a Jewish home when the time comes.

...Through the work of Jewish women in establishing Jewish homes – being the *akeres habayis* ("mainstay of the home"), the matter of ויעש להם בתים ("He made houses for them"[57]) is also accomplished. As *Rashi* explains, according to the teachings of our Sages, this is the meaning of בתי כהונה ולוי' ומלכות ("houses of *Kehunah*, the Levite, and royalty)": Royal houses – home of the kingship of David *Malka Meshicha* (King *Moshiach*), and houses of *Kehunah* – יראה כהן בציון (a *Kohen* will be seen in *Tzion*, in the third *Beis Hamikdash*).

---

51 *Toras Menachem*, vol. 3, p. 153.

52 *Berachos*, 59b.

53 *Yevamos*, 62a, *Rashi*.

54 *Hisvaaduyos* 5742, vol. 4, p. 2023.

55 *Bereishis*, 1:28.

56 *Tehillim*, 45:14.

57 *Shemos*, 1:21.

Naming the Child

... As[58] for her question regarding a suggestion as to what to name the child that was born, may he live:

The response of my father-in-law, the Rebbe, on this matter is known: He does not get involved in these matters. [This lack of involvement] is understood in light of the Arizal's words[59] that parents are given the thought from Above as to what to name the boy or girl that is born, a name connected to this child's *neshamah*, so that the letters of the name are connected to the *chayus* (life-force) of the *neshamah* and body... [The *neshamah* is connected to the body through the letters of one's Jewish name.]

Adding a *Shabbos* candle

One[60] candle is added for each child [that is born] in order to illuminate the *mazal* of each one.

The importance of nursing

Regarding[61] nursing the baby yourself, this is very correct. This is especially so as in the past few years even doctors in the United States have begun to speak and write about how beneficial this is for the mother and the baby.

[For more on the topics of pregnancy, childbirth, circumcision, pidyon ha'ben, and the birth of girls, see the books Shevach Habris and Kovetz Minhagim. For information on conceiving a child with the holiest garments for the neshamah, see sefer Kedoshim Tihiyu by T. Hendel (Hebrew)].

---

58 *Likkutei Sichos,* vol. 12, p. 182. From a letter of 27th of Sivan, 5714.

59 *Shaar Hagilgulim,* ch. 23, *Emek Hamelech,* 1:4. Cited in *Ohr HaTorah,* end *Bereishis*.

60 *Likkutei Sichos*, vol. 11, p. 289.

61 *Shaarei Halacha U'Minhag*, vol. 4, p. 43.

CHAPTER 3

Chinuch from the Youngest Age

"But Chana did not go up, for she said to her husband: 'Until the child is weaned; then I shall bring him.'"

Shmuel, 1:22

Yeshivah fund at *bris*

My[62] father-in-law had the custom that whenever he was invited to a *bris*, at which he was of course honored to be the *sandak*, at the beginning of the meal he would give a sum of money to the *yeshivah*. He would say that this money was a deposit toward the payment of the tuition, for the child, when he grows older. Since "one must use his teacher's words," on the occasion that I was present, the *bris* took place in Warsaw. He gave twenty gold pieces, and he said, "This is a deposit for *Tomchei Temimim*, for tuition."

(From a *sicha* at a *bris milah*): At a *bris milah* we say, "Just as he has entered into the Covenant so may he enter into Torah, *chuppah* and *maasim tovim*" (p. 141). It is our custom to make an advance payment on tuition fees for the boy's studies. (Here the Rebbe gave a sum of money and said): *This is for the Yeshivah.*

(Hayom Yom, Adar Sheini 28)

Surrounding a Child with Kedusha from the First Moments of Life

Children are influenced by everything around them

Toras[63] *Emes* ("the Torah of Truth")[64] tells us that as soon as a baby emerges into the air of the world, he is influenced by everything happening around him. This is the case even when it could be thought that the environment has no effect, since the baby doesn't understand a thing.

That is to say: Not only is the baby influenced by the food and drinks that it consumes, for that is obvious, since the food and beverages become its flesh and blood! But more than this, all that happens in the surroundings of the baby influences the baby's soul, and this comes to be expressed years later.

62 *Igros Kodesh*, vol. 10, p. 339.

63 *Hisvaaduyos* 5742, vol. 4, p. 2190.

64 Blessings on the Torah.

Surely the mode of conduct of the parents has a far greater influence on the baby, even when he is very little.

First steps in *chinuch*: *Mezuzah*, *Shir Hamaalos*, thanking Hashem

The[65] *chinuch* ליראה את ה' ולאהבה אותו ולזכרו תמיד ("to fear Hashem, love Him, and remember Him always")[66] begins the moment a baby is born. This is accomplished through having a *mezuzah* on his door, *Shir Hamaalos,* and so on, and by the father and mother as well as all who surround the baby blessing, praising, and thanking *Hakadosh Baruch Hu* in response to seeing his movements, development, delighting in the baby, and so on.

Kashrus, *Shir Hamaalos*

There[67] is a *din* in *Shulchan Aruch:*[68]

> ומכל מקום לא יניקו תינוק מן הנכרית ... דחלב נכרית מטמטם הלב ומוליד לו טבע רע וכן לא תאכל המינקת אפילו ישראלית דברים האסורים וכן התינוק בעצמו כי כל זה מזיק לו בזקנותו
>
> A baby should not nurse from a gentile woman ... The milk of a gentile woman numbs the heart and produces a bad nature. In addition, the baby should not be nursed by a Jewish woman who eats forbidden foods, and similarly the child should not [eat forbidden foods] because all this harms him when he ages.

This is part of education: The father and mother need to ensure that their child's food and beverages are kosher. Similarly, there is a *minhag Yisrael* to hang the *kapitel* of *Shir Hamaalos* near a woman giving birth. One reason for this is that it protects from undesirable matters. An additional reason,

---

65 *Hisvaaduyos* 5741, vol. 1, p. 316.

66 *Shulchan Aruch Admor HaZaken, Orach Chaim* 46:1.

67 *Shaarei Halacha U'Minhag, Yoreh Dei'ah,* p. 221.

68 *Yoreh Dei'ah,* 81:7.

connected with *chinuch*, is that the first thing the child sees should be something of *kedusha*.

The child was just born and cannot yet distinguish between light and darkness, between sweet and bitter. Still, since he will go out into the world and has eyes with which to see the world, we need to make an effort to place before his eyes the letters of *alef beis,* which combine to give existence to the entire *seder hishtalshelus* (the chain of spiritual worlds).

Being careful to avoid *cholov akum* and *pas akum*

Chinuch[69] includes being meticulously careful to avoid foods that may contain: 1) "חשש דחשש חלב עכו"ם" (the very remote possibility of *cholov akum*) and 2) "חשש דחשש פת עכו"ם" (the very remote possibility of *pas akum*).

Cholov Yisrael and *emuna*

...*Cholov*[70] *Yisrael* in particular has an effect on the strengthening of *emuna.* "Milk that was milked by עכו"ם (non-Jews) – that *Yisrael* did not supervise"[71] – brings one to have doubts in *emuna* (*chas ve'shalom*), and this is easy to understand.

... According[72] to the known story* from my father-in-law, the Rebbe (and a similar one was also printed), *cholov akum* awakens doubts in *emuna.*

> *[There[73] is a well-known story about an individual who came with his son-in-law, who was a big *lamdan,* to the Alter Rebbe in Liozna. The man complained that his son-in-law had always exhibited good conduct but recently had started to have doubts in his *emuna,* and the father-in-law himself had suffered greatly from this. The Rebbe told the son-in-law that he had unknowingly eaten *cholov akum* and gave him a *tikkun* (spiritual rectification) for this, and he recovered spiritually.]

---

69 *Heichal Menachem*, vol. 1, p. 224.

70 *Igros Kodesh,* vol. 22, p. 132.

71 *Avodah Zarah* 35b.

72 *Igros Kodesh,* vol. 16, p. 243.

73 *Sefer Hamaamarim Yiddish*, p. 57.

[In[74] response to a family whose son suffered from a rash on his skin, the Rebbe replied:] "They transgressed unintentionally by eating food to which *shemitah* applies."

[Upon receiving their request for a *tikkun* for this, the Rebbe responded:] "Serve Hashem with *simchah* (which also breaks the boundaries in the realm of שגיאות מי יבין (errors))."

Kashrus affects *middos*

Since[75] every food a person eats becomes his "flesh and blood,"[76] the Torah forbade certain foods in order that the characteristics of the forbidden foods, which are undesirable, will not become part of a person's nature.

Hiddurim in *kashrus*

This[77] is in response to her question ... in which she writes about the state of her children's health, may they live, and she concludes with a question about what she should do regarding foods whose *kashrus* is not *mehudar*, and she thinks that this food could increase her children's appetites.

In general, *hiddurim* with food (as is quoted in several Torah sources) affects not only the observance of that *mitzvah* [of *kashrus*], rather since each item of food [we eat] becomes thereafter the blood and flesh of the body, which [in turn] connects itself with the *neshamah*, [therefore] the *kashrus* and refinement of the foods also influences the personality and good *middos* of the person eating the food. Therefore, each additional *hiddur*, refinement, and cleanliness of a food should be considered as an addition in the form, fineness, and refinement of the personality and *middos*. If this is true of adults, it applies even more to children, as their personality is developing...

According to the above, my opinion is evident: Since this is not a matter upon which one's entire health depends, *chas ve'shalom*, and is only meant to add flavor to the food and to add to the [children's] strength, a *hiddur* regarding

---

74 *Likkutei Sichos*, vol. 36, p. 298.

75 *Likkutei Sichos*, vol. 1, p. 223.

76 Cf. *Tanya* ch. 7.

77 *Igros Kodesh*, vol. 18, pp. 109-110.

food should not be dropped. Surely other suggestions and methods can be found in order to increase their appetites and improve their health, not at the expense of *kashrus* and *hiddur.*

***Shir Hamaalos*, lullabies**

There[78] is an age of *chinuch*, but even before this, from the moment the baby comes into the world, the father and mother make an effort that the baby will always be in a Jewish environment, one of Torah and *mitzvos*. This is part of the general idea of *chinuch*.

There is a known *minhag Yisrael* to hang a *Shir Hamaalos* in the room of the child as soon as he is born. In the same way, there is a custom of Jewish women to sing lullabies about כי טוב סחרה מכל סחורה\די תורה איז די בעסטע סחורה ("Torah is the best merchandise"). And this is before the child knows to distinguish good from bad, before he begins to talk; it even applies to a newborn baby. It is known what the *Rashba* wrote about the importance of being careful to continue the customs of *nashim z'keinos be'Yisrael.*

Baby's ears should cleave to words of Torah

In[79] the past there was a custom among Jewish women – and if only they would continue with it today! – to soothe their babies to sleep with songs about the greatness of Torah. ….

When Rabbi Yehoshua ben Chananya was still a little baby, his mother would take him to *shul* so his ears would cleave to words of Torah.[80] The *Mishnah* praises his mother, saying, "Praiseworthy is the woman who gave birth to him."[81]

From this comes an instruction for every mother: She should not wait for her child to grow and begin to go to *cheder* to begin telling him about Hashem, Torah, and *mitzvos.* Rather, the time to educate is when the baby is still in the cradle, so that his ears will hear Torah.

---

78 *Hisvaaduyos* 5743, vol. 3, p. 1217.

79 *Sichos Kodesh* 5741, vol. 1, pp. 246-247.

80 *Talmud Yerushalmi, Yevamos* 1:6.

81 *Avos,* 2:9.

Shir Hamaalos, pesukim by heart

Chinuch[82] begins from the time of birth, through *Shir Hamaalos* and the like, and when they begin to talk, through learning *pesukim* "by heart, slowly and gradually." After that, they learn the letters of Torah in order to accustom them to read the Torah, and so on (as is explained at length in the beginning of *Hilchos Talmud Torah* of the Alter Rebbe).

The *neshamah* absorbs

Lullabies[83] that women sing to babies should be those of *kedusha* content, such as תורה היא הסחורה היותר טובה ("Torah is the best merchandise").

Some claim that a newborn baby doesn't see or hear what is happening around him. ... However, even if the surroundings do not reach the physical eyes and ears of the baby, we know with certainty that they reach – through his physical eyes and ears – into his *pnimiyus.* His *neshamah* sees and hears, and what's more, it absorbs. All this leaves a strong impression on the baby for life.

Children understand everything

ולכן אין התינוק יכול לדבר, אף שמבין הכל ("...This why an infant cannot speak, even though it understands everything")

(Tanya, Iggeres Hakodesh, Epistle 5)

Bringing children to hear Ten Commandments

Some[84] ask, "What is the point in bringing babies to hear the Ten Commandments? They do not understand it."

In this regard, the Torah gives us an explicit instruction, telling us[85] that when Rabbi Yehoshua ben Chananya was a baby in his cradle, his mother

---

82 *Hisvaaduyos* 5749, vol. 3, p. 75.

83 *Hisvaaduyos* 5747, vol. 2, p. 647.

84 *Likkutei Sichos*, vol. 23, pp. 257-258.

85 *Talmud Yerushalmi, Yevamos* 1:6.

would bring him to the *beis midrash* to hear the learning "in order that his ears would cleave to words of Torah." She is praised with the words אשרי יולדתו ("praiseworthy is the one who gave birth to him")[86] because the Torah that he heard influenced him to become one of the greatest Torah scholars of his generation. ...

The baby was brought to a *beis medrash* (house of Torah study), where grasping the information is fundamental to learning it.[87] How much more so is this instruction applicable to [the baby] hearing the public reading of the Torah scroll, for even though he doesn't understand it, in doing so he is fulfilling the *mitzvah* of Talmud Torah both *mide'oraysa* (on the biblical level) and *miderabanan* (on the rabbinic level).

Washing *negel vasser*

The Alter Rebbe writes in his *Shulchan Aruch:*

> The spirit of *tumah* does not desire to dwell in a place unless it is a vessel of *kedusha*, a place from which *kedusha* has departed. This is the case regarding Jewish bodies when they sleep and their holy *neshamah* departs from the body, and then the *ru'ach* of *tumah* dwells upon the body. When the *neshamah* returns to the body, the spirit of *tumah* departs from the whole body and remains only on the hands.
>
> For this reason, it has been the custom to be lenient when children who have not reached the age of *chinuch* touch [objects], since the completion of and the main entering of the *nefesh hakedosha* (holy soul) into a person is at thirteen years of age and a day for males, and twelve [years of age] for a female.

86 *Avos*, 2:9.

87 *Hilchos Talmud Torah l'Admor HaZaken*, 2:13.

The beginning of the entry of the *nefesh hakedosha* is in the *chinuch* of Torah and *mitzvos*, in which the *chachomim* have obligated us... He who is careful about a baby [regarding morning *negel vasser*] from the *bris* and onwards, "קדוש יאמר לו – 'holy' shall be said of him." [This *pasuk* is originally found in *Yeshayahu* 4:3, and *Rashi* comments there: "They will all be *tzaddikim*."]

(*Orach Chaim, Mahadura Tinyana*, sec. 4)

Negel vasser affects a child's health

Washing[88] *negel vasser* is very important for the health of the child.

Child has a _nefesh Elokis_ from time of birth

Regarding[89] what the Alter Rebbe writes in *Shulchan Aruch:*[90]

> The beginning of the entering of the *nefesh hakedosha* (holy Jewish soul) is in the *chinuch* of Torah and *mitzvos*, in which the *chachomim* have obligated us, as well as with *mitzvas bris milah.*

There are stages through which the *nefesh hakedosha* enters into the body until the body itself becomes *kadosh*.* However, certainly this *nefesh hakedosha* exists and enters into the child from the moment he enters into the air of the world.

*This is also true at the time of sleep, as is understood from the content of the *halacha* about being careful not to touch an infant before washing *negel vasser*, because when the *neshamah* comes back into the body every morning, the spirit of impurity departs from the entire body but remains on the hands, until one washes *negel vasser*.

88 *Sefer HaZichronos (Yiddish)*, vol. 2, p. 435.

89 *Hisvaaduyos* 5751, vol. 1, p. 315, fn. 71.

90 *Orach Chaim, Mahadura Tinyana*, sec. 4.

Surround the child with objects of *kedusha*

There[91] is a common practice in the world that images of animals, such as dogs, cats, lions, and so on, are hung around the baby's room. These are all impure animals.

We need to conduct ourselves differently. Instead of these images, our children should have a *tzedakah* box, a *bencher*, *kriyas Shema,* or *alef beis* and so on, so that when the child looks around, he sees things related to Torah.

Just as a *mezuzah* is placed in a double covering in order to avoid *halachic* problems, this should also be done with a *bencher*, *kriyas Shema,* and *alef beis.* They should be bright and colorful in order to be pleasing to a child.

First the child will glance at these *kedusha* objects, and then will come the hand motions. When the child begins to talk, he will take an interest in these things. He will then be explained that we have Torah, and that Torah is the greatest *sechorah* (merchandise), and when he grows up, he will be given this wonderful *sechorah*.

Immediately buying a letter in a *Sefer Torah*

When[92] a Jewish child is born, efforts should be made immediately to give him merit by buying for him a letter in a *Sefer Torah.* This [should be done] even before naming the child, and after he is named, his (or her) name should be added.

Regarding[93] a baby, who is not able to be involved in this himself, his parents can buy him a letter in a *Sefer Torah*...

Yet, it would be appropriate that this action (placing the money into an envelope, writing the child's information, writing the address, etc.) should be done in front of the baby, since everything that the baby sees and hears, even when he is a day old, leaves a lasting impression.

---

91 *Sichos Kodesh* 5736, vol. 2, p. 170.

92 *Hisvaaduyos* 5744, vol. 2, p. 827.

93 *Sichos Kodesh* 5741, 13th of Nissan.

Father teaches child *Torah tziva lanu Moshe*

...I[94] want to share with you in a matter that has preoccupied my mind in recent weeks, namely, the inadequacy of attention given to the Chinuch of children of pre-Bar (Bas) -Mitzvah age, down to the very little ones. Even in circles where serious attention is given to older boys and girls, there is a prevalent tendency to take the Chinuch of the little ones more lightly.

This attitude is rather surprising, for the Torah has quite strong views on the role of the youngsters. Suffice it to cite the rule laid down by our Sages that as soon as a child begins to speak, his father must begin to teach him Torah, specifically the verse תורה צונ לנו משה מורשה קהילת יעקב -"The Torah which Mosheh commanded us is the heritage of the congregation of Jacob" (Deut. 33:4). At first glance, there is a very long way between a two-year old toddler, just beginning to speak, and the Torah which Mosheh Rabbeinu received at Sinai when he was 80-odd years old and at the height of his greatness. Yet, this is precisely what the Rabbis had in mind: to put this toddler in immediate relationship with the Torah which Mosheh received at Sinai. So much so, that the Alter Rebbe, founder of Chabad, begins the Laws of Talmud-study in his Shulchan Aruch with this very rule laid down by our Sages.

Chinuch from age three

Our[95] Rebbes have instructed that from age three, [for boys] the day of the *opsherenish* and leaving the *peyos*, נהגו להדר להרגיל את התינוק בענין נשיאת ט"ק וברכות השחר וברהמ"ז וק"ש שעל המטה ("it is customary to be *mehader* to accustom the child to wear a *tallis katan*, say the morning *brachos*, *Birkas Hamazon*, and the bedtime *Shema*"). ... This doesn't mean that before this

94 Letter of the Rebbe from Rosh Chodesh Menachem Av, 5733, reprinted with permission from chabad.org.

95 *Hisvaaduyos* 5742, vol. 2, p. 708, *Hisvaaduyos* 5749, vol. 1, p. 37.

age one should not be *mehader* in these matters; rather, from age three the *hiddur* in these areas is *essential* [of course, in a pleasant, peaceful manner[96]]. However, even before this age it is understood that it is worthwhile to be *mehader* in these matters.

Modeh Ani

It[97] is a *minhag Yisrael* to educate a baby to say *Modeh Ani* when he begins to talk, and [some] *nashim tzidkaniyos* (righteous women) even have the *minhag* to recite *Modeh Ani* with, as well as on behalf of, the baby even earlier.

Kissing the *mezuzah*

In[98] recent generations, scientific advances have come to recognize what is known in Torah and *Chassidus:* that even what a one-day-old baby sees and hears impacts him when he gets older.

For this reason, parents in a Jewish home make sure that the baby kisses the *mezuzah* on the doorpost of his room before going to sleep. In the *mezuzah* is written שמע ישראל ה‘ אלוקינו ה‘ אחד ("Hear, Yisrael: The L-rd is our G-d, the L-rd is one").[99] This causes it to be ingrained in the child that ה‘ אחד, the One G-d, is protecting him and everything in his room (as the *Zohar* states,[100] the *mezuzah* protects all the people in the home, even when they leave their house).

Saying names of holy *Yidden*, *shevatim*, *Avos*, *sefarim*

In[101] the past it was customary to educate children (who were not yet able to intellectually understand) to repeat the names of holy *Yidden* as well as of the *shevatim*, of our *Avos* and *Imahos,* and the names of holy *sefarim*.

---

96 *Mishlei,* 3:17.

97 *Hisvaaduyos* 5742, vol. 2, p. 708, *Hisvaaduyos* 5749, vol. 1, p. 37.

98 *Hisvaaduyos* 5747, vol. 2, pp. 647-648.

99 *Devarim,* 6:4.

100 *Zohar* 3:263b, 266b.

101 *Hisvaaduyos* 5750, vol. 1, pp. 181-182.

Avoiding impure animals

It[102] is quoted in holy *sefarim* that whatever one sees and gazes upon has an impact upon the person. Seeing holy things has a positive impact on a person, while seeing images in the form of animals that are *tamei* (impure) has a negative impact on a person. ...

There are also sources in *nigleh* (the revealed dimension of Torah) stating that sight can impact a person positively or negatively. For example, there is a *halacha* in *Shulchan Aruch:* [103] "After immersing in a *mikvah,* women should be careful that the first thing they encounter is not an impure creature such as a dog or donkey. ... If she encountered such things, a G-d-fearing woman should return and reimmerse herself." The reason for this is that seeing impure things has a negative impact on the fetus, while seeing holy things has a positive impact on the fetus.

The Torah's teaching, חנוך לנער על פי דרכו גם כי יזקין לא יסור ממנה ("Educate the child according to his way, so that when he grows old, he will not depart from it"),[104] implies that being careful about this matter [what one sees] is especially important during the age of *chinuch.* This is because things are engraved into children's thoughts through sight at this age, and this affects them for life. ...

When a baby is given toys in the form of animals, efforts should be made that they be only *tahor* animals, birds, fish, etc.

When the child gets older and begins to learn the shapes of letters, and is shown various shapes to make it easier to grasp the shape of the letters, efforts should be made that only *tahor* animals are shown. ...

Any magazines, advertisements, etc. that have animals on them, especially those meant for children of *chinuch* age, should be comprised of *tahor* animals....

However, when the animals come to aid in Torah study, to illustrate the story in *Tanach* and *Midrashim,* and so on, the above does not apply.

---

102 *Hisvaaduyos* 5744, vol. 1, p. 487 ff.

103 *Hisvaaduyos* 5744, vol. 1, p. 487.

104 *Mishlei,* 22:6.

Care in this area is especially important now since we are in the time of *Ikvesa DeMeshicha* when את רוח הטומאה אעביר מן הארץ ("I [Hashem] will remove the spirit of impurity from the land").[105] Therefore, we need to prepare for the coming of *Moshiach* by "tasting" from what will be in the future, by influencing those that surround us to use only images that are *tahor* and holy.

Dressing like a *Yid*

A child stood, waiting to receive a coin from the Rebbe. He was dressed in a *Tzivos Hashem* cap and a shirt that had a childish *goyishe* character on it. The Rebbe asked him if he is in *Tzivos Hashem*, and when the boy nodded yes, the Rebbe asked why he was wearing such a shirt…

(*Kovetz Pninei Hasor*, p. 42)

Clearly the son of a *chassid*

From[106] this [that according to *Rashi*,[107] Yitzchak looked identical to Avraham so that all could recognize that Avraham was his father] we can derive a lesson in the area of *chinuch. Chinuch* should be in such a way that העידו הכל אברהם הוליד את יצחק ("All could testify that Avraham gave birth to Yitzchak"): When we look upon a Jewish child, כל רואיהם יכירום ("all who see can recognize")[108] that he is the son of Avraham... and it should be seen and recognized, as well, that he is the son of a *chassid* and a *tomim*, to the point that the only difference between him and his father is in age. His father already has the beard of a mature man, while his has not yet begun to grow, for he is a child.

This is accomplished through beginning his *chinuch*, from the moment he enters the air of the world, in such a way that [parents] implant in him the fundamental principle that of all our *avodah* is ליראה את ה׳ ולאהבה אותו ולזכרו תמיד

105 *Zechariah*, 13:2.

106 *Hisvaaduyos* 5751, vol. 1, p. 316.

107 *Bereishis* 25:19, *Rashi*.

108 *Yeshaya*, 61:9.

("to fear Hashem, love Him, and remember Him always"),[109] and that regarding this basic idea, all (מגדול ועד קטן from big to small) are equal.

Button right to left

How[110] to use a button: When a button is sewn on the *left* side of the garment, a hole is made on the *right* side. Through this, the left side is connected with the right, in such a way that the right side goes *over* the left. This connects the matters of the left with matters of the right, which represents the dimension of *kedusha.* In order to make this connection, a "hole" should be made in the right side, etc. – and all interpretations [of the concepts of "left," "right," and "hole"] are relevant here.

Brachos

One hundred *brachos* a day

The[111] importance of reciting מאה ברכות בכל יום ("one hundred *brachos* every day")[112] applies to each and every *Yid,* and can be performed with ease. [This applies to] men, women, and even children. Even before the ages of *bar mitzvah* and *bas mitzvah*, we teach them to recite one hundred *brachos* every day. [This applies even to] the smallest children who have not yet reached the age of *chinuch*, and even to children just beginning to speak: we teach them to recite *brachos* (and to respond *amen)* until they become accustomed to reciting *brachos,* so that it is second-nature to them.

Answering *amen*

Our[113] Sages have remarked, "When does a child come to (merit) *Olam Haba* (the World to Come)? When he answers, '*amen...*'"

---

109 *Shulchan Aruch Admor HaZaken, Orach Chaim* 46:1.

110 *Hisvaaduyos* 5744, vol. 3, p. 1672.

111 *Hisvaaduyos* 5751, vol. 1, p. 315.

112 *Menachos,* 53b. *Shulchan Aruch Orach Chaim* 46:3. *Shulchan Aruch Admor HaZaken, Orach Chaim* 46:1.

113 *Hisvaaduyos* 5751, vol. 1, p. 315, fn. 68.

Teaching the meaning of *brachos*

When[114] babies begin to speak, we teach them to recite *brachos* and answer *amen* until reciting *brachos* becomes common practice for them. [This refers] not only to reciting *brachos* verbally, but also and most importantly, in a way that penetrates one's entire existence – one's desire, will, intellect, and emotions. We achieve this by educating them on the meaning of the *brachos* – ליראה את ה' ולאהבה אותו ולזכרו תמיד על ידי הברכות שמברך תמיד ("to fear Hashem, love Him, and remain conscious of Him at all times through the *brachos* we recite").[115]

Giving sweets to children

Not[116] only are we particular to make sure children recite the *brachos* and warn them not to eat without a *bracha, chas ve'shalom;* we also accustom them to recite many *brachos* by giving them sweets.

Birkas Hamazon

It[117] is emphasized that children should be taught *Birkas Hamazon* (a *bracha* that is an obligation from the Torah[118]) in such a way that they can understand intellectually that they should bless and thank *Hakadosh Baruch Hu* for their physical sustenance.

---

114 *Hisvaaduyos* 5751, vol. 1, p. 315.

115 *Shulchan Aruch Admor HaZaken, Orach Chaim* 46:1.

116 *Hisvaaduyos* 5751, vol. 1, p. 315, fn. 67.

117 *Sefer HaSichos* 5752, Vol. 1, pp. 88-89.

118 *Berachos,* 48b.

CHAPTER 4

The Child's Room

"Make for Me a sanctuary"

Shemos, 25:8

Room full of *sefarim*

It[119] is very important for children to have *sifrei kodesh* in their bedroom, as the very presence of *sefarim* in their room makes a strong impression on them. Of course, this doesn't mean that parents should suffice with one *sefer* in order to fulfill this obligation, or place in the room only the one *sefer* that is essential (like the *Siddur* used to *daven* in that room).

Rather, it should be a בית מלא ספרים (home *full* of *sefarim).*[120] This means that the *sefarim* are the עיקר (primary component) of the home, while all the other items in the house are secondary to the *sefarim* – so that the house is מלא ספרים.

The same is true of the child's bedroom. Although there are other things in the room, such as a bed, table, etc. (and *kedusha* objects such as the *tallis katan* for a boy and *Shabbos licht* for a girl), the main purpose of the room is to be a חדר מלא ספרים. Each and every item in the room is only for Torah and according to Torah (such as the table, upon which only kosher food is eaten according to *Shulchan Aruch* and upon which only *sifrei kodesh* are read).

Therefore one should "fill" the room with at least a *Chumash*, *Siddur,* and *Haggadah* of *Pesach.* ... It would be even better to add a *sefer Tehillim.* If the *Tehillim* is attached to the *Siddur*, it should have its own *shaar blatt* (title page), to emphasize that it is its own *sefer*, and not only part of the *Siddur.*

Pushka nailed to the wall

...The[121] [child's] room should contain a *tzedakah pushka,* a *Siddur,* and a *Chumash;* then he will automatically remember matters of Torah and *mitzvos.* ...

The *tzedakah pushka* should be nailed to the wall, turning the entire room into a חדר של צדקה (room of *tzedakah)...*

Efforts should be made to put the *tzedakah pushka* in a noticeable place. Then, when the child has a guest who is unaware of such things for whatever reason, the guest will ask, "What's this?" as is the nature of a child when he

---

119 *Hisvaaduyos* 5747, vol. 2, p. 648.

120 Cf. *Medrash Tanchuma, Korach* 2.

121 *Hisvaaduyos* 5748, vol. 4, p. 346.

sees something new. His host will respond that with a *Siddur* one *davens* to Hashem, from a Torah *sefer* one learns the Torah of Hashem, and with a *tzedakah pushka,* one fulfills the great *mitzvah* of giving money to the poor.

This will immediately awaken in the guest his Jewish nature ... and he will decide to do the same in his own room. Since a child's nature is to be impatient, when he sees something good he does it immediately, especially since his host will encourage him to do so. The guest will immediately take out money from his pocket to put into the *tzedakah pushka*.

A *Mikdash* for Hashem

There[122] is a famous saying of our Sages[123] on the *pasuk* ועשו לי מקדש ושכנתי בתוכם ("Make for Me a sanctuary, and I will dwell within them") [normally translated "in their midst" – the midst of the Jewish people].[124] They say: בתוכו לא נאמר אלא בתוכם – בתוך כל אחד ואחד מישראל ("It is not written, 'within *it* [the *Mishkan*],' but 'within *them*' – inside every single *Yid*").

As we have discussed on several occasions, every *Yid* – man, woman, and child – should make of their home, room, possessions, and so on a *Mishkan* and *Mikdash* for *Hakadosh Baruch Hu.* [It should be] a house of Torah, *tefillah,* and *tzedakah.* This is accomplished through a child's establishing in his room a place for a *Chumash*, *Siddur,* and *tzedakah* box, and writing on them לה' הארץ ומלואה ("The world and all that fills it belongs to Hashem")[125] before writing his name. In general, all the details in the life of a *Yid* should be permeated with *kedusha* and G-dliness, because אני נבראתי לשמש את קוני ("I was created to serve my Maker"),[126] and in this way a Jew turns all aspects of his life into a *Mishkan* and *Mikdash* for Hashem.

There is an additional spiritual *avodah* of guarding the *Mikdash* because of the *kavod* of the *Mikdash* and the *kavod* of the *Shechinah:* "guarding" one's *sifrei kodesh* and all one's *kedusha* objects, for they are the *Mishkan* and

122 *Hisvaaduyos* 5750, vol. 3, p. 89.

123 *Reshis Chochmah, Shaar Ha'ahavah*, ch. 6.

124 *Shemos,* 25:8.

125 *Tehillim,* 24:1.

126 *Kiddushin,* 82b.

Mikdash in one's life. They should be especially precious to a *Yid* – more than his mundane belongings.

Every Jewish child is "judge" and "officer" over his room

Every[127] Jewish child should be the "judge" and "officer" over his own personal conduct and his room: the room with his *sefarim*, *tzedakah pushka,* and other belongings. [He should ensure] that everything is put in its proper place, that the *sefarim* are clean, and that each book is available when he needs to learn from it. [The child ensures that] ... on *Shabbos* and *Yom Tov* [the *tzedakah pushka*] is placed in a location high up and out of reach, so that it is possible to see it and remember the *mitzvah* of *tzedakah*; however, they will wait until after *Shabbos* or *Yom Tov* to actually give *tzedakah.* He will also arrange the other objects in his room so that they are available when needed, but if they are *Muktzeh,* then on *Shabbos* and *Yom Tov* they will be placed high up out of reach, so that they won't be touched. The children should influence their friends to do the same with their belongings in their own rooms.

A clean, illuminated, and holy room

It[128] is incumbent upon every person, including the smallest children, that each individual contemplate that their home, as well as every Jewish home, and for children, also the classroom where they learn in school, and so on, need to be clean, illuminated, and holy.

Making the room a place of Torah, prayer, and acts of loving-kindness

Every[129] boy and girl should have a personal *Siddur* and write לה' הארץ ומלואה[130] ("The world and everything in it is Hashem's") inside the front cover. The child

127 *Hisvaaduyos* 5749, vol. 4, p. 215.
128 *Igros Melech*, vol. 2, p. 420-421.
129 *Likkutei Sichos*, vol. 14, pp. 279-280.
130 *Tehillim,* 24:1.

will see this while *davening* each day and will remember that the whole world belongs to *Hakadosh Baruch Hu.* Under the *pasuk* לה' הארץ ומלואה, the child should write his Jewish name and this will indicate that he devotes himself to Hashem. It will also remind him of his Jewish name. …

In addition, each child should have a personal *tzedakah pushka.* Each weekday, the child should put a coin *(bli neder)* into the *pushka.*

In this way, the child will have objects to use for each of the pillars of Torah, *tefillah* (prayer), and *gemilus chassadim* (loving-kindness). The *Siddur* is for *tefillah;* and since the *Siddur* also contains Torah *pesukim*, it also stands for and is used for learning Torah. The *tzedakah pushka* represents and is used for *gemilus chassadim.* The world is supported upon these three principles and acts.[131]

Children should be encouraged to use *sefarim*

Surely[132] it should be explained to the children that they should not worry that in using their *sefarim* so much, the *sefarim* may become worn out and ripped, for they are promised that [in such a case], new *sefarim* that are even nicer will be bought for them.

In regard to infants, the fear of ruining and ripping *sefarim* is greater, as our Sages say[133] on the *pasuk* ודגלו עלי אהבה ("He skips over Me with love"),[134] ...ודילוגו עלי אהבה אפילו התינוק מדלג על האזכרה ("Even when a Jewish infant [unknowingly] jumps *(daleg)* on the written Name of Hashem … His jumping upon Me is love!"). The reason for this is that Torah (referring to *sefarim*) exists for the sake of the *Bnei Yisrael* – צו את בנ"י, דבר אל בנ"י ("Command the *Bnei Yisrael*," "Speak to the *Bnei Yisrael*").[135]

---

131 *Avos,* 1:2.

132 *Hisvaaduyos* 5748, vol. 2, pp. 172-173, fn. 89.

133 *Shir HaShirim Rabbah.*

134 *Shir HaShirim,* 2:4.

135 Cf. *Tana Devei Eliyahu Rabbah* 14, 31. *Bereishis Rabbah* 1:4.

CHAPTER 5

Instilling a Love and Awe for *Hakadosh Baruch Hu*

"...To love G-d, your G-d, to walk in all His ways, and to cleave to Him."

Devarim, 11:22

Emuna, the Foundation of Chinuch

The world has a *Baal Habayis*

The[136] true, firm foundation of *chinuch* is the knowledge that יש בעל הבית לבירה זו ("This world [lit: city] has a *baal habayis*").[137] He is not only like a *baal habayis* who purchases a ready-made palace; rather, בראשית ברא אלוקים את שמים ואת הארץ ("In the beginning, Hashem created the heavens and the earth").[138] *Hakadosh Baruch Hu* is the Creator of the world, and He conducts the world with *hashgacha pratis* over every detail... This knowledge is what influences the person to behave in the appropriate way.

"An Eye that sees and an Ear that hears"

A[139] child's nature is to be spoiled. His parents accustom him to be this way, and habit becomes nature, or at least second nature. This nature could well lead a child to a feeling of entitlement. As a result, if he has something of his own, fine; but if not, he will take what belongs to another! He might come to the conclusion that "What's mine is mine and what's yours is mine"![140]

When attempts are made to teach him that he should restrain himself and not indulge because at the street corner there stands a police officer who may punish him with imprisonment when he sees him stealing, the child has a solution: He will steal when the police officer is not looking!

The only solution [to avoid this kind of conduct] is to permeate the child with the recognition that there is "an Eye that sees, an Ear that hears, and all your actions are recorded in a book."[141]

---

136 *Hisvaaduyos* 5743, vol. 2, p. 899.

137 *Bereishis Rabbah*, 39:1.

138 *Bereishis,* 1:1.

139 *Hisvaaduyos* 5743, vol. 3, p. 1342.

140 *Avos,* 5:10.

141 *Avos,* 2:1.

Opportunity to do *teshuvah*

[Children[142] should be taught the reality that this world is not a place where "everything and anything goes."] There is a Creator Who runs the world. There is "an Eye that sees, an Ear that hears, and all your actions are recorded in a book."[143] The reason Hashem doesn't punish the person as soon as he does something wrong is that Hashem, in His kindness, is providing the opportunity to do *teshuvah*.

Begin *chinuch* with *kabbalas ol*, not intellect

My[144] father-in-law, the Rebbe, related that when his children were small, he hired a *melamed* for them. This *melamed* believed that children need not be told matters of *Yiddishkeit* that are shocking, or miracles that are not understood by the intellect. In his view, these matters are for adults who already understand that which can be understood by intellect, and only then can they grasp miracles. However, for a child, it would be overwhelming. The *melamed* thought that children should only be taught matters of *Yiddishkeit* that are logical. As soon as the Freirdiker Rebbe discovered the approach of this *melamed*, he was fired.

[*Chinuch* should] begin with *emuna* and *kabbalas ol*, not with intellect. Matters that are understood intellectually should also be fulfilled out of *kabbalas ol*, just as we should fulfill matters that are beyond human understanding. So too with the matter of *chinuch:* we should tell children of wondrous things that are beyond intellect, and this implants within them *emuna*. Any claims that this is not the correct order, or asking why it is necessary to start out with things that are overwhelming and the like, come from the *yetzer hara*, מלך זקן וכסיל ("The old and foolish king").[145]

---

142 *Hisvaaduyos* 5743, vol. 3, p. 1342.

143 Ibid.

144 *Likkutei Sichos*, vol. 19, pp. 91-92.

145 *Mishlei* 4:13.

Emuna is indivisible

My[146] saintly father-in-law, the [previous] Rebbe, related:

There was a *melamed* (teacher) who, while teaching *Chumash* and *Tanach* to young children, would endeavor to garb the various miraculous stories in somewhat more realistic, rational terms. When, however, he would encounter issues that he failed to grasp intellectually, he would omit them.

The *melamed* maintained that his conduct was legitimate, seeing as how the appropriate approach to education ought to be one of *chanoch l'na'ar al pi darko* – educating a child "according to his way.'"

That is, he continued, it is particularly difficult for young children, (especially young girls,) to grasp wondrous concepts. Therefore, one should impart these gradually: first the concepts existing within the natural order, then the miracles implemented within nature, and finally, the miracles that transcend nature.

When word of this reached the Rebbe Rashab, he rejected this approach completely.

At first glance, one could argue that the *melamed* actually had a point. After all, the importance of educating a child "according to his way" (in this case, gradually) is pointed out in numerous places, beginning with the *Rambam*, who maintains that one should teach children by motivating them with various incentives relative to their age. A younger child is rewarded with sweets; an older child is encouraged with the promise of buying him shoes, awarding him with honors, and so on, until ultimately one teaches him to study Torah *lishmah* – for the sake of Heaven.

In addition, similar principles seem to be applied to *Chassidus* – the inner part of Torah – as elucidated in the section *Chinuch katan* in *Tanya*. What, then, is the fallacy of this approach?

The response to this is as follows: Only ideas that can be divided such as intellectual matters can be divided into segments and conveyed gradually by first explaining simpler principles and then gradually conveying deeper concepts. A child is first taught the simpler aspects of Torah and is eventually introduced to more complex issues.

---

146 *Toras Menachem* 5721, p. 310-312, The Rebbe's Holy Care, Issue 4

Faith, however, is indivisible. Faith cannot be conveyed in segments. It is either conveyed in its entirely or not conveyed at all.

Thus, an attempt to convey faith part by part – in addition to failing to achieve one's goal – would be only detrimental. Either the child is taught that the Almighty is the one singular being of existence, is in ultimate unison with existence, and is infinite, or the child is not taught faith at all. For a portion of faith is, in fact, no faith at all! On the contrary, when one attempts to present miracles in rational terms, this only serves to convey a conflicting message.

Thus, the ultimate objective of teaching faith to children is to achieve the goal that even once the child grows intellectually and endeavors to comprehend everything within the scope of reason, he should maintain a core, simplistic faith in the Almighty that transcends the intellect.

This is the authentic meaning of the verse, *Chanoch lana'ar al pi darko – gam ki yazkin lo yasur mimenah*[147] – "Educate a child according to his way, so when he grows old he will not deviate from it."

It is precisely when a child is young that one must implant within him/her an instinctive faith in the Almighty as He transcends nature, fortifying the faith of the child so that even when "he grows old" he will maintain an intrinsic faith in the Almighty, beyond reason.

Not to be alarmed by the concealment of this world

A[148] Jewish child should be taught not to be alarmed by the Divine concealment in the world;[149] what the world says should not matter to him. [Instead, he should pay attention] only to the will of the Torah. This resolution should be so strong within him to the point that "even when he grows old, he will not depart from it."[150]

147 *Mishlei*, 22:6.

148 *Likkutei Sichos*, vol. 15, p. 134.

149 Cf. *Likkutei Torah*, *Shelach* 37d.

150 *Mishlei*, 22:6.

Yiras Shamayim

One[151] should not compromise on matters relating to *yiras Shamayim,* and the like, especially in matters of *chinuch*, where every move and change affects the students, who will soon be building Jewish homes according to the way that they were taught.

Instilling *Yiras Shamayim*

She[152] should make efforts to ingrain in them matters related to *yiras Shamayim.* This includes that they wear a *yarmulka* and *tallis katan* and be careful to recite *Modeh Ani*, *brachos*, *Birkas Hanehenin*, *Shema Yisrael,* and the like.

Sleeping with a *yarmulka*

A[153] child may ask: "During the time of sleep one does not feel anything, so what difference does it make how one goes about sleeping?"

A Jewish child must sleep with a *yarmulka* because Torah is "our life" at every moment which we live. This applies to the time he sleeps as well. He is living, and so he should be permeated with Torah.

There is also the question: The covering of the head is connected to one's *yiras Shomayim*. When one sleeps he has no intellect or emotion, so what connection is there [between covering one's head and *yiras Shomayim*]?

The explanation is: We were chosen from among all of the nations. This "chosen-ness" is not related to intellect and emotion, but rather, a Jew's very body was chosen. Since he is a Jewish body even when he sleeps, he therefore "feels" — by way of covering his head— the fear of heaven even during the time of sleep.

Explaining to a child that Hashem is One

When[154] teaching a child the *passuk* of "*Shema Yisrael - Hashem echad*", one explains that the Almighty is the *Melech Malchei Hamelachim* – the King over

---

151 *Igros Kodesh*, vol. 17, p. 109.
152 *Igros Kodesh*, vol. 5, p. 330.
153 *Sichos Kodesh 5736*, vol. 1, p. 89
154 *Toras Menachem*, 5714, p. 148, The Rebbe's Holy Care, Issue 7

all the "kings of kings." At an early age this suffices for the child to understand the unity of G-d: there are "kings," there are "kings of kings," and the Almighty is the "King" over all other "kings of kings," and no other "king" is equivalent to Him.

When the child grows older, his previous understanding is no longer sufficient. One then explains to him that in truth, there is no sovereignty apart from the Almighty. That is, in addition to His being the "King of all kings," He is the only Master present in all of existence. Everything else is just like the "axe in the hand of the lumberjack," which has no freedom to choose and simply carries out the will of its possessor. In fact, in this regard, the unity of the Almighty is greater, being that the "axe" itself is created by G-d.

In due course, when the child grows older, one explains to the child that in addition to the presence of no sovereignty other than G-d, there is, in fact, no existence outside of G-d.

Morality depends upon belief in Hashem

The[155] Ten Commandments begin with the *mitzvos* to believe in Hashem and not to worship any other deity. This sequence emphasizes that if we wish to ensure that children do not transgress "do not murder," "do not steal," and "do not covet," their entire education should be based upon belief in G–d's existence and rejection of anything that detracts from this belief.

To our sorrow, recent experience has shown that the same nation [Germany] that championed various philosophies and ideals [but without belief in G–d] ultimately sunk to the basest barbarity. Torah, however, which is "a teaching of life,"[156] guarantees not only eternal life in the World to Come, but also a life worthy of its name in this world.

An increase in one family members' *yiras Shamayim*

Since[157] family members are connected to each other not only physically but also spiritually, it is clear and simple that when one family member increases

---

155 *Igros Kodesh*, vol. 22, pp. 236-237.

156 *Amidah* liturgy.

157 *Igros Kodesh*, vol. 23, p. 376

in *yiras Shamayim,* this affects the other family members. This is especially so in regard to the parents' behavior and its impact upon the children. The more the parent increases in *yiras Shamayim*, the greater the impact will be [on the children].

Teaching *hashgacha pratis*

The[158] Baal Shem Tov once sent Rabbi Chaim Rappaport [a great Torah scholar][159] to a certain spot, and at that place he quenched his thirst from the wellspring. Afterwards, the Baal Shem Tov told him that this wellspring had been waiting since the Six Days of Creation for Rabbi Chaim Rappaport to come and recite a *bracha* on the water from that spring.

Similarly, … a Jewish boy or girl is walking on the street, becomes thirsty, and wants to drink water, and not only in order to quench his or her thirst, but in order to have a clear mind for learning Torah. At that precise moment, a truck passes by selling kosher drinks. The Jewish boy or girl should know that although the person selling the drinks does not know the child at all, knows nothing about their thirst and how much more so does he not know that a Jewish child will be passing by on his exact route – despite all this, it is no coincidence; rather, it is by *hashgacha pratis.*

Hashem orchestrated all the details so that the man selling the beverages would wake up at a certain time that day and go out with his truck at the precise moment when the Jewish child would be there, so that the truck would arrive and the two would meet. All this happened so the child would have something to drink and would not be uncomfortable due to thirst, and in this way, he can have a clear mind to study Torah... And the truth is that that street corner where the child made the *bracha* on the water and drank had waited since the Six Days of Creation for a Jewish child to come to that spot and bless Hashem! …

A Jewish child should be taught that Hashem עושה נפלאות גדולות ("performs great wonders and miracles")[160] and arranges all the particulars of

158 *Sichos Kodesh* 5741, vol. 1, pp. 245-247.

159 *Likkutei Dibburim,* vol. 4, 596a ff.

160 *Tehillim,* 136:4.

the world in order to fulfill his needs, such as food, drink, and the like.

In fact, we should tell a Jewish child that *Hakadosh Baruch Hu* עושה נפלאות גדולות ("performs great wonders and miracles") not only because this is the correct approach to *chinuch*, but because it is the truth. As our Sages teach, כל אחד ואחד חייב לומר בשבילי נברא העולם ("Every person must say: 'For my sake, the world was created'").[161]

A child who is told this and given this kind of *chinuch* [to recognize *hashgacha pratis]* will relate to the world, and his portion of the world in particular, in an entirely different manner.

Various[162] matters of *pnimiyus haTorah [Chassidus*] are now explained even to children, in a way that they can understand. In addition, they are told stories that teach them instructions connected with the *neshamah* of Torah *[Chassidus]*. For example, [children are told about] *hashgacha pratis*,[163] about the Baal Shem Tov's teaching of continuous creation [of the entire world] at each and every moment from *ayin* (nothing) into *yesh* (something), literally.[164] These concepts can even be explained to little children, even before the age of five or six. On the contrary, little children do not need a long explanation of the concept of continuous creation at each and every moment just as the first time [it was created], since they do not discern between the renewal of something that previously existed and something that is entirely new. ... A child readily accepts that every teaching in Torah and *Chassidus* is given by the *Echad ve'Yachid*, the One to whom he *davens:* Hashem's Essence.[165]

A *Yid* does not make calculations (statistics, probabilities, etc.)

The[166] youth should be told to set all calculations aside. A member of a nation not governed according to the natural order since its very birth; a member of

---

161 *Sanhedrin*, 37a.

162 *Hisvaaduyos* 5749, vol. 3, p. 314.

163 *Keser Shem Tov, Hosafos* 119.

164 Cf. *Tanya, Shaar Hayichud Veha'emunah,* ch. 1.

165 Cf. *Derech Mitzvosecha, Shoresh Mitzvas Hateffillah* ch. 8.

166 *Toras Menachem,* vol. 21, p. 159.

the most ancient religion, that has the oldest Torah, and which experienced many years of *nisyonos* and difficulties, whose entire existence is only through miracles – a member of such a nation is not connected with any calculations, and he has no reason to think about such things.

When parents guide the child in such a way while the child is still young, so that the child knows that he is above calculations and that he has an eternal connection with the Creator, then *Hakadosh Baruch Hu* promises, ביצחק יקרא לך זרע ("For by Yitzchak, your seed will be called"):[167] The parents will have true *nachas*, spiritually and materially.

Child's speech lacking in *emuna*

An[168] instruction to every teacher and educator: Pay special attention to the tone of the student's speech and questioning, that it does not have a tinge or a trace that is not in the spirit of *emuna*. If [the educator] detects such undesirable wording, *chas ve'shalom*, he should be like Rabbi Yehoshua, as his name implies, י-ה יושיעך ("Hashem will bring you salvation").[169] He should to try to do everything in his power to rescue the student by encouraging him to be careful to avoid *cholov akum* and other similar things that are prone to cause undesirable thoughts. …

Rashi's intention here is also to give instruction to a child who is בן חמש למקרא ("at five years of age [a child is brought] into the study of scripture"): [170] When a heretic asks [the child] such a question [not in the spirit of *emuna*], he should not enter into an argument with him. At most, he should direct him to the *chachomim* of *Yisrael* in his generation who are similar to Rabbi Yehoshua ben Karcha, who held debates and responded to the arguments of heretics.

---

167 *Bereishis*, 21:12.

168 *Hisvaaduyos* 5751, vol. 1, p. 201, fn. 88.

169 *Bamidbar* 13:16, *Rashi*.

170 *Avos*, 5:22.

"The world was created for me" – expressed appropriately

The[171] adage, "Every person must say: 'For my sake, the world was created"[172] applies to children as well. On the contrary, a child naturally feels that the entire world was created for him, even though children need the assistance of their parents at every step of the way. ... However, they should be educated to express this feeling in the appropriate way.

Instilling Important Values

A new channel

A[173] new channel in *chinuch* has been revealed in our times. Through the proper *chinuch*, it is now possible to break through the boundaries of the nature of a Jewish child and accustom the child to yearn for *ruchniyus* (spirituality) to such an extent that the child's heart is deeply permeated with an intense desire for Hashem to reveal Himself to him.

When a Jewish child is not grieved over the lack of Hashem's revelation to him, this is not because he is unable to reach this level, but because his educators [parents and teachers] are not speaking to him about these matters sincerely, with words that emanate from the heart.

Yearning for Hashem to the point of tears

Every[174] *Yid*, even a child, can be "lovesick."

Since a child's desires are more intense than an adult's (as we see, when a child wants something, he demands it with all his strength, he cries, and so on), so too, the state of being "lovesick" is closer to him.

---

171 *Hisvaaduyos* 5750, vol. 2, p. 139.

172 *Sanhedrin*, 37a.

173 *Likkutei Sichos*, vol. 15, p. 133.

174 *Hisvaaduyos* 5748, vol. 3, p. 291.

"A child desires small things of little value, as his intellect is underdeveloped and he does not yet appreciate commodities that are more precious and expensive." Even so, through a proper *chinuch,* a child can be influenced to desire loftier things. As is known, my father-in-law, the [Previous] Rebbe, related the story about his father, the Rebbe Rashab, who, when he was four or five years old, entered his grandfather's room during the week of *parshas Vayera* and began to cry, saying, "Why did Hashem appear to Avraham *Avinu,* but He did not reveal Himself to us?"

This teaches us that through a proper *chinuch,* one can influence a little child of four or five years old to the point that he desires the revelation of G-dliness, and to the point that he will even cry that it has not been revealed to him, which is what it means to be "lovesick."[175]

Chelek Eloka mi'maal mamash

It[176] is crucial to tell and explain to children that they have within them a *neshamah* that is a *chelek Eloka mi'maal mamash* ("a part of Hashem above"),[177] a *neshamah* that stood at *Har Sinai* at the Giving of the Torah, and that for it, the fulfillment of Torah and *mitzvos* is a matter of life, for Torah is חיינו ואורך ימינו ("our life and the length of our days").[178] [When this is explained to them,] they will naturally request and demand that their parents give them the most fundamental thing upon which their life depends.

Sense of pride in *Yiddishkeit*

Yidden[179] are always a minority among the nations of the world, and so too, in America. It is natural for a minority to develop an inferiority complex in relation to the majority. Therefore, it is essential to ingrain in a child, from the earliest age, a sense of pride in our heritage and customs, as well as a strong Jewish identity, so that instead of hiding their Jewishness, they can be proud of

175 Cf. *Likkutei Sichos*, vol. 15, p. 129 ff.

176 *Hisvaaduyos* 5748, vol. 3, p. 472.

177 *Tanya* ch. 2, beg.

178 *Devarim* 32:47. Evening liturgy.

179 *Moreh LeDor Nevoch*, p. 177.

it without any inhibitions, in spite of the mocking of non-Jewish neighbors, and the like. To do this it is necessary, above all, to instill in the child the right feelings toward true Jewish values by inculcating in them a preference for the spiritual over the material.

Pride in being different

The[180] purpose of a *Yid* is not to be *kadosh* on his own but, as is written about Avraham *Avinu:* אשר יצוה את בניו ואת ביתו אחריו ושמרו דרך הוי' ("He commanded his sons and his household after him, that they keep the way of Hashem").[181] In connection to this comes the second command: איש אמו ואביו תיראו ("Every man shall fear his mother and his father"). This *pasuk* hints at the obligation of *chinuch*: A child's first educators are his mother and father. Parents need to ingrain in their children the feeling that they are different from the entire world, for they are the members of a *goy kadosh* (holy nation).

The order of the *pasuk* is "mother and father." The mother is mentioned first because she is the *akeres habayis,* and so the *chinuch* is primarily in her hands.

The bearer of a sacred tradition

Jews[182] have always been "a minority among the nations", even in the best of times. At the same time "their laws differ from those of any other people," and they differ not only in regard to special occasions, or special aspects of life, such as Yom Kippur, but they differ in their *Shabbos* or Rosh HaShanah and way of life, and in every aspect of the daily life. For the Jew the Torah and Mitzvos are the guide of daily happiness, and this is the simple life and the source of life and true meaning of "*Toras Chaim*"- "Law of Life," and

180 *Likkutei Sichos*, vol. 1, p. 255.

181 *Bereishis,* 18:19.

182 *Letters from the Rebbe*, vol. 2, pp. 8-9.

the definition of the mitzvos as the essence of Jewish life, "whereby Jews live."

It is clear that being in the minority, Jews must have special reinforcements from childhood and on, in order to be able to hold their own in the face of overwhelming odds.

If it was difficult enough to live as a Jew in countries where Jews were persecuted or confined to ghettos, there was one redeeming factor at least, namely that under those circumstances Jewish adherence and loyalty to the Torah and mitzvos was not put to the test. An individual Jew could sever his ties with his people, but that involved a sudden and complete break; it was therefore rare and extreme. But in free countries, and under the present economic and social conditions, there are no outside barriers separating Jew from gentile; the road to assimilation is wide open, and the danger is all the greater since the process is a gradual one. No sudden break with tradition is entailed, but a gradual deviation, step after small step, leads in that direction.

There is a well-known parable for this, about the boy who strayed from the road and later found himself in the midst of the woods. He got there by making a small false step off the road, which let to another and yet another.

The conditions and environment in a country such as this call, therefore, for an even greater spiritual reinforcement of the Jewish boy and girl than ever before and elsewhere. This reinforcement must be of such strength and duration that the Jewish child will always be conscious of the fact that no matter what the environment is, he is the bearer of the sacred tradition of the Divine Torah and Mitzvos and belongs to a people that is holy and different. For this, it is essential that right from the earliest childhood to adolescence the Jewish child should receive the fullest possible Jewish education, throughout his formative years.

Jewish pride: The key to influencing non-Jews

Some[183] argue, "How can we influence non-Jews when we make it clear to them that the Jewish people behave in such a way that 'Their laws are different from [those of] all the nations'?"[184]

This very claim was put forward by Haman! The result of this claim was that when Haman's name is mentioned, even among non-Jews, the appellation "*wicked*" is added!

Haman argued: "How can the Jews follow laws different from all the non-Jews, when 'they are scattered and dispersed among the nations'?[185] This is contradictory![186] On account of this behavior, they forfeit the right to exist in our country." Haman promoted this argument until he succeeded at influencing the non-Jews not to disrupt his plans!

In spite of this, as the Scroll of Esther relates, the Jewish people, known as "the nation of Mordechai,"[187] emulated the behavior of "Mordechai the Jew,"[188] of whom it is written, לא יכרע ולא ישתחוה ("he would neither kneel nor prostrate himself").[189] Even "at the king's gate"[190] it should be evident that this is "Mordechai the Jew," and Haman must know that Mordechai will "neither kneel nor prostrate himself"!

The Jew's intention in refusing to submit to Haman is not to harm him or fight against him, but only to act in the way befitting for a Jew, according to the instruction of G–d, Who endowed him with his soul, and created his body.

---

183 *Hisvaaduyos* 5742, Vol. 2, pp. 954-958. Cf. *Hisvaaduyos* 5743, Vol. 1, pp 394-395.

184 *Esther,* 3:8.

185 Ibid.

186 I.e., if they are among the nations, they must follow the nations' customs.

187 Ibid. 3:6.

188 Cf. ibid. 2:5.

189 Ibid. 3:2. Mordechai refused to bow before Haman, for such an action could have been construed as idolatry, either because Haman wove an image of an idol on his clothes (*Esther Rabbah* 7:6), or because Haman fancied himself a deity (*Esther* 3:2, *Rashi*).

190 Ibid. 2:21.

When Jews behave in this way, all the provocations raised against them before the king and the top ministers will remain external and temporary. Ultimately the truth will prevail, for "truth will sprout forth from the earth"[191]!

As the Scroll of Esther relates, in the end, Mordechai's refusal to kneel and prostrate brought him honor, to the point that "the king took off his ring, which he had taken from Haman, and gave it to Mordechai,"[192] and instructed all the countries to assist the Jews in all areas, especially in matters related to observance of Judaism.

The Scroll of Esther should not be studied as a matter of history; rather, it holds an eternal lesson:

When a Jewish child lives in a neighborhood along with non-Jewish children, his mother or father might "pity" him, and tell him that since he is in an environment of non-Jews ("they are scattered and separated amongst the nations"),[193] and he encounters them on the street, it is inadvisable for him to appear different from everyone else – whether by his *tzitzis* protruding openly, or by refusing to eat a non-kosher candy that the non-Jewish child gives him. It is not worthwhile for him to behave in such a way that דתיהם שונות מכל עם ("their ways are different from every nation"),[194] they tell him, because this might anger the non-Jew, or at least diminish the non-Jew's respect for him.

However, the story of the Scroll of Esther teaches every Jewish mother that to hide the Jewish identity of one's child flies in the face of the child's very being.

They worry about the child's welfare, and protecting his honor in the eyes of his non-Jewish friends, and of a girl, in the eyes of her non-Jewish friends, and that the non-Jewish children should not persecute or beat the Jewish children, G–d forbid. However, the only way to attain this is for the Jewish child to show them that he does not deceive them, and he behaves like a Jew!

When a Jewish child walks with a *yarmulka* on his head, and checks right away upon being given a candy that it is kosher, and then tells the non-Jewish

---

191 *Tehillim*, 85:12.

192 *Esther*, 8:2.

193 *Esther*, 3:8.

194 Ibid.

child that before he eats a candy he blesses Hashem—this is the approach that will cause the non-Jew to respect him!

When the non-Jewish child asks: "Why do you recite a blessing before eating?" the Jewish child responds: "There is a G–d in the world!" When asked, "What is the connection between G–d and eating a candy?", the Jewish child responds [by explaining the meaning of the blessing]: "שהכל נהי' בדברו" ("everything was created by Hashem's word"). This candy is now in Brooklyn, Washington, or the like. Yet although it was apparently created by the factory workers, in reality "Everything was created by His word"—this candy was created only because so was the desire and word of G–d! Then the non-Jewish child will also understand that one should bless G–d before eating, just as one should say "thank you very much" upon receiving a gift.

First the child thanks Hashem for the candy, and only then may he eat it. Only a child who is not at all *aidel* (refined) could eat before expressing thanks. However, an *aidel* child knows that first one expresses thanks for a gift, and only then does he enjoy it!

Thus, the Scroll of Esther is clearly teaching us a lesson of eternal relevance, for Jewish children encounter non-Jewish children daily.

When a Jewish mother is approached and the above message is conveyed to her concerning the way that she should educate her children, she may argue, "Where is it written explicitly in *Shulchan Aruch* that when a Jewish child walks down the street, his Jewishness should be recognizable?!"

The reason this is not written explicitly in *Shulchan Aruch* is that it is self-evident!

However, when the evil inclination dominates, the person argues that since we do not find this written explicitly in *Shulchan Aruch*, and not even in *Kitzur Shulchan Aruch*, it is irrelevant to him!

He is not fussed by the "fanatics" who behave in this way, for he does not want to associate with fanatics!

One should answer as follows: This conduct is not "fanatic"; this is the true nature of every single Jew. He is a member of the "one nation,"[195] which

195 Ibid.

was created by G–d in a way that protection of his existence, health, and honor in the eyes of the nations is attained when he acts according to the verse, דתיהם שונות מכל עם ("their laws are different from every nation"),[196] not when the nations of the world see that he strives to deceive them and conceal his true identity from them!

One need not seek for this notion in the *Code of Jewish Law*, for it is written explicitly in the Scroll of Esther: When Mordechai sat "at the king's gate", he acted as he wished: He openly displayed his identity as "Mordechai *the Jew*," and he "would neither kneel nor prostrate himself." This approach led "his fame to spread throughout all the countries,"[197] until he became the viceroy—the one through whom Achashverosh governed all the countries of his empire!

This demonstrates that even when the Jewish people are in exile, and "still servants of Achashverosh"[198]—i.e., there is the Persian king, the ministers, and there are Jews among the ministers—when the Jew neither kneels nor prostrates himself to secular culture, he will be promoted to the position of viceroy.

This too is for the benefit of all the "one hundred and twenty-seven countries,"[199] for when the viceroy is a G–d-fearing Jew, all the countries will be governed appropriately.

In order for the Jew "at the king's gate" to "neither kneel nor prostrate himself," we must educate him in this spirit from childhood, as it is written, "Educate a youth according to his way", and then "even when he becomes old, he will not stray from it."[200]

Thus, the Jewish mother should educate her child not to be ashamed of his Jewishness. On the contrary, one should inculcate the child with Jewish pride in being privileged that G–d created him as a son of Avraham, Yitzchak, and Yaakov, or her as a daughter of Sarah, Rivkah, Rochel, and Leah. And

---

196 Ibid.

197 Ibid. 9:4.

198 I.e., still subordinate to the rule of the non-Jews. Cf. *Megillah* 14a.

199 Ibid. 1:1.

200 *Mishlei,* 22:6.

when the non-Jewish child asks him, "to which nation do you belong?" He should tell the truth with pride: "I am a member of the Jewish nation," "one nation" that is "scattered and dispersed among the nations"!

It is certainly forbidden to lie about this, for one lie leads to another, and so on. The non-Jewish children around him will lose confidence in him, for they see that he is ashamed of his identity, and of the identity of his parents, grandparents, and nation! It is clear just how much the children in his neighborhood will then respect and value him!

One should teach a child from childhood that his path in life is based upon a feeling of Jewish pride, and this will automatically lead him to build a Jewish home, one about which Hashem says, "I will dwell in their midst."[201] This home will be obviously Jewish, for at the entrance a *mezuzah* is affixed, in the house there are holy books, in the kitchen a division is evident between vessels of milk and meat, and so on.

When Hashem then chooses him to represent Jews and non-Jews, and to represent them in the leadership and administration of a neighborhood, city, or an entire country, he will follow the path of honesty—i.e., he will not hide the truth, nor will he be ashamed to follow the path of honesty! Only such conduct will bring people to genuinely reckon with his opinions, and not do so merely out of duress. Then he will succeed at establishing and introducing positive, ethical laws in the neighborhood, city, or entire country.

Then "his fame spreads throughout all the countries," and everyone respects and reveres him—as an individual, but primarily as a member of the "nation of Mordechai," who will neither kneel nor prostrate himself. Obviously one who serves in the government needs to know how to "neither kneel nor prostrate himself," for then even if people try to bribe him, we can rely that he will "neither kneel nor prostrate himself."

---

201 *Shemos*, 25:8.

Living like a *goy* is spiritual death for a *Yid*

[About[202] the command of: כל הבן הילוד תשליכוהו וכל הבת תחיון ("All the baby boys should be thrown into the Nile river, and the girls should be kept alive"),[203] the Rebbe says regarding the words וכל הבת תחיון:]

[*Par'oh*] instructed that the remaining [Jewish] children, who would remain physically alive, the Egyptians should "make them live" [i.e., the girls] by educating them to follow the Egyptian way of life in order to kill their *neshamos.* ... This is even worse than killing their bodies, for "spiritual death is worse than physical death."[204]

Should children play ball?

After[205] a child has already concluded his Torah studies and desires to play "ball", it would certainly be inappropriate to chastise him until he no longer wishes to play. Rather, the proper approach to similar matters such as utilizing rewards to propel a child to study is, as *Rambam* explains, "'teach a child according to his way,' through using an inviting, sympathetic yet firm hand, awarding the child with 'nuts and monetary rewards.'"

Indeed, because the child naturally wishes to play "ball," one must teach the child that the activity of playing ball itself should be "for the sake of heaven." In fact, the child ought to be explained that in order for you to study Torah better, it is necessary for you to engage in physical exercise and 'run around' a bit. This is the appropriate way to explain this to children.

The parents, however, ought to be explained that playing "ball" is equivalent to taking a 'pill.' When in need of ingesting medication, one certainly does not reject it but gives the medication to he who needs it. Nonetheless, it is clearly noted that this is no remedy for a healthy person. Similarly, it is

---

202 *Likkutei Sichos,* vol. 1, p. 111.

203 *Shemos,* 1:22.

204 *Derech Chaim,* ch. 1. Cf. *Rashi* on *Devarim* 23:9, "One who causes another to sin is worse than one who kills him."

205 Sicha, Parshas Shemini 5740, *The Rebbe's Holy Care,* Issue 17

exclusively the child who is taught to play ball for the sake of Heaven, simply because this may prove to be the most relevant and spiritually fulfilling message for his present spiritual standing. The "medication" is for him. However, for one who recognizes the significance of Torah-study and fulfillment of the *mitzvos*, engaging in such activity would be equivalent to ingesting medication which has been prescribed for another, making it lethal. Obviously, when explaining sports to a child, one cannot present the concept of playing ball as being compared to medication. Yet this must be one's approach to the issue.

That being said, I must unfortunately point out the following: With the aforementioned, I do not intend to encourage people to begin (tonight, after *Shabbos*) to inquire how to play "football", for such behavior would indicate childish intelligence. For if one understands the virtue of Torah-study and the fulfillment of the *mitzvos*, it would certainly be foolish to forfeit an opportunity to engage in their study and observance for playing ball instead! In addition, it would certainly be inappropriate for one who recognizes the significance of Torah study to suggest that one may first play ball and subsequently attain the virtue of repentance (*teshuvah*). For one who deliberately sins with the intent to subsequently repent is not granted the opportunity to repent from on-high. In fact, such an approach counters the Divine intent, and is antithetic to the entire Torah. Of what 'sin' is 'playing ball'? In this instance, it is a matter of relinquishing the opportunity to study Torah to play ball instead. It is only a child (either in age or in intelligence) who has yet to recognize the significance and virtue of Torah study, who must be taught "according to his way" to play ball, but to play 'for the sake of Heaven'.

There[206] is an additional approach to playing ball for a Divine purpose that can, in fact, be explained to children. While playing ball with a Gentile, the motivating objective of the Jewish child should be for *Yiddishkeit* to triumph. The child should be taught that this can be achieved by wearing '*tzitzis*', eating kosher food, and 'davening' before the game, and upon being victorious, proclaiming '*Boruch* Hashem!'. For the child thus shows the Gentile as well as the entire world that although he conducts himself as a Jew, it is he

[206] Sicha, Parshas Shemini 5740, *The Rebbe's Holy Care,* Issue 17.

who managed to score the goal and win the game. It's especially because he conducts himself as a Jew that he can be the best at playing ball!

Striving to grow

Every[207] educator instills in their student the awareness that a person grows and must mature, rising higher and higher, and not stand in one place in his accomplishments. For this, the educator adduces proof from the physical body, which also grows.

This is a fundamental principle in *chinuch*. A child cannot be told, "Now that you have reached your perfection for today, stop here. You need not continue learning in school tomorrow." On the contrary, even though he remembers everything he was taught, since he is a living person, he must increase his knowledge, improve his *middos* (character traits), actions, learning, and so on.

Even when it comes to העלאה בקודש (increasing in *kedusha*), one cannot suffice with a one-time action. Rather, every single day, the student is required to increase further in *kedusha* than his level on the previous day.

We see this clearly when a child returns home from school. If the parents act as they should, they immediately ask the natural question: "What did you learn today?" This question means, "What is new in your learning today compared to what you learnt yesterday?"

... This principle is a constant foundation of *chinuch:* One must change from day-to-day and constantly aspire to grow in *kedusha*... חנוך לנער על פי דרכו (כדי שגם) כי יזקין לא יסור ממנה ("Raise a child according to his way, [so that] even when he grows old, he will not depart from it").[208] In other words, a child is taught when he is young that he should rise in *kedusha* all the days of his life, and even כי יזקין (when he ages), meaning when he reaches high levels of *chochmah*, according to the saying זקן זה שקנה חכמה ("An 'old person' is one who has acquired wisdom"), he still has the obligation to rise in *kedusha*. This is all the more true in light of the precise wording שקנה חכמה ("who 'bought' wisdom"),[209] which implies that the wisdom becomes his personal possession, and does not remain comparable to an item borrowed temporarily.

---

207 *Hisvaaduyos* 5744, vol. 1, pp. 105-106.

208 *Mishlei*, 22:6.

209 *Kiddushin*, 32b.

Children are *shluchim*

Every[210] single *Yid* is a *shaliach* (emissary) of *Hakadosh Baruch Hu* to make for *Hashem Yisborach* a *dirah betachtonim* (a dwelling place in the lowest world).[211] In addition to this, some have merited to become "*shluchim*" ["ones who are sent out"] in actual practice, for they were sent to a certain place in order to be involved in disseminating Torah and *Yiddishkeit*, and in disseminating the wellsprings outward.

The *avodah* of *shlichus* is carried out by the *shluchim* and all the other household members: the wife, sons, daughters, and even babies. Although they have not yet reached complete understanding, their actions are considered actions.[212] What's more, infants have the advantage of being sincere, for it is the way of little children to do everything with sincerity.

Even[213] the smallest child [is the *shaliach* of Hashem, making this world a dwelling place for *Hakadosh Baruch Hu*] – when he recites the blessing, "*Shehakol nihiyoh bidvaro.*" Even when a newborn baby lies in a bassinet with a *"Shir Hamaalos"* hanging next to him, or next to the mother who just gave birth to him, the baby is fulfilling the *shlichus* of *Hakadosh Baruch Hu* in this world by bringing matters of *kedusha* into the hospital. This *[shlichus]* applies to every Jewish child and every single *Yid*, in accordance with his individual circumstances.

Influencing their friends

By[214] nature, children befriend other children their age (or a little older or younger). A child wants to show off how in certain areas, he has the ability to rule over and dominate his fellow. This nature should be utilized for *kedusha* [by explaining to the child that] he should educate his friends. When children meet their friends at school, at home, or even on the street, they should take the opportunity to influence [them] in matters of *Yiddishkeit*, Torah, and *mitzvos* applicable to them.

---

210 *Hisvaaduyos* 5750, Vol. 3, pp. 135-136.

211 *Midrash Tanchuma, Naso* 16. *Tanya* ch. 36.

212 Cf. *Chulin* 12b ff.

213 *Hisvaaduyos* 5750, vol. 2, p. 433.

214 *Sichos Kodesh* 5736, vol. 2, pp. 146-147.

A child should be aware that when he knows a fact or topic in the written or oral Torah that his friends do not yet know, he should teach them about this matter.

Since קנאת סופרים תרבה חכמה ("Jealousy among scholars causes wisdom to proliferate"),[215] the other child will also be motivated to act in this manner, to explain, and to teach yet another child a teaching in Torah that he knows but of which his friend is still ignorant. He will do this with great enthusiasm, as is the nature and virtue of children that they do everything with passion and excitement, not in a measured and limited way.

The result of raising children with a boundless passion for Torah matters, one that is above limitations, is that גם כי יזקין לא יסור ממנו[216] – even when they grow older, they will remain connected with the [positive] abandonment of limitations and constrictions, above and beyond measure and limitation.

Children should teach other children

With[217] regard to children, each boy and girl should make an effort, in addition to his or her studies at school or Yeshivah, to establish a class to teach other children lessons of the Torah that he or she has studied. In particular, since the nature of children is to have a passion for influencing other children, it is necessary to utilize this nature for the study of Torah.

Saving *Yidden*

During[218] Avraham *Avinu's* life (before his *bris milah),* he was very involved in publicizing Hashem in the world, as it is written, הנפש אשר עשו בחרן ("The souls which they made in Charan"), שהכניסו תחת כנפי השכינה אברהם מגייר את האנשים כו' ("They brought them under the wings of the *Shechinah;* Avraham would convert the men ...").[219] In the words of the *Rambam,*[220] "He began

215 *Bava Basra,* 21a.

216 *Mishlei,* 22:6.

217 *Sefer Hasichos* 5750, vol. 2, p. 502.

218 *Hisvaaduyos* 5749, vol. 1, pp. 333-334.

219 *Bereishis,* 12:5, *Rashi.*

220 *Mishneh Torah, Hilchos Avoda Zara* 1:3.

to proclaim in a loud voice to the entire world, informing them that there is one G-d, and it is fitting to worship him. He would go from city to city and from kingdom to kingdom, gathering the inhabitants in each place, until he reached *Eretz Kenaan*... until he gathered tens of thousands..."

...Regarding one's obligation to be involved in spreading Torah and *Yiddishkeit*, the very fact that one sees a *Yid* in a state of *pikuach nefesh* (danger to [spiritual] life) is by *hashgacha pratis* (according to the Baal Shem Tov's famous teaching).[221] This is clear proof that this task is incumbent upon the observer, that influencing this Jew is part of his role and *shlichus*. He has surely been given the abilities necessary to do this, for "Hashem only demands according to one's ability."[222] Therefore, he should set aside all his personal affairs and run to perform an act of *chessed* for this *Yid*, to draw him close to Hashem, Torah, and *mitzvos*.

...It should be emphasized that what we are saying about the dissemination of Torah and *Yiddishkeit* and the dissemination of the wellsprings applies to every single *Yid* – old and young; men, women, and children. Every single *Yid* can be influenced, and every single *Yid* can and should influence others. If someone claims that he does not know [enough to do this] and the like, in every single place, someone can be found who can teach him, which will enable him to influence others. [This applies] even to children, for in our times, matters of *Chassidus* have been explained in such a way that even little children can understand.

Encouraging others to increase in *mitzvos*

Special[223] emphasis should be placed on the words of our *Navi*, the vision of Yeshayahu ben Amotz: ציון במשפט תפדה ושביה בצדקה ("Zion shall be redeemed through justice and her captives through righteousness").[224] ... This means that by studying Torah and fulfilling its *mitzvos*, particularly the *mitzvah* of *tzedakah*, we hasten the *geulah*. The matter of *tzedakah* involves... giving *tzedakah* both

221 *Keser Shem Tov, Hosafos* #119-129.

222 *Bamidbar Rabbah* 12:3.

223 *Likkutei Sichos*, vol. 13, p. 269.

224 *Yeshaya*, 1:27.

with the body and with the *neshamah*. "*Tzedakah* with the body" is understood simply, by giving *tzedakah* to the poor or to a *tzedakah* box. "*Tzedakah* with the *neshamah*" means to make efforts so that acquaintances and friends increase in matters of Torah and *Yiddishkeit*, through each person being a *dugmah chayah*, and speaking with them about this with words that emanate from the heart.[225]

Instilling the attributes of compassion and *bittul*

Teaching[226] a boy or girl to donate of their own money to another, ("[money] with which one could buy sustenance for life [i.e., food]"[227]), and especially teaching [the child] to perform acts of *gemilus chassadim* with his body [such as helping out another, or giving of his time] – all this ingrains in a child the attributes of humility and *bittul*. ...

> **A sensitivity for *kedusha***
>
> As[228] we can see, in a *chassidishe chinuch*, even before the child knows how to distinguish good from bad, he is educated immediately to have א חסידישן קאך ("a chassidic passion") in matters of *kedusha*, in a way that transcends boundaries and limitations. He is taught that these teachings are directed at *him*, and so he should act accordingly.

Bringing children to *farbrengens*

Little[229] children, three years of age, should be brought [to *farbrengens*] to squeeze themselves in between the *chassidim*.

...A *chassid* once related how a *Yid* would bring his little child to a *siyum* on *erev Pesach*. Someone asked him, "Does your child understand?" [The father] responded, "And they – the adults – they do understand?!"

---

225 Cf. *Sefer HaYashar* of *Rabeinu Tam*. Quoted in *Shelah*, 69a.

226 *Likkutei Sichos*, vol. 16, p. 626.

227 *Tanya*, 48b.

228 *Hisvaaduyos* 5742, vol. 3, p. 1456.

229 *Toras Menachem*, vol. 5, p. 180.

[The Frierdiker Rebbe relates:][230]

Once when I was a baby, on one of the nights after *Sukkos,* my father took me to a *farbrengen* of *chassidim* that was being held in the *ulam hakatan* (the "small hall" in the village of Lubavitch). My mother, who was worried about me, said, "Doesn't the child need to sleep?" My father responded, "Don't worry; let him sleep in the *beis midrash* (Torah study hall), and when he grows older, he won't want to sleep."

When[231] I was a little child, *chassidim* once *farbrenged* on *Simchas Beis HaSho'evah*, and I was also there...

Then when I fell asleep in the *Sukkah,* my mother came in to take me home. My father did not allow her, saying, "Don't worry; he should be amongst *chassidim,* and *Hashem Yisborach* will help him." He then blessed me with a long life.

Once[232] at a *farbrengen* for *Simchas Beis HaSho'evah,* I fell asleep in the *Sukkah*. My mother came out there in order to take me home. My father did not allow it, saying, "So he'll sleep!"

My mother responded, "Is this the fulfillment of כרחם אב אל בנים ("A father has compassion for his children")? The Torah verse doesn't say כרחם אם ("a *mother* has compassion"), but כרחם אב" ("a *father* has compassion").

My father answered, "This is the *true* meaning of a father having compassion on his children."

"It's cold here," my mother protested. "He could catch a cold."

"He won't catch a cold," my father said. "Let him sleep amongst the *chassidim*; he will warm up, and this heat will last him for many generations."

This is *mesirus nefesh* for *chinuch.*

230 *Yud Beis Tammuz* 5708.

231 *Sefer Hamaamarim* 5711, p. 90.

232 *Sichas Leil Beis Sukkos*, 5707.

Expectation for *geulah*

Students[233] should be educated in a manner that arouses within them the expectation of *geulah* through *Moshiach tzidkeinu*, for whom we wait every day. As *Rashbi* stated:[234] "how precious *Yisrael* are to *Hakadosh Baruch Hu*, that in each place that they are exiled, the *Shechinah* is with them. And when they are redeemed, the *Shechinah* is with them, as it is written, 'Hashem will return your captives.'"[235]

The *Beis Hamikdash* will very soon be rebuilt

We[236] need to know that one of the main ways to nullify the decree... is to gather Jewish children and to teach them Torah and about *Yiddishkeit*:

They should be told that the bringing of the complete redemption is in [each] individual's hands and therefore there is no reason to despair, since once *Bnei Yisrael* do *teshuvah,* we will immediately be redeemed.

They should be told that the *Beis Hamikdash* will speedily be rebuilt and we all need to be prepared to serve Hashem!

Faces radiating *geulah*

אל תגעו במשיחי: אלו תינוקות של בית רבן ("'Do[237] not touch my anointed ones':[238] these are the school children").[239]

One of the explanations of this (in addition to the interpretation of the commentators) is that the *chinuch* of children should be handled in such a way that the children are permeated so completely with the faith in *Moshiach* that when one glances at a Jewish child, what does one see? *Moshiach*!

---

233 *Likkutei Sichos*, vol. 17, p. 507.

234 *Zohar* 1:257a; *Megillah* 29a.

235 Devarim, 30:3.

236 *Likkutei Sichos*, vol. 36, p. 266.

237 *Hisvaaduyos* 5752, vol. 1, pp. 148-149.

238 *Divrei Hayamim,* 16:22.

239 *Shabbos,* 119b.

Their entire existence is *Moshiach* and the revelation of אתה הראת גו' אין עוד מלבדו ("You were shown that… there is nothing else besides Him").[240]

Hashem's army

The[241] children of our generation are called (with the consent of *Gedolei Yisrael)* by the name *Tzivos Hashem.*

The name *Tzivos Hashem* demonstrates that children are devoted and nullified entirely to *Hakadosh Baruch Hu*, similar to (and more than) soldiers to their commanders. This conforms with the wording of the text during the exodus from *Mitzrayim,* הוציא ה' את בני ישראל מארץ מצרים על צבאותם ("Hashem took the children of *Yisrael* out of the land of Egypt with their legions"), which implies a level [of dedication] higher than that found under the limitations of an army.

Davening

Modeh Ani

The[242] day of every *Yid*, including a little child, begins with declaring *Modeh ani lefanecha...* for he is taught in such a way that every area of *Yiddishkeit* applies to him. He recites it not with the lips alone, but in a way of כל עצמותי תאמרנה ("all my limbs will declare"):[243] His entire body sways in declaring, "*Modeh ani lefanecha…*"

Reciting *Birkas Hamazon*

We[244] educate children to recite the *Birkas Hamazon* (Grace after Meals), a blessing whose obligation is biblical, and in a way that they understand intellectually that they should bless and thank Hashem for physical sustenance.

---

240 *Devarim,* 4:35.

241 *Hisvaaduyos* 5752, vol. 1, p. 149.

242 *Hisvaaduyos* 5751, vol. 4, p. 310.

243 *Tehillim,* 35:10.

244 *Sefer Hasichos* 5752, vol. 1, pp. 88-89.

The[245] *Minhag Yisrael* (Jewish custom) is well known that before a child is able to recite the *Birkas Hamazon* in its entirety, he may recite a portion of it. It is the custom in several congregations to recite only the first blessing, *Birkas Hazan,* with the child.

Thanking Hashem for all one's possessions

Furthermore,[246] [children should be taught to thank Hashem] not only for food that gives vitality to the body and becomes their flesh and blood, but also for the physical objects in the home, as is emphasized in the *mitzvah* of *mezuzah*. Every single Jew holds the *mezuzah*, even in infancy, for we see how Jewish children are drawn by nature to kiss the *mezuzah*. They are lifted up to kiss the *mezuzah* several times throughout the day. This is done especially at the beginning of the day, right upon awakening, and at the end of the day, before they go to sleep. Through it being affixed at the entrance of the home and the entrance to every room, it is apparent that all the objects in the room, the room itself, and the entire home are connected to the one G-d.

The essence of a child's *davening:* Hashem's name should be upon their lips

[The[247] Rebbe discussed the plight of Jewish children in public schools, who lack a Jewish education.] The call of the hour is to strive with all one's strength to keep this coal [of faith] from being extinguished, *chas ve'shalom*. ...

At the very least, [these children should make sure to engage in] proper *davening* every day, so that the name of Hashem will constantly come forth from the mouths of children... Regarding the conduct of the Baal Shem Tov, one of the holy ways of serving Hashem for which he is famous was to strive for Hashem's name to be on everyone's lips, including simple people, women, and children. He accomplished this by inquiring how they were doing so they would respond "*Baruch Hashem*" and the like.

245 *Sichos Kodesh* 5737, vol. 1 p. 460.

246 *Sefer Hasichos* 5752, vol. 1, p. 89.

247 *Igros Kodesh,* vol. 22, p. 475.

Learning the simple explanation of the *tefillos*

The[248] Tzemach Tzedek directed all the *melamdim* who learned with his grandchildren to teach them the simple meaning of the words of *tefillah*, in addition to their regular learning. Once a month, they would come to the Tzemach Tzedek to be tested in this.

Skipping sections to keep up with the *minyan*

Regarding[249] his question about what should be done about boys who come late, for if they are not told to skip the order of *davening* before *Hodu*, they will be unable to *daven* with a *minyan*.

The saying of our Sages, איזהו חכם הרואה את הנולד ("Who is wise? The one who looks ahead at the outcome of a course of action"),[250] is relevant in every single area, including this one. It is clear that it is indeed the law that one should skip over portions (as in the *sefer Shaarei Tefillah* of Rabbi Yaakov Rokei'ach, where ninety-one opinions who believe so are quoted). However, one should look ahead [at the results of teaching the youth to do so]. After a short while – as we have already seen from experience – the *heter* (dispensation) to skip over the sections before הודו [leads] afterwards to [skipping] *Pesukei De'zimrah* as well, and afterwards, etc. In particular [this is problematic] since his question is regarding youth.... Practically, even though one cannot *pasken* and publicize something differing from the *din*, it is necessary to do everything possible to prevent them knowing about the *heter* to skip sections. This is similar to the Torah's teaching to desecrate one *Shabbos* in order to keep many *Shabbosos*...[251]

---

248 *Hayom Yom*, 8 Teves.

249 *Igros Kodesh*, vol. 7, p. 139. Cf. *Igros Kodesh*, vol. 18, p. 81.

250 *Tamid*, 32a.

251 *Shabbos*, 151b.

Teaching a student to have *kavanah* in *davening*

The[252] desire of the students to *daven* a little longer on *Shabbos* should be honored. However, they should be guided [on how to do this]. They should also be supervised, to [ensure that they] fulfill the instruction of having their thoughts on appropriate matters and not thoughts that stray from here to there. Although one cannot know the thoughts of another person,[253] one can oversee this by asking a question beforehand – on *erev Shabbos* or on *Shabbos* before *davening* – to inquire what [the student] will think about, and so on, or by instructing beforehand that it would be correct [for the student] to reflect upon a certain matter (which corresponds to the weekly *parshah* or the meaning of the words [of *davening*]).

Don't dampen youthful enthusiasm

You[254] write that you are unhappy that the students are davening at length, since it doesn't coincide with their conduct in other areas, and you are worried that they are being "showoffs." Your arguments may be correct; however, it's obvious to anyone who studies the nature of today's youth that they in particular are going through a period of crisis. Therefore, one should be very careful to avoid anything that might weaken the strength of their opposition to the "winds [of heresy] blowing in the world." So even when it comes to matters that are premature for them to get involved with on their present level, since it increases their ability to stand firm against the "winds blowing outside," [by depriving them of it,] you carry the responsibility for removing or weakening the matter.

If you believe that there is a contradiction between their davening at length and their conduct in other areas, then effort should be made, in a calm but firm manner, to influence them to improve in those areas as well. However, don't stop the davening at length, since eventually this will increase their *yiras Shamayim* (fear of Heaven) and remove them further from worldly pleasures, even if only on a superficial level.

---

252 *Igros Kodesh,* vol. 14, p. 319.

253 Cf. *Pesachim* 54b.

254 *Igros Kodesh,* vol. 5, p. 325.

Tefillin

One does not bless *Shehecheyanu* when putting on *tefillin* for the first time

[Our] [255] custom is not to recite *Shehecheyanu* when putting on *tefillin* for the first time.

Why does a child preparing for the *mitzvah* of *tefillin* not make a *bracha* as with the *chinuch* of other *mitzvos?*

He[256] asks: A child recites *brachos* upon all the *mitzvos* that he performs, even though he performs these *mitzvos* only for *chinuch* purposes. However, when he begins to put on *tefillin,* we learn that our custom is that "Two months before he reaches thirteen years [he begins to wear *tefillin],* at first without a *bracha...*"[257] This was the directive of the Rebbe, my father-in-law. What is the reason for this difference?

The simple answer is that when performing other *mitzvos,* the child recites a *bracha* for *chinuch* purposes. There is no deficiency in the way that the child performs the *mitzvah* as compared to the way an adult fulfills the same *mitzvah.* However, with donning *tefillin* one should be precise about the placement and tying of the *tefillin,* as well as other details, and a child cannot be relied upon to do everything properly even after he has been taught for a few days... because, due to his young age, he does not recognize how precious and great is the matter.

However, when he is taught all this over a period of weeks [and he perfects his skill over time, he will be ready to recite the *bracha*]. According to *nigleh* and *Chassidus,* the essence of the *mitzvah* of *tefillin* is to subdue the mind and heart,[258] as is also stated in *Shulchan Aruch.*[259] Spiritually, the main purpose [of *tefillin]* is *hamshachas hamochin* (drawing down the intellect) which represents maturity,

255 *Likkutei Sichos*, vol. 11, p. 289.

256 *Likkutei Sichos,* vol. 19, p. 442.

257 *Hayom Yom,* 2 Av.

258 *Tanya,* 56b.

259 *Bach* on *Tur*, *Orach Chaim*, 625.

and this is why *chinuch* is less applicable to *tefillin.* In contrast, regarding the other *mitzvos,* maturity is only a precondition to becoming obligated in the *mitzvah,* but not related to the essence of the *mitzvah.*

Why is the amount of time to don *tefillin* without a *bracha* not specified?

[You[260] ask] regarding the instruction of my-father-in-law, the Rebbe (in *Hayom Yom)*[261] that when beginning to put on *tefillin,* the exact time period is not specified as to how long this is done without a *bracha.* [You also inquire about] the reason for beginning without a *bracha:*

It can be said simply: [the boy wears *tefillin* without a *bracha*] until he becomes accustomed to being thoroughly precise in the donning of the *tefillin* in accordance with details of the *mitzvah*, as otherwise he would be making a *bracha levatalah* (a blessing said in vain). Since not all boys are alike in this regard, there is no set time for donning *tefillin* without a *bracha.*

Chol HaMoed within two months before *bar mitzvah*

[When[262] *Chol HaMoed* days fall within the two months before the *bar mitzvah,* during the period when one begins to don *tefillin*], he can begin a week earlier than usual. May it be held at a good and auspicious time.

Tzitzis

When he begins to walk

When[263] he begins to walk [unassisted], he should be dressed with *tzitzis.*

---

260 *Igros Kodesh*, vol. 14, p. 63.

261 *Hayom Yom,* 2 Av.

262 *Igros Kodesh*, vol. 23, p. 89.

263 *Igros Kodesh Admor HaRashab*, p. 905, *Hisvaaduyos* 5748, vol. 2, p. 421, fn. 27.

Protects the child

Regarding[264] their son's fears... may he live, he should wear a *tallis katan* of the correct measure* and have it explained to him that the *tallis katan* protects and guards the wearer, because the *tzitzis* testify that he is a servant of Hashem.

> *Regarding[265] children who reach the age of *chinuch*, from age six until age thirteen, one can be lenient and rely on the opinion of those who say that the measure of the garment that obligates the wearing of *tzitzis* is one *amah* by one *amah*.

Brings to the keeping of all Hashem's *mitzvos*

The[266] *mitzvah* of *tzitzis* is equal to all the *mitzvos*.[267] When a *Yid*, even a child who has reached the age of *chinuch*, wears a *tallis katan (tzitzis)*, he fulfills what is written וראיתם אותו וזכרתם את כל מצוות ה׳ ועשיתם אותם ("you shall see it and remember all Hashem's *mitzvos*, and you shall do them").[268] That is to say, the *tzitzis katan* – not only the *mitzvah* of *tzitzis gadol* – serves as a reminder. What's more, it reminds [the person] and brings to the fulfillment of all of Hashem's *mitzvos*. Moreover, this [brings about the same result] for every single *Yid* who sees the *tzitzis*.

Draws down Hashem's *Malchus*

It[269] is obvious that every *hiddur* possible, in whatever the *mitzvah* may be, is most correct. Surely this applies regarding *tzitzis* and *tallis*, as our Sages say, זה א-לי ואנוהו ("This is my G-d and I will beautify Him")[270] – "beautifying Him with *mitzvos* – with beautiful *tzitzis*"[271] [and the same principle applies

---

264 *Likkutei Sichos*, vol. 3, p. 273.
265 *Shulchan Aruch Admor HaZaken*, *halachos* of *tzitzis*.
266 *Hisvaaduyos* 5748, vol. 2, p. 421.
267 *Nedarim*, 25a.
268 *Bamidbar*, 15:39.
269 *Igros Kodesh*, vol. 14, p. 329.
270 *Shemos*, 15:2.
271 *Shabbos*, 133b.

to other *mitzvos*]. It is known that the spiritual meaning behind wrapping oneself in *tzitzis* is "to elicit Hashem's attribute of *Malchus* ("royalty") upon the person – which is the *Malchus* of all the worlds – to connect it with us through this *mitzvah.*"[272]

Therefore, any *hiddur* possible in this *mitzvah* can affect all of one's matters. This includes using lamb's wool that is suitable without any doubt, *avodah* that is *lishmah* [i.e., the preparation of the *tzitzis* must be done with proper intent for the *mitzvah*] in all details, and more, as is explained in the *Shulchan Aruch* of the Alter Rebbe, *Divrei Nechemiah,* and other sources.

Instilling a passion for Torah

Kissing *Sefer Torah* with affection

Even[273] the smallest child, who has not yet begun to study Torah, knows the importance of Torah. The child is brought to *shul* to kiss the *Sefer Torah* lovingly, with the same affection that he kisses what is most precious to him, namely his father and mother. What's more, because his parents and teacher give him the proper *chinuch*, he may sense that he should kiss the *Sefer Torah* with even more affection than he kisses his parents.

Understanding Torah

[Before[274] a child reaches the age of five] his mother, father, or older siblings teach him *pesukim* from Torah, whether in *lashon hakodesh* or another language. [The language doesn't matter,] the goal is for the child to understand as much as possible.

When a child learns and understands the words of Torah properly, because his parents chose good educators for him and made efforts for him to understand the words of Torah, then the Torah fills his entire existence. He is then able to understand that it gives him *chayus* (inspiration), as the

272 See *Tanya,* ch. 41, beg.

273 *Hisvaaduyos* 5749, vol. 1, p. 203.

274 *Hisvaaduyos* 5751, vol. 1, p. 156.

verse states, חיינו ואורך ימינו ("[the words of Torah are] our life and the length of our days").[275]

Explaining to a child on their level

Explaining[276] something to a little child in words that he can understand should not mean telling him something untrue, *chas ve'shalom*. After all, little children too need to be told explanations from Toras Emes ("the Torah of Truth").[277] Rather, the explanation should be vested in words that he can understand. ...

This is especially so according to the known statement told by my-father-in-law, the Rebbe, in a *sicha* he delivered about the virtue of receiving an *aliyah laTorah* (ascent to the Torah): When one learns a matter in Torah that the *nefesh* below does not understand, when he rises to the Torah, all the levels in his soul rise above: the *ru'ach* of the *neshamah* rises to the world of *Yetzirah,* and so forth, until the *yechidah* rises to worlds that are infinite, and there the matters he learned are understood.

The same is true with children: even though they do not understand the *pnimiyus* of the matter, the matter exists to them all the same, and it leaves an impression on their soul.

Recently, the wisdom of the nations of the world has also reached this conclusion (and they speak about it as though it is their own revelation). They agree that things that happen to a child immediately after his birth leave a lasting impression and have an effect upon him when he matures as well.

---

275 *Devarim* 32:47. Evening liturgy.

276 *Sichos Kodesh* 5736, *Rosh Chodesh Iyar.*

277 Blessings on the Torah.

Speaking only words of Torah

Parents[278] need to strive toward the goal that their children live up to the *pasuk* לדבר בם - ולא בדברים אחרים ("'You should speak words of Torah'[279] – and not of other [mundane] things"[280]).

Although sometimes there is talk of other things, it is מלאכתך ארעי (temporary)[281] and only a preparation for having a better understanding of Torah or to be able to speak words of Torah with more vitality.

This applies to sons and daughters equally. Although with respect to *limmud haTorah* there is a major difference between sons and daughters, the Alter Rebbe writes at length and in detail that in all areas related to *Yiras Shamayim* there are no differences between a man and woman (see *Hilchos Talmud Torah*, end of Chapter 1).

Giving children *sefarim* as gifts

It[282] is fitting and correct to utilize the *minhag Yisrael* of giving *sifrei kodesh* as gifts; including to small children as well, on their joyous occasions or before a *Yom Tov* and so on.

When children meet, they should learn Torah

...It[283] is worthwhile to strengthen the custom that when two children meet, it be שנים שיושבים ועוסקים בתורה ("two who sit and are involved in Torah")[284] [i.e., they should discuss Torah]. All the more so when there are more than two children, and more than three. Through this, Torah is further ingrained into the lives of the children, and it gives them life.

---

278 *Sichos Kodesh* 5728, vol. 2, p. 430.
279 *Devarim,* 6:7.
280 *Yoma,* 19b.
281 Cf. ibid.
282 *Hisvaaduyos* 5752, vol. 2, p. 76.
283 *Hisvaaduyos* 5751, vol. 1, p. 156.
284 *Avos,* 3:6.

Learning with a *chavrusa*

The[285] instruction of our Sages that one should make a point to study [Torah] with a companion is well-known.[286] Surely he can find a *chavrusa* (study partner) in the place where he lives. It is possible that [in the past] the circumstances did not suit his needs in this regard – that is, either he had no *chavrusa,* or the individual was not a fitting *chavrusa*. This detracts from the success of one's learning. It is obvious that even if one has no *chavrusa,* it is still necessary to learn Torah. It is also clear that despair and low spirits do not come from "the side of *kedusha.*" As we see with our own eyes, this is not the way to inspire diligence, as is explained in several sources, including the *Tanya.*[287]

Sensitive topics in *Chumash/Nach*

In[288] learning *Chumash* and *Nach* (נ"ך), no matters should be skipped over, such as Yehuda and Tamar, David and Bas-Sheva, and the like. The material should be learned according to the foundations of our Sages.

Spreading the wellsprings to children

[This[289] is a response] regarding their question, "Is the spreading of the wellsprings [of *Chassidus*] also applicable to children of a tender age or to those who have not yet received a fitting *chinuch?*"

It is understandable that the spreading of the wellsprings applies to every single *Yid* [including children]. However, it is also understandable that one must use a channel and terminology that is appropriate to each person, according to their level of understanding and circumstances.

Regarding this, we learn from my father-in-law, the Rebbe, the *Nasi* of the Jewish people, who publicized both deep and intellectual *maamarim* in *lashon hakodesh* and also *maamarim* that are easy to understand and to apply to one's

285 *Igros Kodesh*, vol. 14, p. 414.

286 *Taanis,* 7b.

287 E.g., *Likkutei Amarim,* ch. 26.

288 *Hosafos Le'Sichos Kodesh* 5728, vol. 1, p. 506.

289 *Igros Kodesh*, vol. 18, p. 191.

avodah, which he publicized them in *Yiddish,*[290] ... and in other languages as well. All this he did in the context of spreading the wellsprings, but the form was tailored to fit to the recipient.

Learning *Chassidus* from age five

According[291] to the saying of the *Mishnah*, "*Ben chamesh shanim le'mikra*" ("At five years of age [a child is brought] into the study of scripture")[292] and it is explained in *Likkutei Torah...* that *pnimiyus haTorah* (*Chassidus*) is included in *mikra* (scripture). (See also *Hilchos Talmud Torah* of the Alter Rebbe, ch. 4, end of section 1.)

Studying the Chassidic Torah Portion

Many[293] *chassidim* had the custom of studying each and every week (and especially on *Shabbos*) the "*chassidisher parshah*" ("*chassidic Torah portion*"). During the winter *Shabbosos* they studied *Torah Or*, and on the summer *Shabbosos* (as well as at the end of the winter), they learned *Likkutei Torah.* Some had the custom to learn it, superficially at least, with members of their family, including also their children of *bar mitzvah* age (or younger).

Father tests children in their learning

According[294] to *minhag Yisrael* of past generations, on *Shabbos* the father tests his children on their Torah study throughout the week and especially on the weekly *parshah* that was learned in *cheder*.

---

290 *Yiddish* was the language spoken by the majority of Jews who lacked a Torah education, as well as educated Jews, in that generation.

291 *Igros Kodesh,* vol. 3, p. 407.

292 *Avos,* 5:22.

293 *Hisvaaduyos* 5749, vol. 1, p.315, footnote 29.

294 *Hisvaaduyos* 5750, vol. 3, p. 364. Cf. *Hisvaaduyos* 5750, vol. 3, p. 172.

Ink written on new paper

The[295] *Gemara* relates:[296]

> Acher would ride on a horse on *Shabbos*, and Rabbi Meir would walk behind him and learn Torah from him. When [Acher] reached the boundary of *Shabbos* [beyond which one may not go], he said to Rabbi Meir, "Meir, go back, for I have already estimated by the footsteps of my horse that the boundary of *Shabbos* finishes here."

This emphasizes two details:

1. Even while Acher rode on a horse on *Shabbos*, "Rabbi Meir would walk behind him and learn Torah from him."
2. Acher himself warned Rabbi Meir not to accidentally violate the prohibition of going beyond the boundary of *Shabbos*, although this prohibition is only rabbinic.

Here we see the greatness of Elisha ben Avuyah [i.e., Acher]: Even after he abandoned Torah observance, he would teach Torah to Rabbi Meir, of whom it is written, "he illuminated the eyes of the Sages in Jewish law,"[297] and to such an extent that "his colleagues were unable to truly grasp his wisdom."[298]

The reason for this is apparent from Elisha ben Avuyah's very own words: "One who studies Torah while young – to what may he be compared? To ink written on new paper."[299]

Elisha ben Avuyah studied a vast amount of Torah in his childhood; as the *Gemara* relates,[300] his father said, "Since such is the power of Torah ... I

295 *Hisvaaduyos* 5742, vol. 3, p. 1456.
296 *Chagigah*, 15a.
297 *Eruvin*, 13b.
298 *Ibid*. 13a.
299 *Avos*, 4:25.
300 *Yerushalmi, Chagigah* 15:1.

am setting aside my son for Torah." Therefore, the Torah that he learned in his childhood stayed with him forever, since it was similar to "ink written on new paper," which lasts.

This demonstrates to what extent it is necessary to expend effort for the Torah study of children. In addition to it being a positive *mitzvah* from the Torah for the father to teach Torah to his little child (see beginning of the Alter Rebbe's *Laws of Torah Study)*, and as is explained in the writings of the Tzemach Tzedek (on *Mishneh Torah,* beginning of *Laws of Torah Study)*, that even a child has an inherent obligation to study Torah on his own – "once he recognizes." One should make great efforts in this because of the great advantage of a child's Torah learning, which is like "ink written on new paper."

Buying a letter in a *Sefer Torah*

An[301] entirely new initiative is being suggested: A *Sefer Torah* should be written, and its letters will be only for *Tzivos Hashem*, boys and girls before *bar mitzvah* and *bas mitzvah.* Each one of them should have a letter. Since a *Yid* should not "[eat] the bread of shame,"[302] he can purchase one himself and [this *mitzvah*] will be performed in the most perfect way possible.

Each boy and girl should give an equal amount. Since we are in the United States, and the suggestion came from the United States, each child should pay one dollar.

If a child doesn't have such a large amount of money in his possession, we will trust him to pay this sum from the time that the writing of the *Sefer Torah* begins. The main issue is that he pays before the *Sefer Torah* is completed.

...All should donate the same amount, and in other countries an amount equal to a dollar should be given. If it is difficult to give precisely the amount of one dollar, each person should give a cent or two more, an amount such that it is not significant that one gives more than does the other.

---

301 *Sichas Yud-Alef Nissan,* 5741, vol. 3, p. 131.

302 *Yerushalmi, Orla* 1:3.

[One[303] hastens the *geulah* through] buying a letter in a *Sefer Torah* that is written in everyone's merit – all *Bnei Yisrael, shlita* – since our Torah is *Toras Emes* ("the Torah of Truth")[304] and it is eternal... One may also give the merit to a person who is somewhere else at this time (by buying him a letter in a *Sefer Torah*), [thus loving] one's fellow as oneself, if for whatever reason one doesn't do this oneself...

Efforts[305] should be made to strengthen the campaign so that each and every Jew will buy a letter in one of the *sifrei Torah haklaliyim*, in accordance with the *dvar Malchus* above that כל א' מישראל יש לו אות א' בתורה ולכן נהגו כל ישראל לכתוב אות בתורה כו' – ("Every single *Yid* has a letter in the Torah,[306] and therefore all *Yidden* have accustomed themselves to each write a letter in the Torah") – and through this, all *Bnei Yisrael* become one entity.

Obviously it is not enough to write one *Sefer Torah* to unite all *Yisrael*, and it's not enough to write even two *Sifrei Torah*, as the letters in two *Sifrei* Torah are equal to the number six hundred thousand (as each one has half the amount of six hundred thousand). Efforts should be made that each and every *Yid* should buy a letter in a *Sefer Torah*, and the number of *Bnei Yisrael* is a few times six hundred thousand, may they increase.

As is explained in the *Tanya,*[307] when we say that there are six hundred thousand Jews, this refers to the six hundred thousand *neshamos klaliyos.* These six hundred thousand *neshamos* are root *neshamos.* Each root divides into six hundred thousand sparks, and each spark is one *neshamah,* and so on.

A letter in a *Sefer Torah*- even before the child is named!

...When a Jewish child is born, efforts should be made to immediately give him the merit and buy a letter in a *Sefer Torah* for him. This [should be done] even before naming the child. (A boy is named at the time of the *bris milah*,

303 *Likkutei Sichos,* vol. 24, pp. 583-584
304 Blessings on the Torah.
305 *Hisvaaduyos* 5744, vol. 2, p. 827
306 Cf. *Megaleh Amukos* 186.
307 Chapter 36.

which is the time of תחלת כניסת נפש זו הקדושה [the beginning of the entry of the *holy neshamah* into the body]. A girl is named at the first possible Torah reading. And regarding the entering of the holy *neshamah* into a girl's body, a woman is born "circumcised," so to speak.) After the naming ceremony, the name of the child should be added regarding his or her ownership of a letter in the *Sefer Torah*.

It[308] is worthwhile, and most correct, that immediately after a boy or girl is born, a letter in a *Sefer Torah* be purchased on his behalf ... This draws down success and *bracha* into the child's life, materially and spiritually.

In addition, through this the child unites with all *Bnei Yisrael* in the entire world, and beyond – with all generations, since each *Sefer Torah* is copied from a *Sefer Torah* before it, spanning back all the way to the *Sefer Torah* that was written by Moshe *Rabeinu*. (This refers to the twelve *sifrei Torah* that Moshe gave to each tribe, along with the *Sefer Torah* that was placed in the *aron* forever, as is quoted in *Rambam*'s introduction.)

Learning *mishnayos* by heart

The[309] notion of purifying the air through reciting words of Torah by heart, especially *mishnayos* by heart, should be publicized.

The[310] intention in founding groups [to learn] *mishnayos be'al peh* was not that only *yeshivah* students would learn *mishnayos* by heart, but that the groups would include all Jews. People should run a campaign so that *everyone* will be involved by each one learning by heart his portion of three to five chapters a year (such as the weekly *Mishnah*). Each person should repeat what he already knows when he walks outside, stands in a store, sits on a train, and at every other opportunity, in order to purify the air.

308 *Hisvaaduyos* 5746, vol. 4, p. 287.

309 *Igros Kodesh*, vol. 1, p. 39.

310 *Igros Kodesh*, vol. 1, p. 105.

The Rebbe's twelve *pesukim*

... Torah[311] learning is חיינו ואורך ימינו ("our life and the length of our days").[312] It is not only wisdom and knowledge; rather, Torah is our *life*. Therefore, learning Torah must affect one's entire life, as *Rambam* teaches,[313] that a true *chochom* is also recognizable by [the way he] eats, strolls, and so on.

This applies to every single *Yid,* even little boys and girls. Therefore, we are suggesting that children recite by heart certain *pesukim* from the written Torah, teachings of our Sages from the oral Torah, and passages from *pnimiyus HaTorah* (the inner, mystical dimension of Torah).

One should influence the child so that at every free moment he should say or think [the *pasuk*] and also explain the *pesukim* and teachings of our Sages to his friends. The advantage of this is that when Torah matters are ingrained in the children's memories, it affects them, each according to their level to reach the wondrous level of *Toraso umanuso* ("Torah is their craft"[314] – a lofty level of devotion to Torah), [which is manifest] בשבתך בביתך ובלכתך בדרך ובשכבך ובקומך ("when you sit in your house and when you walk on the way; when you lie down and when you rise up").[315] It even extends to the point that when he plays with a friend, he will be reminded of a *pasuk* from the written Torah, oral Torah, or from *Tanya.*

The advantage is emphasized as well in a teaching of the Alter Rebbe in *Likkutei Torah,* end of *parshas Kedoshim,*[316] on the *pasuk* והדרת פני זקן ("you shall revere an elderly person"),[317] that when one memorizes a teaching from the oral Torah, this teaching remains with him in a complete way even when he is involved with another matter. ...

The intention is not for children to merely recite matters of Torah without understanding them... for these selected passages can be explained to every

311 *Sichos Kodesh* 5736, p. 148, *Sichas Rosh Chodesh Iyar.*

312 *Devarim,* 32:47. Evening liturgy.

313 *Mishneh Torah, Hilchos Dei'os* 5:1.

314 *Shabbos,* 11a.

315 *Devarim,* 6:7.

316 30d.

317 *Vayikra,* 19:32.

child, including the smallest child, in order that they will permeate his mind so he can "live" with them. [This way,] even when he is playing, he will remember this Torah idea and it will not only affect him, but he will explain the matter to his friend [and have an impact upon the friend as well]. …

תּוֹרָה צִוָּה לָנוּ מֹשֶׁה מוֹרָשָׁה קְהִלַּת יַעֲקֹב (דברים לג, ד)

The Torah that Moshe commanded us is the heritage of the congregation of Yaakov – *Devarim* 33:4

Our Sages say[318] that when a child begins to speak, his father teaches him the *pasuk, Torah tziva lanu Moshe, morasha kehilas Yaakov.* [319] With this *pasuk,* the *chinuch* of the child begins.

Even a little child should know that the Torah in its entirety has been given as an "inheritance" [to him]. The preciousness of Torah should be explained to him so that just as he feels how precious are his toys and other belongings he cherishes greatly, so does he feel about his "inheritance" of the Torah.

שְׁמַע יִשְׂרָאֵל אֲ-דֹנָי אֱ-לֹהֵינוּ אֲ-דֹנָי אֶחָד (דברים ו, ד)

Hear 0 Yisrael, the L-rd is our G-d, the L-rd is One – *Devarim* 6:4

The child should begin to say the *pasuk* of *Shema Yisrael* at the earliest age possible during the day and at night. It would be even better for him to recite the entire *parshah* of *kriyas Shema*; nevertheless, at least he should recite the *pasuk* of *Shema Yisrael.*

The meaning of the *pasuk* should be explained according to the child's understanding and level of communication. To an adult we explain[320] that the word "אֶחָד" consists of three letters: 'א' ,ח' ד. The 'ח corresponds to the seven firmaments and the earth; the 'ד corresponds to the four winds [directions] of the world; and the 'א hints to Hashem, *Alufo shel olam* ("Master of the universe"), Who is the Ruler of the entire world: the seven firmaments, the earth, and the four directions.

318 *Sukkah,* 42a. *Mishneh Torah, Hilchos Talmud Torah* 1:6.

319 *Devarim,* 33:4.

320 *Orach Chaim* 61, *Beis Yosef* s.v. *kosav Semak.*

Moreover, just as the letter "א" is the first letter of the *roshei teivos* (acronym) "אחד," so do the seven firmaments, the earth, and the four directions of the world emanate from *Alufo shel olam.*

This is also the way that we should explain the matter to children. Although they see the heavens, the earth, and the four directions [as a part of nature], they should know that ה' אלוקינו ה' אחד – that Hashem runs it all.

When this is explained well to a child, in words that the child can understand, it will lead to ואהבת את ה' אלוקיך,[321] love of Hashem in the child's heart, just as it is demanded of the adults that by meditating on the *Shema Yisrael,* they come to ואהבת את ה' אלוקיך. ...

בְּכָל דּוֹר וָדוֹר חַיָּב אָדָם לִרְאוֹת אֶת עַצְמוֹ כְּאִלּוּ הוּא יָצָא מִמִּצְרַיִם (פסחים פ"י, מ"ה)

In every generation one must look upon himself as if he personally went out of Egypt. – *Pesachim* 116b

The concept of our Exodus from *Mitzrayim* should be fixed in one's memory, למען תזכור את יום צאתך מארץ מצרים כל ימי חייך ("so that you shall *remember* the day you left Egypt all the days of your life"),[322] and therefore it is appropriate to include a teaching of our Sages that deals with *Yetzias Mitzrayim.*

There is a special connection between the Exodus from Egypt and children, which is why the Exodus is especially emphasized in matters related to *chinuch.* This is expressed on the night of the 15th of Nissan [Pesach] during the *Seder,* when all types of children are present: כנגד ארבעה בנים דברה תורה ("the Torah speaks of four children"),[323] the wise son, and the other children. During the *Seder,* we do various things in order to surprise the children and prompt them to ask questions, since the story of *Yetzias Mitzrayim* is meant to be told specifically to the children.[324] The *chinuch* of the night of the 15th of Nissan is a preparation for the entire year, in which the *chinuch* of the children should continue in the same manner.

---

321 *Shemos,* 6:5.

322 *Devarim,* 16:3.

323 *Haggadah,* sec. beg. *baruch haMakom.*

324 *Shemos,* 13:8.

The meaning of this teaching of our Sages is that one should see and imagine to himself how Hashem is taking *us* out of *Mitzrayim*. This can be explained easily to children, as we say in the *Haggadah*: ואילו לא הוציא הקב"ה את אבותינו ממצרים הרי אנו כו' משועבדים היינו ("Had *Hakadosh Baruch Hu* not taken us out of Egypt... we would continue to be slaves"),[325] so it is really as though *Hakadosh Baruch Hu* took us out of Egypt.

[The love for Hashem] comes as a result of our feeling that we would do anything for the One Who did us such a kindness as to take us out of Egypt!

כָּל יִשְׂרָאֵל יֵשׁ לָהֶם חֵלֶק לָעוֹלָם הַבָּא, שֶׁנֶּאֱמַר: וְעַמֵּךְ כֻּלָּם צַדִּיקִים
לְעוֹלָם יִירְשׁוּ אָרֶץ, נֵצֶר מַטָּעַי מַעֲשֵׂה יָדַי לְהִתְפָּאֵר
(סנהדרין פ"י מ"א)

All Yisrael have a share in the World to Come, as it is stated,[326] "All Your people are *tzaddikim*. They shall inherit the Land forever. They are the branch of My planting, thes work of My hands, in which [I] take pride." – *Sanhedrin* 90a.

The Alter Rebbe writes in his *Siddur*:[327]

> It is customary to recite one chapter of *Pirkei Avos* every *Shabbos* between *Pesach* and [*Shemini*] *Atzeres* at *Minchah*, and before it, the *Mishnah* כל ישראל. Some have the *minhag* to do this for the duration of all the *Shabbosos* of the summer.

According to all customs, *Pirkei Avos* is learned during the *sefirah* days with the addition of the introduction to *Pirkei Avos*...כל ישראל ; the precise wording is כל ישראל – "all Yisrael," including children.

Like the earlier ones, this teaching of our Sages can be explained to all children, even those very young.

---

325 *Haggadah*, sec. beg. *avadaim hayinu*.

326 *Yehoshua*, 20:22.

327 In the preface to *Pirkei Avos*.

Every child should know that he is נצר מטעי מעשה ידי להתפאר ("the work of My hands, in which I take pride").[328] Even a child understands that as much as his physical father and mother are great and important, the greatness of "our Father in Heaven" is incomparably greater. And he has merited to be the work of Hashem's hands in which He takes pride!

In the merit of this, the child receives a חלק לעולם הבא ("a portion in *Olam Haba*"), which is an eternal world. This means that his connection with *Hakadosh Baruch Hu* will be eternal!

As was said, these things can be comprehended even by a very little child who has reached an elementary level of understanding.

... A child can be taught that through proper conduct, he will merit to sit with all the *Gedolei Yisrael* in the World to Come, but that if his conduct is somehow lacking, he will remain sitting embarrassed among other children who misbehaved. Moreover, this will take place in the World to Come, which does not change because it is eternal. When the child receives such an explanation, this will inspire good conduct, out of love and a desire for Torah, *mitzvos,* and matters of *Yiddishkeit* in general, including the *mitzvah* of "honor your father and mother."[329]

כִּי קָרוֹב אֵלֶיךָ הַדָּבָר מְאֹד בְּפִיךָ וּבִלְבָבְךָ לַעֲשׂוֹתוֹ (דברים ל, יד)

It is within your close reach to follow the Torah in speech, feeling, and deed. – *Devarim* 30:14

On the title page of *Tanya*, the Alter Rebbe writes – as my father-in-law, the Rebbe, explained that the title page was written by the Alter Rebbe as well) – that the book of *Tanya* is founded on the *pasuk* כי קרוב אליך הדבר מאוד בפיך ובלבבך לעשותו ("For this thing is very near to you, in your mouth and in your heart, that you may do it"), [to which the Alter Rebbe adds:] "to explain clearly how it is exceedingly near."

The Torah says that *Yiddishkeit* is very close and easy for a Jew to fulfill. What's more, it is close to one's heart (בלבבך). The simple meaning here, as is explained in the continuation of *Tanya,* is that every *Yid,* in every place and

328 *Yeshaya,* 60:21.

329 *Shemos,* 20:12.

time, is "close" [i.e., it is attainable and easy for him] to serve *Hakadosh Baruch Hu* "with his heart." This applies to us as well, since "the Torah is eternal."[330]

This idea can even be explained to a very young child. Although his heart is drawn after material things – toys, games, and the like – he should know that "This thing is very near to you, in your mouth and in your heart, that you may do it." He need only think about the preciousness of matters of Torah and *mitzvos,* and he will feel a desire for these things.

וְהִנֵּה ה' נִצָּב עָלָיו וּמְלֹא כָל הָאָרֶץ כְּבוֹדוֹ וּמַבִּיט עָלָיו וּבוֹחֵן כְּלָיוֹת וָלֵב, אִם עוֹבְדוֹ כָּרָאוּי (תניא, פרק מ"א)

Hashem stands over him, and the whole earth is full of His glory, and He searches his mind and heart (to see) if he is serving Him as is fitting. – *Tanya*, Chapter 41

At the beginning of chapter 41 of *Tanya*, the Alter Rebbe states that והנה ה' נצב עליו ומלא כל הארץ כבודו ומביט עליו ובוחן כליות ולב אם עובדו כראוי ("Hashem stands over the person, and the whole earth is full of His glory, and He searches his mind and heart (to see) if he is serving Him as is fitting").

The wording of the Alter Rebbe, "ה' נצב עליו" hints at a wondrous matter.

The *Midrash*[331] explains the *pasuk,* והנה ה' נצב עליו to mean that *Hakadosh Baruch Hu* so to speak stands and grasps onto Yaakov, like a rider on a chariot.

The Alter Rebbe makes an amazing statement: Every *Yid*, in whatever state he may be, should know that *Hakadosh Baruch Hu* "stands over him." This means that Hashem's "standing" over the *Yid* is a merit for him; Hashem is "supported" by his behavior, on whether in his "mind and heart, he is serving Hashem as is fitting.

Moreover, the word נצב (stands) comes from the expression נצב מלך ("a *king* stands"),[332] which implies that whether *Hakadosh Baruch Hu* stands firm – the strength of His *Malchus* – depends upon the conduct of every *Yid.*

This too can even be explained to a very little child, as befits his understanding, by using examples from material and physical matters.

330 *Tanya,* ch. 17.

331 *Bereishis Rabbah,* 9:3.

332 *I Melachim,* 22:48.

This is all the more true given that the father and mother of the child, who are deeply connected to the *chinuch* of their child, will make great efforts to pass on this message to their children. They will reach out to each child according to his personality and circumstances, but in a complete way, so that it will affect his day-to-day conduct, in ways of pleasantness[333] and with love. ...

We[334] have already discussed the suggestion and request that every Jew recite words of Torah by heart, so that when he doesn't have a *sefer* in his hand to look at, he will be able to remember the words of the oral and written Torah, at least one *pasuk, maamar Chazal,* and more. He should repeat it until it is engraved in his memory, and this will translate later into action – both in his conduct and in the conduct of those in his surroundings. In addition, it is worthwhile that two *pesukim,* two teachings of our Sages be added, and two passages from the Alter Rebbe that appear in chapter 33 of his *Tanya*, which have a direct connection to daily life.

בְּרֵאשִׁית בָּרָא אֱ-לֹהִים אֵת הַשָּׁמַיִם וְאֵת הָאָרֶץ (בראשית א, א)

In the beginning Hashem created the heavens and the earth. – *Bereishis* 1:1

The first *pasuk* in the written Torah is בראשית ברא אלוקים את השמים ואת הארץ. It states that *Hakadosh Baruch Hu* created the world, the heavens and all that are in them, and the land and all that is in and upon it.

This verse has direct relevance to our day-to-day conduct.

A little boy or girl, and even an adult, are liable to become afraid when looking around at the big world, which contains elements that are not as they should be.

This *pasuk* comes to teach and remind that there is a Master and Creator in this world – *Hakadosh Baruch Hu,* Who gave us the Torah. Through Torah we can control the world, drawing blessing and success into "the land" – in all matters on the earth below and "in the heavens" for Hashem above [by following the will of *Hakadosh Baruch Hu*].

---

333 *Mishlei,* 3:17.

334 *Sichos Kodesh* 5736, vol. 2, *Sichas Lag Ba'omer.*

וְשִׁנַּנְתָּם לְבָנֶיךָ וְדִבַּרְתָּ בָּם בְּשִׁבְתְּךָ בְּבֵיתֶךָ וּבְלֶכְתְּךָ בַדֶּרֶךְ וּבְשָׁכְבְּךָ וּבְקוּמֶךָ (דברים ו, ז)

And you shall teach [the Torah] to your children, and you should speak about it when you are home and when you travel, before you lie down to sleep and when you wake up. – *Devarim* 6:7

The second *pasuk* that should be recited by heart comes as the continuation of *Shema Yisrael.*

Children, boys and girls, should approach their parents and say to them, ושננתם לבניך ("And you shall teach [the Torah] to your children"), meaning they are requesting that every father and mother do what they can, to the best of their ability, to teach Torah to their children. This applies whether they are literal children or "'your children' – 'these are the students"[335] – all those who need to be taught another Torah teaching.

This learning should be in such a way that it will fulfill the continuation and conclusion of that *pasuk:* בשבתך בביתך ובלכתך בדרך ובשכבך ובקומך ("when you sit at home and when you travel, before you lie down to sleep and when you wake up"), which implies that the lessons should be learned and reviewed by heart, and will be ingrained in their hearts and minds until they are involved in it without pause. This means that when they – the children, students, and parents – are in a state of "returning home," "on their way," and "lying down to sleep and waking up," then even when they lie down to go to sleep, it will be with a Torah saying, and their awakening from their sleep will be with a Torah instruction.

When children request this of their parents from the depths of their hearts, as is customary for children, then their request will surely be granted. During the summer, the parents will send their children to a camp where the spirit of Torah prevails, as well as conduct according to Torah. As the new school year approaches, they will enroll their children in a school that teaches Torah, *mitzvos,* and matters of *Yiddishkeit.*

---

[335] *Sifri* and *Rashi* on the verse.

יָגַעְתִּי וְלֹא מָצָאתִי – אַל תַּאֲמִין, לֹא יָגַעְתִּי וּמָצָאתִי – אַל תַּאֲמִין, יָגַעְתִּי וּמָצָאתִי – תַּאֲמִין. (בבלי מגילה ו:ב)

If someone says, "I have worked hard and I have not been successful," don't believe him. If someone says, "I have not worked hard and I have been successful," don't believe him. If someone says, "I have worked hard and I have been successful," believe him! – *Bavli, Megilah* 6b.

Even if a child remembers that at one point in his life he did something that he shouldn't have, he should not fear (thinking that this proves that he is incapable of following the instructions of the Torah). This should certainly not weaken his resolve in his activities in matters of Torah, *chas ve'shalom.*

If he asks, "How can it be? Did it not happen that he failed?" He should review the teaching of our Sages above, לֹא יָגַעְתִּי וּמָצָאתִי – אַל תַּאֲמִין ("If someone says, 'I have not worked hard and I have been successful,' don't believe him"). This implies that if one has not found in his soul the strength necessary to behave properly according to Torah and *Yiddishkeit*, clearly the only reason for this is that he did not invest the proper effort!

If he will only invest the proper effort, he will clearly find within his soul the strength needed for this, as it states at the beginning of the saying, יָגַעְתִּי וְלֹא מָצָאתִי – אַל תַּאֲמִין ("If someone says, 'I have worked hard and I have not been successful,' don't believe him").

וְאָהַבְתָּ לְרֵעֲךָ כָּמוֹךָ – רַבִּי עֲקִיבָא אוֹמֵר, זֶה כְּלָל גָּדוֹל בַּתּוֹרָה (ירושלמי נדרים ט, ד)

Rabbi Akiva says that "Love your fellow as yourself" is a great basic principle of the Torah. – *Yerushalmi, Nedarim* 9:4

...One should not suffice with merely working on oneself; rather, one should influence one's friends – and a girl, her friends – in those areas where change is needed, as well influencing one's entire surroundings.

This teaching of our Sages also means that one's influence on another and on the environment should be full of enthusiasm, with the same passion, wholeheartedness, and effort as the person directs toward himself. The reason is that ואהבת לרעך כמוך ("Love your fellow as yourself")[336] is a basic and fundamental

[336] *Vayikra,* 19:18.

principle in learning and teaching. From this it also follows that just as one toils hard to learn and teach oneself, so should one toil hard to teach a fellow Jew.

וְזֶה כָּל הָאָדָם וְתַכְלִית בְּרִיאָתוֹ וּבְרִיאַת כָּל הָעוֹלָמוֹת, עֶלְיוֹנִים וְתַחְתּוֹנִים, לִהְיוֹת לוֹ יִתְבָּרֵךְ דִּירָה זוֹ בְּתַחְתּוֹנִים (תניא פרק ל"ג)

The purpose of the creation of every person and of all the worlds is to make a dwelling place for Hashem in this lowest world. – *Tanya*, Chapter 33

This is a teaching of the Alter Rebbe from chapter 33 of his *sefer haTanya*.[337] One should explain to a child that matters of Torah and *mitzvos* are the greatest *shlichus* that a *Yid* has been given. This is כל האדם ותכלית בריאתו, the entire objective and purpose for which man was created, and ובריאת כל העולמות – the purpose for which all the worlds were created.

As the verse continues, להיות לו דירה זו בתחתונים, the entire purpose of the creation of the world is in order that a Jew, through Torah and *mitzvos,* should make of himself, his home, and the entire world a place where Hashem can dwell exactly as a person dwells in his private home.

יִשְׂמַח יִשְׂרָאֵל בְּעוֹשָׂיו, פֵּרוּשׁ שֶׁכָּל מִי שֶׁהוּא מִזֶּרַע יִשְׂרָאֵל יֵשׁ לוֹ לִשְׂמֹחַ בְּשִׂמְחַת ה', אֲשֶׁר שָׂשׂ וְשָׂמֵחַ בְּדִירָתוֹ בְּתַחְתּוֹנִים (תניא פרק ל"ג)

The Jews should rejoice in their Maker. Every Jew should share in Hashem's joy, Who rejoices and is happy in His dwelling place in this world. – *Tanya* ch. 33

This lesson is another message from the teachings of the Alter Rebbe in the same chapter, and it comes in continuation to the passage immediately preceding. It states that everything we do (according to what was explained above) should be done in a manner of ישמח ישראל בעושיו, with *simchah* and enjoyment, and not as a person does something he is commanded to do, without experiencing pleasure from it, or experiencing only a little bit of enjoyment.

The Alter Rebbe goes on to explain that this lesson applies to כל מי שהוא מזרע ישראל ("every descendant of *Yisrael*") – every single member of the Jewish nation. It doesn't matter at all what his circumstances were the

337 Cf. *Midrash Tanchuma, Naso* 16. *Tanya* ch. 36.

day before, or what his *chinuch* was a day ago, or even a moment ago. Since he is a "descendant of *Yisrael*," he has the *shlichus* "to rejoice with the *simchah* of Hashem" in making a dwelling place for *Hakadosh Baruch Hu* in this world through matters of *Yiddishkeit*, Torah, and *mitzvos*.

In other words, in addition to the command that rests on each individual boy and girl, whether a child in years or in knowledge, to be involved in all the matters described in the previous passage, since this is "the purpose of the creation of every person and of all the worlds," he has another command to fulfill. He should meditate on this concept and, through this meditation, come to great *simchah*, and be involved in all these activities with great *simchah*.

Moreover, this joy is not only their own, but the joy is בעושיו (in their Maker), in the *simchah* of *Hakadosh Baruch Hu*, Who created the heavens and the earth and chose כל מי שהוא מזרע ישראל ("whomever is among the descendants of *Yisrael*") to transform the world into a dwelling place for Him.

All this begins with little children, who also stand in a state of great joy, knowing that *Hakadosh Baruch Hu* is rejoicing together with them – and what's more, that this is the joy of *Hakadosh Baruch Hu*. Then all the above matters are done with *simchah*, strength, and enthusiasm, and thus everything they do is even more successful.

Children's Torah learning hastens the *geulah*

So[338] great is the merit of Jewish children through learning Torah and giving *tzedakah*, that they bring the *geulah* and salvation to our entire nation and hasten the true and complete redemption through our righteous redeemer.

---

338 *Likkutei Sichos*, vol. 16, p. 622.

Hiskashrus to the Rebbe

Encouraging children to devote themselves to the Rebbe

[This[339] answer is] regarding what he writes that his son... does not have such a passion in his learning.

He should explain to him, with words that are appropriate for him, that our times are entirely different [from previous generations]. He should know that my father-in-law, the Rebbe, is the *Nasi* and head of all his *chassidim* and those connected to him. Since it is absolutely certain that the head [the Previous Rebbe] is healthy and strong, it possesses in a perfect state all the strength and life-force associated with every single man and woman connected to him. It depends entirely upon them [to devote themselves to him and thereby access these strengths]. ...

If he will meditate upon this even for a short while, he will surely see the great responsibility placed upon him. Then, to the degree compatible with his state of health, he will devote himself, and devote his entire existence, to the will of my father-in-law, the Rebbe, and to fulfilling his words and instructions as found in his *sichos* and letters, the communal ones as well as the individual ones. In these writings, every single *Yid*, male and female, can find instructions for his path in life.

There is no need to be surprised, and ask how a little child can have a relationship with such a great Rebbe, for this is explained in several places in *Eitz Chayim* and also in the *maamar of Chai Elul* of this year [5710], chapter 7. ...

Assign an essay about the Rebbe's *inyanim*

In[340] connection with the upcoming tenth of *Shvat (yohrtzeit* of the *Rebbe Rayatz),* it should be suggested to the girls, at least the older ones among them, that each one should write an essay on some area of the *avodah* of my father-in-law, the Rebbe, his *sichos,* and so on...

339 *Igros Kodesh*, vol. 3, pp. 461-462.

340 *Igros Kodesh*, vol. 10, pp. 238-239.

Students of the Rebbe are like his children

The[341] Torah considers one who teaches his fellow Jew's son Torah to be as if he gave birth him.[342] This is especially so with a *chassid* and Rebbe: it is not "as if," but he *literally* gave birth to him.

Consulting with the Rebbe and following his instructions

The[343] *chassidishe Ba'alei Batim* of the previous generations implanted within their children – without distinguishing between boys or girls – an inherent devotion and attachment to the Rebbe.

Consequently, for all of their concerns, family affairs, and issues of livelihood, they consulted with the Rebbe and followed his instructions, and this was beneficial both for themselves as well as for their families.

---

341 *Igros Kodesh*, vol. 3, p. 422.

342 *Sanhedrin*, 19b.

343 *Sefer Hasichos* 5700, p. 163, The Rebbe's Holy Care, Issue 6.

CHAPTER 6

Methods in Early Education

"Educate the youngster according to his way; then, when he grows old, he shall not depart from it."

Mishlei, 22:6

Make learning tangible

In[344] this connection, it is well to bear in mind the general rule, especially in regard to children, that any idea or knowledge—if it is to be truly absorbed and of lasting benefit—must not remain in the realm of thought or pure knowledge, but must be immediately related to and connected with actual experience in some tangible expression in the child's life. In this way, it can be expected that the knowledge plus experience which the child attains in school will be lasting and effective also outside the walls of the school...

Engraving Judaism in the child's nature

One[345] should educate a Jewish child in a manner of "engraving." From a very young age, one should accustom the child to fulfill *mitzvos* in a way that becomes part of his nature and habit. For example, as he wakes up from his sleep, he instinctively recites *Modeh Ani*.

The reason is that he is still a small child and not yet able to comprehend the meaning of the *mitzvos;* therefore, the way to lead him to perform the *mitzvos* is through "engraving" [embedding] it in his nature so that he does so instinctively. This is the simple meaning of the statement, "when he would reach *Modim* [in davening], his [head] would instinctively bend over."[346]

Chinuch through Stories

Utilizing stories

[As[347] a part of] *chinuch,* one should tell stories. A child is often afraid of learning something difficult, fearing that he will be unable to understand

[344] Letter from 15th of Elul 5733, written to Shaliach in Madrid

[345] *Sefer HaSichos* 5749, vol. 2, pp. 472-473.

[346] *Talmud Yerushalmi, Berachos* 2:4, end. Cf. *Shabbos* 118b, *Tosfos s.v. iyun.*

[347] *Hisvaaduyos* 5745, vol. 4, pp. 2302-2303.

it with his mind; stories banish this fear. Stories arouse the interest of the child, so he wants to hear more and more. The words of verse, שאל אביך ויגדך זקניך ויאמרו לך ("Ask your father and he will tell you; your grandparents, and they will explain it to you").[348] This is to say that the child himself asks to be told story after story about what happened to the *Yidden*. ...

This applies to all matters of Torah: "Torah" is derived from the word *horaah* (instruction).[349] As is known and explained in several sources,[350] all of the Torah's instructions are transmitted by way of stories. The advantage of this approach to *chinuch* is that when a lesson is communicated in the form of a story, the child will more readily take it to heart.

Implanting *emuna* through miracle stories

We[351] should begin *chinuch* with *emuna* and *kabbalas ol*, not intellect. Even matters of intellect should be fulfilled out of *kabbalas ol*. ... The first stories that children are taught should be of supraratational miracles. This is the way to implant *emuna* within them.

Choosing the right stories

The[352] stories told to children should be stories taken from the oral and written Torah, or true stories told about *tzaddikim*. We should not be telling children old wives' tales as others do.

The[353] custom of proper Jewish mothers is that instead of telling children "stories" and "news" from the newspaper or the like, they relate stories from

348 *Devarim*, 32:7.

349 Cf. *Zohar* III, 53b. *Gur Aryeh*, *Bereishis* 1:1, in the name of *Radak*.

350 Preface of *Ramban* to *Chumash; Sefer Hamaamarim* 5568, p. 159 ff.

351 *Likkutei Sichos*, vol. 19, pp. 91-92.

352 *Sichos Kodesh* 5741, vol. 1, p. 246.

353 *Hisvaaduyos* 5746, vol. 3, p. 394.

the Torah (including topics that they have not yet been taught in *cheder)* with enthusiasm and passion, as though they are כחדשים (like new),[354] until they become "alive." In this way, the children receive a true Jewish *chinuch* that will affect them for life.

Only true stories

When[355] a child is told a true story, this positions him [on a foundation of] truth and peace. However, when a child is told a story that is not true, this turns him into a superficial and dishonest person.

Before age five, *chinuch* is mainly through Torah stories

Before[356] the child reaches *ben chamesh le'mikra* ("at five years of age [a child is brought] into the study of scripture"),[357] *chinuch* occurs mainly through relating stories of the Torah: the written and oral Torah, *aggados,* and *midrashei Razal* from *Ein Yaakov.*

A child can relate to *mesirus nefesh* better than an adult

My[358] father-in-law, the Rebbe, instructed that even children should be taught the *parshah* of *Akeidas Yitzchak,* and the like. Some mistakenly think that this will scare the child. However, by nature a Jewish child feels and understands the concept of *mesirus nefesh* (self-sacrifice). In fact, a child can relate to it even better than can an adult.

---

354 *Rashi* on *Shemos* 19:1, 11:13, *Devarim* 26:16.

355 *Sefer Hasichos* 5704, p. 143.

356 *Hisvaaduyos* 5748, vol. 3, p. 307.

357 *Avos,* 5:22.

358 *Hisvaaduyos* 5749, vol. 1, p. 349.

Tell stories at every opportunity

The[359] way of teaching *Chassidus Chabad* is to supervise with special attention the conduct of each individual household member: the wife, the sons, and daughters. During every opportune time, such as the *Shabbos kodesh* and *Yom Tov* meals, stories and ways of conduct that demonstrate *middos tovos* and *ahavas Yisrael* should be told. The stories and *niggunim* will bring richness to the conduct of *chassidei Chabad.*

Often a woman could be heard, while doing housework, cooking, baking, or cleaning the home, telling little children *chassidishe* stories. This left a strong impression on the children.

[The Frierdiker Rebbe relates:][360]

When I was a child, my father taught me using stories from *Chumash, Nevi'im,* and tales from *Ein Yaakov.* When I was a little older, he also told me about our teacher, the Baal Shem Tov, our teacher the *Maggid* of *Mezeritch,* and the Alter Rebbe. Sometimes he would explain the story to me along the lines of a person's *avodah* to refine and correct the *middos*. He did this in such a way that I grasped it and it was engraved in my memory. He would conclude almost every time by saying, "This is how *chassidim* who are *baalei avodah* educate their little children and grandchildren."

---

359 *Sefer Hamaamarim, Admor HaRayatz* 5711, p. 59.

360 *Sefer HaSichos* 5701, p. 101.

Chinuch in a Way of "The Right Hand Draws Near"

Influencing children

In[361] order for *chinuch* to succeed, it should be accomplished out of *ahavas Yisrael*, "the right hand draws near."[362] Even though it is sometimes necessary to implement "the left hand pushes away" – for "one who withholds his rod, despises his child"[363] – it is done with the left hand, the less dominant hand, and it is only done very rarely. ... When we approach children *be'darkei noam* (pleasantly) and peacefully, we influence them more successfully and quickly than through other means.

Should always choose the pleasant and peaceful path

Regarding[364] what he writes about his relationship with his daughter ... may she live, there is a known *psak din* of our holy Torah with respect to both oneself and toward *Bnei Yisrael:* the paths [one takes] should be pleasant and peaceful.[365] The *psak din* that one should always follow the approach of "the right hand drawing near"[366] is known. If for some reason it is necessary to demonstrate that the [child's] conduct was completely not as it should have been, there are multiple ways of doing so, as is easy to understand.

Refrain from scaring a child

Chinuch[367] should be conducted through love and closeness. Experience shows that this approach is more effective than educating through fear and intimidation. In general, one should refrain from scaring a child, so that he may live his life and make use of his abilities with inner peace and *simchah*, enabling him to use his potential to the maximum.

---

361 *Hisvaaduyos* 5743, vol. 1, p. 318.
362 *Sanhedrin,* 107b.
363 *Mishlei,* 13:24.
364 *Igros Kodesh*, vol. 17, p. 6.
365 *Mishlei,* 3:17.
366 *Sanhedrin,* 107b.
367 *Hisvaaduyos* 5750, vol. 3, p. 194.

The negative is external and temporary

Chinuch[368] should be imparted out of closeness, ימין מקרבת ("the right hand draws near"),[369] and only then is it possible to think about the approach of שמאל דוחה ("the left hand pushes away"), in order to release the grip of undesirable traits from the child. Even then, one must chastise only with the left hand, which is the weaker hand. This means that [although one gives consequences,] one does not do so with the same amount of enthusiasm, devotion, and tumult that is usually required in *chinuch*.

The reason for this is that the undesirable things are nothing but a foreign entity that has attached itself [to the Jew] from the outside. However, the essence of each and every *Yid* has no connection whatsoever with undesirable matters, so even if something alien becomes attached to him, this is only temporary.

Beginnings are difficult

The[370] purpose of *chinuch* is to become accustomed to something new. Since "all beginnings are difficult,"[371] to begin something new requires more lofty *kochos* than those one usually uses. The same is true regarding *chinuch*, and so, when we begin to teach a child, we begin by giving him many gifts [i.e., prizes], things that are precious to him, "to accustom him to start out in his studies."[372] ... I.e., "one educates by giving him something additional, like closeness or a gift."[373]

368 *Hisvaaduyos* 5746, vol. 3, p. 617.

369 Ibid.

370 *Hisvaaduyos* 5748, vol. 2, p. 123.

371 *Shemos*, 19:5, *Rashi*.

372 See *Rambam's Commentary on Sanhedrin*, chapter *Chelek*, beg.

373 *Likkutei Torah*, *Naso* 29a ff.

Gevurah does not apply to a baby

The[374] order of "the left hand pushes away and the right draws near" [375] does not apply to a baby. With babies, one must begin with the right hand embracing, for otherwise one could well distance him completely from learning. Drawing the child near – "the right hand" – is a necessary preparation before one begins to influence.

Corporal punishment

...He[376] is correct that the punishment of the rod[377] is not the right path to use in *chinuch.* Most often the loss outweighs the benefit, and this suffices for those who understand. We see clearly that force that is vested in ways of pleasantness[378] has a greater impact.

Potching in school

Reprimanding[379] by hitting in a *yeshivah* is completely out of the question. First, it is more destructive than productive... Other modes of punishment should be sought out, like sending the child away from school for a certain amount of time [suspension], or entirely [expulsion]. Or another method, which is mentioned in the *sichos* of my father-in-law, the Rebbe, is to forbid them from being present during the telling of stories of *tzaddikim* and the like, which are activities in which they desire to participate. Above all, by increasing supervision over the students, there is hope that the [undesirable behavior] will decrease on its own, until it stops altogether.

---

374 *Likkutei Sichos*, vol. 17, p. 74.

375 Ibid.

376 *Shaarei Halacha U'Minhag,* vol. 3, p. 192.

377 I.e., strict discipline. Cf. *Mishlei* 13:24.

378 Ibid. 3:17.

379 *Igros Kodesh*, vol. 21, p. 195.

Tracht gut, vet zein gut

...Even[380] regarding *[chinuch]*, the saying of our Rebbe, our holy *Nasi, Tracht gut vet zein gut* ("Think positively, and this will ensure a positive outcome")[381] applies. According to the simple meaning of the words as well, when one views the conduct [of the children] with a positive eye, then their conduct toward the onlooker will be in accordance – and how much more so their manner of speaking with him. Whenever one can influence with words of closeness, it is understandably far greater than conduct in the opposite manner.

Giving sweets to a child

A[382] child is not drawn to [Torah] study through commands, and how much more so not through the rod, but by being given sweets and so on. Specifically, one should give him sweets that he can appreciate at his present level, not items to save for the future [when he will appreciate them]. [Using incentives is necessary even though] it is true in general, a very young child is able to have *kabbalas ol* [obedience], and he can be coerced. How much more so in the matter under discussion [motivating the child to study Torah] should this be the approach [incentives, not penalties].

Hold back from reprimanding

...According[383] to what is explained in *Tanya* and *Chassidus* in general regarding the matter of המוח שליט על הלב ("the mind rules over the heart")[384]... sometimes it is necessary to exercise restraint over the feelings of the heart, and it is crucial

380 *Igros Kodesh*, vol. 16, p. 49.

381 *Igros Kodesh Admor HaRayatz*, vol. 2, p. 537. Cf. *Likkutei Sichos*, vol. 36, p. 4.

382 *Igros Kodesh*, vol. 21, p. 260.

383 *Igros Kodesh*, vol. 11, pp. 135-136.

384 Cf. *Tanya*, ch. 12.

to hold oneself back for the time being, even from giving reprimands that would be valid according to the Torah. ...

Indirect influence is received more readily and deeply

The[385] nature of youth and children is that influence that comes indirectly is received more readily and more deeply than influence that comes through imposing upon them the yoke of a command or a decree.

Discipline

Discipline is the foundation for success

It[386] is known that discipline is the foundation for success in learning and conduct.

Kabbalas[387] *ol*, discipline, and order are the foundations for success in learning.

The middle path

Regarding[388] his question as to whether he should take the approach of "the strong hand," etc.: In general, according to the well-known instruction of the great teacher [*Rambam*] in *Hilchos Dei'os*, it is best to take the middle path. The problem is that doctors in the United States, especially regarding children, are advising adults to fulfill the desires [of the children] to an extreme. Only recently have they started to rethink the correctness of this method. Since the advice of the doctors is needed [in this situation], it is understood that their opinions should be taken into consideration. However, first one should explain to them the point mentioned above of the "golden path," the middle road, especially when one sees undesirable results [from other methods]. He should fulfill the instructions of doctors, but should not be so "*mehader*" (excessively careful) in doing so.

---

385 *Igros Kodesh*, vol. 18, p. 296.

386 *Igros Kodesh*, vol. 10, p. 86.

387 *Igros Kodesh*, vol. 13, p. 162.

388 *Igros Kodesh*, vol. 18, p. 298.

Reprimanding the Torah way

It[389] is possible that because of the love [he possesses for his child], and אהבה מקלקלת את השורה ("love distorts the boundary line")... when it comes to the *mitzvah* of הוכח תוכיח את עמיתך, ("you shall reprimand your fellow"), he may abstain from reprimanding, even in private, especially regarding children, because he will want to increase in the *mitzvah* of ואהבת לרעך ("You shall love your fellow"),[390] love that is misplaced. Regarding this he is told, לא תוסף עליו ("You shall not add to [the Torah]"), and there must be הוכח תוכיח ("You shall reprimand your fellow").

So, too, at the other extreme: He may reprimand loudly, publicly, and in a humiliating way. Regarding this he is told, לא תגרע ממנו ("You shall not take away from [the Torah]"), from ואהבת לרעך ("You shall love your fellow"). First one should rebuke himself, [and then], calmly and using gentle language, [he will rebuke his fellow]). Only afterwards "if he does not repent, he should be reprimanded publicly"...

It is important to be careful with the main issues, in the direction of "the right hand draws near,"[391] as well as in the direction of "the left hand pushes away," so that his behavior is in complete accordance with *Toras Chayim*,[392] an instruction for life, and *Toras Emes*,[393] the Torah of Truth (and especially in accordance with the sections of *Orach Chayim* and *Choshen Mishpat* in the *Shulchan Aruch).*

Shielding a child from negative external influences with rebuke

It[394] is necessary to protect a child from undesirable outside influences. This is done through rebuke and the like, but only in a manner of "the left hand pushes away." The rebuffing is done with the less dominant hand... and not with the same force as the measure used for "the right hand draws near." ...

When a child is educated (and a person is educating himself) in the said way, step after step, level after level, he satiates himself with Torah and *mitzvos*.

---

389 *Igros Melech*, vol. 1, p. 247ff.

390 *Vayikra,* 19:18.

391 *Sanhedrin,* 107b.

392 See the *Amidah* liturgy, s.v. *Sim shalom*.

393 Blessings on the Torah.

394 *Igros Melech*, vol. 2, pp. 143-144.

Mussar is not the way of Chabad

He[395] surely knows the way of Chabad, which is not the way of *mussar* (harsh reproof). [It is true that according to the path of Chabad] at times words are said in order to wake a person up, and expressions are used that don't give one pleasure [to hear]. [However, these things are not said] because someone enjoys preaching *mussar*, but in the hope that it will make a difference – that by uttering these words, if necessary, the situation will change.

Emphasis on the positive

The[396] main thing is – unlike the way of *baalei mussar*, with their emphasis on lengthy explanations and descriptions of the *ra* (bad) – that one's main efforts and explanations [to a child] should be about the virtue of true goodness. Simply put: Efforts should be made to *farbreng* with them a lot – in topics appropriate to their level of understanding, of course – telling stories, singing Chabad *niggunim,* dancing, and so on.

Prioritize answering *rasha,* but don't reward insolence

The[397] order in which *Rashi* enumerates the four sons is the same order that exists in education. Meaning, when all four [sons] are sitting together and uncertainty arises about whom to respond to first, *Rashi* tells us the order: first is the *tam* (simple son), and then the *rasha* (wicked son). …

Between the first two, the *rasha* is of primary concern, for … if we do not respond [to his inquiry], he will not practice. So this is "separating him from a prohibition,"[398] which is of primary concern. We find this principle in *halacha* as well, that even if one is in a place where it is forbidden to speak words of Torah, if one's intent is to separate a fellow Jew from sin, it is permitted [to speak words of Torah]. …

---

395 *Igros Kodesh*, vol. 11, p. 6.

396 *Igros Kodesh,* vol. 12, p. 378.

397 *Sichos Kodesh* 5728, vol. 2, pp. 41-42.

398 Cf. *Berachos,* 19b.

Nevertheless, the *rasha* is not listed first, "so that the sinner not be rewarded."[399] And to respond to the one with *chutzpah* first is contrary to all principles of education. Since the others will think that he was answered first because he is insolent, therefore there was a need to place a different son before the *rasha*.

Having a fixed schedule

It[400] is clear that in *chinuch* there must be a set *seder*... for proper *chinuch* is impossible if there is no set and firm schedule. This should be taken into consideration first and foremost, because this is fundamental...

In[401] response to your letter about your son... may he live: As I understand, the true reason that supervising him all day and getting him to follow a set schedule is difficult for him is that apparently he did not experience this at home.

Thus, it should be ensured, through peaceful and pleasant means,[402] that he stays there [at camp] until the time that school begins. Surely as time passes, it will be easier for him to adjust to the new conditions. This can have a positive impact throughout the year, enabling him to accept discipline and follow a schedule, not only during school hours, but also at home. This is the most important thing for a child. On the psychological level as well, when he knows that it was decided that he should stay there, he will decide in his own mind to stay. From your letter, it seems that he hopes that through phone conversations he will be released from the camp and from discipline in general.

It is not good for children to have too much free time

Regarding[403] his student... it seems that one of the areas requiring correction is... that he has free time at his disposal, and he can make use of the time as he

---

399 *Yevamos*, 92b.

400 *Igros Kodesh*, vol. 9, p. 274.

401 *Igros Kodesh*, vol. 17, p. 287.

402 *Mishlei*, 3:17.

403 *Igros Kodesh*, vol. 14, p. 148.

wishes, or leave it empty. "Free time leads to [boredom, and boredom leads to sin"[404]]. Beyond this, he seems to have no specific plan regarding his future.

Efforts[405] should be made to do whatever possible that the children not have free [empty] time; rather, they should be involved in *limmudei kodesh,* reviewing their studies, and the like. May *Hashem Yisborach* grant him the merit to succeed at breaking the ice that seems to exist in your community in this matter. The coldness should be transformed into warmth, and the light of *kedusha,* in turn, into *chassidishe* warmth and light.

Saying *Tehillim* in free time

The[406] tradition passed down from the Baal Shem Tov to recite the *kapitel* corresponding to one's age is applicable to every Jew, including children.

However, it would be correct to teach them to recite the *kapitel* in their spare time, when they are not involved in [other] matters in which their *chinuch* obligation is greater.

It[407] would be worthwhile for each and every one to say (from time to time, such as on *Shabbos*, etc.) a *kapitel* of *Tehillim* corresponding to her age [at age 1, *kapitel* 2; at age 2, *kapitel* 3; etc.].

Simchah should not be expressed as wild behavior

There[408] are times that the *yetzer hara* interferes. When he sees that a child (or adult) is in a state of *simchah*, it tries to confuse and entice him to turn the *simchah* into wild behavior, so that the happy child will lose his self-control and turn into a *pereh adam* ("a wild person"), upsetting the military-like mood

---

404 *Kesubos*, 50b.

405 *Igros Kodesh*, vol. 14, p. 43.

406 *Hisvaaduyos* 5749, vol. 3, p. 399.

407 *Igeres Hachinuch* p. 209 – a handwritten response with regard to girls in kindergarten.

408 *Hisvaaduyos* 5744, vol. 1, pp. 269-270.

of obedience appropriate for Torah and *mitzvos*, as a member of *Tzivos Hashem* (Hashem's army). …

One should always remember that one's *simchah* should stem from Torah and *mitzvos*, and therefore there is no question about it: one cannot abandon one's self-discipline. On the contrary, at a time of *simchah* and personal satisfaction from belonging to *Tzivos Hashem,* one should be even more careful than usual to follow the directive of *Hakadosh Baruch Hu* and fulfill his mission.

Therefore, even when the child is in a state of *simchah*, he does not forget to recite *brachos*, and when he is thirsty and drinks water, he recites *Shehakol nihiyoh bidvaro* before drinking the water.

Ruling over instincts, lusts, and natural inclinations

One[409] of the foundations of *chinuch* is to educate the student and prepare him for proper conduct in his life when he becomes older... so that he will know how to relate to his desires and lusts. …

A student should be educated to be an *adam* (person) befitting that title, which is different from living the life of an animal, where everything is permissible. An *adam* is higher than an animal in that he is not enslaved to his instincts, lusts, and natural inclinations; he tries to restrain and rule over them.

A[410] Jew possesses: 1) a *nefesh HaElokis* (G-dly soul); 2) a *nefesh hasichlis* (intellectual soul); 3) a *nefesh habehamis* (animalistic soul); and 4) a body. …

The purpose of the *nefesh hasichlis* is to bring understanding to the *nefesh HaBehamis* through intellect, guiding it in how to act. Now a child, whether in years or in knowledge, has emotions that are powerful and intellect that is underdeveloped. If the *nefesh hasichlis* is drawn after *taavos* (lusts), even those that are permissible, like an animal, this is a fall from its level, and it is considered "dead."[411] This is the purpose of *chinuch:* to set the child on the correct path.

---

409 *Igros Kodesh,* vol. 22, pp. 494-495, 497.

410 *Igros Kodesh*, vol. 2, p. 5.

411 Cf. Zohar 3:135b. *Eitz Chaim, Shaar Sheviras Ha'kelim*, ch. 2. *Likkutei Torah, Chukas* 56d ff.

The[412] goal of *chinuch* is to lay solid foundations upon which the rest of the child's life is based. These are foundations that will not change because of the vicissitudes of time and place.

Therefore, a child is taught according to the foundations of *chinuch*: the foundations of righteousness and honesty, Torah and its *mitzvos,* and the Thirteen Principles of Faith, in a way that זאת התורה לא תהי' מוחלפת ("The Torah will not change").[413]

Then, when a child comes with a complaint that at this moment, he has a certain desire or lust, we tell him that the above foundations are not subject to change for any reason.

The Torah must be recognizable in the way he eats, sleeps, travels...

The[414] true meaning of *chinuch* is a "way of life," meaning that the *chinuch* does not only apply to a certain number of hours during the day, but it is **constant**. As we see from experience with true educators, they don't care only about the students' acquisition of a great deal of (proper) information. Rather, they teach them to be recognizable in their conduct: in their eating, sleeping, traveling, and all matters that the *Rambam* includes in *Hilchos Dei'os* through which one can distinguish the wise person.

Rambam writes these *[halachos]* regarding a *chacham* (wise person); nevertheless, by contemplating this briefly, one can discern how the same details apply to the *chinuch* of a little child as soon as he reaches [the level of maturity required] for a certain matter [to apply to him]. After all, as was said, a true educator cares how his child – and one's students are considered as one's children – conducts himself at every moment.

---

412 *Hisvaaduyos* 5744, vol. 1, p. 105.

413 Ninth of the Thirteen Principles of Faith.

414 *Sichos Kodesh* 5736, vol. 2, *Sichas Rosh Chodesh Iyar*

Teaching *derech eretz* during mealtimes

Mealtimes[415] are a time of emotional closeness, and so they should be utilized to instill *chinuch* for *derech eretz,* in accordance with the customs and laws of *Yisrael.*

Cleanliness

Physical[416] cleanliness is related to inner cleanliness,[417] for through careful conduct in this area on the physical level, one brings additional *kedusha* and *taharah* to one's soul. This is true since physical cleanliness makes a person a more fitting vessel for *ruchniyus* and the refinement of his *neshamah.*[418]

Never Teach or Say to a Child an Untruth

When a child learns it is permissible to lie

It's[419] obvious that deception in general is forbidden, for "One should distance oneself from falsehood."[420] We should even be very careful not to tell children falsehoods when we have good intentions. The reason is that eventually the child will realize that he has been told a lie, which will leave the impression that it is permissible to lie, and there is no way to know how the *yetzer hara* will take advantage of this.

---

415 *Igros Kodesh*, vol. 14, p. 409.

416 *Likkutei Sichos,* vol. 32, p. 68.

417 Cf. *Moreh Nevuchim,* 3:33.

418 Cf. *Sefer Hamaamarim Kuntreisim,* vol. 2 323a.

419 *Hisvaaduyos* 5744, vol. 2, p. 1248. Cf. *Hisvaaduyos* 5748, vol. 3, p. 307, fn. 8.

420 *Shemos,* 23:3.

Truth will not sprout from lies

We[421] should be careful not to tell children things that are untrue. Some mistakenly believe that it is permissible to interpret a text in a way that is untrue, *chas ve'shalom,* and that later, when the child grows older and can understand, we will explain to him that since then he was little, and he couldn't understand the true explanation, we had to tell him an untrue explanation. However, when one implants the opposite of truth, truth cannot possibly sprout from it. Truth grows only from truth!

There is a *minhag Yisrael,* which is Torah,[422] to throw candies at a child when he is brought into *cheder.*[423] How can we tell a child that the *Malach Michoel* is the one throwing the candies, when it is his father, mother, older brother, older sister, or teacher?

Some explain it by saying that since he is a little child, we can tell him that the *Malach Michoel* is throwing the candies.

This explanation is incorrect, for this is a *minhag Yisrael,* which is Torah, and Torah is *Toras Emes* ("the Torah of Truth"),[424] so how can we tell the child an untruth? And then turn this into a *minhag Yisrael!* Yet we see that in this way, pious children grow up.

The explanation: When parents throw him the candies, they act as the emissaries of the *Malach Michoel,* and the *Malach Michoel* is the שַׂר (chief angel)[425] of the child whom we are bringing to *cheder.*

One must fulfill promises to a child

When[426] one promises to give a child a reward if he learns, he must fulfill the promise. It is mentioned in *sefarim* that one should be careful not to make a promise to a little child and then not follow through. One should be

---

421 *Sichos Kodesh* 5739, vol. 1, pp. 609-610.

422 *Menachos* 20b, *Tosafos,* s.v. *nifsal. Maharil,* cited in *Rema* on *Yoreh Dei'ah,* 376:4. See *Likkutei Sichos,* vol. 22, p. 56.

423 *Sefer HaSichos* 5701, p. 30.

424 Blessings on the Torah.

425 *Daniel,* 10:21.

426 *Sichos Kodesh* 5736, vol. 2, p. 278.

especially careful with the very youngest ones, since with older children one can sometimes not fulfill one's word when it is necessary to promote peace;[427] however, little ones do not understand compromise. When a child is promised something and the promise is not kept, he loses all trust in his caregiver, for he sees dishonesty.

By Personal Example – Dugmah Chayah

Parents must set a living example

Parents[428] need to be a living example of what they require from their child. Otherwise, the child will not accept their demands.

When parents make demands, they must ensure that their words are דברים היוצאים מן הלב ("words that emanate from the heart") in order that they will be נכנסים אל הלב ("enter the heart").[429] They should influence and ingrain in their children that their conduct should be in a manner of לדבר בם (speaking words of Torah[430]) not only in school, but also בשבתך בביתך ובלכתך בדרך ובשכבך ובקומך ("when you sit in your house and when you walk along the way, when you lie down and when you arise").[431]

The first condition to succeed in *chinuch*

Hashem[432] *Yisborach* should help you and your husband to fulfill all that was said. However, the first condition in order to be able to do this successfully, is that you need to strengthen yourselves in *Yiddishkeit*, true *Yiddishkeit*. Through this one can hope that the talks with your children will be accepted by them, as a result of the children seeing that their parents themselves conduct their lives in this way wholeheartedly.

---

427 Cf. *Yevamos*, 65b.

428 *Shaarei Chinuch* p. 132.

429 *Sefer HaYashar* of Rabeinu Tam. Quoted in *Shelah*, 69a.

430 *Yoma*, 19b.

431 *Devarim*, 6:7.

432 *Igros Kodesh*, vol. 8, p. 19.

Behavior should not contradict what they teach their child

It[433] is obvious that the parents' conduct should not contradict what they teach their child, for otherwise the child will ask, "Why do my parents demand that Torah matters should be 'like new'[434] (exciting) for me, while they suffice with the minimum to fulfill their obligations?" On the contrary, parents need to set a *dugmah chayah* (living example).

This doesn't only apply when a child reaches the age of *chinuch*; it begins even before the child has any understanding. Even a newborn infant is influenced by his parents' behavior, and this affects his future conduct.

Children notice everything

First[435] of all, a child should be accustomed to and educated in a way that establishes a strong foundation for him, [a knowledge and sense] that he is a child of Avraham, Yitzchak, and Yaakov, and she is a daughter of Sara, Rivkah, Rochel, and Leah. These will be their *Avos* and *Imahos* for the rest of their lives, and these are the *Avos* and *Imahos* of their parents, grandparents, and all *Yisrael* going back to the beginning [of the Jewish people].

However, in order for this feeling to permeate the children, their teachers must behave in accordance with it. One cannot trick a child. When he sees that he is told one thing, but he "catches" the teacher or parent acting differently, not only does this weaken the matter for him, but he also loses his trust in the parent and teacher!

Even when it seems that [the parents] are only compromising in order to make more money that will go toward *chinuch* and the welfare of the child, since this wealth comes from an undesirable source, it is not wealth that will be of true benefit to him.[436] What's more, eventually the truth will come out and the children will figure out how the money was made.

In order to influence a child, one must set a living example, for children notice everything! At times the child comments [on inconsistencies]

---

433 *Hisvaaduyos* 5744, vol. 3, p. 1534.

434 *Rashi* on *Shemos,* 19:1, 11:13, *Devarim,* 26:16.

435 *Hisvaaduyos* 5744, vol. 1, pp. 113-114.

436 Cf. *Koheles,* 5:12.

immediately, and at other times he doesn't comment until later. Sometimes he remembers this quite a while in the future, but he notices!

Setting an example

He[437] surely knows that the best way to influence another is by showing an example himself in the way that he conducts his life. When one wants another to grow by one handbreadth, he must himself grow by two handbreadths.

I think it is unnecessary to remind him that if this effort is worthwhile regarding another *Yid*, how much more so regarding a son or daughter, for parents spare no effort as long as they can add strength and fortitude to the edifice being built by their son or daughter, so that it be built upon a firm, solid foundation.

The students will take it a step further

When[438] he makes demands of his students and *mekablim,* he should be a *dugmah chayah* not only for what he demands of them, but also for the entire way of life he is speaking about. As our Sages put it, he should be טופח ע"מ להטפיח ("moist enough to transmit moisture [meaning that he can only inspire others to an average level of inspiration if he is exceptionally inspired, just as a material must be extra moist in order to moisten something else]).[439] The students learn by *kal vachomer* [an a priori logical inference]: if it is permissible for their teacher to commit a certain sin, then it is permissible for the student in several more areas.

Learning Alef beis

Learn letters at age two

Children[440] begin to learn the letters of Torah at around age two.

437 *Igros Kodesh,* vol. 5, p. 135.

438 *Igros Kodesh*, vol. 22, p. 343.

439 *Berachos,* 25b.

440 *Hisvaaduyos* 5750, vol. 3, p. 246.

Teach letters and *nekudos* separately

Of[441] course, children should be taught the letters and the *nekudos* (vowels) separately, as it is known that *Gedolei Yisrael* and our Rebbes waged war over this, in order to ingrain in children the *kedusha* (holiness) of the letters and the *kedusha* of the *nekudos*.

Does not delay progress, instills *yiras Shamayim*

The[442] instruction of our Rebbes is to learn the letters on their own, the *nekudos* on their own, and then afterwards to combine them together. There are people who mistakenly think that learning in this way delays the progress of the child, but on the contrary: through learning specifically in this [traditional] way, the child is ingrained with the essence of the *alef*, *Alufo shel olam* (the Master of the world) and the word *Anochi* ("I," the first word of the Ten Commandments).

This letter encapsulates the first of the *Aseres HaDibros* (Ten Commandments), which includes within it all the *Aseres HaDibros*, which in turn includes within it the entire written Torah, and so too the entire oral Torah.

If the child begins to learn the letter *alef* with the *nikkud komatz*, without first learning the *alef* on its own, the opportunity to implant this in the heart of the child has been missed.

After a few letters, one may teach those letters with the *nekudos*

After[443] the child has learned a few letters, one may start to teach those letters with the *nekudos* (as opposed to waiting until all the letters have been learned).

Do all *nekudos* need to be learned before learning with letters?

In[444] response to his question as to whether one may teach children the letters they already know with *nekudos* before they have learned all the *nekudos*:

---

441 *Igros Kodesh*, vol. 8, p. 82.

442 *Hisvaaduyos* 5742, vol. 4, p. 2123.

443 *Shaarei Halacha U'Minhag* 10, p. 194.

444 *Igros Kodesh*, vol. 8, p. 39.

There is no rule about this, although it seems it would be easier for the child to learn all the *nekudos* together rather than to interrupt in the middle to learn other material. However, this is a question for educators and should be resolved as is fitting for the children in the class and the way in which [the teacher assesses that] the children will absorb the material best.

Letters should not be embellished

The[445] first letters a child is shown when learning *alef beis* must be in the true form of the letters. They should not be embellished, as this may give the impression in the mind of the child that the embellished form is the true form of the letter.

Learning letters from a *sefer*

Minhag[446] *Yisrael* is to begin learning *alef beis* from the letters printed in a Torah *sefer* from which one can learn a topic in Torah, as opposed to a chart where only the letters are found.

Learning letters from the *shaar blatt* of *Tanya*

My[447] father-in-law, the Rebbe, relates in one of his journal notes that when he began to learn *alef beis*, he was shown the letters from the page of the *shaar blatt* (title page) of *Tanya*.

We need to understand: What is the connection between learning the form of the *osiyos* of the *alef beis* and the *shaar blatt* of the *sefer Tanya?*

The *sefer Tanya* discusses *Hakadosh Baruch Hu* as well as various ways of serving Hashem, and it is based on the *pasuk* כי קרוב אליך הדבר מאד בפיך ובלבבך לעשותו ("For the thing is very close to you, in your mouth and in your heart, to do it").[448] ...

---

445 *Shaarei Halacha U'Minhag* 10, p. 194.

446 *Hisvaaduyos* 5747, vol. 2, p. 449.

447 *Hisvaaduyos* 5743, vol. 2, p. 792.

448 *Devarim,* 30:14. Quoted in the title page of the *Tanya*.

From this we learn a wondrous lesson. When we start to teach Torah to a Jewish child, beginning from the form of the letters of the *alef beis,* we immediately connect it to the Written Torah of *Chassidus, sefer Tanya*, by showing him the shape of the letters in the title page of *sefer Tanya*. We explain to him that this *sefer* talks about Hashem and *avodas Hashem* – more than this the child cannot yet understand – and from this *sefer* he is shown the form of the letters of the *alef beis*. ...

In this way, even the beginning of study of the form of the letters is permeated with the teachings of *Chassidus.*

The deeper meaning behind the forms of the letters

Children[449] should be taught the *pnimiyusdik* (inner) meaning behind the forms of the *osiyos* (letters).

For example, "What is an *alef?* A dot above, a dot below, and a line in between – this is an *alef*."[450]

A child must know that the *alef* of Torah is a *Yud* [alluding to Hashem's Essence] above, a *yud* [the essence of the soul of every Jew] below, and a line of faith that joins them.

Another version: A *Yud* above – this is the soul; a *Yud* below – this is the body; a line of *yiras Shamayim* in the center."

In this way, the child should be taught the rest of the *osiyos.*

The order of the *nekudos*

The[451] order of learning the *nekudos* should be according to the order on the *alef beis* chart (as is printed in the *Siddur*). Besides for the reasons having to do with their *kedusha*, it is also in order not to confuse the order [which can happen] if they learn part of the *alef beis* with the parents occasionally, or from other educators. This is particularly relevant since the custom is to start with *komatz* and not *patach*, as children are used to hearing from home, "*Komatz, alef, oh.*"

---

449 *Sefer HaSichos* 5748, vol. 2, p. 502, fn. 44.

450 *Hayom Yom* 8 Adar 1.

451 *Shaarei Halacha Ve'Minhag, Yoreh Dei'ah*, p. 197.

Colorful or black on white?

In[452] response to a question as to whether *alef beis* should be colorful or black letters on a white background: it depends what will be more effective in exciting the interest of the students.

If a person desires to use only black letters so that they resemble the letters written in *sifrei Torah* and *mezuzos,* it is noteworthy to mention that the breastplate of the *Kohen Gadol* had separate individual letters on colorful stones.

Letters and *nekudos* originate from *Har Sinai*

I[453] received your letter... and was pleased to read that you teach your class according to the *mesorah* of our holy ancestors, *komatz, alef, oh.*

It is known that the holiness of the *osiyos* of the *alef beis* and the *nekudos* originate from Moshe *Rabeinu,* who received these from Hashem at *Har Sinai.* This is plainly understood in the *Zohar* and in *Tikkunei Zohar.* It applies not only to the letters and *nekudos* themselves, but even to their names. In the abovementioned sources, it is written that the names of the *nekudos* are actually the *roshei teivos* (acronyms) of the names of *malachim,* etc.

Guardian angels

The Frierdiker Rebbe discusses the effect of these angels in his notes: The Alter Rebbe instructed that one should teach children *alef beis* with nekudos, "*komatz alef– oh,*" "*komatz beis – buh.*" Special care must be taken that the children read clearly. An angel is created from each word, and these angels protect the children and their parents. *(Perspectives Magazine 17, Merkaz Anash)*

Let the child know

When[454] a child learns *alef beis,* he must feel that he is learning Hashem's wisdom.

---

452 *Igros Kodesh*, vol. 23, p. 83.

453 *Igros Kodesh*, vol. 13, p. 93.

454 *Likkutei Sichos*, vol. 4, p. 477, Perspectives Magazine 17, Merkaz Anash

Inherent holiness

Regarding[455] your question whether there is holiness to the letters and if it is mentioned in *Shulchan Aruch*: It is actually written in a book even before the *Shulchan Aruch*, that is the *Gemara Shabbos* (104a), and in several places in the holy *Zohar* and *Tikkunei Zohar*, and likewise concerning the *nekudos*...Now, all of the above is extremely simple and logical. The fact that there are some who question it and argue against it, is only because it is their excuse to justify to themselves, how they dare to transgress the Torah's instruction. Ashamed to say that they can't withstand their temptation, they rationalize and take the burden off their shoulder by casting doubt on the matter itself.

The Radatz would learn *mishnayos* with his grandson. Once, his grandson did not understand what his grandfather was saying, so the Radatz comforted him, "*Heilige osyois*," the letters are holy.

(*Toras Menachem,* vol. 1, p. 79), *Lma'an Yishmeu,* vol. 326

Destroying the pure hearts

Chadorim[456] and teachers who don't teach in the proper manner – "*komatz alef oh, komatz beis buh*" – but, instead, teach them to say, "uh, buh," similar to how mundane languages are taught, are profaning the shining holiness of the letters, and are breaking and destroying the inborn pure and genuine hearts of the children.

Risk of becoming a heretic

The[457] *alef beis* letters are literally vessels to receive the light of the Torah. However, this is only so if the child recites "*komatz alef oh, komatz beis buh.*" If the child merely verbalizes the sounds without saying "*komatz alef,*" he is at risk of becoming a heretic *rachamana litzlan*. But if he is taught to say "*komatz alef*" he will remain a believer in Hashem.

---

455 *Igros Kodesh*, vol. 11, p. 9, Perspectives Magazine 17, Merkaz Anash

456 *Sefer Hasichos* 5701, p. 88, Perspectives Magazine 17, Merkaz Anash

457 *Sefer Hasichos* 5689 p. 44, Perspectives Magazine 17, Merkaz Anash

CHAPTER 7

Chinuch Al Taharas Hakodesh

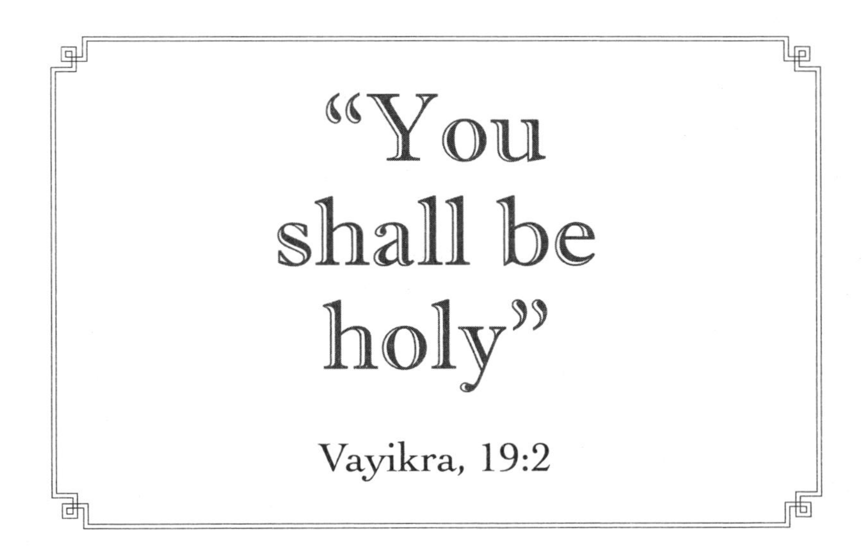

Negative outside influences

A[458] common mistake that parents make in raising their children is the hope that their children will reach a certain standard when they grow up and become independent, so they limit their education during childhood and adolescence to a certain measure and standard. Yet they fail to take into account that if they want their child to reach a certain standard when he becomes independent, then during the age of education he should be taught in a way that after the outside negative influences detract from the accomplishments of his education, what will remain is the standard that they hoped for [i.e., parents should raise their children at a much higher standard in order to compensate for the environment].

An[459] essential point: [The parents] also need to take into account the strong pressures and influences that their children are exposed to on a regular basis in school and in the community in which they live and grow. When these influences are negative, they need to give their children an adequate dose of vaccine so that they can withstand these temptations.

Yiddishkeit in the strongest measure

One should not think that a child should be given a "diluted" *Yiddishkeit*, and that afterwards when he grows, he will be given more. This might have been true if we were discussing an issue that is entirely logical and calculated; however, in all areas pertaining to *Bnei Yisrael* – who are above and beyond natural calculations – we have an instruction from a story in Torah. The order in Jewish *chinuch* is that when the child is only eight days old, he should already be given the strongest measure of *Yiddishkeit*: he should already be interwoven [with Hashem] in an eternal bond. This bond is not only for one year, ten years, or twenty years – rather, it is an eternal covenant.

What does it mean that children too need to be given *Yiddishkeit* in the strongest measure?

---

458 *Likkutei Sichos*, vol. 38, p. 170

459 *Moreh LeDor Nevoch*, p. 177.

From a young age, children need to have it explained to them that the Jewish nation in general—and every *Yid* in particular—is not connected with natural calculations.

A lesson from the circumcision of Yitzchok and Ishmael

The[460] circumstances surrounding Yitzchok's birth were supernatural and miraculous. His Bris (circumcision) took place when he was eight days old, and his upbringing was fraught with difficulties and trials.

Quite different was the case of Abraham's son Ishmael, whose birth was quite normal, and who was circumcised when he was thirteen years old, i.e., at a mature age.

Yet it was Yitzchok whom G-d chose to be Abraham's true heir, from whom the Jewish people would descend.

Thus, the Torah teaches us that when new generations are to be born who are to ensure the Jewish continuity and future, the approach must not be based on natural considerations and human calculations. For Jewish existence is not dependent upon natural forces, but upon G-d's direct intervention and providence.

Similarly, the education and upbringing of Jewish children is not to be determined by the same considerations and criteria as in the non-Jewish world. Jewish parents do not wait until the child becomes mature enough to determine his behavior and find his own way to Yiddishkeit. He is given the strongest and fullest possible measure of Jewish training from infancy. Only in this way is it possible to ensure the "everlasting covenant" with G-d, to come through all difficulties and trials with strength, and endowed with G-d's blessings materially and spiritually.

---

[460] Letter of the Rebbe from 1st day of the Week of Vayera 5730, reprinted with permission from Chabad.org.

Beginning *chinuch* with *hiddurei mitzvah*

The[461] *chinuch* of children should begin immediately with *hiddur mitzvah*, as it is the nature of children that they accept every good matter, matters of true goodness, all matters of Torah and *mitzvos*.

Chinuch for *minhagei Yisrael*

My[462] father-in-law, the Rebbe, related[463] regarding his father, the Rebbe Rashab, that when he started going to *cheder*, his grandfather, the Tzemach Tzedek, threw candies upon him and told him that *Malach Michoel* was the one who threw these at him. This made the candies very precious to the child, so he saved them and did not eat them.

On *Erev Pesach*, when it was customary to check the pockets of little children, the Tzemach Tzedek called in the Rebbe Rashab and asked about the candies, at which point the Rebbe Rashab had no choice but to eat them. …

From this incident, we can see just how great are the efforts one should invest in *chinuch*, and not only in matters of *deOraysa* and *deRabanan*, or even *hiddur mitzvah*, but even in Chassidic *minhagim*. The story teaches us that every *mitzvah* or custom should be done according to its authentic form [without modifying it for the child].

One must do so not only when doing so is easy, but even when it involves *mesirus nefesh* – *mesirus ratzon* – on behalf of the child. We find this as well in a number of stories regarding the *chinuch* of my father-in-law, the Rebbe, himself. [One should not think] that these stories apply only to special people, [such as] the *Nesi'im* of *Yisrael*. The very fact that these stories were publicized indicates that they are an instruction for every single *Yid*, as the [Frierdiker Rebbe] writes at the end of the *sicha* [in which he related the above story]: "We need this type of *chinuch*."

---

461 *Sefer Hasichos* 5749, vol. 2, p. 632.

462 *Likkutei Sichos*, vol. 16, pp. 129, 138.

463 *Sefer HaSichos* 5701, p. 30.

We gain the strength to do this from our Rebbes, our *Nesi'im*, for בתר רישא גופא אזיל ("the body follows the head"),[464] to follow in the ways that they taught us, forever.

Minhagim have the greatest impact on a child

The[465] order of the Four Questions according to *Minhag Chabad* is: *matbilin* (dipping), *matzah*, *maror*, and *mesubin* (leaning).

It seems difficult to understand: Isn't this order incorrect in terms of importance, since *matzah* is a Biblical obligation, *maror* is a Rabbinic obligation, while dipping is merely a *minhag?*

Some say that Biblical *mitzvos* should be fulfilled vigorously, to the point of *mesirus nefesh.* Rabbinical *mitzvos* also should be fulfilled with great vigor, for they are included in the *mitzvah* of לא תסור ("do not deviate")[466] and as *Rambam* explains at length[467] regarding the topic of fences, Rabbinical *mitzvos* in particular are included in לא תסור. However, when it comes to *minhagim* (Jewish customs), although it is a good idea to keep them, one is not obligated to sacrifice oneself for them.

Some claim even more: We need to educate children in the path of Torah, and it is very difficult to succeed in every detail. Sometimes it is worthwhile to forgo *minhagim* and devote oneself to inculcating only the most fundamental matters within the children.

In response to this, we can derive a lesson from the order of the questions on the *Seder* night: The first thing the child asks about, the first thing that he notices and that leaves an impression on him, is not a Biblical or a Rabbinic precept, but a *minhag Yisrael.* This is what catches his eye and has the greatest influence upon him.

If a child's conduct and the conduct around him is similar to that of the non-Jewish environment, then it will not help that he has set times for learning Torah, and that he *davens* and performs *mitzvos.* Since his conduct

---

464 *Eruvin,* 41a.

465 *Toras Menachem*, vol. 16, p. 198.

466 *Devarim,* 17:11.

467 *Mishneh Torah, Hilchos Mamrim* 1:1.

resembles that of those in his surroundings, and he is not clearly recognizable as being Jewish, and in his presence people do not experience the matter of המבדיל ... בין ישראל לעמים ("You distinguish between *Yisrael* and the other nations")[468] and אתה בחרתנו מכל העמים ("You chose us from all the nations")[469] ... this brings about, as well, that the child himself will not feel the *kedusha* in the *mitzvos* that he performs and in the Torah that he learns.

When something is lacking in the foundation – the *kedusha* of Torah and the *kedusha* of *mitzvos* – then over time, *chas ve'shalom*, their fulfillment may well also come to be lacking.

Ingraining *minhagim* in little children

Surely[470] it is unnecessary to emphasize the greatness of ingraining the laws and customs of *Yisrael* in the memory of *Bnei Yisrael.* Although at the age of kindergarten this isn't [done] through [formal] learning, we see from experience that with little children, accustoming them to the laws and customs of *Yisrael* has a greater impact than the [formal] learning of the laws and customs.

This is especially true when along with these laws and customs, [the parent or teacher adds] a story and explanation appropriate to the children's comprehension level that adds depth in their understanding of the laws and customs.

A lesson from Kimchis: Striving for more

Our[471] Sages tell us[472] about the wondrous *tznius* of a woman by the name of Kimchis. She had seven sons, and all served as *Kohen Gadol.* The *Chachomim*

468 *Havdalah* liturgy.

469 *Amidah* liturgy for *Yom Tov.*

470 *Igros Kodesh*, vol. 14, p. 71.

471 *Toras Menachem*, vol. 20, pp. 69-70. *Likkutei Sichos*, vol. 2, pp. 319-320.

472 *Yoma*,47a.

asked her, "What did you do to merit this?" She said to them, "All my days, even the walls of my home never saw my hair."

[This story holds much to learn about the virtue of *tznius*, but one can learn even more about devotion to *chinuch banim.*] Why couldn't Kimchis have sufficed with her sons becoming regular *kohanim?* ...

[The answer: *It was within her ability to do so.*] Therefore, when a woman has the ability to educate her children and bring them to high achievements, this very potential proves that it is her duty to do so, and if she doesn't fulfill this task, in a sense she has not fulfilled her duty at all, for she has not fulfilled the will of the Creator. ...

Jewish women in particular were commanded regarding this, since the *chinuch* of sons and daughters depends upon them. They should know that it is incumbent upon them to behave on such a level that they will be able to raise sons to be *Kohanim Gedolim*.

Every detail is important

Right[473] from infancy, children should be given a complete *Yiddishkeit*, with no compromises or *heteirim.* ... Hence, our *chachomim* invested tremendous effort to ensure the purity of the *chinuch* of Jewish boys and girls. They waged war so that no detail of *chinuch* would be compromised, even details that didn't seem so important. They knew that the years of *chinuch* affect the entire life of the boy or girl, and that children must be given the firmness and inner weaponry with which to overcome all the battles they are to encounter along their way in life.

---

473 *Toras Menachem*, vol. 10, pp. 288-289.

A scratch on a seed

A[474] man is like a tree.[475] If a tree is scratched once it is already grown, the scratch only affects a limited area and doesn't harm the tree. But when a seed about to be planted is scratched, the tree that grows from that seed may well be a *baal mum* (blemished).

Likewise regarding *chinuch.* If in middle age, after half one's life has passed by, it seems to a person that he must agree to compromise, this is only a blow to a few years. He lived for forty years without compromising, so if he fails and compromises for one year, the previous forty years serve as a source of strength to enable him to move past the compromise and to return to observing *Yiddishkeit* completely.

However, when we are talking about children – and there are those who want to raise them with compromises – the passion and zeal for *Yiddishkeit* is robbed of them for a lifetime! The scratch and deficiency that is created in their *neshamah* in their young years can cause them to grow into a blemished *Yid*, *Rachmana litzlan* (G-d forbid)!

Ammunition to stand up to challenges of this generation

Parents[476] should not be satisfied with giving their children the level [of *Yiddishkeit]* that *they* believe is sufficient for the children. This is because once the children become independent, their level of *Yiddishkeit* is what will remain, in most cases, after falling from the level that the parents gave them. For various reasons, there are already deficiencies in [what the parents transmit], and significant deficiencies. If what the parents give their children is not transmitted with sufficient liveliness and passion, then as children they will also be lacking somewhat, and what will remain afterwards?!

Especially considering that the younger generation has many more tests and difficulties in *Yiddishkeit* than the youth in previous generations. They

474 *Toras Menachem,* vol. 10, p. 289.

475 *Devarim,* 20:19. Cf. *Taanis* 7a.

476 *Igros Kodesh,* vol. 8, p. 18.

need stronger ammunition – which strengthens one's connection to Torah and *mitzvos* – even more than one, two, and more generations ago.

A small deviation from the path

A[477] person does not take the incorrect path all at once and end up in the depths of the forest. Rather, it starts from one small step astray in the wrong direction. The sooner he catches himself straying from the path, the easier it will be for him to return to the correct path.

This fundamental principle is especially important in relation to the Torah *chinuch* of a Jewish child. It is important to start from the nursing years with all the details, without compromise. At times it may seem as if a certain detail in *chinuch* is not so important that one should insist upon it with all one's might. Or perhaps one may think that it can be postponed until a later time. However, in reality this is not so, for in the future the matter will be much more difficult to straighten out and correct. The same applies in the positive direction as well: each improvement, even of the smallest nature, during childhood will lead to a tremendous increase and growth during the adult years.

This is also one of the main foundations that our Rebbes, our *Nesi'im* ... considered to be the foundation of a Torah *chinuch* for all Jewish children: ... That from the very beginning, *chinuch* should be entirely according to Torah – *Toras Chayim* ("the Torah of life"),[478] *Torah temimah* ("the pure Torah") – which is complete in all its particulars and without compromise.

Compromises have proven to be ineffective

We[479] see clearly in recent years how all those who agreed to compromises years ago, thinking that this would win over the young generation and attract them to *Yiddishkeit* – while all those already in the *frum* camp would remain complete – that not only did they lose the youth whom they wanted to lead in the way of compromise, but they even implanted weakness in the youth who were under their influence and who were [initially] intact in their *Yiddishkeit*.

---

477 *Likkutei Sichos*, vol. 20, pp. 645-646bv

478 See the *Amidah* liturgy, s.v. *Sim shalom*.

479 *Toras Menachem*, vol. 10, p. 291.

In contrast, those who, ten, fifteen, or twenty years ago followed the approach that it is forbidden to compromise on any detail, especially in *chinuch* – they are the ones who succeeded.

When[480] my father-in-law, the Rebbe, came to America, Poland, and elsewhere, some were hesitant about promoting a path of meticulousness in Torah observance, thinking that no one would be interested. Instead, they advocated promoting the way of compromise. Ultimately, it became clear that the path of my father-in-law, the Rebbe, not to allow compromises and leniencies, is the successful path, and not only in quality, but also in quantity, for there have been many students.

The reason is that when educators compromise, the students see that they are not being given an education that is inherently true; rather, they are being treated in accordance with the winds of the time. However, when no leniencies are given, the students feel as if they are being given something fundamental and truthful that is not subject to change according to the winds of the time. This in itself attracts people.

An additional advantage [to not compromising on standards] is this: Human nature is that when a person knows he won't be able to have any impact [by challenging something], then from the outset he doesn't argue against it. So when people know that here, in this *yeshiva,* no compromises will be made, from the very beginning the parents will not put up an argument. Instead they will think, "Oh well, so my child will be a bit more religious [than I am]."

Aside from all the above reasons, אין חכם כבעל הנסיון ("There is no wise person as one with experience").[481] And experience clearly shows, again, that all who followed the path of compromise eventually went further and further to the left. While all those who traveled the path of refusal to compromise are the ones who succeeded, in both quality and quantity.

---

480 *Toras Menachem,* vol. 14, pp. 136-137.

481 *Akeidah, Parshas Noach,* gate 14, preface 3.

Young people seek truth

Young[482] people cannot tolerate compromises. Only when they are given the word of Hashem in its complete and pure form does it capture their hearts. The truth is not as some believe, that leniencies and compromises will win over the trust of the youth. It is by imparting a traditional *chinuch* without compromises that the recipient is given a life of true happiness, both materially and spiritually.

Health of body depends on health of *neshamah*

Mothers[483] who want their children to be physically healthy – which everyone certainly wants – and to have fulfilling lives materially and spiritually, need to know that this depends on the health of the *neshamah*, which causes the body to be healthy as well.

Even non-Jewish sages, *lehavdil*, state that the health of the body depends upon the health of the *neshamah*. When the *neshamah* is healthy, the nerves are healthy, and the body is healthy too. The difference is that with the Jewish nation this is possible only through *chinuch* and life according to Torah.

A mother may ask: What is the connection between a life according to Torah and the health of the body? The health of the child depends on proper diet, sleep, and the like. What connection is there between the health of the child and *kashrus, kriyas Shema, brachos, tzitzis,* growing *peyos,* and learning *alef beis*?

It is important to know that since *Hakadosh Baruch Hu* created the world, and He is the Master over the entire world, He is the Master also, over the *neshamah,* as well as over the body, and the way that *Hakadosh Baruch Hu* ruled is what must be done.

For example, we see that a person who has designed a large factory knows better than anyone else how the factory should be run. There are details that

---

482 *Igros Kodesh*, vol. 13, p. 195.

483 *Likkutei Sichos,* vol. 2, p. 574.

in the eyes of others may seem small and insignificant, but the designer knows that each of these details affects the entire factory.

An *akeres habayis* too does not trust another person to run her home. She wants everything to be run in the way she understands, because she alone knows exactly what her husband, children, and home need.

If this applies to a home or a factory, how much more so does it apply when speaking of a child – and when speaking not only of the child himself, but also of his children and their offspring for all generations. Certainly no one is allowed to interfere with "how it is run," and one should behave only in the way established by *Hakadosh Baruch Hu*, the Master and Ruler of the world. This is crucial for the child himself and for many future generations.

We must know that Hashem, Who is in charge of heaven, is also in charge of the United States and any other country. In order for a child to be one hundred percent healthy, his *chinuch* should be one hundred percent according to Torah.

Parents would not settle for a child to be fifty percent healthy, *chas ve'shalom*, or for the child to be healthy half of the day and not so healthy, *chas ve'shalom*, for the other half. Parents devote their lives so that their children will be completely healthy physically, without compromise.

However, Hashem established matters such that the children's physical health depends on *chinuch* that is complete and without compromise, not fifty percent – half for Hashem and half for material matters. When the *chinuch* is one hundred percent for Hashem, the children will be one hundred percent healthy.

Teach one step at a time

[I[484] answer regarding] your question about your hesitation in teaching Torah without compromises, and your fears that if you are stringent with the children, they may not accept at all, and for this reason compromising may be preferable.

My suggestion for the said children is *not* to make compromises. That is to say, do not tell them that it is permissible to transgress, *chas ve'shalom,* some of the *mitzvos* as long as they fulfill other *mitzvos.* In addition to the prohibition against lying, this is a matter of misrepresenting the Torah, making changes

---

484 *Igros Kodesh,* vol. 17, p. 225.

in our religion, and the like. Rather, explain to them that right now we are teaching them about this *mitzvah*, but they should know that there are more *mitzvos*. However, since it is not possible to teach them all topics at once, they are being taught one step at a time.

They should also be taught about *teshuvah*: If *chas ve'shalom* a person did not withstand a test and did not follow what is written [in Torah], he is still obligated as before in *all* the *mitzvos* of the Torah, for ישראל אע"פ שחטא ישראל הוא ("Even if a *Yid* sins, he is still a *Yid*").[485] Explain that even after such an occurrence, the *tikkun* (spiritual rectification) of *teshuvah* is available.

Chinuch also needs a *hechsher*

There[486] is a known saying of my father-in-law, the Rebbe, in his first years after coming here: עס איז דא השגחה אויף וואס מען לייגט אין די טעפלאך, פארוואס איז ניטא קיין השגחה וואס לייגט מען אין די קעפלאך ("There is supervision over what we put in our pots, but why is there no supervision over what we put in our [children's] heads?!").

Chinuch and Parnassah

Par'oh Melech Mitzrayim

A[487] "*Par'oh Melech Mitzrayim*" exists even now: It is the control and conduct of the country that advocates sending the Jewish children into the river of the customs and norms of the country, drowning them in the river which, according to this opinion, brings *parnassah*.

...When the question of the *chinuch* of children arises, one should remember that it is forbidden to drown them in the "Nile" – the *avodah zarah* of that country. [In America, that *avodah zarah* is] searching for "*tachlis*" [i.e., a future career]. The only way to live is [by giving the children] a full *chinuch* as decided upon in our Torah – *Toras Chayim* ("the Torah of life").[488]

---

485 *Eruvin*, 19a.

486 *Igros Kodesh*, vol. 4, p. 227.

487 *Likkutei Sichos*, vol. 1, pp. 112-113.

488 See the *Amidah* liturgy, s.v. *Sim shalom*.

...One should know that Hashem sustains and provides for all, and if we do what He wants ... [in terms of Jewish education], He will do what we ask of Him – both for ourselves and for our children. ...

In every single country, and especially in America, one should pay no attention to the preoccupation of the country to make calculations regarding plans for earning *parnassah.* Children should be educated according to the way Hashem commanded, and Hashem will provide for the children, as well as for the parents.

It is specifically by *not* reckoning with the decrees of *Par'oh* [which pressures us to give up a proper Torah education] that we save our children, and this brings the *geulah* for the entire Jewish people through *Moshiach Tzidkeinu,* in the very near future.

University

[Studying[489] in university] is a severe *issur* (prohibition) and [spiritual] danger, and the danger is great. Moreover, it is known that exposing oneself to danger is even worse than violating a prohibition.[490] The entire atmosphere and weltanschauung of the environment in these institutions nowadays is permeated with the denial of *hashgacha pratis* (Divine Providence), the notion that no entity or force can interfere with natural law, so much so that this is accepted as axiomatic and thus not even requiring proof, and as the foundation of all the studies, which need not even be explicitly mentioned.

In most of these institutions heresy, idolatrous religions, and the like are taught.[491]

In the vast majority of these institutions, the boundaries of shame and modesty do not exist, to the extent that they belittle and mock those who maintain such boundaries. On the contrary, the more lecherous one is, the more highly he is regarded.

---

489 *Likkutei Sichos,* vol. 15, p. 43.

490 *Chullin,* 10a.

491 See *Mishneh Torah, Hilchos Avoda Zara,* 2:2, "Hashem commanded us not to read ... and not to think ... so that we not come to ask concerning the method of worshiping it ..." See there further, and ibid. 2:3.

The appalling situation in the campuses, dormitories, promenades, and so on, is infamous. One need not elaborate concerning shocking phenomena in general, and certainly not when it has reached the awful extent that it has in this case.

As for the famous claim that he or she will not be harmed and will overcome the test, and so on, the simple answer to this is also well-known. Even a perfectly righteous person, on the last day of his one-hundred-and-twentieth year on the earth [i.e., immediately before his passing], begins his day, before all his other prayers, by pleading before G–d: אל תביאנו לידי נסיון ("Do not bring us to a test").[492] This matter deserves further elaboration, but now is not the occasion to elaborate upon this.

Learning[493] in college is not merely a matter of learning facts. It entails being exposed to certain circles and activities that are antithetical to the values and faith of the believer. It would be like taking someone from a warm environment and casting him into cold water – "shock treatment" – several times a day. How long would he be able to survive?

In addition to this, the studies in university are set up to be at an age in which one's personality is not yet sufficiently developed, usually before the age of thirty, and the exposure [to negative influences] then is more dangerous.

Few come out unscathed

I[494] am aware, of course, that there are boys who together with their *yeshiva* education attend college. I have occasion to meet with them and I can assure you that very few come out unscathed from the tremendous conflicts involved. Even those who on the surface appear to be wholesome have no peace of mind, and very, very few indeed of those who mixed *yeshiva* with college have remained completely wholesome inwardly as well as outwardly.

492 In the morning blessings *(Berachos* 60b). Cf. *Sanhedrin* 107a.

493 From a private audience with the Rebbe in 5715 (1955), printed in *Dem Rebben's Kinder* p. 211.

494 Letter from the 23rd of Sivan 5708 – reprinted with permission from www.Chabad.org.

Overwhelming forces to confront at every turn

...When[495] a Jewish boy completes his compulsory education, it is an absolute must that for a couple of years, at least, he should dedicate himself to the exclusive study of the Torah and sacred subjects, in a most conductive atmosphere of a Yeshivah without distraction of secular studies, all the more so as the teenage years are crucial and formative and of lasting effect, in the crystallization of the character.

This would have been my opinion even if college entailed no more than a distraction of secular studies. Actually, there is much more involved. Theoretically, a college and its faculty should not try to impose any particular views, much less a way of life, on the students. Actually however, the student cannot help by being impressed, on the conscious and subconscious level, by the views, outlook and way of life of his professors. These as well as the whole atmosphere of a college, are unfortunately not compatible with the Jewish way of life and frequently, if not always, quite contradictory to it. This is so even in colleges which are theological, or having so-called religious studies.

Needless to say, the whole atmosphere of college is in violent conflict with the *Shulchan Aruch* way of life, whereby the Jew is totally committed - in every detail and aspect of his personal daily life - to the Torah and Mitzvos and the service of G-d, as is written "You shall know him in all your ways," to which a whole chapter in *Shulchan Aruch, Orach Chaim* (Ch. 231) is devoted.

In other words, the Jewish boy (or girl) entering college, yet desiring to retain the Jewish way of life in accordance with the Torah, finds himself tossed about in the raging waves of confict between two contradictory worlds. He is at a further disadvantage in finding himself in the minority camp, since

495 *Letters from the Rebbe*, vol. 2, pp. 9-10.

those sharing his views and convictions are few on the college campus, while the forces pulling in the opposite direction are overwhelming; forces he must confront at every turn - among the student body, faculty members, textbooks, newspapers and periodicals. It is doubtful whether even an adult and mature person who is subjected to such "shock treatment" day after day would not be shaken; how much more so a teenager.

Secular learning

...It[496] is not the role of Chabad to found schools for the learning of secular studies, not even when [this learning] is secondary. The exception to this – and this is only as a result of being forced – is what was done in the United States under my father-in-law, the Rebbe, that until the age that the government mandates it, they learn only the minimum secular education required by the law. Otherwise it would not be possible [legally] for the *chadorim* and lower classes to exist... This is not the case with regard to the trade school and for grades of students who have already passed the age of mandatory secular education, yet some parents or a movement of those close to Chabad [are advocating for children] to learn secular knowledge as well. This is a change that should not be agreed to.

It is understood that the above applies to secular studies in general. However, when the secular studies are secondary to the trade being taught in the school, they do not constitute secular learning for its own sake; rather, they are a branch of the study for the trade [and therefore acceptable].

...Surely it is unnecessary to point out again that this trade school should not be a place to escape to from the Talmud Torah *yeshivas* of Lod. Admission to the trade school should come only after students have learned for a period of time in the *yeshivos* of Lod, and other students should only be accepted as an exception.

496 *Igros Kodesh*, vol. 9, pp. 188-189.

Minimize secular learning

It[497] would be correct for them to minimize secular learning and not be stuffed full with it until the known age [age nine or twelve[498])]. "The street will already take care of it" [meaning, he will "pick it up" from the "outside"]. They should increase in *limmudei kodesh* (Torah study).

Makes a child's mind impure

The[499] first three years of age, which is when a child begins to learn, is the time that is the main foundation of his future success. Yet it is specifically during these years that people take their child and contaminate ["make *tamei*"] his mind with "English," "grammar," and the like!

If only the adults, too, would not know these matters! How much more so the children [should not study secular subjects] until the age of nine years, or until twelve years – and I would say that it applies to the following years as well, if not for the fact that תפסת מרובה לא תפסת ["If you try to hold too much, you end up losing everything"[500] – if one places too great a demand upon people, no one will listen, so this is the Rebbe's compromise].

This comes at the same time that *Hakadosh Baruch Hu* says that He needs neither *Gan Eden* nor the *Beis Hamikdash;* He wants nothing but "*veshachanti besocham*" ("I will dwell in their midst"). [501] *Hakadosh Baruch Hu* desires to dwell specifically *in the mind of a Yiddishe child* – and this mind is taken and contaminated with external [secular] knowledge.

The truth is that the parents want the child to study *only* secular subjects! It is only because there is some *zeideh* (grandparent) who demands that the child learn *Yiddishkeit,* or because they fear a *Yid* who sits in New York [i.e., the Rebbe], that they teach him Torah at all!

They claim that after the child learns "English" and the like, he will be able to earn a *parnassah* (livelihood) and he will be more "set" for life. This

---

497 *Igros Kodesh*, vol. 8, p. 24.

498 Cf. *Toras Menachem* 5715, vol. 1, p. 74.

499 *Toras Menachem* 5715, vol. 1, pp. 73-75.

500 *Rosh Hashanah,* 4b.

501 *Shemos* 25:8. Cf. *Reshis Chochmah, Shaar Ha'ahavah*, ch. 6.

claim has no substance, since no one knows the future; all of one's conduct should be according to Torah.

Every single thing of value is written in the Torah. If there were some material benefit to be had from acquiring secular knowledge, there would be a law in the Torah commanding one to gain secular knowledge. Since no such law exists – and in fact, the Torah states explicitly that this study is forbidden because it contaminates the *ChaBaD* [*Chochmah, Binah,* and *Daas* – the intellectual faculties] of the soul[502] – this means that there is no benefit in it materially! On the contrary!

They think that they can outsmart *Hakadosh Baruch Hu*, such that they will pay no attention to the route that *Hakadosh Baruch Hu* sets forth in His Torah in order to succeed. Instead, they will search for their own route, to learn "English," and they decide that through this the child will be successful. They should remember that *Hakadosh Baruch Hu* created the world five thousand, seven hundred, and fourteen years ago [from the time the Rebbe delivered this *sicha*], and since then He has been running it according to His will. From now on as well, the world will continue to be run according to His will: according to Torah.

...The parents come and steal the pure years from their children – they steal a portion of their children's lives!

... By what right do the parents steal from their children their days?! Was it for this purpose that *Hakadosh Baruch Hu* gave them children – for the parents to take their lives from them?!

Mathematics is also considered secular learning

Regarding[503] what is written in *Tanya* at the end of Chapter 8 about the wisdom of the nations of the world, [you ask] whether this applies [only] to philosophy or to other wisdom as well:

It seems that you wish to distinguish between them. You believe that philosophy would be prohibited as it deals with matters that go against religion, while in contrast, the wisdom of mathematics [is not problematic]. However,

---

502 Cf. *Tanya* ch. 8, end.

503 *Igros Kodesh*, vol. 11, p. 403.

[the Alter Rebbe] is plainly referring to all wisdom [including mathematics]... for there he writes *"chochmos"* ("wisdoms," in the plural). Also, he states that the *tumah* (spiritual impurity) from learning these various *chochmos* comes from *kelipas nogah,* which means that he's not referring to the wisdom of heresy, which is an actual prohibition.

[The Rebbe is saying that all secular knowledge contaminates the mind spiritually, even if it's not technically forbidden to study, as is philosophy.]

Introducing secular studies into curriculum

Concerning[504] what you write about altering the curriculum of *Tomchei Temimim* to introduce secular studies into it, even though you suggest doing so only for certain specific classes, I do not know what to make of the audacity in this [suggestion] ... to think of changing the curriculum of *Tomchei Temimim* which has existed as it is for a number of years...

The skills will be acquired with ease

With[505] regard to what you write, that many skills are necessary to fulfill the demands of this world [i.e., to earn a *parnassah*], to our regret, matters such as [the knowledge needed in order to make *parnassah*] can be acquired much more easily by the youth than *limmudei kodesh*. Therefore, a short time after they leave the walls of the *yeshivah* – after receiving sufficient immunization against harmful spiritual influences – it will be easy for them to acquire the skills truly necessary to organize themselves and earn an actual *parnassah*.

At least several years devoted to Torah study without interference

...It[506] is my definite and considered opinion that all Jewish children, upon completing their compulsory secular education, should devote at least several years to the exclusive study of the Torah, without the interference of other studies, not even

---

504 *Igros Kodesh*, vol. 11, pp. 249-250.

505 *Igros Kodesh*, vol. 14, p. 102.

506 *Letters from the Rebbe*, vol. 2, pp. 11-12.

training for a trade, in order to obtain the maximum insurance against all risks and dangers that their future life may hold, when they attain adulthood and settle down to a family life.

To put the matter in bolder relief, by way of illustration. Take the general attitude to polio, G-d forbid, and the precaution taken against it. Fortunately, the incidence of polio is not widespread, and where it strikes, it cripples only part of the physical body; yet though the odds are far-fetched, it would be reckless not to take the necessary precaution. Unfortunately, the victims of college education are numerous indeed and most widespread, by far in the majority, and the harm is even more far-reaching.

Another point which is often the subject of misconception: the importance attached to a college degree from the economic point of view. Statistics show that the majority of college graduates eventually establish themselves in occupations and business not directly connected with their courses of study in college. The moral is obvious.

Reserving the first portion of one's income for *chinuch*

From[507] the income one earns, one should first set aside the sum of money needed to pay for the *chinuch* of one's sons and daughters in the path of Torah and *mitzvos*. ... The household expenses should only be taken from the remainder of one's income.

Chinuch expenses do not diminish *parnassah*

Hashem[508] runs the world and grants the needs of *Yidden* and all creations, for He alone is the One Who sustains all. Clearly, therefore, it is not possible that

---

507 *Toras Menachem*, vol. 19, p. 194.

508 *Igros Kodesh*, vol. 9, p. 174.

acting in accordance with His will, by giving one's children a Torah education, would adversely affect one's *parnassah*.

The opposite is true: When we strengthen ourselves and act in accordance with the will of the Creator, even though it may seem to come with difficulties, we merit the fulfillment of Hashem's promise, אם בחוקותי תלכו ("if you act in accordance with My statutes") – which *Rashi* interprets to mean toiling in Torah, for learning Torah comes through great efforts – then ונתנה הארץ יבולה ("the land will give forth produce"),[509] and Hashem will give *parnassah* in even greater measure.

When parents provide proper *chinuch*, Hashem provides for all their needs

This[510] is a lesson for Jewish women in this generation. They should strive to give their children a genuine *chinuch* based on the foundations of *ahavas* and *yiras Hashem*. They should spare no effort to ensure that their children receive the best possible education. They should not be satisfied with an average *chinuch*, but should strive for the very best possible *chinuch*, for it is the way of parents to strive to give their children the very best. If this is even true of physical matters related to the physical body, it applies all the more so to spiritual matters related to the *neshamah*, which is "truly a part of Hashem above."[511]

Even if giving the best *chinuch* comes at a greater expense than an average *chinuch*, this is not a reason to attempt to save money and *chas ve'shalom* decrease the quality of *chinuch*, for the money that goes towards the *chinuch* of one's sons and daughters is given to parents as a "deposit" from Hashem – to be used specifically for the *chinuch* of one's sons and daughters in the path of Torah and *mitzvos*.

When parents fulfill their duty to educate their children in the path of Torah and *mitzvos*, then Hashem fulfills all their material needs, with abundant *parnassah*, and the like.

---

509 *Vayikra*, 26:3-4.

510 *Hisvaaduyos* 5743, vol. 3, pp. 1482-1483.

511 *Tanya*, ch. 2, beg.

Put differently, our Sages say:[512] "There are three partners in the creation of man: the father, the mother, and *Hakadosh Baruch Hu*." The partnership is divided so that providing for the spiritual needs of the child (the *chinuch*) is the job of the parents, meaning that *Hakadosh Baruch Hu* entrusted them with the most precious deposit possible [a Jewish child], who is "truly a part of Hashem above," in the hope that they would fulfill their role to ensure that the child's soul will shine in him openly, so that it be apparent in him that he belongs to the "kingdom of priests and holy nation."[513] In contrast, the material needs of the child – providing his food, *parnassah*, health, and the like – are the responsibility of *Hakadosh Baruch Hu*. When parents uphold their responsibilities in the partnership in the appropriate way – by educating their children in the path of Torah and *mitzvos*, then Hashem fulfills His portion of the partnership in a fitting way, as well.

Hashem has no shortage of money

Do[514] not worry "from where will the money come for the *[chinuch]* expenses..."

Since the *chinuch* of Hashem's children is a matter about which He gave us commandments, and לי הכסף ולי הזהב נאום ה' צבאות ("Hashem proclaims: 'The silver belongs to Me, and the gold belongs to Me'"),[515] surely there will be no lack of money, and [the administrations of the schools] will be able to bring in boys and girls with no limitations whatsoever.

There is a well-known saying of our Sages: קצובים –חוץ מהוצאת בניו לת"ת ("[The amount Hashem] stipulates for us is a fixed portion, but the [amount given to provide] for the expenses of one's child's *chinuch* for Talmud Torah is not [fixed]").[516]

512 *Kiddushin*, 30b.

513 *Shemos*, 19:6.

514 *Likkutei Sichos*, vol. 13, pp. 272-273.

515 *Chagai*, 2:8.

516 *Betzah*, 16a.

When[517] Chana brought her son Shmuel to the *Mishkan Shiloh*, the Torah relates[518] that she said: אל הנער הזה התפללתי ויתן ה׳ לי את שאלתי אשר שאלתי מעמו וגם אנכי השאלתיהו לה׳ (רד״ק: החזרתי לו השאלה שהוא נתן לי) כל הימים אשר הי׳ הוא שאול לה׳ ("For this child I prayed, and Hashem granted me the request that I asked of Him. And I have also lent him to Hashem; all the days he lives, he is borrowed by Hashem").

...According to the interpretation on the verse ושאלה אשה משכנתה ומגרת ביתה גו׳ ("Each woman shall ask from her neighbor..."),[519] שאלה means a gift.

...This implies that one's child should be presented as a gift to *Hakadosh Baruch Hu*. This teaches us a lesson about trust in *Hakadosh Baruch Hu*. We should trust that He will provide for a child's material and spiritual needs. Since one is giving the child to Hashem as a gift, He will surely care for all of the child's needs, for לי הכסף ולי הזהב ("gold is Mine and silver is Mine").[520]

Instructions for a trade school

...The[521] same applies with regard to the trade school—it is irrelevant that some people call it a high school. What I discussed here with Rabbi Young was founding a trade school, not a high school for secular studies, or even for secular and Jewish studies together. Thus, there should be room for the students to study topics relevant to their work, as you write in your letter. However, there is no room in this school for studying topics in order for the students to be eligible to receive a high school diploma, or the like. In this area as well, you will surely begin with a peaceful opening, and in a pleasant manner, although it is impossible to compromise on the principle.

I enjoyed what you wrote that the Jewish studies and prayer take up much more time than the study of a trade and related topics, and you will surely keep this up.

---

517 *Hisvaaduyos* 5744, vol. 1, p. 158.

518 *I Shmuel*, 1:27-28.

519 *Shemos*, 3:22.

520 *Chagai*, 2:8.

521 *Igros Kodesh*, vol. 9, pp. 188-189.

CHAPTER 8

Chinuch Milestones

"At five years of age, the study of Scripture [should be commenced]; at ten – the study of *Mishnah;* at thirteen – to [the obligation to observe] the *mitzvos*; at fifteen – the study of *Gemara*; at eighteen – marriage; at twenty – pursuit [of a livelihood]..."

Avos, 5:22

Birthday

The joy on a birthday

An[522] unborn child's life force is not his own, for his soul is not yet united with his body, even though it is found within it.[523] Rather, it is his mother's, and therefore לאו נפש הוא ("he is not a *nefesh* [life]"). Hence, the joy on the anniversary of his date of birth, for on this day [he received his own life force, his soul, and] he became an independent living being, a *nefesh*.

Customs for first birthday

When[524] the child reaches his first birthday, his parents should follow the birthday customs*, adding in Torah learning and giving additional *tzedakah* in the child's merit. The main thing for the parents is to contemplate the great privilege and good fortune with which they were blessed. *Hakadosh Baruch Hu* entrusted them with caring for a *neshamah* in a holy body, and trusted them with caring for this precious deposit properly by giving him the proper *chinuch* to follow the path that leads to the house of Hashem. ... This *chinuch* will also turn the child into a "candle to illuminate" the world with the light of *Chassidus*. Therefore, when the child's date of birth arrives, parents should increase in all of these matters.

*Birthday customs

1. To[525] have an *aliyah* to the Torah on the *Shabbos* before one's birthday; when one's birthday falls on a day the Torah is read, one should also have an *aliyah* on the day of the birthday.
2. To give extra *tzedakah* before davening *shacharis* and *minchah*. When a birthday falls on *Shabbos* or *Yom Tov*, one should give *tzedakah* on *erev Shabbos* or *erev Yom Tov* (and it would be good to give afterwards as well).

---

522 *Likkutei Sichos*, vol. 24, p. 180.
523 Cf. *Sanhedrin* 91b.
524 *Hisvaaduyos* 5742, vol. 4, p. 2190.
525 *Sefer Hasichos* 5748, vol. 2, p. 406 -407.

3. To increase in *tefillah* – to have extra *kavanah* in *davening*, meditate on the greatness of Hashem, and so on, and recite the whole *Sefer Tehillim* ([if that is impossible, as many as one can, and] at least one *sefer*).
4. To learn the new *kapitel* of *Tehillim* one begins to say on his birthday, which corresponds to the person's age [(age plus one)].
5. To add a shiur in *Toras hanigleh* and *Toras hachassidus* in addition to one's set Torah learning, three *shiurim* in *Chumash*, *Tehillim* and *Tanya*, which apply to all, and the daily portion of *Rambam*.
6. To learn a *Maamar Chassidus* by heart (the entire *maamar* or a portion of it) and to recite it to one's friends (publicly) on the birthday itself or close to the date, and specifically on the *Shabbos* that is after the birthday (during *seudah shlishis*).
7. To increase in activities done on behalf of others – spreading Torah and the wellsprings (of *Chassidus*) to the outside, out of *ahavas Yisrael*.
8. To spend time in seclusion, reviewing one's memories in order to see what needs to be corrected: a person should do *teshuvah* and correct his conduct. That is to say, one should meditate on his conduct of the past year and to take on good resolutions for the coming year.
9. A person should take upon himself/herself to be more careful, or add an additional *hiddur* in a specific matter (according to his level, of course), as one does on Rosh HaShanah.
10. One should make a *farbrengen* with one's family members, friends, and acquaintances - a praise and thanks to Hashem (and, if possible, say *Shehecheyanu* on a new fruit or garment, with the *simchah* of Torah and the *simchah* of *mitzvah*).

The mother makes the birthday into a *ruchniyus* matter

In[526] recent years, the good custom has been adopted to turn a birthday into a matter of *kedusha*.[527] This is especially relevant to Jewish women, for it is their responsibility to make the effort to ensure that children's birthdays be a matter of *kedusha*, particularly by giving additional *tzedakah*. It would be even better for each child to give *tzedakah* from his own money as well (once the child reaches an age at which this is applicable).

The Frierdiker Rebbe's directives

My[528] father-in-law, the Rebbe, publicized directives that should be carried out on one's birthday (which in previous generations were known only to a select few): One should search his memory for what should be corrected, and he should do *teshuvah* for and correct [those matters]. Similarly, the custom was to increase in giving *tzedakah* before *Shacharis* and *Minchah* (if the birthday falls on a *Shabbos* or *Yom Tov*, this is done on the day before), as well as increasing Torah learning, *nigleh* and *Chassidus*.

The Rebbe's directives

...On[529] one's birthday, a person should increase in Torah, *tefillah* and *tzedakah*, the three pillars on which the world stands, beginning with עולם קטן זה האדם (Man is referred to as a "small world," he should begin with himself). A person should take upon himself *hachlotos tovos* (positive resolutions) to add in matters of Torah and *mitzvos* throughout the year.

...On one's birthday, every single Jew should hold a *farbrengen* of *simchah* together with his family or friends, so that the *hachlotos* (birthday resolutions he makes on his birthday while מזלו גובר ("one's *mazal* is strong")[530] will be

---

526 *Hisvaaduyos* 5749, vol. 4, pp. 380-381.

527 Cf. *Sefer HaSichos* 5748, vol. 1, p. 331 ff.

528 *Hisvaaduyos* 5748, vol. 2, p. 461.

529 *Hisvaaduyos* 5748, vol. 2, p. 461.

530 Cf. *Talmud Yerushalmi, Rosh Hashanah* 3:8, and commentaries there.

made with *simchah* (joy). This will enhance the fulfillment of the *hachlotos* with *simchah* and *chayus* (vitality).

All this applies to every single Jew: men, women, and children, including those of the youngest age, [whose celebrations will be organized] by their parents. Once they are able to understand, they can and should have it explained to them (in a way they will understand) that on their birthday they must renew and increase in all areas of their lives that are good and holy. ...

An additional point relevant to little children: It is their nature to accept everything emotionally and with excitement. This influences their brothers and sisters to desire to celebrate their birthdays in a fitting way, as well. ... Moreover, the sons and daughters will raise a tumult to their parents as well about observance of this practice [i.e., that the parents should make a *farbrengen]*, including making good resolutions on their birthdays.

Taking on positive resolutions in the presence of others has much more strength than a person's making a decision on his own.[531] This way, [as time passes] others can also ask him about his actual fulfillment of the *hachlotos*.

Delivering public words of Torah

There[532] are places where it is customary that when a boy becoming *bar-mitzvah* delivers a speech on a topic in Torah, it is a *pilpul de'Oraysa* (a scholarly explanation). (Furthermore, there are places where it is customary, even in birthday celebrations before [the age of] *bar mitzvah*, that parents and teachers encourage and help the child to speak on a Torah topic, and this includes a *pilpul de'Oraysa.)* Since this *minhag* is spreading and increasing amongst *Yidden,* this indicates that it is a good *minhag*. The *Rambam paskens* that customs that spread among *Yidden* assume the force of a *mitzvas asei* (positive commandment) and a *mitzvas lo taasei* (negative commandment).[533]

---

531 *Sefer HaMaamarim* 5659, s.v. *Heichaltzu* ch. 10.

532 *Hisvaaduyos* 5750, vol. 1, p. 162.

533 *Mishneh Torah, Hilchos Mamrim,* 1:1.

Opsherenish

Yarmulka

Boys[534] should have their heads covered with a *yarmulka* from the time of *opsherenish*, and many begin even earlier.

Sleeping with a *yarmulka*

Surely[535] he will sleep with a *yarmulka* on his head and be told, in words appropriate for his age, about my father-in-law, the Rebbe. The child should know that now, too ... he elicits *brachos* for all those connected to him, especially boys and girls. ...

First haircut

It[536] is a Jewish custom not to trim or cut a boy's hair until he has reached the full age of three years old.

Cutting the boy's hair at that time – an *opsherenish* – is an important Jewish custom, meant to educate the child to leave his *peyos* [uncut]. From the time of his [first] haircut, when the *peyos* are left uncut, the custom is to make a point of training the child to wear a *tallis katan* and to recite the Morning Blessings, the *Birkas Hamazon,* and the Bedtime *Shema*.

Opsherenish not before boy reaches third birthday

[In response to a question about holding an *opsherenish* a few days early to coincide with *Yud Shevat:*]

It[537] is known that it is the "Jewish custom, which has the status of Torah,"[538] that an *opsherenish* is not done before the day that the boy has reached three

---

534 *Igros Kodesh*, vol. 9, p. 181.

535 *Igros Kodesh*, vol. 3, p. 397.

536 *Hayom Yom*, 4 Iyar

537 *Igros Kodesh*, vol. 7, p. 114

538 *Menachos* 20b, *Tosafos*, s.v. *nifsal*. *Maharil*, cited in *Rema* on *Yoreh Dei'ah,* 376:4. See *Likkutei Sichos,* vol. 22, p. 56.

years old. You should act accordingly, and may the *opsherenish* take place in a good and auspicious hour.

Postponing the *opsherenish*

[I[539] am responding] regarding what you write about the *opsherenish* of your son when he reaches three years of age on the 14th of *Shvat*, and you ask whether to postpone the *opsherenish* until the coming *Lag Ba'omer*. It seems from your letter that this is customary among *chassidim* in *Eretz Hakodesh*.

The great value our Sages placed upon this custom is well-known. You also write that some perform the *opsherenish* early, so it coincides with *Lag Ba'omer*, even though the child has not reached the age of three. This does not seem correct to me at all, since even if one were to say that the *opsherenish* in Meron is more important than the child being three, one can delay the *opsherenish*, but not celebrate it early.

As for whether to wait until *Lag Ba'omer:* If it is only a delay of a few days, the *opsherenish* should be postponed, but if it is a delay of a few months, the issue should be examined more carefully, since the *opsherenish* is considered a matter of *chinuch* for *kedusha*. According to the precise wording of my father-in-law, the Rebbe, leaving the *peyos* of the head [uncut] and the beginning of devotion to *chinuch* for a number of years and generations surely awakens a *hamshachah* from above (drawing down of Divine light) to the [child] being taught. When this is delayed, the *hamshachah*, too, comes only after some time, and in the meantime there is a deficiency for those weeks and months.

Learning in the text

As[540] soon as a child turns three, a child should be taught matters that are in the text [i.e., he should be taught with reference to Hebrew words and phrases], in addition to what he is taught *be'al peh* (orally) from when he began to speak, consistent with the famous statement of our Sages.

---

539 *Igros Kodesh*, vol. 14, p. 39.

540 *Igros Kodesh*, vol. 12, p. 288.

Hachnasah LeCheder

Child is given honey cake

The[541] *minhag Yisrael* is to connect the event of the first time that a child goes to *cheder* to study Torah *(areinfirenish)* with food: *lekach* (honey cake). The *lekach* is given after a *pasuk* (verse) of Torah is said.

The child is brought to stand close to a *Sefer Torah*. (For this, one uses a *Sefer Torah* suitable for a child. One does not use a kosher *Sefer Torah* written on *klaf* (parchment), because one takes care not to allow it to come near a baby, so that it remains undamaged.)

Candies from *Malach Michoel*

When[542] a child begins *cheder* at three years of age, we toss candies to him. He is told that they are being thrown by *Malach Michoel*, as is the *minhag Yisrael*. ... The child readily accepts this truth. If only it would be as readily accepted by adults!

This is understood at simple face value not only by a five-year-old child, but even by a three-year-old child – since even when he was two years old, when he began to speak, he was taught "*Torah tziva lanu* Moshe...".[543] This means he is learning the very same Torah that Moshe *Rabeinu* learned from the mouth of *Hakadosh Baruch Hu*, only he is learning it from the mouth of his *melamed*. And since he is learning the Torah of *Hakadosh Baruch Hu*, what is the great wonder that *Malach Michoel* is making the effort to throw him candies? On the contrary, it is a great *zechus* for *Malach Michoel!*

---

541 *Sichos Kodesh* 5752, vol. 1, p. 343.

542 *Hisvaaduyos* 5743, vol. 2, p. 679.

543 *Devarim,* 33:4.

Sending a child to *cheder* before age three

Regarding[544] what you write about starting [your son] in *cheder*, whether you should wait until he has reached three years of age or start earlier – this depends on how his *chinuch* has progressed until now. If care is taken at home to ensure a proper *chinuch*, as is customary in many Jewish homes, there would seem to be no need to rush to start him in *cheder* until the day he is three. If, however, putting him in *cheder* will add to his proper conduct [then it would be desirable]. In that case, it is not so much a matter of *limmud* as it is of *chinuch*. [In the latter case, his going to *cheder]* is no less effective than the *chinuch* he received at home, which is not associated with any date.

Take the child to *cheder besimchah*

The[545] first time we take a child to *cheder*, we do so *besimchah* (joyfully). This is also the way it should be done every day when we send our children to *cheder* to learn: *besimchah*.

We should not worry what will happen when our child grows up by asking, "How will he make *parnassah?"* When we send him to learn Torah, we connect him with the Sustainer of all life, and "the One who gives life will give sustenance."[546] Hashem's promise will be fulfilled: "I will give your rain in its time, and the land will give forth its produce."[547] So, when we send our child out to learn, it should be with the greatest *simchah*, with the knowledge that this is the only path that will lead to fulfillment, and not only spiritually, but materially as well.

---

544 *Igros Kodesh*, vol. 14, pp. 39-40.

545 *Toras Menachem,* vol. 16, pp. 328-329.

546 *Taanis,* 8b.

547 *Vayikra,* 26:4.

Bar mitzvah

Bar mitzvah simchah comparable to *chuppah*

...On[548] the day of a person's *bar mitzvah*, the *simchah* should be as on the day of a *chuppah* (wedding).[549]

Bar mitzvah celebrated on day boy turns thirteen

...The[550] celebration of the *bar mitzvah* should be on the day [of the birthday] according to what is written אני היום ילדתיך... ("Today I have given birth to you").[551]

Must begin to work to reach level of "*adam*"

...The[552] [young man becoming] *bar-mitzvah* ought to know that he should reach the level of the title "*adam,*" which is the highest of the four descriptions: *adam, ish, gever,* and *enosh*[553]... One should work on this immediately and not delay, and then he is helped [by Hashem] to become an *adam.*

Celebrate like a *chassid*

...I[554] do not understand why one would mark the event of coming to the age of *mitzvos* secretly. This was even true in days of old, but particularly in our forlorn generation. To the greatest extent possible, every event related to Torah and *mitzvos* should be strengthened and engraved in the memory of all involved. Of course, my intention in saying this is not to cause the waste of money, but that the celebration be held in the spirit of Torah, and a *chassidishe* celebration. Then those who participate will bless him to grow up to be a *yerei Shamayim, chassid,* and *lamdan.* The saying of our holy Rebbes is known:

וואס א חסידישער פארברייינגען קען אויפטאן קען מלאך מיכאל ניט אויפטאן

---

548 *Likkutei Sichos*, vol. 5, p. 86, fn. *.

549 *Zohar Chadash*, *Bereishis* 15:4.

550 *Likkutei Sichos*, vol. 35, p. 278.

551 *Tehillim*, 2:7.

552 *Igros Kodesh*, vol. 3, p. 350.

553 Cf. *Hayom Yom* 4 Elul.

554 *Igros Kodesh*, vol. 10, pp. 376-377.

("What a *chasssidishe farbrengen* can accomplish, even *Malach Michoel* himself cannot accomplish").[555]

Bar mitzvah boy and family should study ***Tehillim*** and give ***tzedakah***

It[556] is worthwhile and correct for each and every boy becoming *bar mitzvah* to learn on the day of his *bar mitzvah*, which is the day of his *simchah, Kapitel* 14 in *Tehillim* – since he has completed thirteen years and entered his fourteenth year – and *kapitel* 13 for a girl turning *bas mitzvah.*

In addition, on the day of the *bar mitzvah,* the boy becoming *bar mitzvah* should give of his own money to *tzedakah.* If the *bar mitzvah* falls on *Shabbos* or *Yom Tov,* he should give *tzedakah* on *erev Shabbos* and after *Shabbos*, or *erev Yom Tov* and after *Yom Tov.*

It would also be good for the parents and grandparents of the *bar mitzvah* boy, as well as the other relatives, to give *tzedakah* in the merit of the *bar mitzvah* boy.

Should the bar mitzvah boy read the *parsha* for the congregation?

Regarding[557] his letter that the *bar mitzvah* [boy] is planning to read the entire *parshah* for the congregation, my opinion on this is known: that to our regret, in our generation the primary issue has been made secondary, and so too the opposite [the secondary has been made primary]. Included in this is the fact that as a preparation to take on the yoke of Torah and *mitzvos*, the fundamental and primary learning –the *halachos* needed for day-to-day life – is minimized, and this is replaced by matters which are not fundamental. Another point, and this is also important, is that [in previous generations] it was never customary to do this.

---

555 *Igros Kodesh Admor HaRayatz*, vol. 3, p. 412.

556 *Hisvaaduyos* 5748, vol. 4, p. 21.

557 *Igros Kodesh*, vol. 20, p. 118.

Following the local custom

When[558] one comes to a city, one should follow its custom, and every single city has a number of customs that vary from other places [i.e., you can follow a different local custom for marking the *bar mitzvah*, such as saying the *bar mitzvah maamar* or a *pilpul]*. This is easy to comprehend. Of course, the above comes merely as a suggestion and comment, and a recommendation that you investigate again for yourselves whether it is worthwhile [to have your son prepare to read the entire Torah portion in public].

Whichever way you decide, may Hashem help it to work out for the best.

Bas mitzvah

...It[559] is necessary to point out that the day of the *bar mitzvah* should be a *simchah* like the day of a *chuppah*.[560] It would seem, according to the reason given in the above source that this applies to a *bas mitzvah* as well.

However, it should not be celebrated as a *bar mitzvah* is celebrated; rather, it should be celebrated modestly at school, like a birthday, and the parents should buy her a nice gift. ...

[The *bas mitzvah]* should be celebrated as is a *Shabbos* party or a *melaveh malkah*.

Youth

Teenagers are by nature more tense

[Influencing[561] the son in a pleasant manner and maintaining peace] is more the responsibility of the parents than of the son, as the parents are older, and they have far more life experience. ...

Moreover, and this is the main thing: the son is in his teenage years. This means that he is naturally more tense. Not every person merits to have his

---

558 *Igros Kodesh*, vol. 20, p. 118.

559 *Shaarei Halacha U'Minhag, Orach Chaim,* vol. 2, pp. 311-312.

560 *Zohar Chadash, Bereishis* 15:4.

561 *Igros Kodesh*, vol. 24, p. 18.

mind rule over his heart and to attain complete relief from tension. As a person grows and matures, the mind rules over the heart to an ever-greater extent.

Obviously, I don't mean to frighten you, G-d forbid, but I feel compelled to emphasize again that at all times, and especially nowadays, we must be exceedingly careful about anything related to the nerves of the young generation, the boys and girls, considering the state of the health of youth in general, and of their nerves in particular.

You[562] write of your son, and that you are at a loss for advice in dealing with him.

The advice of our Sages is already known that there are three people about whom it is said that, "The right hand should draw close,"[563] one of whom is a child. In your case, you should consult with a psychologist, since often, and perhaps even in most cases, the behavior you describe in your letter is related to tension of the nerves, and often a doctor has the ability to assist significantly. In any case, it seems from your letter that expelling the child from the home could cause the situation to further deteriorate, not be rectified. May you soon be able to share good news about the above. It is understood and obvious that the more you and your family in general increase in matters of Torah and *mitzvos*, the greater will be Hashem's blessings in general, and the fulfillment of your above request in particular.

Youth must be a *dugmah chayah*

The[564] youth have a special role that is easy to comprehend. Above all, they themselves should set a *dugmah chayah* (living example) in their daily conduct, keeping Torah and *mitzvos be'hiddur* (scrupulously), as well as influencing their surroundings in the abovementioned direction and spirit. We have been assured that one who comes to purify himself – as the Alter Rebbe puts it, ליטהר ולטהר ("to purify himself and purify others")[565] – is helped from Above. Through

562 *Igros Kodesh,* vol. 15, p. 224.

563 *Sanhedrin*, 107b.

564 *Likkutei Sichos,* vol. 8, p. 363.

565 Cf. *Yoma* 38b. *Likkutei Torah, Drushim L'Shemini Atzeres* 88b.

this, each and every person does what is in his power to hasten the end of our *galus* and bring closer the coming of *Moshiach Tzidkeinu* and our *geulah.* May we merit the fulfillment of the prophecy, "These days will be transformed into days of happiness and celebration."[566]

Youth sees through hypocrisy

In[567] this generation, the youth themselves ridicule those who walk a path of compromise, saying that if the teachers and educators would themselves believe in what they are teaching, there would be no possibility for compromise. This is especially so in matters connected to Hashem's Torah, as is self-evident that a man of flesh and blood has no authority to compromise in matters of *Hakadosh Baruch Hu.*

Monitoring the environment of youth

It[568] is superfluous to point out the necessity that the students of high-school age always remain in an appropriate environment. This is because at this age [teenage years] they are very impressionable, and events during this time period affect their entire lives.

Youth are craving meaning and purpose

If[569] ever, at any time and place, it was necessary to give meaning to day-to-day life – that is, meaning according to Torah and tradition – it is required all the more in this generation. Many philosophies and ideals, from the extreme left to the extreme right, have resulted in widespread disappointment. This discouragement affects mainly the youth who have not seen life illuminated with the values of *Bnei Yisrael,* the eternal nation. They feel left in a void, empty of all substance. The most undesirable consequences arise when life enters a pattern widely known as "a grey world," and there is no special campaign

---

566 Cf. *Mishneh Torah, Hilchos Taaniyos* 5:19.

567 *Igros Kodesh*, vol. 7, p. 239.

568 *Igros Kodesh*, vol. 9, p. 200.

569 *Igros Kodesh*, vol. 22, pp. 189-190.

providing the opportunity for the youth to reveal their [hidden] inner strengths: the strengths of courage and *mesirus nefesh.*

Parents of these young people ... have a doubled and redoubled obligation to fulfill the deficiencies in their children's *chinuch* up until this point, as per the statement of our Sages, "If not now, when?"[570] What will they respond when their day of judgment comes and their children ask, "Why were we not given eternal and fundamental values that would provide meaning in life and encouragement to battle a difficult and grey existence?"

The youth are ready to transform their entire way of life for Truth

If[571] at all times it has been of vital importance to transmit the Torah and tradition to the young generation, it is especially vital in our present day and age, when we see many of our young people so confused and lost, yet at the same time searching and groping for the Truth. Experience has shown that when one conveys to them a genuine word, they are eager to listen, and ready to take up a challenge even if it means a complete transformation of their way of life. But[572] of course, in order that the message should have a lasting impact, it is not sufficient to give it to them now and then, but they must be provided with the facilities where they could dedicate themselves to the study of the Torah and daily religious experience, in an institution and surroundings which are permeated with the true spirit of *Yiddishkeit* and *Ahavas Yisroel.*

---

570 *Avos,* 1:14.

571 *Letters from the Rebbe*, vol. 2, p. 42.

572 *Letters from the Rebbe*, vol. 2, p. 42.

Extra attention to those susceptible to suffer a crisis

You[573] write about your work with *Bnos Chabad.* Surely you are giving serious thought as to how to improve the areas of which you write in which the situation is not as it should be, especially as it seems from your letter that the problems stem from a lack in vitality [and *chassidishe* warmth]... Since the girls in general, and the girls coming from another country in particular [are in need of special care and attention] – particularly during these transitional years when they are more susceptible to suffering a crisis, *chas ve'shalom* – all efforts to improve their standing are worthwhile, and the merit of any such efforts is too great to describe.

Explaining intimate matters

With[574] regard to speaking to young boys and girls at the age of maturity about the topic of, and problems related to, the *yetzer* [for the opposite gender] and intimate matters: It is difficult to take any particular position. On one hand, our Sages state concerning the verse you quote in your letter, "If there is a worry in the heart (in this case, of the youth), it should be discussed with others."[575] On the other hand, regarding this area, our Sages have said, "There is a small organ in a man; when it is satiated, it hungers, and when it is made to hunger, it is satiated."[576]

As I have observed done in several places, the appropriate solution is for the teachers involved to consult with one another and decide how to proceed regarding a particular male or female student. At most, they should speak to small groups of a maximum of two or three students for whom such a discussion would be suitable, obviously talking with boys and girls separately. However, this should not be done in a publicized manner as is customary in many places.

573 *Igros Kodesh*, vol. 12, p. 191.
574 *Likkutei Sichos*, vol. 22, p. 404.
575 Cf. *Mishlei,* 12:25, *Yoma,* 75a.
576 *Sukkah,* 52b.

Even then, great deliberation is required in order not to cause others, or oneself, to stumble by committing the (Scriptural, or at least Rabbinic) prohibition of being enticed to think forbidden thoughts and the like.[577]

Lower the age of marriage

Here,[578] I feel duty-bound to express the profound pain that I have felt for several years now over the fact that when the mass immigration of our Sephardic brethren to the Holy Land began, it was found "appropriate" to raise the age of marriage in a way contrary to the accepted custom in the lands from whence they came.

If when this decree was made there was doubt as to which is greater – the benefit or the loss [of this change] – the bitter consequences of this decree during these years on account of our numerous sins, and to our great distress, have demonstrated the tremendous damage this change has caused.

Obviously, my intention is not to bemoan the past; however, from time to time new suggestions are raised with regard to raising or lowering the age of marriage, and my opinion is definitely evident from the above. If only Ashkenazic Jewry would also become accustomed to marriage at a very young age, in accordance with the words of Rav Chisda:[579]

> Rabbi Chisda praised Rabbi Hamnuna before Rabbi Huna as a great man. He said to him, "When he visits you, bring him to me."
>
> When he arrived, he saw that he wore no *sudra*. "Why do you have no *sudra?*" he asked. "Because I am not married," was the reply. Thereupon he turned his face away from him. "See to it that you do not appear before me until you are married," he said.
>
> Rabbi Huna was thus in accordance with his views. For he said: "He who is twenty years of age and is not married

577 *Shulchan Aruch, Even HaEzer* 23:3; cf. *Tanya* ch. 11.

578 *Likkutei Sichos*, vol. 22, p. 404.

579 *Kiddushin,* 29b.

spends all his days in sin." "In sin?" Can you really think so? But say [that it means that he] spends all his days in sinful thoughts.

Rava said, and the School of Rabbi Yishmael taught likewise: "Until the age of twenty, the Holy One, blessed be He, sits and waits. When will he take a wife? As soon as one attains twenty and has not married, He exclaims, 'Blasted be his bones!'"

Rabbi Chisda said: "The reason that I am superior to my colleagues is that I married at sixteen. And had I married at fourteen, I would have said to Satan, 'An arrow in your eye.'"

Without undue haste

You[580] ask my opinion as to whether you should interest yourself about a *shidduch* for your daughter who will soon be turning seventeen, or whether you should wait:

In my opinion, you should not conduct yourself in any of the two extremes, [i.e., neither to be too hasty in your quest, or completely put it off]. Rather, you should interest yourself in this matter, but in a calm manner, and without undue haste. Surely, at the proper time, *Hashem Yisborach* will reveal the path with regard to this matter.

[*For a more comprehensive picture of the Rebbe's perspective on dating, engagement, and marriage we recommend reading* ***Eternal Joy***, published by Sichos in English Publications.]

Addressing *tznius inyanim*

I[581] have pleasantly received his sefarim: "*Taharas Yom Tov*" - five volumes - as well as the notification that he is going to publish a sixth volume. They are based on the Sefer: "*Yesod Yosef*" which speaks about "*Shmiras Habris*" and "*Tikkun Hapgam*", *chas ve'shalom*, even though it is not the custom within Anash to publish specific sefarim that explain the reason for the sin, and not even to

---

580 *Igros Kodesh*, vol. 6, p. 72.

581 *Igros Kodesh*, vol. 9, p. 24-25.

specifically speak about it publicly with much exposure. The reason for this is based on the words of the Tzemach Tzedek: "The contemplation and fear of the sin can by nature cause the emission of semen just like sinful thoughts." ...

In this country, within known sects where there has been a great breach in this sin, it is like an "open valley" in their eyes. More so, some of the doctors—who are quacks and who permit the prohibited—instruct those who come to them to do it regularly. They mock those who refrain from it and they explain that not only is it permissible, but it is a *mitzvah, rachmana litzlan*. With the multitude of our sins, there is nobody who will speak out, rebuke, and reveal the disgrace. Not even to explain at least the destruction of the body and its strength as well as the destruction of life that comes through it. In addition to the impurity it brings to the soul and its descent... In the words of the Alter Rebbe: "It is more heinous... and [the individual's] sin is greater with regard to the enormity and abundance of the impurity of the *kelipos* he begets, and multiplies them to an exceedingly great extent."[582]

There is reason to suggest to publish and publicize the greatness of the sin and its blemish, and to specifically speak in this regard, only for the purpose of saving the soul of the youth of Israel from descending... and primarily to strengthen and expand through this the attention of the teachers, the *Rosh Mesivta*, and *Rosh Yeshiva* to the situation therein, since, in a substantial and important measure, it is dependent upon them to fix this preposterous situation. In accordance with this measure, they are to blame. As it says: "He who is able to rebuke..." "Hashem's desire shall prosper in his hand," "To cause the community to be meritorious." To inspire them "To do justice (which is mercy) for the oppressed." "Which refers to the sparks of holiness that are "oppressed" through the evil deeds of individuals." (See the Siddur of the Mitteler Rebbe), until Hashem will gather the dispersed of his nation, through *Moshiach Tzidkeinu*, speedily in our days, Amen.

---

582 Tanya, End of Ch. 7.

Endeavors and toil will not be expended in vain

Surely[583], you will utilize your influence over your son to influence him to increase in matters connected with *yiras Shamayim*... There are parents who are either embarrassed to speak of these matters with their children, or they say to themselves that surely it will have no effect. Just as it is a *mitzvah* to say [some things], it is a *mitzvah* not to say [some things]. However, according to what my father–in-law, the Rebbe, said a number of times, this is not the case; endeavors and toil will not be expended in vain. This is true, even when [the efforts] are done by a regular Jew; how much more so, when inspiring things are said by a father, who, according to *Chassidus*, is one with his son. His words will be accepted, and especially in such a case where surely the words will come from the heart, as it says in our liturgy, כרחם אב על בנים ("like the compassion a father has for his son").

583 *Igros Kodesh*, vol. 5, p. 323-324.

CHAPTER 9

Chinuch of Girls

"Far beyond pearls is her value."

Mishlei, 31:10

A newborn girl is named at first possible Torah reading

Our[584] custom is to name a girl during the first possible Torah reading, even if it is a weekday, and not to wait for *Shabbos.* If only this custom of giving a girl her name at the earliest opportunity would spread to all groups of Jews, for this matter is also connected with the hastening of the *geulah.* Our Sages say, "*Moshiach* will not come until all the souls have come into bodies,"[585] and the connection of the *neshamah* to the body is through the letters of one's [Jewish] name.

Importance of *chinuch* of girls

...My[586] father-in-law, the Rebbe,[587] instructed that it is necessary to devote oneself to the *chinuch* of daughters just as to the *chinuch* of sons, and to strive to save the daughters of *Yisrael* as much as possible: three, two, and even one!

Le'Torah, le'chuppah, ule'ma'asim tovim!

With[588] regard to daughters, it is also important to emphasize the need to educate them *le'Torah, le'chuppah, ule'ma'asim tovim* ("To Torah, the marriage canopy, and good deeds"),[589] since women are also obligated to study the *halachos* applicable to them. Moreover, through this learning they fulfill the *mitzvah* of Torah study, which is a *mitzvah* from the [written] Torah [albeit as an optional *mitzvah* in which they are not obligated].[590]

---

584 *Toras Menachem,* vol. 3, p. 364.
585 *Yevamos* 62a.
586 *Toras Menachem,* vol. 3, p. 24.
587 *Igros Kodesh Admor HaRayatz*, vol. 7
588 *Hisvaaduyos* 5749, vol. 3, p. 75.
589 Cf. *Hayom Yom,* 25 Av.
590 See *Likkutei Sichos,* vol. 3, p. 469.

Chinuch of girls affects entire system

You[591] will surely recognize that the *chinuch* of daughters is among the greatest responsibilities, as it is written, חכמת נשים בנתה ביתה ("The wisdom of a woman builds her home"),[592] and that *Matan Torah* depended on the women.[593] Thus, the existence of *all* kosher *chinuch* institutions and their success in the *chinuch* of the students [i.e., even boys] depends to a large measure on the existence of schools for the *chinuch* of girls.

Proper *chinuch* endows a Jewish girl with special sensitivity

Parshas[594] *Terumah* tells about the building of the *Mishkan* and *Mikdash.* This should remind us—and emphasize the importance—of *n'shei u'bnos Yisrael* in all aspects of Jewish life. They set the tone and direct the way.

As the Torah relates, women were the first to take part in the building of the *[Mishkan,* the] holy place for Hashem's *Shechinah,* while they refused to take part in the sin of the golden calf, which represented the very opposite.

Through the proper *chinuch* in the spirit of Torah, a Jewish girl senses with an inner, divinely-endowed sensitivity what is holy and should be supported, as well as what is harmful and to be distanced from Jewish life.

In our times, when society's definition of good and bad, as well as light and dark change frequently, it is more crucial than ever before for a *bas Yisrael* to receive a Torah *chinuch al taharas hakodesh,* so that she will be able to assume her proper role as *akeres habayis.* In her hands, to a large measure, lies the future of *beis Yisrael.*

Educating girls to be *Yiddishe kinder*

When[595] it comes to the *chinuch* of girls, it is not a matter of Torah study and amassing knowledge; rather, it is about ensuring that they will be *Yiddishe kinder* (Jewish children). Most of the time, the girls live in an environment in

591 *Igros Kodesh*, vol. 2, p. 81.

592 *Mishlei,* 14:1.

593 Cf. *Shemos Rabbah,* ch. 28.

594 *Igros Kodesh*, vol. 12, p. 310.

595 *Reshimos* vol. 3, p. 261, cited in *Shaarei Chinuch,* pp. 266-267.

which people are immersed in worries about *parnassah* – "making a living" – or, on the other extreme [when there is an abundance of *parnassah,* they are preoccupied with] "having a good time." They do not see at all [the importance of maintaining a distance from the ways of the nations] ונפלינו אני ועמך מכל העם אשר על פני האדמה ("I and Your people will be distinguished from every [other] nation on the face of the earth").[596] They do not see that this is part of one's conduct in the spirit of *Yiddishkeit.* They associate *Yiddishkeit* only with limitations and self-affliction ["this is forbidden" or "that is forbidden," and so on]. ...

This is one of the roles of the "Beis Rivka" and "Beis Sara" institutions founded and run by my father-in-law, the Rebbe: to engrain in the hearts of the students that they are *Bnos Yisrael,* to explain to them the *kedusha* that this entails and the goodness and purity that go along with this, and to explain to them the responsibility placed on them.

***Shabbos* candles**

...This[597] *mitzvah* [of lighting *Shabbos* candles] applies to every *bas Yisrael* (Jewish girl) and even to a three, two-and-a-half, or even one-year-old girl who has begun to talk and is able to light and recite the *bracha.* She has the merit and ability to illuminate the entire room and home, whether she lights in her own room or in the family dining room, together with her sisters and, even more importantly, together with her mother (who lights after her children, so she can help them light).

Since there is no limit to the amount of light [that can be brought into the world], with each candle that is lit, more light is added. The great *simchah* and glowing face of the small girl, even a one-year-old, upon seeing her candle lit and illuminating [its surroundings] is visible to all. The girl's beaming face radiates true happiness, for it is the nature of children that their behavior is never feigned, and everything they do is done with sincerity and truthfulness.

---

596 *Shemos,* 33:16.

597 *Hisvaaduyos* 5749, vol. 4, p. 378.

A light that lasts from *Shabbos* to *Shabbos*

[The[598] fact that Rivkah *Imeinu* lit *Shabbos* candles at age three] teaches us a clear lesson that the obligation to light candles applies not only to girls before marriage, but even to little girls (not [yet] obligated in *mitzvos),* from the age of three and up. If they already understand the meaning of lighting *Shabbos* candles, they should be taught to do so. This also applies when the mother (or others) lights in the home as a *mitzvah* for which she is obligated.

...It is certain that Avraham *Avinu* lit *Shabbos* candles every *erev Shabbos* [after Sarah's passing]. The Torah testifies that he reached old age and was blessed with everything; surely this includes [blessings in] the spiritual sense as well. Yet, despite this, his lighting of the candles did not carry with it the wonder of נר דלוק מערב שבת לערב שבת ("a candle that remained lit from *erev Shabbos* to *erev Shabbos"),*[599] as was the case with the candles of Sarah and later Rivkah, from the moment she began to light at age three.

We see from this the immense power of the *mitzvah* of the *Shabbos* candle-lighting of Jewish girls. Even those who are very young – three years old – are called "the daughters of Sarah, Rivkah, Rochel, and Leah." Their lighting of candles illuminates the home for the duration of the entire week, until the following *erev Shabbos.*

On a deeper level, this same reality exists when every Jewish girl lights candles, even though it is not seen by the physical eye. Since מעשה אבות (the events that occurred to our forefathers) סימן (are a sign [that the matter will repeat itself]) and a transmission of the abilities needed לבנים (to their descendants).[600] Therefore every single girl who is "the daughter of Sarah, Rivkah, Rochel, and Leah" has the ability to affect the entire week through her *mitzvah* of lighting *Shabbos* candles.

Furthermore, there is an additional wondrous quality to the candle-lighting of little girls: When our Sages praise the "breath of Torah-learning,"[601]

598 *Likkutei Sichos*, vol. 15, pp. 170-173.

599 *Bereishis,* 24:67.

600 Cf. *Bereishis,* 12:6, *Ramban. Bereishis Rabbah* 40:6.

601 *Shabbos,* 119b.

saying that it sustains the world, they immediately elucidate that this refers to the breath of little children, breath that is free of sin.

This demonstrates the great virtue in the lighting of a candle, or any action done by a hand that has not sinned.

Yet we must understand further: This virtue exists in every *mitzvah* that a child performs as part of his or her *chinuch*. Why isn't this discussed in *sefarim?!*

The reason that it was only the candles of Sarah and Rivkah that "remained lit from *erev Shabbos* to *erev Shabbos*" – and likewise, the candles of all their descendants, all Jewish girls and women – and that this miracle did not occur when Avraham *Avinu* lit his candles, is connected with the Torah-ordained roles of men and women in the home. Our Sages state[602] that the role of a man in the home is מביא חיטין ("He brings the wheat") – he provides [the basic material for sustenance] in the home, while the task of the wife, "a helpmate to complement him,"[603] is to work with the wheat and turn it into edible food.

The way that *Hakadosh Baruch Hu* established the nature of the world is that "It is man's way to conquer,"[604] to bring things from the outside into the home.

In contrast, of the woman, [Torah tells us,] כל כבודה בת מלך פנימה ("all the glory of the King's daughter is within").[605] She is the *akeres habayis* ("mainstay of the home"), and so her role is inside the home: to work with and transform what is brought in from the outside in such a way that it becomes fit for use by *adam* (man), until ultimately this sustenance becomes fitting, so to speak, for *Adam Ha'Elyon* (*Hakadosh Baruch Hu*).

This is why Avraham's candle-lighting did not cause the candles to physically illuminate the home in a supernatural manner, for there was no connection between candle-lighting and his role.

It is specifically Sarah, Rivkah, and all the daughters of Sarah, Rivkah, Rochel, and Leah – all Jewish women and daughters – who are charged with the *shlichus* and role to be involved with the needs of the home, and work with the physical dimension of the home. They have the mission and power

602 *Yevamos,* 63a.
603 *Bereishis,* 2:18.
604 *Yevamos,* 65b.
605 *Tehillim,* 45:14.

to illuminate the entire home, all the time, through their candles, so that it is recognizable throughout the week that this is a home in which a daughter of Sarah and Rivkah lit a *Shabbos* candle.

Based on the above, we can understand on a deeper level the order of the three details that *Rashi* brings in his commentary: "A candle remained lit from *erev Shabbos* to *erev Shabbos,* a blessing was found in the dough, and a cloud hovered above the tent."

The commentators say that these three details correspond to the three *mitzvos* assigned especially to Jewish women: *challah*, *niddah* (*taharas hamishpachah*), and lighting *Shabbos* candles:

- Keeping the *mitzvah* of lighting the *Shabbos* candles brings about the state of "a candle that remains lit from *erev Shabbos* to *erev Shabbos.*"
- Care in the *mitzvah* of taking *challah* brings a ברכה מצוי' בעיסה ("a blessing in the dough").
- Through meticulousness in the *mitzvah* of *niddah,* one merits an ענן קשור על האהל ("a cloud over the tent") – the purity brings the "cloud" of the *Shechinah* [to rest upon the home].

Rashi brings all these three details in the chronological order of the fulfilling of these *mitzvos*. A girl begins lighting the *Shabbos* candle immediately when she reaches the *chinuch* age ("a candle that remains lit from *erev Shabbos* to *erev Shabbos*"). Later, when she grows a bit, she begins to help with the housework and is also involved in the preparation of the dough ("a blessing found in the dough"). Lastly, if she is married, she fulfills the *mitzvah* of *niddah* – *taharas hamishpachah* ("a cloud over the tent").

From all that has been said above, one can understand the great merit in investing the effort so that every Jewish girl who reaches the age of *chinuch* lights a candle every *erev Shabbos kodesh* and *erev Yom Tov*.

Through this candle, we will merit, as it is written in *Yalkut Shimoni,*[606] to witness the "*neiros Tziyon*" that *Hakadosh Baruch Hu* will show us in the very near future, at the time of the true and complete redemption.

---

606 *Bamidbar, Behaaloscha,* beg.

Blessing *Shehecheyanu*

...It[607] is worthwhile and proper for girls to begin lighting [*Shabbos* candles] on a *Yom Tov* so that they can bless *Shehecheyanu* while also [keeping in mind that it is for] the beginning of the fulfillment of the *mitzvah* of lighting *Shabbos* and *Yom Tov* candles. Those who are eager to begin earlier should buy the girl a new garment [on which she can recite *Shehecheyanu]*.

One candle

... I[608] advised to light *only* one candle until marriage.

Their very own candle and candlestick

The[609] youngest girls, as well, when they are taught to light *Shabbos* candles, use their own candlestick and their own candle, and they recite the *bracha* on their own... exactly as the mother, grandmother, and great-grandmother do. They are all united in their joy at meriting to illuminate the home together. Each additional light adds a *bracha* of *Hakadosh Baruch Hu* in the merit of the candle now being lit by another little girl. Of course, this adds to the merit of all the older family members, who helped and [continue to] help throughout the time the girl is receiving her *chinuch* on this path.

Chinuch of *kashrus*

...In[610] regard to *kashrus* of food and beverages, although both men and women are obligated in this *mitzvah*, in practice the main fulfillment depends on and is carried out by the woman. This begins with the *mitzvah* of *challah* 'ראשית עריסותיכם ... תתנו לה ("the choicest of your dough ... set aside for Hashem").[611] This imbues all areas of eating and drinking in the home with the

---

607 *Hisvaaduyos* 5750, vol. 3, p. 225, fn. 38.
608 *Likkutei Sichos*, vol. 11, p. 289.
609 *Hisvaaduyos* 5748, vol. 3, p. 371.
610 *Hisvaaduyos* 5749, vol. 4, p. 379.
611 *Bamidbar*, 15:20.

feeling that the first portion [in both time and quality] is given to *Hakadosh Baruch Hu* (since every *seudah* is referred to as "bread"[612]).

It is the custom of Jewish women to educate their daughters in matters related to the *kashrus* of food and beverages while they [the daughters] are helping with meal preparation.

Helping the mother

It[613] is understood that this matter [*chinuch* in the spirit of *Yiddishkeit]* also applies to girls before marriageable age, for they must prepare to fulfill their primary role when the time comes – to establish a *Yiddishe* home. Then every one of them will become an *akeres habayis* and will need to educate the members of her household in the spirit of *Yiddishkeit.* Therefore, they need to begin [training] in all these matters even before marriage by helping their mothers.

Bnos[614] *Yisrael* have a connection to בנתה ביתה ("building the home")[615] – the *chinuch* of children. In the time preceding marriage, they are preparing for their important role and *shlichus* for the Jewish nation: to build a Jewish home in the appropriate way, and to raise children in the appropriate way. Even small daughters, by helping their mothers with the *chinuch* of their younger brothers and sisters, become their mothers' partners in building the home.

Accustoming herself to be a *dugmah chayah*

In[616] order to enable her to fulfill her role as *akeres habayis*, even while she is still a small girl – and how much more so when she grows several years older – she should accustom herself to being a *dugmah chayah*. That way, when the time comes, she will set a living example and illuminate her entire surroundings, beginning with her own children.

---

612 *Bereishis,* 31:54, *Rashi.*

613 *Hisvaaduyos* 5745, vol. 2, p. 1350.

614 *Hisvaaduyos* 5748, vol. 4, p. 341.

615 *Mishlei,* 14:1.

616 *Hisvaaduyos* 5746, vol. 3, p. 618.

Playing with a doll and what it teaches

One[617] of the most beloved toys of a little girl, among both the Jewish people as well as *lehavdil* the nations of the world, is a doll – plastic or wood in the form of a baby.

The lesson from this: We remind and prepare the girl so that when she grows up, and *Hakadosh Baruch Hu* blesses her with a home and with children of her own, she will run her home and raise her children according to the will of *Hashem Yisborach*.

Small girls should also be brought to *shul*

Common[618] practice, with the consent of *Gedolei Yisrael*, is that small girls also come to *shul* with their fathers, and not only to the woman's section, even after the age of three. This is the case as long as they have not yet reached the age of *chinuch* [to conduct themselves as women] and an understanding in this matter.

The founding of "Bais Rivkah" and "Bais Sarah"

[After miraculously escaping war-torn Europe and arriving safely in the United States, the Rebbe was appointed by the previous Rebbe to be the chairman of Merkos L'Inyonei Chinuch, the educational arm of the Chabad Lubavitch movement.

During the year 5706 (1946), the Association of Bais Rivkah Schools, under the auspices of Merkos L'Inyonei Chinuch, held its annual dinner. As the representative of Merkos, the Rebbe addressed the function. The following is adapted from the Rebbe's address, recorded by the Rebbe in his personal diary:]

When my saintly father-in-law, the [previous] Rebbe, visited the United States 16 years ago in 1930, he took great interest in the condition of Jewish education here.

---

617 *Likkutei Sichos*, vol. 14, p. 106.

618 *Hisvaaduyos* 5749, vol. 1, p. 39, fn. 25.

Subsequently, upon his return six years ago (on the ninth of Adar, 5701 (1941), he observed the developments that had ensued in the interim, and after a period of preparation, he founded the network of schools for girls called "Bais Rivkah" or "Bais Sarah."

However, as is the case with any new project, many objected to his activities, showering him with all sorts of questions and queries. Their primary and most potent argument was rooted in the dictum of our Sages[619] that women are exempt from the study of Torah. In fact, our Sages tell us, "One who teaches his daughter Torah, teaches her foolishness[620]". ...Yet, considering the present circumstances, the above discussion is clearly irrelevant. This is due to the fact that the education of Jewish girls today no longer involves a question of whether their Torah study is legitimate. Rather, the entire issue is a question of assuring the continuity and survival of Jewish children.

This is because, in most circumstances, they are raised in an environment submerged in the pursuit of "earning a living," or conversely (when the livelihood is ample), in an environment of ambition to simply "have a good time." Consequently, they fail to sense the theme expressed in the verse, *Viniflinu ani v'amcho mikol ho'om asher al p'nei hoadamah*[621] – "And I and your nation shall be made distinct from every people upon the face of the earth." From their perspective, Judaism is synonymous with restrictions, prohibitions, and so forth – perhaps even personal suffering.

Certainly, when they participate in a charitable endeavor, irrespective of the beneficiary, they maintain that in doing so they have already fulfilled their duty completely, both toward the Almighty and toward their fellow man.

This is the function of the "Bais Rivkah" and "Bais Sarah" schools, founded by my saintly father-in-law, the [previous] Rebbe, : to impress upon the hearts of the students that they are *b'nos Yisrael* – Jewish daughters, and to explain to them the sanctity of *Yiddishkeit*, the virtue and purity that it yields, and the responsibility that each one of them bears.

---

619 *Kiddushin*, 29b.

620 *Sotah*, 21b.

621 *Shemos*, 33:16.

That being said, the response to the second question posed is also obvious. People asked, "Are you founding a school to create 'Rebbetzins'?"

Our aim is that every student should recognize her duty as a *bas Yisrael*, being a member of the Jewish nation, and one who will establish a Jewish home in the future as a Jewish mother. …

…Surely, for the sake of saving even one soul from straying from the path of Torah and *mitzvos*, we must grant all we can toward this end. This is true in particular for girls, in whom we hope to see the fulfillment of the verse, "The wisest of women, each one builds her home[622]" – on the foundations of Torah and *mitzvos*.

Tznius

From three years and a day

According[623] to the *Shulchan Aruch*, a girl should already conduct herself in a manner of *tznius* from the age of three years and a day. This surely applies to a girl ten years and older. ...

But do not be oppressive about this ... and speak in a pleasant manner.

From the most tender age

A[624] Lubavitcher *chassid* once asked the Rebbe, "From what age should *tznius* be taught, and how should it be done?"

The Rebbe responded, "Go and ask ... son of ..." (and named a Chabad *chassid)* who was successful in the *chinuch* of his daughters.

That *chassid* had been careful with his daughters' *chinuch* from the most tender age, dressing them with long skirts that covered their knees while seated, sleeves that covered the elbows, and long socks. *Baruch Hashem,* he merited that all his daughters married *rabbanim* who were *geonim* and *chassidim.*

622 *Mishlei,* 14:1

623 *Likkutei Sichos*, vol. 18, p. 448.

624 *Sefer Madrich L'Imahos Be'Chinuch*, Yosef Hartman, pp. 82, 86.

Tznius: Minhag hamakom

My[625] opinion is known in this matter: the measure that [applies] equally to every Jewish girl and in every place is that the knees should be covered even when seated.

The above is, again, the *minimum* requirement for all.

However, there are places where this requirement is insufficient. In matters of *tznius*, there are certain boundaries that may not be changed regardless of the location, and then there are additional practices that depend upon the *minhag hamakom* (the custom of that community). [In certain places where customs are different, the *minhag hamakom* would require one] to be more stringent, but never more lenient, of course. It is for the *rav* (community rabbi) of that place to determine and instruct what should be done in practice.

Another point to add, and this is also primary, is that when we say that it is necessary to be stringent according to the circumstances of the place, this may not constitute merely a stringency, as the circumstances of the place may mean that a particular mode of dress is *assur min haTorah* (Scripturally forbidden).

The Jewish girl must set the example, and not follow others' way of dress

When[626] Dina saw another girl wearing a short dress, and she thought to herself, "I, too, can wear such a dress," the result was ותצא דינה ("and Dina went out"). This was a mistake, because Dina [the young girl in the Torah, and in a broader sense, every young Jewish girl] should not be learning from others how to dress; all other girls should be learning how to dress from her.

Dina's grandmother, Sarah [*Imeinu*], was different. She lived in a different era [so she was indeed able to live in the big world and influence her surroundings, as it is written], "Avraham converted the men, and Sarah, the women."[627] For a little girl, however, who is still a child in terms of her intellect and *yiras Shamayim,* to become familiar with the latest styles of dress and what *bnos ha'aretz* ("the native girls") have to say is inappropriate.

---

625 *Igros Kodesh,* vol. 27, p. 256.

626 *Sichos Kodesh* 5732, vol. 1, pp. 94-95.

627 *Bereishis* 12:5, *Rashi.*

The very fact that the Torah demands this indicates that we have the ability to do it.[628] If the girl is in a school in which others act inappropriately, [her parents should] establish another school!

There is a famous letter in which the *Rambam* wrote his daily schedule. The *Rambam* spent most of the day in the company of non-Jews, as he was one of the important people attending the Sultan. Yet when the *Rambam* writes about appropriate conduct for a *Yid,* he rules explicitly that one should dwell among G-d-fearing people, and if he can't find such a community, he should exile himself to a desert. How much more so in this situation, where other schools already exist that are befitting for the daughters of Sarah, Rivkah, Rochel, and Leah [so the girl should be sent there].

We must know that Dina [i.e., a Jewish girl] has no connection to the *bnos ha'aretz,* and the Torah tells us what [a calamity] resulted. [This separation must be accomplished,] however, in a pleasant and peaceful manner.

When Hashem blesses *Yidden* with children, He also grants the parents the ability to educate their children, or the means to hire someone suitable to educate them according to Hashem's will. ...

When we march forward with *simchah,* which breaks all boundaries and obstacles, we will then have a *Yiddishe* (Jewish) year, maximizing our impact wherever our influence can reach. We will then be able to raise children worthy of being named "sons of Avraham, Yitzchak, and Yaakov" and "daughters of Sarah, Rivkah, Rochel, and Leah," who will be "the army of Hashem." We will then be able to march proudly to greet *Moshiach Tzidkeinu* with the true and complete redemption.

Conduct of a *bas Yisrael*

[What[629] do we learn from the story of Shlomis bas Divri? (*Parshas Emor*)]

...The intention of what is written is not to speak pejoratively [about Shlomis], but to inform us of the *halacha* and to teach us a lesson from a biblical story, ... to warn us [about the importance] of being careful regarding the conduct and *tznius* of a *bas Yisrael.* She should not be "chatty," even in the

628 *Bamidbar Rabbah,* 12:3.

629 *Likkutei Sichos,* vol. 37, pp. 68-69.

manner of asking "How are you?" of every person. [She should not be] overly talkative, because this kind of conduct can result not only in her own demise, but even in giving birth to a son who blasphemes, G-d forbid.

Beyond this, the fact that as a result of this action she gave birth to a son who blasphemed is very surprising, for she didn't fail in this area intentionally. She mistakenly believed that being שואלת בשלום הכל ("Asking every person, 'How are you?'") was not a matter of פריצות (promiscuity), but merely friendly conduct toward others. Nevertheless, what emerged from it was a son who blasphemed, may Hashem save us. Hence, this story is coming to warn that every person should be exceedingly careful in *tznius*.

Learning *Gemara*?

In[630] response to your letter from the seventh of Iyar, in which you write that as a [female] teacher in Beis Yaakov, you want to know if the rumor is correct that it has become permissible for *Gemara* to be taught to girls. However, you do not go into detail about which *Gemara,* and in what way the teaching would take place.

The necessary pedagogical methods depend upon the personalities, talents, and knowledge of the girls being taught. The foundational principles upon which to decide the details of this are based on what is explained in the *Laws of Torah Study, Yoreh De'ah* 247:3 and the commentaries there. You will find the summary and final conclusion in the *halachos of* Talmud Torah of the Alter Rebbe, author of the *Shulchan Aruch,* at the end of chapter one:

> "Women, too, are obligated to learn those *halachos that they need* to know, such as the laws of *niddah,* immersion [in a mikvah], salting [meat], the prohibition of *yichud,* and the like, **all** positive, non-time-bound *mitzvos* and **all** negative *mitzvos,* both scriptural and rabbinic, for they apply [to women] just as they apply to men."

630 *Igros Kodesh*, vol. 7, pp. 247-248.

In addition to this, in our times knowledge of the foundations of our faith have become flimsy in the minds of the [Jewish] masses, particularly among the youth, and the shrewdness from the outside has affected them. Hence, it is especially necessary to teach them [Torah], especially girls, for in a few years' time, the management of the entire home will depend upon them. They each need to be informed of the beauty of Torah, and to be familiar with the world-view of our holy Torah regarding the issues and problems that they will face in daily life: as a wife to her husband, and as a mother to her children. The recent years have demonstrated just how important this knowledge is.

Accordingly, in recent years it has become impossible for women to be without at least a basic knowledge of *Chassidus,* which brings one to deeper feeling in matters between man and Hashem, love of Hashem, awe of Hashem, love of one's fellow Jew, love of Torah, and so on. If this knowledge is imperative for individual men and women, it is all the more vital for those involved in *chinuch*, who have a special influence on the young generation. Consequently, when a teacher is guilty of even a minor error or slight deviation from the correct path, it is bound to inflict great damage upon all their students. It is unnecessary to elaborate upon this.

Focus on sections with practical relevance

Regarding[631] your question about learning *Gemara* with an eleven-year-old girl, if it can be easily arranged, you should set out to learn sections related to practical matters, for this is in the realm of learning for women, as is explained in the *halachos* of Talmud Torah of the Alter Rebbe at the end of chapter 1, see there. There are many such tractates and sections, and [this is] especially [important] as she is soon to reach the age of accepting the yoke of *mitzvos* at age twelve (*bas mitzvah*).

---

631 *Igros Kodesh*, vol. 14, p. 99.

CHAPTER 10

Obligations of the Parent

"There are three partners in the making of man: Hashem, his father, and his mother."

Kiddushin, 30b

Every investment in *chinuch* makes a world of difference

Surely[632] there is no need to emphasize to someone like him the great importance of *chinuch. Chinuch* can be compared to caring for a soft seed or sapling. Every improvement and additional nurturing act brings about results that are באין ערוך (of incomparable excellence) once the seed or sapling becomes a fruit-bearing tree. And so too, the opposite, *chas ve'shalom.*

Dressing children in expensive clothing

Parents'[633] primary devotion should be to provide their children with *chinuch* according to Torah and *mitzvos* so that their children will grow to be *chassidim, yerei Shamayim,* and Torah scholars, through which they bring eternal good fortune to both the children and the parents.

However, when parents are instead preoccupied with dressing their child in expensive clothing, so that their child will be better-dressed than the neighbors' children, this kind of satisfaction can last a day, a week, a month, or a year. However, afterwards, when the child grows older, it will be apparent that he wasn't given true good fortune, which would have led to a lifetime of happiness.

Raising a sincere *Yid*

Regarding[634] the prayer of Chana for a child, ונתת לאמתך זרע אנשים ("give your maidservant a male offspring"),[635] the *Gemara* states[636] that she requested that he be מובלע בין אנשים ("concealed among people" [meaning he should not stand out]).

That is to say: Chana did not ask that her son – her only son – become the leader of all the exiled *Yidden*; this was not of value to her. Rather, she asked that he be obscured among people, and in this way specifically he would make the impact he needed to make, even though this meant he would not be greater than the rest of his generation regarding the education he received.

---

632 *Igros Kodesh*, vol. 26, p. 380.

633 *Toras Menachem*, vol. 19, p. 65.

634 *Toras Menachem*, vol. 27, pp. 340-341.

635 *I Shmuel,* 1:16.

636 *Berachos,* 31b.

Thus Shmuel was educated in the היכל ה' (the *Beis Hamikdash*) – not necessarily to be the greatest *ga'on* (genius), but to be camouflaged among people and to know that כל הימים אשר הי' הוא שאול לה' ("All the days of his life, he is 'borrowed' by Hashem"),[637] that he belonged to Hashem and to no one else!

Because Chana took this path, Shmuel became in his generation like Moshe and Aharon in their generation. Not only that, but שמואל שקול כנגד משה ואהרן ("Shmuel is considered equal to both Moshe and Aharon combined").[638]

[Chana simply wanted a *tomim,* not a *ga'on.* She wanted her child to feel and be taught that he is here on "borrowed time," not that he should work at being better than others.]

Hashem gives children to parents as a deposit to give the proper *chinuch*

There[639] is a well-known saying of our Sages:[640] "There are three partners in the creation of man: the father, the mother, and *Hakadosh Baruch Hu.*" The partnership is divided so that providing for the spiritual needs of the child (the *chinuch)* is the job of the parents. Meaning that *Hakadosh Baruch Hu* entrusted them with the most precious deposit possible, [a Jewish child], who is "truly a part of Hashem above,"[641] in the hope that they would fulfill their role to ensure that the child's soul will shine in him openly, so that it be apparent in him that he belongs to the "kingdom of priests and holy nation."[642] In contrast, the material needs of the child – providing his food, *parnassah*, health, and the like – are the responsibility of *Hakadosh Baruch Hu.*

637 *I Shmuel,* 1:28.

638 *Berachos* ibid. *Medrash Tanchuma, Korach* 5. *Bamidbar* 16:7, *Rashi.*

639 *Hisvaaduyos* 5743, vol. 3, p. 1482.

640 *Kiddushin,* 30b.

641 *Tanya,* ch. 2, beg.

642 *Shemos,* 19:6.

Parents do not own their children

Some[643] parents think that they own their children, to do with them as they please. If they wish, they will raise the children in the spirit of Torah and *Yiddishkeit*, and if not, they will offer them to *Molech* (an *avodah zarah* deity), G-d forbid! The truth is that parents do not own their children. Hashem gave them their children in safekeeping, to raise and educate appropriately, through *chinuch* in the spirit of Torah and *Yiddishkeit.* However, when parents educate children in other ways, the results are clear to see that the *chinuch* is destructive, and we need say no more about this saddening and alarming matter.

This point should be explained to parents until they recognize the great need for *chinuch* in the spirit of Torah and *Yiddishkeit.*

The *mitzvah* of *chinuch* is compared to the *mitzvah* of *tefillin*

All[644] of *Bnei Yisrael* were at *Matan Torah,* even newborn infants; therefore the *mitzvah* of *ve'ahavta... be'chol me'odecha* ("You shall love Hashem ... with all your might")[645] applies to children as well. My father-in-law, the Rebbe, taught, [646] "Just as putting on *tefillin* every day is a *mitzvah de'Oraysa* (from the Torah), so is one obligated to think every day for a half-hour about the *chinuch* of one's children."

How is *tefillin* connected to *chinuch*? By putting on *tefillin,* one subjugates one's intellect and emotions to Hashem. [647] This is what *be'chol me'odecha* means. One should give one's children *chinuch* in a manner of *be'chol me'odecha,* so that they too will serve Hashem in a way of *be'chol me'odecha.*

Parents' involvement with school

It[648] is clear and obvious (and a great wonder that I need to be asked about this):

643 *Hisvaaduyos* 5744, vol. 1, p. 504.

644 *Sichos Kodesh* 5740, vol. 3, p. 217.

645 *Devarim,* 6:4.

646 *Hayom Yom,* 22 *Teves.* Cf. *Igros Kodesh Admor HaRayatz*, vol. 13, p. 47.

647 *Shulchan Aruch, Orach Chaim,* 25:5. *Shulchan Aruch Admor HaZaken, Orach Chaim,* 25:11.

648 *Heichal Menachem,* vol. 1, pp. 126-127.

1. Parents must *take an interest* in the way their children are educated. When something is not clear, they can ask questions and make suggestions.
2. This does not *at all* mean that every father and mother of the student is the administration of the school or are above the administration.
3. For the benefit of the student, the institution, and so on, all this should be undertaken without tumult, disputes, and so on, especially when those involved are affiliated with Chabad, and especially since this is an explicit command: אוהב שלום ("love peace").
4. When one has a difference of opinion with the administration and so on, the *Shulchan Aruch* rules explicitly: "[Conduct yourselves] according to the *beis din* of the community."
5. For parents to involve the student in all this is to act in direct opposition to the goal of providing a proper *chinuch*, in direct opposition to the welfare of the student, and in direct opposition to the *Shulchan Aruch*, and so on.

Parents should consult with the administration

It[649] is difficult for parents to be objective regarding their children. Therefore, you should consult with the administration of the school in which your son learns.

Parents are often not reliable in assessing their children

I[650] am responding to your letter... in which you write about the *chinuch* of your son... and explanations regarding the matter.

Since a decision about this is based on a variety of factors, and especially on the characteristics of the child, it would be proper to consult with those who know your son and these factors. Very often in such situations, the parents are particularly not reliable in assessing their own children. The concern is not only that they can predisposed to the right, but also at times, because of their

649 *Igeres Hachinuch*, p. 235, from a handwritten response.
650 *Igros Kodesh*, vol. 20, p. 284.

closeness, the opposite as well [excessive strictness], in accordance with [the saying], "A person does not consider himself to be a [*rasha*, but a] *tzaddik* out of his closeness to himself".

The responsibility for the chinuch of children is the parents'

To[651] our deep sorrow, there are parents who take care of all the physical needs of their child – food, beverages, clothing, toys, and the like. However, when it comes to the most important thing – shaping the child's character so that he becomes an *adam* as befits that title, who behaves in an honest manner – to this they pay little attention. They are preoccupied with *parnassah* and the like, and they rely on the school to instill such values and behaviors.

About this, the Torah, *Toras Emes* ("the Torah of Truth")[652] and *Toras Chayim* ("the Torah of life")[653] emphasizes that the main responsibility of *chinuch* lies on the *parents'* shoulders. The school acts merely as the emissary of the parents. Even when parents send their children to school, the responsibility remains on the shoulders of the parents.

While school is necessary, it is not sufficient. ... The parents need to give the child everything that is in their ability to give.

Tzedakah to *chinuch* institutions

It[654] is worthwhile to give *tzedakah* – at least a portion [of the *tzedakah* one gives] – to a *chinuch* institution in one's own city.

Parents Want the Best for Their Children

Parents have *mesirus nefesh* for children

One[655] of the most important things in the life of a person is his relationship with his children. It may even be said that a person's true character is evident in

---

651 *Hisvaaduyos* 5744, vol. 3, p. 1434.

652 Blessings on the Torah.

653 See the *Amidah* liturgy, s.v. *Sim shalom*.

654 *Hisvaaduyos* 5747, vol. 2, p. 651.

655 *Hisvaaduyos* 5744, vol. 1, p. 105.

his relationship with his children. Even in situations in which a person would suffice with the minimum if it were only for his own sake, when it comes to his children, his attitude is different. If he is befitting of the title *adam*, he wants only the best for his children and spares no efforts – to the point of self-sacrifice – to provide for his children, and not just the basic necessities, in both material and spiritual matters.

From the *chinuch* one gives his children, it is apparent where he himself stands

At[656] the time of *Matan Torah, Bnei Yisrael* said, "Our children will be our guarantors."[657] Hashem accepted this, for they said to Him, "Look at the *chinuch* that we give our children, and You will see that You can rely on us to give us the Torah."

The explanation: One can discern a person's level from the way he treats his children. It is human nature that whatever one is lacking, he desires to correct in his children.

Every person has a goal in life, but אין אדם מת וחצי תאותו בידו ("A person does not pass away having fulfilled half of his desires"),[658] so he does not succeed in reaching the goal he set for himself. Thus, he places some of the blame on himself. Then (although only to a minor extent), he rationalizes that *Hakadosh Baruch Hu* is at fault. In addition, certain people got in his way. Still, he does not deny the truth that he himself is at fault in this; he simply rationalizes that he bears only very limited responsibility for it. Therefore, when it comes to the *chinuch* of his children, he wants to correct what he was lacking so that it will not be lacking in his son's life.

For these reasons, when we want to know where a person stands, one cannot determine such a thing from observing his personal life, because he has a *yetzer hara* and he may not have managed to control it so well. However, when it comes to *chinuch,* a person spares no money (if we are speaking of parents worthy of their title and role). Furthermore, regarding his child's *chinuch*, it

---

656 *Sichos Kodesh* 5729, vol. 2, p. 158.

657 *Shir HaShirim Rabbah,* 1:4.

658 *Koheles Rabbah,* 1:13.

is not possible to say that his *yetzer hara* is an obstacle, because every person is able to rule over himself and overcome his lusts in order to avoid harming his child, since a person is more worried about harm coming to his child than about harm that might come to himself.

Parents want their children to outdo them

We[659] see that it is the nature of a person to do everything in his power for his child to be a true *lamdan* – and not only as much as his father, but even more than his father. Likewise with a daughter: the mother wants her daughter to excel in matters of *Yiddishkeit* and light, and even outdo the mother.

When a child is given a true Torah *chinuch*, the life of the parents can be considered "life"

Why[660] is the order [of blessings] in the *Gemara* בני חיי מזוני ("children, health, and livelihood")? One would think that the order should in the reverse, because first Hashem gives life, then sustenance, and then, only after marriage, does Hashem give children.

However, when we meditate upon this, we see tangibly how if parents are proper parents, and they behave properly, feeling proper human emotions, then only when children are רויחי ("abundant," meaning that the children are raised on the right path) can abundance in "life" and abundance in "sustenance" be of true value.

We see this in the words of Avraham, "the first Jew," before he had a son. He had heard all of *Hakadosh Baruch Hu*'s *brachos*, and he had said of himself, אנכי עפר ואפר ("I am but dust and ashes"),[661] implying that he was a servant of Hashem who would not have spoken to Him in a way that emphasized his own selfish existence.

---

659 *Hisvaaduyos* 5749, vol. 3, p. 211.

660 *Shaarei Chinuch,* p. 104.

661 *Bereishis,* 18:27.

Yet when it came to having children, Avraham said to Hashem: "What can You give me seeing that I am to go childless?" Of what value are all other blessings if "to me You have given no offspring, and my steward inherits me"?[662] In other words, of what benefit is "life" and "sustenance" and all the blessings – one needs children!

Chinuch requires toil and great efforts

In[663] order for children and students (also called בנים[664]) to turn out the way they should requires great efforts. Even if a person has children so well-disciplined that he can say just one word and it suffices, he should not think he has fulfilled his obligation. The fact that he has attentive children and influence over his students is a blessing that he was given from Above. It is not a result of his own efforts, and in addition to this he must invest his own effort. His efforts should be in the category of עמל (toil), toil to the extent that Torah considers it toil.

Mesirus nefesh for every Jewish child

On[665] the *pasuk* ויגש אליו יהודה ("And Yehuda approached him"),[666] the Sages say[667] that in Yehuda's approaching Yosef, Yehuda was prepared for anything, even to wage war.

Why did Yehuda endanger himself to such an extent for Binyamin? The text continues, כי עבדך ערב את הנער ("For your servant is responsible for the child") – this is why he was prepared to wage war. Even though all his other brothers were alive and well, he had *mesirus nefesh* for one Jewish child, because he had taken this responsibility upon himself.

This holds a lesson for every single parent: Hashem has charged him with the responsibility to care for every single one of his children, to the point of

662 *Bereishis*, 15:3.

663 *Toras Menachem*, vol. 16, pp. 205-206.

664 *Sifri* on *Shemos*, 6:7.

665 *Likkutei Sichos*, vol. 1, pp. 94-95.

666 *Bereishis*, 44:18.

667 *Bereishis Rabbah*, 93:6.

mesirus nefesh – even for one child, so that nothing will happen to him that shouldn't happen to a *Yiddishe* child.

By having *mesirus nefesh* for *chinuch* so that our sons and daughters receive a pure and holy upbringing, we attain what is written at the end of *Parshas Vayigash,* ויפרו (ויתר על כן:) וירבו (עד) מאד ("They were fruitful and (even more so) they multiplied greatly").[668]

Mesirus nefesh **for grown children**

When[669] Avraham sent his servant Eliezer to bring Rivkah to Yitzchak, *Rashi* tells us, שטר מתנה כתב ליצחק על כל אשר לו, כדי שיקפצו לשלוח לו בתם ("He wrote a gift deed to Yitzchak for everything he owned, so that they would hasten [lit., jump] to send him their daughter").[670]

This teaches us the extent of the devotion a parent should have to the *chinuch* of their child. Yitzchak was a grown man at the time, over thirty-seven years of age. He was able to "stand on his own two feet," was established in his path, and had even passed the *nisayon* of the *Akeidah,* as it is written, וילכו שניהם יחדיו ("The two went forth together"), [which is explained to mean] בלב שוה ("with one accord" [lit. with an equal heart]).[671] For just as Avraham passed the *nisayon* (test) successfully, so did Yitzchak, and to such an extent that he became an עולה תמימה ("a perfect burnt offering").[672]

Yet although Avraham was successful in his *chinuch* of Yitzchak, and Yitzchak was already close to the age of forty and well-established, Avraham continued to care for him and direct his path. He did so to the point of *mesirus nefesh:* He actually gave all his belongings to Yitzchak so he could succeed in finding a suitable *shidduch* – without leaving a thing for himself!

---

668 *Bereishis,* 47:27.

669 *Sichos Kodesh* 5730, vol. 1, pp. 209-210.

670 *Bereishis,* 24:10, *Rashi. Bereishis Rabbah,* 16:59.

671 *Bereishis,* 22:8, *Rashi.*

672 Ibid. 26:2, *Rashi.*

Lesson from Chana: There must be an everlasting bond between parent and child[673]

When Chana brought her son, Shmuel, to *Mishkan Shiloh,* we learn from the text[674] that she said: אל הנער הזה התפללתי ויתן ה׳ לי את שאלתי אשר שאלתי מעמו, וגם אנכי השאלתיהו לה׳ (רד״ק: החזרתי לו השאלה שהוא נתן לי) כל הימים אשר הי׳ הוא שאול לה׳ ("For this child I prayed, and Hashem granted me the request that I asked of Him. And I have also lent him to Hashem; all the days of his life, he is 'borrowed' by Hashem").

In this matter of אנכי השאלתיהו לה׳ ("I have also lent him to Hashem"), there are two interpretations. The first interpretation[675] is כאדם המשאיל כלי לרבו(like a person who lends a vessel to his teacher), from the word שאלה (a loan).

The lesson from this interpretation is that… Chana only lent Shmuel to Hashem, but her connection to him remained – he still belonged to her. This teaches a lesson about the everlasting bond that must exist between a mother and her son, between parents and their children.

673 *Hisvaaduyos* 5744, vol. 1, p. 158.

674 *I Shmuel,* 1:27-28.

675 Cf. *Rashi.*

CHAPTER 11

The Role of the Mother

"The women's wisdom builds her home"

Mishlei, 14:1

The advantage of *chinuch* given by a woman

With[676] regard to children, Jewish women have a special mission and privilege.

Women are called the "*akeres habayis*" because they are the עיקר הבית ("the primary part of the home"). It is clearly apparent that the main *chinuch* of the טף – i.e., not only little children, but even of the littlest infants – is not through the father, a *melamed*, a *rosh yeshivah,* or the *rav* of the city – but the mother. Specifically, the *chinuch* of the littlest children is almost entirely in the hands of the wife.

The *chinuch* given by mothers has a special advantage, for it is based on love and affection toward the children. The *derech* of the father, on the other hand, is one of *yirah* and *kavod,* awe and respect. Therefore it is said of women, חכמת נשים בנתה ביתה ("The wisdom of a woman builds her home"),[677] because her *chinuch*, her building of the home, is done wisely, through love and affection.

This approach to *chinuch* by women is the path that has been learned from the matriarchs of the Jewish nation, Sarah, Rivkah, Rochel, and Leah.

Compassion, humility, and *gemilus chassadim*

I[678] would like to emphasize in this letter the special merit (and responsibility) of *n'shei Yisrael* in general, and *n'shei u'bnos Chabad* in particular. … As we see, the younger years [of a child's life] in particular depend mainly or entirely on the wife.

Jewish women exemplify, in a much stronger measure than do men, the three attributes in which the Jewish people excel: compassion, humility, and *gemilus chassadim* (kindness).

The attributes of compassion and *gemilus chassadim* are of the utmost importance in the *chinuch* of children.

May *Hashem Yisborach* help them to do the above with the proper health and good-heartedness, permeated with *chassidishe* light and warmth, and may He bless them with success.

---

676 *Hisvaaduyos* 5748, vol. 4, p. 341.

677 *Mishlei,* 14:1.

678 *Igros Kodesh*, vol. 20, pp. 141-142.

Woman's focus and passion direct the home

The[679] woman is called the *akeres habayis* because she is the *"ikar"* (primary part) of the home. The *ratzon* and conduct of her husband and children depend upon her *ratzon* [what excites her, what her focus is]. From this we learn two things: First, just how great is the responsibility that *Hakadosh Baruch Hu* placed upon the wife; and second, since *Hakadosh Baruch Hu* placed this kind of responsibility on the Jewish woman, he certainly endowed her with the abilities to fulfill her *shlichus* in the best manner possible.

Woman have special traits necessary for *chinuch*

...The[680] area of *chinuch* is particularly relevant for *n'shei Yisrael*, for they were endowed with the special traits necessary for *chinuch*.

As we see from experience, during the child's first years, the *chinuch* depends entirely upon the mother. Only later does the father participate as well, and even then, the mother's role is extremely important.

Although[681] the mother is not commanded regarding the *mitzvah* of *chinuch* as the father is, the fact remains that, practically speaking, the majority of *chinuch* is given by the mother, the *akeres habayis*.[682]

In fact, there is an advantage in the *chinuch* and rebuke of women. Women, by nature, relate in a gentle way, with a feeling of closeness, love, and affection, more so than do men. Experience shows, and this is especially the case in recent generations, that it is the approach of closeness and love in particular that leads to a more successful *chinuch*.

679 *Igros Kodesh*, vol. 4, p. 11.

680 *Hisvaaduyos* 5746, vol. 3, p. 617.

681 *Hisvaaduyos* 5750, vol. 3, p. 171.

682 Cf. *Shaloh, Shaar Ha'osiyos* 44a, cited in *Chanoch La'naar* p. 34 ff.

Hashem entrusted *chinuch* to the Jewish woman

All[683] that is holy in the nation of the G-d of Avraham and fundamental for the house of *Yisrael* in raising and educating an upright generation, regarding *kashrus* of food and the lofty purity of the holiness of *Shabbos*, was entrusted and endowed by the revered and awesome G-d to Jewish women to guard and to cultivate.

To the woman who fulfills her obligation and calling in the area of family life, directing her household and the *chinuch* [of her children] according to the Torah, the verse can be applied: חכמת נשים בנתה ביתה ("The wisdom of a woman builds her home").[684]

The fetus develops inside the mother

[In[685] answer to the question as to why Jewishness is matrilineal.] A fetus is built entirely from a minute drop of semen into a sophisticated body – and the structure of the body also influences the characteristics of the *nefesh* to an important degree – all by the mother. During the time that it is a fetus, it eats what its mother eats, and so forth.[686] [The mother has a significant impact on the baby] to the point that it is perceptible that the spirituality of the mother (and if she is happy, fearful, and the like) influences and molds the personality of the fetus, and whether it will be born complete and healthy.

The lesson from the law that Jewish identity is matrilineal

Jewish[687] identity is determined by the mother. If the mother is Jewish, the child is Jewish. It doesn't matter where the father stands [spiritually], or what he wants. ...

From this we can understand the great merit and responsibility placed upon the mother in regard to *chinuch*. To bring up a child to be a Jew depends upon the mother.

---

683 *Hayom Yom*, 26 *Adar* II.

684 *Mishlei*, 14:1.

685 *Likkutei Sichos*, vol. 14, p. 205.

686 *Niddah*, 30b.

687 *Sichos Kodesh* 5729, vol. 2, p. 113.

The *Yiddishkeit* of the next generation is in the Jewish woman's hands

The[688] extent to which our Sages exalted the glory of Jewish women and girls is known. The Sages emphasized women's extreme importance in the life of our nation, to the point that they even stated that when *Hakadosh Baruch Hu* came to give His nation the Torah of life, which provides instruction in daily life, He turned to the women first; as our Sages teach, כה תאמר לבית יעקב - אלו הנשים, ותגיד לבני ישראל - אלו האנשים ("This you shall say to *Beis Yaakov* – this refers to the women, and tell the *Bnei Yisrael* – this refers to the men").[689]

If this was true in all times and periods [throughout Jewish history], how much more so does it apply in our times, when the environment and the "street" are not as they were in the past – saturated with *Yiddishkeit* and a life of Torah – but on the contrary, and sometimes society even fights against it. The entire *chinuch* of the sons and daughters of *Yisrael* in the spirit of Torah and *mitzvos* takes place in *chinuch* institutions that are run *al taharas hakodesh,* and inside the home. We can tangibly observe that for various reasons – living conditions, the husband's preoccupation with *parnassah*, and so on – the *chinuch* in the home depends mainly on the *akeres habayis,* the *eim habanim* (the mainstay of the home, the mother).

Nurturing a love for *Yiddishkeit* from the youngest age

Concerning[690] the education of Jewish children – the primary component which sets up the foundation for life – we see that their education is contingent upon the efforts of the child's mother, especially with regard to young children. In fact, the younger the child is, the more its education is dependent on the mother.

For it is the Jewish mother in particular who implants within her child – from the very youngest age onward – the vitality and spirit of *Yiddishkeit.* It is on this foundation that her sons and daughters grow up to be engaged in the study of Torah and the fulfillment of its *mitzvos* in a wholesome, beautiful manner in all respects, both spiritually and physically.

---

688 *Igros Kodesh*, vol. 23, p. 184.

689 *Rashi* on *Shemos* 19:3, from *Mechilta*.

690 *Sefer Hasichos* 5752 vol. 2, p. 357, The Rebbe's Holy Care, Issue 3.

This means that in addition to succeeding in teaching her children the regular observance of Torah and *mitzvos*, the Jewish mother imparts to her children a unique enjoyment and warmth toward Torah and *mitzvos* through her innate refined and loving nature, characteristic of Jewish women, so that her child's involvement with Torah and *mitzvos* should be in a good and pleasant manner to the degree that one can point to her children and say, "This is my G-d and I will beautify him.[691]"

This is exhibited, for example, by the good custom of Jewish mothers to sing to their very young children, even while they still lie in the cradle, that Torah is the best thing, the sweetest thing, the most beautiful thing, and so on.

This, in turn, inculcates in the child, - even when the child grows old (*lo yasur mimenah*), "he will not deviate from it,"- a deep love and cherishing of Torah and *mitzvos*.

The mother reveals Hashem in the home

The[692] woman is the *akeres habayis.* She is the one responsible for the home to be illuminated with an internal Jewish light and warmth, so that the Jewish home is protected from winds foreign to *Yiddishkeit* that blow in the outside world and endanger the *Yiddishkeit.*

For this purpose, the Jewish woman has been endowed with a greater measure of emotion and warmth. For this reason, she is fit to arouse and reveal the inborn and inner emotions of *ahavas Hashem, ahavas haTorah,* and *ahavas Yisrael.*

She reveals the *pnimiyus* (that which is hidden beneath the surface), until the point where the *pnimiyus* rules over the external in day-to-day life. This brings with it the reward, "measure for measure,"[693] that Hashem's *hashgacha* (Divine Providence), which is the essence of goodness, but is also *pnimiyus* and concealed, becomes revealed goodness that is manifest and visible in all one's day-to-day needs: health, *parnassah,* and *nachas* from one's children.

---

691 *Shemos,* 15:2.

692 *Igros Kodesh*, vol. 20, p. 226.

693 *Sanhedrin,* 90a.

Making the home a *chassidishe* home

It[694] is truly in the hands of the *akeres habayis,* and within her capacity, to make her home into a *chassidishe* home, to the point where the child can actually sense it.

The purpose of a woman's *kinus*

It[695] is apparent that the main *chinuch* of small children is not so much in the hands of the father, the big brother, or the school teacher, but rather, in the mother's hands. Similarly, it is in the hands of the big sister, who is preparing for her primary role in the *chinuch* of children, when she will merit to be an *akeres habayis* in her own home.

This is the goal and purpose of this *kinus* (gathering): that a woman should encourage and strengthen her friend in all matters of *Yiddishkeit,* and especially in the role of women in the *chinuch* of sons and daughters.

...this applies to every *kinus* of *N'shei U'bnos Yisrael,* at every time ...

Mother instills in children a passion for Torah study

Just[696] as women are not obligated in the *mitzvah* of Torah study, so are women not commanded to teach Torah to their children.[697] However, when a woman helps her sons or husband to be involved in Torah, she shares in their reward.[698] ...

By a mother's taking an interest in the learning of her sons, asking them to review their learning with her when they return from *cheder, Talmud Torah,* or *yeshiva,* then – in addition to the advantage that they are reviewing their learning – there is a particular advantage in their learning with their mother.

---

694 *Hisvaaduyos* 5719, p. 276.

695 *Hisvaaduyos* 5745, vol. 5, p. 2997.

696 *Hisvaaduyos* 5750, vol. 3, pp. 171-172.

697 *Mishneh Torah, Hilchos Talmud Torah* 1:1. *Hilchos Talmud Torah l'Admur HaZaken,* 1:14.

698 *Sotah,* 21a.

The mother has a special warmth and passion in her learning (compared to the father, whose learning with his children is more to test them, as is the custom that fathers test their sons on *Shabbos* and so forth). In this way, the mother increases the *chayus* (liveliness) and passion in the learning of her children, as we can see from experience.

Encouraging her husband, brothers, and children to learn

As[699] we have discussed at length in the past, one of the roles of *n'shei u'bnos Chabad* is to encourage and strengthen their husbands, brothers, and children to study Torah. [Torah study] is an obligation for every single man, young and old, rich and poor, and the like. The learning should take place every day in the greatest measure possible and, as with all matters of *Yiddishkeit,* with *simchah* and passion.

The special connection between women and ensuring that Torah study occurs is:

1) Very often, the reason for the lack of Torah study in the proper measure is the husband's worries about *parnassah* matters, and how he will support the home, family, and all their needs. Often, this is nothing but a false perception that this work is necessary.

Therefore, it is especially necessary and important for the woman, the *akeres habayis,* to encourage her husband and even demand from him to study Torah day after day, and to study as much as possible, even if this means certain material sacrifices in the way her home and family is run. [Ultimately,] the learning is the sure way to bring wealth to the entire family.

2) Even if the wife's encouragement and demands of the husband to continue learning properly are expressed in words only from time to time, her daily presence is a constant reminder to her husband.

3) By encouraging and demanding that her husband study Torah – and by sending the children to kosher *chadorim* and *yeshivos* – a woman has a portion in their Torah study, i.e., in their *mitzvah* of Torah study.

---

699 *Igros Kodesh*, vol. 20, pp. 330-332.

Therefore, they also share in the reward for this *mitzvah,*[700] which is greater than the reward for other *mitzvos.*

This is in addition to the women's learning the *halachos* needed for their everyday lives, as is explained in the *halachos* of Talmud Torah (end of the first chapter).

My request is that during these days women should start a special movement and initiative to encourage their husbands, brothers, and children to strengthen and increase in their daily study of both the revealed parts of Torah and of *Toras haChassidus,* and to do so with passion and *simchah.*

The mother provides the spiritual sustenance

Our[701] Sages relate[702] that Abba Chilkiya and his wife [Shelmrus] both gave *tzedakah.* When there was a lack of rain, they both *davened* for rain, but her prayers were accepted before her husband's. Our Sages explain that Abba Chilkiya's *tzedakah* was in the form of money, and then with that *tzedakah* money, the poor needed to buy the food to satiate their hunger, while his wife would give the actual food to the poor.

In another source, our Sages say, עושה צדקה בכל עת זה הזן בניו ובנותיו כשהם קטנים ("'One who performs charity at all times':[703] This refers to one who supports his sons and daughters in their infancy").[704] This means that the concept of *tzedakah* applies not only to strangers, but also to one's own children. This refers not only to material *tzedakah*, for spiritual *tzedakah*, which includes the *chinuch* of one's children, is also considered *tzedakah.*

Just as regarding material *tzedakah,* the husband gives the poor person the means of obtaining food, while the wife gives the food itself, so too is it regarding spiritual *tzedakah,* the *chinuch* of children. The husband, the father, gives the children the means to obtain a *chinuch*, while the mother gives the spiritual food itself.

---

700 *Sotah,* 21a.

701 *Likkutei Sichos*, vol. 2, p. 580 ff.

702 *Taanis,* 23b.

703 *Tehillim,* 106:3.

704 *Kesubos,* 50a.

For although the father has a *mitzvah* of ושננתם לבניך ("And you shall teach them to your children"),[705] in most cases it is not the father himself who teaches his children; rather, he hires a teacher for them.

It is told[706] that one day the Alter Rebbe called one of his *chassidim* and said to him, "I have the obligation of ושננתם לבניך, ("And you shall teach them to your children"), and you have the *mitzvah* to provide *parnassah* for your household members. Let's trade: I will provide the *parnassah* for your household members, and you teach my son *Berel* (The Miteler Rebbe)."

Hence, the father does not give the spiritual sustenance itself; the teacher does this through the money that the father gives to him.

It is not so with the mother: The mother gives her children the spiritual sustenance itself. She teaches the child to wear a *tallis katan*, to wash *negel vasser*, to recite *brachos,* and so on. Afterwards as well, when the child grows and learns in *Talmud Torah* or *yeshivah*, he can, during the time he is home, lose or fail to retain what he receives from these institutions. The mother must then be careful to direct him toward proper conduct.

Mothers should study *Chassidus*

Our[707] generation has merited that the study of *Chassidus* is spreading among Jewish women and girls, beginning with the study of the *Tanya* and the like.

Not only do they study basic topics, but even particulars, and they reach a thorough understanding. Study of *Chassidus* on this level is attainable to women, for "more understanding was granted to a woman than to a man."[708] We see this from experience in the present generation, and surely they will continue in an even greater measure, and steadily increase in both quality and quantity. …

It is necessary [for the mother] to be knowledgeable and grasp not only simple matters of *Yiddishkeit,* the *"alef beis"* of *Yiddishkeit*, and of course the basics, but also to be knowledgeable in Torah in general, and especially in *pnimiyus haTorah* (*Chassidus*), in accordance with "Know the G-d of your

705 *Devarim,* 11:19.

706 *Hayom Yom* 8 Adar I.

707 *Hisvaaduyos* 5746, vol. 3, p. 521.

708 *Niddah,* 45b.

father, and serve Him with a complete heart."[709] This will bring one's success in *chinuch* of children to be broader and deeper. ...

It is clearly apparent, especially in this generation, that when an educator is knowledgeable in matters of *Chassidus*, knowledge of Hashem, love and fear of Him, and the like, along with the knowledge of *seder hishtalshelus* (the chain of spiritual worlds), *taamei hamitzvos* (the reasons for the *mitzvos),* and so forth, his work in *chinuch* is not only more comprehensive and deep, but this also elevates his prestige in the eyes of the student. His influence is therefore incomparably more successful.

Mother permeates home with G-dliness

The[710] husband's role is to give general guidance, in the form of a concise point, by declaring that the running of the home, the *chinuch* of the children, and the conduct of every household member should be as is fitting according to *Shulchan Aruch*.

The wife's role is to then bring this down into the details. She implements this in all the particulars of the running of the home, in all the particulars of the children's *chinuch,* and in all the particulars of the conduct of the household members. Within even the minutest detail of daily life, the family members should experience the matter of שמע ישראל ה' אלוקינו ה' אחד[711] that the husband recited in the morning. This is dependent upon the *akeres habayis;* she is the one who permeates day-to-day life with this notion and brings it into practice in all the particulars of the conduct of the home. ...

We see this principle clearly ... in the first Jew, Avraham *Avinu*. When it came to *chinuch,* Avraham *Avinu* issued the general instruction [to his family]: אשר יצוה את בניו ואת ביתו אחריו ושמרו דרך ה' לעשות צדקה ומשפט ("He commanded his sons and his household after him, so that they would keep the way of Hashem, performing righteousness and justice").[712] However, the particulars of *chinuch* – such as how to educate Yitzchak and which friends to protect him

709 *I Divrei Hayamim,* 25:9.

710 *Toras Menachem,* vol. 31, p. 138.

711 *Devarim,* 6:4.

712 *Bereishis,* 18:19.

from – were all attended to by Sarah. Due to her role, Avraham was told, כל אשר תאמר אליך שרה שמע בקולה ("Whatever Sarah tells you, hearken to her voice").[713]

The pictures on the walls, all that enters the home affects *chinuch*

The[714] way the home is run, which pictures hang on the walls, and all the particulars of the home, play a very important role in the *chinuch* of a baby. This influence is no less vital than the *chinuch* a child receives by being taught Torah and the like. The decorations and furnishings of the home – and how much more so, the things that enter the home, such as food and beverages – are entirely the privilege and the responsibility of the woman, the *akeres habayis.*

The *kashrus* of the food affects *chinuch*

[One[715] of the ways in which the Jewish woman establishes the next generation of *Yidden* is through care in providing kosher food. She nourishes her family members] through serving kosher foods and drinks whose characteristics, when absorbed, affect the nature of the body. This is in accordance with the *Ramban's* explanation[716] that one of the reasons for the prohibition of eating the flesh of cruel animals is that doing so imbues a cruel nature within the person eating it. When the food and drink are kosher, the person's flesh, bones, and blood are "kosher," and this influences the way that one fulfills *mitzvos.*

The health of the children's bodies and *neshamos*

...Just[717] as a mother cares for the health of the bodies of her children, so too, she must care for the health of the *neshamos* of her children. I hope that you utilize the influence that you have over your sons and daughters...

---

713 Ibid. 21:12.

714 *Sichos Kodesh* 5733, vol. 2, p. 264.

715 *Hisvaaduyos* 5744, vol. 1, p. 130.

716 On *Vayikra,* 11:13.

717 *Igros Kodesh*, vol. 4, p. 434.

There are mothers who think that their children will not listen to them, and so they do not speak with them about *Yiddishkeit*; others are embarrassed to speak. Both of these attitudes are false. There is no room for embarrassment when a matter affects the health of children's *neshamos*. I am sure that when children are spoken with once, and then again, and it is explained to them in suitable words that the only way for *Yidden* to have true happiness and to merit a home which embodies true happiness is through the path of *Yiddishkeit*, Torah, and *mitzvos*, eventually they will be affected.

Making her home into a *Mishkan*

...Being[718] an *akeres habayis*, the woman's main involvement is with matters of the home. The wisest person *[Shlomo HaMelech])* has described the ways and conduct of the *Eishes Chayil*,[719] which applies to each one of the daughters of Sarah, Rivkah, Rochel, and Leah, and this is recited at the beginning of the *Shabbos*, and in the home.

Even while she is involved with other matters – טרף לביתה, ("food for her household"), דרשה צמר ופשתים גו' הייתה כאוניות סוחר גו' סדין עשתה ותמכור וחגור נתנה לכנעני ("she seeks wool and flax ... [she is] like the merchant ships ... she makes linen garments and sells them and delivers girdles unto the merchant") – i.e., sometimes she needs to do business with non-Jews); and regarding her activities of *tzedakah* and *chessed*, כפה פרשה לעני וידי' שלחה לאביון ("she holds out her hand to the poor and extends her hand to the destitute") – her main concern is always צופי' הליכות ביתה ("watching the conduct of her household").

The poet [King David] says, "All of the King's daughter's glory is internal":[720] the true glory of a *Bas Melech* (princess) – which refers to each one of *n'shei u'bnos Yisrael* – is *pnimah* (internal), by her making of her inner heart, and the inside of her home, into a *Mishkan* (Sanctuary) and *Mikdash* (Temple) for *Hashem Yisborach*.

It is clearly and openly recognizable that the home is run by an *akeres habayis* whose inner heart is a *Mishkan* and *Mikdash* for Hashem, and her actual

718 *Hisvaaduyos* 5747, vol. 3, pp. 344-345.

719 *Mishlei*, 31:10-31.

720 *Tehillim*, 45:14.

conduct conforms to the instructions of the Torah. This matter is expressed in the conduct of the entire household: the husband, the sons, and the daughters. Their conduct in thought, speech, and action is permeated with creating a *Mishkan* and a *Mikdash* for *Hashem Yisborach.* Even the objects and vessels in the home, the vessels for eating and the like, are permeated with *kedusha* and G-dliness, as befits a home that is made into a *Mishkan* and *Mikdash* for *Hashem Yisborach.* [Of such a home Hashem says,] "I will dwell within them."

Cleansing in the *kiyor* before entering the home

In[721] our times, the Jewish home should be established and built in such a way that *Hakadosh Baruch Hu* can dwell within it. [This applies] not only on *Shabbos* and *Yom Tov,* but also on every day and night throughout the entire year.

Therefore, in a Jewish home—which is a *Mishkan* for *Hakadosh Baruch Hu*—there are all sorts of roles and jobs that need to be performed. However, before approaching any kind of *avodah*, if one desires to do it according to the will of Hashem, there should be a "cleansing" with the *kiyor* (sink) and its basin. In other words, it is necessary to remove the dust, mud, and all the unclean, impure things that can adhere to a person from the street, so that they remain outside and do not enter the home.

With regard to making the *kiyor* and its basin, *Hakadosh Baruch Hu* relates in His Torah[722] that the *kiyor* was made from the mirrors that *n'shei Yisrael* donated for the building of the *Mishkan.*

...Every Jewish woman is an *akeres habayis*, and the conduct of the Jewish home depends on her. She should ensure (and this applies to her as well as to her husband and children) that when they enter from the street, where winds blow – sometimes positive winds, and sometimes winds that can bring into the home matters that are not blessed for a *Yid* – the *kiyor* and its basin should first be used for cleansing before entering the home. This is a matter that is truly of great value.

---

721 *Toras Menachem,* vol. 36, p. 367.

722 *Rashi* on *Shemos* 38:8.

Bringing the *geulah*

It[723] would be fitting to reflect upon the fact that that the birth, salvation, and *chinuch* of the redeemer of *Yisrael* came from the devotion of two Jewish women: a mother and daughter – Moshe's mother, Yocheved, and sister, Miriam. This was at a time when the decrees of *Par'oh*'s enslavement reached the peak of their difficulty, to the point that even the strongest in the generation became dispirited. Yet these two women, mother and daughter, were not discouraged. "The Jewish wet-nurses" continued their work with true *mesirus nefesh* to *give life* to the children. In the depths of *galus*, they established the generation of *geulah*. With their dedication and courage, they saved not only the women, but the men as well, until they merited that through them, the redeemer of *Yisrael* came to take the Jewish people from slavery to freedom.

So too, is it in the final generations of this bitter exile, and in our generation in particular. The same role, responsibility, and merit that was the portion of the women of the first *galus* were bequeathed to the women of this last *galus*, as my father-in-law, the Rebbe, frequently emphasized in writing and in his oral discourses.

Mesirus nefesh for her children

What[724] characterized Chana was her *mesirus nefesh* for her children. First, nothing else satisfied her, and she did everything in her power to give birth to a Jewish child! She then devoted herself to the *chinuch* of the child and sacrificed going to *Mishkan Shiloh* in order to educate and raise her son properly.

Here there exist two opposite concepts: By *not* going to *Mishkan Shiloh*, Chana brought her son to reach such a high level that וישב שם עד עולם ("he would abide there [in Shiloh] forever").[725]

...The *shlichus* that has been placed on her is to establish the next generation of Jews, sons and daughters, until their presence is in a manner of ומלאו את הארץ ("They will fill the land").[726]

---

723 *Igros Kodesh*, vol. 22, p. 424.

724 *Hisvaaduyos* 5744, vol. 1, pp. 129-130.

725 *I Shmuel*, 1:24.

726 *Bereishis*, 1:28.

This is accomplished by first building a *kosher* home, a *pure* home (through Family Purity), and an *illuminated* home – with *Shabbos* candles, the candles of *Rosh HaShanah, Yom Kippur, Shemini Atzeres, Simchas Torah,* and so on.

Akeres habayis ensures that stability of home is not shaken

When[727] it seems that there is an inadequacy in the [family's] physical needs, and even if this is in fact the reality *chas ve'shalom*, it is the role of the *akeres habayis* to ensure that this does not affect the stability of the home. The atmosphere should always be permeated with the light of Torah and *mitzvos,* and *bitachon*, *simchah,* and contentment. This [atmosphere] impacts every individual household member as well as the unit as a whole. [As a result,] the husband and children will be healthy and will gain encouragement and strength in their affairs outside the home: for the husband, in matters of *parnassah;* and for the children, in their *chinuch* institutions.

Since the merit and responsibility for this is great, the *akeres habayis* is surely given the strength necessary to fulfill it in the fullest measure. This also applies to *bnos Yisrael* as they prepare to fill their role as *akeres habayis.*

A mother's emotional state

The[728] success of children's *chinuch* is connected to their emotional state. [Therefore, it is important] that [even when the parent faces difficulties,] they see their mother going about her affairs with contentment and inner peace, and that she encourages them so that they too can live in contentment and happiness.

The atmosphere of the home

Since[729] each and every [Jewish woman] is an *akeres habayis*, the entire atmosphere of the home depends upon her.

---

[727] *Likkutei Sichos,* vol. 17, p. 523.

[728] *Likkutei Sichos,* vol. 35, p. 269.

[729] *Hisvaaduyos 5748,* vol. 3, p. 366.

Interferences to her role as a mother

It[730] is known that among the main obligations of a woman and mother – and this is also her merit – is to conduct her home in accordance with the instructions of our Torah and its *mitzvos*, in the *chinuch* of sons and daughters, and so on. From the above it follows that anything that interferes with this, even if it only causes a weakening [in her ability to carry out her role in the fullest], should be rejected completely, since this prevents her from fulfilling the duty with which she has been charged by the Giver of the Torah and Creator of the world.

A lesson from Chana: The priorities of an *akeres habayis*

In[731] the *haftorah* [of *Rosh HaShanah*], we read about how both Sarah and Chana conceived on *Rosh HaShanah*. This is why the *haftorah* of the first day of *Rosh HaShanah* relates the story of Chana.[732] Although this is the general point, it follows that since it has become a part of Torah, all of the details told about Chana contain a lesson—and a broad lesson—that we can apply throughout the year – and since we *can* apply it, we *should.*

How much more so does this apply to the *haftorah*, and [even to] a peripheral part of the *haftorah* – it always contains a lesson, as mentioned, for Torah is eternal. We have often discussed the teaching of the Baal Shem Tov[733] that when one has just seen or just heard something, it surely holds a lesson that is relevant now, to [the time] when one saw or heard it.

This story, which contains numerous details, relates a wondrous thing about Chana, from which we can learn a fundamental lesson concerning how every Jewish family should behave.

The story begins by relating how Elkanah would make an annual trip to Shiloh, and he would take along his entire family. The *Midrash* states, as does the *Yalkut Shimoni*, that he would take along his brothers and sisters.[734]

---

730 *Igros Kodesh*, vol. 14, p. 436.

731 *Sichos Kodesh* 5734, vol. 1, pp. 24-29.

732 *I Shmuel*, ch. 1

733 *Keser Shem Tov, Hosafos* #119-129.

734 *Eliyahu Rabbah*, sec. 9.

Every year, he would go down a different path [to reach Shiloh], and the *Midrash* explains his intention in doing so: Since his journey to Shiloh was a pilgrimage, in the places that he would stop over on the way, he would stop in an open area, making a lot of noise because he would arrive with his entire family, with his male and female relatives.

When he was asked, "Where are you going?" and "Whom are you taking with you?", he would respond that he was going with his entire family on a pilgrimage to Shiloh, for at that time the Divine Presence was revealed in the *Mishkan* at Shiloh in a way comparable to the way it was later in the *Beis Hamikdash.* This created a tumult in the cities through which he would pass, to the point that a large number of their residents went along as well. Therefore, Hashem told him that since he vigorously encouraged Jews to go along with him to Shiloh, he would to receive a certain reward, as is explained at length in that *Midrash.*

Even of one Jew who goes on a pilgrimage it is written, "All your males will display themselves before the face of Hashem, your G–d,"[735] which the Talmud interprets[736] to mean, "Just as they came to see [G–dliness], so did they display themselves [before G–d]." This means that he would see Hashem, as it were, and Hashem would see him.

How much more so when it came to Elkanah and his family – including Chana – who brought along many Jewish men and women [to Shiloh], one can understand what wondrous [Divine revelation] they experienced when they arrived in Shiloh.

Then the *haftorah* relates how Chana bore a child, and when the pilgrimage time came, Elkanah assumed that Chana would go along. However, Chana declined. This time she wouldn't go to Shiloh; she would remain home. Since she had a child, she needed to wait until "he is weaned," i.e., until she has raised him, and she would be able to go along with her child to Shiloh. But until then, she would stay home.

Chana was a prophetess, as the end of the *haftorah* relates. This means that not only did she see G–dliness in Shiloh in the way that other Jews saw

---

735 *Mishpatim* 23:17.

736 *Chagigah* 2a.

it, but she also saw it as a prophetess sees it, meaning that [when experiencing this revelation,] she had true pleasure, true understanding, and the greatest possible feeling.

As the *haftorah* records, and the *Midrash* in particular, Elkanah was wealthy, and so he would have been able to bring with him various servants and wet-nurses so that Chana would be able to take the child along and be confident that the journey wouldn't harm him. Chana could have taken Shmuel along to Shiloh. However, obviously the care and attention one can give while one is alone at home is not comparable to [and far greater than] when one travels, even with all the servants and conveniences.

This is as far as [the effect of the journey on] Shmuel is concerned. However, there was another option. Chana could have taken – as it's called in this country – a babysitter for those few weeks while she would go to Shiloh and back. Since she would go to Shiloh and absorb even more G–dliness and prophecy, her child would ultimately also benefit from what she gained.

But the *haftorah* relates as a simple fact – and Elkanah appreciated this, for he didn't argue with her at all – that Chana said that by being at home during these two years (and usually a child is weaned after two years), and not going to Shiloh for two years, she would be able to ensure the proper rearing of Shmuel, at least somewhat more than she could if she would travel – and even if she would travel on a path leading to Shiloh.

Chana succeeded, and when she later brought Shmuel, "He (Shmuel) remained there (in Shiloh) constantly." And she testified, "It was for this boy that I prayed." This was the power of her self-sacrifice in not going in Shiloh for two years: in order to ensure that Shmuel would receive everything [he needed]. Although she could have made extra-sure of that while on the trip as well, she still stayed home. Through this she merited not only to deliver the entire prophecy mentioned later – which means that Hashem approved of her choice – but it was also established, and established in Torah.

There are a few details in the life of Chana that are recorded in Torah, but only several verses describe the life of Elkanah and Chana. The reason for this is that this is the part that is relevant as a lesson to all future generations, and the two verses describing how Chana didn't go to Shiloh were included in Torah because they contain a lesson for all generations.

A Jewish woman or mother, or one who is preparing to be a mother, may be occupied with all kinds of good things, for "here we are not discussing fools" – we're discussing intelligent people. Yet the *haftorah* tells us that even though we are speaking of a prophetess, who wanted to go to [such a holy place as] Shiloh – which would have been a binding custom according to *halacha* [since she had been doing so regularly until then], and Chana would have needed a dispensation from three rabbis or one expert rabbi – nevertheless Chana did all these things for the sake of the advantage to be gained by Shmuel's not being brought along to Shiloh. While at home, she would be able to devote herself to him exclusively, and in this way he would benefit more than he would have otherwise.

This serves as an example for all Jewish women throughout all the generations. Some mistakenly think that a woman should feel inferior to a man; therefore, she should strive to fight a war: Just as a man is eligible to a certain position, and just as a man can accomplish certain tasks, she should also be able to work in that position and she should also be able to perform those tasks. She should be able to leave the home very early and come home, completely exhausted, very late, for she must demonstrate and prove how she isn't inferior to him...

But the *haftorah* tells us that this is completely incorrect. This is an inferiority complex, and a false assessment of the mission with which Hashem has charged a woman. Hashem gave her something even greater than a pilgrimage to Shiloh, and even greater than vigorously encouraging Jewish communities to go to Shiloh. That is all second-rate when compared with what a woman can accomplish when she stays home and ensures that the home is built on the foundations of Torah and *mitzvos* in general, and especially with regard to educating boys and girls.

As we have often discussed, when we start to count the Jewish people, Torah tells us immediately – although in *Chumash*, we are not told how many people were in each family; we are only told how many people were in each tribe, and the census of the entire Jewish people, so it is the tribe that is emphasized – that the foundation, survival, and structure of the Jewish people, Judaism, and Torah depends upon "their families." This means that the family should be built as Hashem established it – that the man does his part, the woman does hers, and her part is no less important. If anything, her part is even more important than is the man's when it comes to children.

As we see, unfortunately – now is a time when one should only speak favorably about Jews, so this will be brief and general – what happened when some women were forced due to reasons of livelihood to become busy with jobs, business, and livelihood, and therefore had to leave the home. Society then came to think that a woman's perfection is to be found in imitating a man.

We see what it led to: A separation between the different worlds – between the mother, the father, and the children, so that each one not only knows nothing about the others, but doesn't understand the others. As mentioned, [at this time] we should only speak positively about Jews.

This mistake should be changed at its very root, with the husband doing his part, and the woman hers, as the "mainstay of the home." If anything, her role is *more* important; not only is she not somehow not valuable, but on the contrary, she is the one entrusted with educating the boys and girls from their infancy and childhood, and from their very birth, and even from nine months earlier, because "[the embryo] eats from what its mother eats."[737]

To think that she will reach perfection by forgetting about all of this and demonstrating that she can be a successful professional, as it's called, or a successful breadwinner, and so on – this is in fact a descent and a fall for her. Not only has she lost her self-respect and incorrectly assessed her talents, but [this also has a detrimental effect upon] the survival of Jewish families, G–d forbid.

It pains the heart to look at what is going on, and what should be fixed. Yet instead, there are Jews who have nothing else to concern themselves with but tearing even more women away from their role, and seeking halachic dispensations and [inventing new] customs so that they too can become a *gabai* in a synagogue, an assistant in a synagogue, and be counted in a *minyan.* They're making a whole parade, saying that in so doing, they've elevated women to their true level, and so they should be thanked. These women are going around and celebrating that *now* they've reached their perfection, not considering – aside from the fact that this flies in the face of Jewish custom

737 *Niddah,* 30b.

and Torah law – how this affects the fundamental unit of the Jewish family, which is the foundation of the entire Jewish people.

The woman should occupy herself with her main work, and her main work and her main task is educating [her children], which is the idea of the [role of the woman as] "mainstay of the home." She shouldn't degrade herself to [what for her would be] trivialities by imitating another. Nor should she declare that since we live in an environment in which [the woman's staying home] might be interpreted differently, she should abandon her own children so that others will be able to say that she was elevated – she was counted for a *minyan,* she was appointed *gabai,* or she was bestowed honor with a certificate that no one cares about (even if it would be acceptable according to Jewish law).

What is this coming to replace? It's being put forward and recommended instead of the ultimate mission with which Hashem charged women – to maintain the Jewish people by [ensuring that] there are children and grandchildren whom we can bring in Shiloh and declare, "It was for this boy that I prayed," as is told at length later in the prophecy of Chana.

Again, this is not the time to speak at length about undesirable things; [my intention is] to focus on the positive aspect of this: that although according to Jewish law it was completely acceptable for Chana and Peninah [Elkanah's other wife] to go along with Elkanah – and the *Midrash* says that the sisters went along as well, even though women are not obligated to go on a pilgrimage, and they only go to accompany their husbands – [Chana still chose not to go along once Shmuel was born].

This is what the *haftorah* tells us on *Rosh HaShanah,* and we must take this lesson to heart for all the days of the year: that a Jewish mother – or a girl who is preparing to become a mother when Hashem blesses her with children – should know that nothing else [is as important]. Even when it comes to going to Shiloh "to see the face of Hashem, your G–d," Hashem, your G–d says that there is an even higher level: When Hashem blesses one with children, and Hashem blesses them with a home, then all other things should be set aside, and the main purpose of the wife is to be the "mainstay of the home." That is her greatness, role, and mission. No one else can do it.

She shouldn't imitate and run after others who don't know what they want and who cause others to be confused because they think that it will lead to some benefit. Rather, a woman should know that her primary mission is to serve as the "mainstay of the home."

On the contrary, through this she will then be able to come with her children to Shiloh and meet the *kohen gadol*, and tell him, "It was for this boy that I prayed" [just as Chana said to Eili]. Then this boy will become like Shmuel, of whom it is said that he equaled Moshe and Aharon (the exact meaning of this is explained in the commentaries). And he will then anoint David, King of the Jewish people, who was the first redeemer, the king from whose seed (from the seed of David and Shlomo) *Moshiach* comes forth, and this is the beginning of the coming of *Moshiach*.

This was entrusted into their hands; it is in the control of every Jewish "mainstay of the home." The permission and ability has been granted. Women were given the entire wherewithal to carry out their mission in the loftiest manner possible, and with joy and a glad heart. When they fulfill their task and mission completely, they establish "the seed blessed by Hashem" with which we will soon go to greet our righteous *Moshiach*, with the true and complete redemption, very soon.

Women and Work

Involvement in *chinuch*

[The[738] following was written in response to the question of the principal of Beis Rivkah in Brooklyn, regarding what the Rebbe mentions in the *sicha* of 6 Tishrei and *Motza'ei Simchas Torah* 5734, that *n'shei Yisrael* should be involved in the *chinuch* of their children and not go out to work.]

Was Beis Rivkah not established by our Rebbes, our *Nesi'im*, so that there be [female] teachers and [female] instructors and the like, so what is the question?!

They [the Rebbes] also demanded involvement in *N'shei Chabad;* however, it must be in the right time, and in the right quantity, and so on, according to the individual circumstances of every individual woman.

---

738 *Heichal Menachem*, vol. 2, p. 103.

The reason for the role of *akeres habayis*

The[739] Alter Rebbe writes in his *Shulchan Aruch*[740] that the reason that women are advised and cautioned regarding the *mitzvah* of lighting *Shabbos* candles more than men are, is that they are "found at home and involved with the needs of the home."

The reason for this – their being "found at home and involved with the needs of the home" – is that they don't come into contact as much with the outside world, and therefore they are not influenced by the outside world. Thus, they are more capable of fulfilling the role of *akeres habayis* and running a Jewish home in the appropriate way, which also involves their adding to the husband's *shleimus* (completeness).

Conditions of the Rebbe for going out to work

The[741] main role of a married *bas Yisrael* is to be a proper *akeres habayis*, running the home in general, and especially the raising of and *chinuch* of the children. This is also consistent with what is said, "All of the King's daughter's glory is internal."[742] It was barely made permissible [for women] to be involved *outside* – and this is for the *chinuch* of *Bnei Yisrael*, because women have a special motherly feeling for the children, and their influence is greater and deeper. Other conditions of great necessity under which the *Chachomim* permitted women to work outside the home are:

1) in order to relieve the husband (who devotes himself to Torah study) from the understandable worries of *parnassah* (pursuing a livelihood) or 2) when the husband is unable to provide sufficient *parnassah* despite his efforts in this, as is written: שארה כסותה לא יגרע ("He shall not diminish her sustenance, garments..."),[743] and he needs the help of his wife to provide *parnassah* for the home.

Do you have one of the above situations?

---

739 *Hatzne'a Leches*, p. 267, from *Sichas Yom Simchas Torah* 5725.

740 *Orach Chaim* 263.

741 *Hatzne'a Leches*, p. 257, a handwritten response of the Rebbe

742 *Tehillim* 45:14.

743 *Shemos*, 21:10.

(Regarding what is written about the *Eishes* Chayil [which also applies to others like her], סדין עשתה ותמכור ("She makes a cloak and sells it"), surely this does not contradict the conditions above, which are taken from *Shulchan Aruch,* from the *halachos* of *tznius,* and so forth). I will mention her at the gravesite (*tziyon*) of my father-in-law, the Rebbe.

A mother's primary priority

This[744] is to acknowledge receipt of your letter of the 30th of Nissan [April 27], which reached me with considerable delay. In it you write about [a woman in your community] who would like to open a shop and, presumably, would want to manage it personally.

Although it is generally difficult to give advice in such a situation from a distance, and not knowing the person – I do not think, generally speaking, that it would be advisable for her to undertake such a responsibility, in view of the fact that she has [...] children of school age and has also to take care of household responsibilities in her important role as *akeres habayis.* Even if, as you write, she can get adequate help in the house and there would be no problem with childcare, it cannot be a substitute for the personal attention and care that the children need in their upbringing and *chinuch.* These considerations surely have top priority, and all other considerations can only be secondary.

To be sure, if one has time to spare, it should be utilized in the best possible way, but one should not confuse the order of priorities.

First and foremost, a mother

You[745] write about your present frame of mind and lack of fulfillment in having to devote all of your time to domestic responsibilities, taking care of the children, and so forth.

---

744 Letter of the Rebbe, 9 Sivan, 5739 – reprinted with permission from www.Chabad.org.

745 Letter of the Rebbe, reprinted with permission from www.Chabad.org.

It is a matter of common sense, as well as of considerable emphasis in our Torah, that a woman finds her fulfillment precisely as the *akeres habayis,* and that this is the area where she can truly accomplish great and wonderful things, if only she desires it. It is written that "G-d created man upright, but he seeks many calculations."[746] Thus, in the present abnormal times, it has become a prevalent, though nonetheless erroneous, view that the wife must seek employment, and that this must be outside the home. To be sure, if there were some employment that could be taken up at home to supplement the *parnassah,* that would be well and good, as is mentioned in the well-known chapter of *Eishes Chayil.*[747] However, some women insist upon outside employment, so that this has become the established practice and has become "second nature," to such an extent that it has resulted in a complete reversal of values, making the essential secondary, and the secondary essential, as if a woman can be regarded as a real person only if she goes against her nature and against the natural order of the world.

The above would be true even if the woman had only one or two children to take care of. How much more so when there are, thank G-d, more than a minimal number of children? This is especially true when they are at an age when they depend entirely upon the attention and loving care of the mother. And when one lives in a place where the ability to keep a Jewish home is in itself a challenge – not as it used to be in earlier days and under different circumstances – and when one has, in addition, the great responsibility and privilege to strengthen *Yiddishkeit* with the light and warmth of *Chassidus,* all this certainly requires the mobilization of all of the woman's capacities, ingenuity, concentration, and peace of mind, and there is no satisfaction greater than that which comes from being able to accomplish all the above. It would seem rather doubtful that, after all this, there would be an excess of energy and interest to divert to outside employment and the like.

---

746 *Koheles,* 7:29.

747 *Mishlei,* 31:10-31.

A Mother's Tznius Impacts Entire Home

Tznius of the mother brings the *Shechinah* into the home and *brachos* for the family

It[748] is appropriate to spend some time on the *pesukim* in our *parshah*... which lists the G-dly *brachos* that come as a reward for בחוקותי תלכו ואת מצותי תשמרו ("walk in My statutes and keep My *mitzvos*").[749] The central point of the *brachos* is ונתתי משכני בתוככם...והתהלכתי בתוככם והייתי לכם לאלוקים ואתם תהיו לי לעם ("And I will place My dwelling in your midst... I will walk among you and be your G-d, and you will be My people").[750] Although this *bracha* is connected with the observance of Torah and *mitzvos* in general... the conclusion of the *brachos* emphasizes the special importance of *kedusha, taharah,* and *tznius*. This is because they are the foundation for the *Mishkan* of Hashem and the dwelling of the *Shechinah* among the Jewish people in general and each *Yid*, man or woman, in particular. This matter is emphasized as well in another place in the Torah: והיה מחניך קדוש, ולא יראה בך ערות דבר ושב אחריך ("[Therefore,] your camp shall be holy, so that He should not see anything unseemly among you and would turn away from you").[751]

Our Sages explain in a clear way that *tznius* and *kedusha* need to be kept in all matters – in speech, and how much more so in dress and conduct. On previous occasions, it has been discussed how *n'shei u'bnos Yisrael* set the tone in certain matters of Jewish conduct, as is clearly seen. This is the case especially in the area of *tznius*, as our Sages of blessed memory tell us in many sources, and as they also say, the greatest *nachas* from children, spiritually and materially, is related to the *tznius* conduct of the mother.

---

748 *Likkutei Sichos,* vol. 7, pp. 360-361.

749 *Vayikra,* 26:3-4.

750 Ibid. 26:11-12.

751 *Devarim,* 23:15.

America is no different!

This[752] anecdote has special significance for Jewish women, in some aspects even more than for men. In general, women have a tendency to follow the latest fashion, and it is not uncommon for fashion to be at odds with the dictates of modesty. Women should know that the same Torah and *mitzvos* and the same principle of "the glory of the King's daughter is within" [753] that applied in the Old Country also apply in America. This is the same tradition of pure-hearted Jewish women who were the first to help build the *Mishkan* for the entire Jewish nation, as well as the holy *Mishkan* and *Mikdash* in their own home, so that it be a home about which Hashem can say "I dwell in their midst,"[754] for their home is then a suitable dwelling for the Divine Presence, so to speak. This principle continues to be valid here in America, just as it was once in the Old Country, across the sea.

Tznius is true beauty

[Asher[755] had daughters who were beautiful and would marry *kohanim gedolim* (high priests) ... what is the connection between their beauty and their marrying *kohanim gedolim*? Theirs was a spiritual beauty.]

The true beauty of a Jewish woman is כל כבודה בת מלך פנימה ("All the glory of the King's daughter is within") [756] – the matter of *tznius*, which not only brings to, but also assists the *kehunah gedolah* (high priesthood) [since a *Kohen Gadol* could not do his *avodah* on *Yom Kippur* unless he was married,[757] and a woman is an *eizer kenegdo* ("a helpmate to complement him" [758])].

Through what does one merit this? ... By conducting oneself with *kabbalas ol*, according to the *Shulchan Aruch*, which includes the observance of *tznius*. [Through this] one merits to establish a righteous generation of sons and

---

752 *Likkutei Sichos*, vol. 6, p. 364.

753 *Tehillim*, 45:14.

754 *Shemos*, 25:8.

755 *Likkutei Sichos*, vol. 1, p. 109.

756 *Tehillim*, 45:14.

757 *Yoma*, 47a. *Bamidbar Rabbah*, 1:3.

758 *Bereishis*, 2:18.

daughters occupied with Torah and *mitzvos*. Her sons will even be *kohanim Gedolim:* Sons who enter into the *Kodesh Hakodoshim*, which contains only the *Aron* and the *Luchos* upon which the Ten Commandments are engraved. They are not written with ink, which is a separate entity from the *klaf* (parchment); rather, they are engraved onto the *luchos*, which represents a level at which the Jew and Torah are one.[759]

Tznius indicative of level of *yiras Shamayim*

In[760] a *yechidus* with Rabbi Mordechai Shmuel Ashkenazi and his wife (in *Tishrei* of 5729), the Rebbe said, אבן הבוחן ליראת שמים היא צניעות וטהרה, ("The test which is indicative of [the level of one's] *yiras Shamayim* is *tznius* and *taharah*").

A matter of *kedusha*

[Tznius][761] is the crown and glory of *bnos Yisrael* (Jewish girls), each of whom is called the daughter of Sarah, Rivkah, Rochel, and Leah. This is true of *bnos Yisrael* in every place, and how much more so in *Eretz Hakedosha* (the Holy Land), "the land upon which Hashem's eyes are constantly focused, from the beginning of the year until the end of the year."[762]

There is a well-known commentary of our Sages,[763] of blessed memory, that *kedusha* (holiness) is defined by *tznius*.

This special role belongs to Jewish women, who are called the *akeres habayis*, the foundation of *beis Yisrael*. [This includes] both the individual [home] and the *klal* [Jewish nation]. As great as is the responsibility and role of *n'shei Yisrael* in the matter of *tznius*, their reward is correspondingly great in drawing down *brachos* for the home and family, as is explained in the *Zohar Hakadosh:*[764] *Brachos* from above and below, with wealth, children, and great-grandchildren.

---

759 Cf. *Likkutei Sichos*, vol. 2, p. 320.

760 Printed in *Hakfar Shel HaRebbe*, Issue 3, *Teves* 5770.

761 *Igros Kodesh*, vol. 25, p. 215.

762 *Devarim*, 11:12.

763 Cf. *Nesivos Olam* of *Maharal*

764 3:126a.

Tznius elicits *brachos*

A[765] woman's strengthening herself in the ways of *tznius* is a sure path to health, *parnassah*, and an abundance of true *nachas* from children and grandchildren. This depends on each [woman and girl]. She should do this herself and also influence her close friends to recognize their great potential, as well as the *hatzlacha* that comes along with it.

Not depending on "fashions" of the street

It[766] is necessary to appeal to Jewish mothers and emphasize the importance [of *tznius* and] the danger of laxity in *tznius* in the raising of their daughters.

It is necessary to make aware the administration of girls' *chinuch* institutions of *all* ages to be more careful about the matter of *tznius* in the *chinuch* institutions. They should explain to the students that *tznius* is the most beautiful attribute, the crown of the Jewish daughter and mother.

We must strive to convince all those who appreciate and keep *tznius* that they have a responsibility to influence their sisters, both in word and especially by setting a sterling example, so that they will strengthen modesty in both their home and community.

The time has come for Jewish women and girls to feel Jewish pride and stop depending on the deceptive, alluring, and thoroughly empty "fashions" of the street. These fashions have no substance and are only in the interest of those who profit financially from the industry.

Deficiencies in *tznius* deprive sons of spiritual levels that would be otherwise attainable

...Of[767] course, even if the child won't reach the level of a *Kohen Gadol,* he is still a *Yid,* and he is considered a *Kohen.* Yet we do not know the ways of *Hakadosh Baruch Hu*, and it may have been decreed from Above that the child

---

765 *Igros Kodesh*, vol. 20, p. 204.

766 *Igros Kodesh*, vol. 26, p. 326.

767 *Toras Menachem*, vol. 16, p. 263.

of this woman has the potential to reach the level of a *Kohen Gadol* (spiritually). However, because there is a deficiency in her conduct in the matter of "all my days the walls of my home never saw my hair," she is withholding from her son the great merit that he could otherwise have attained.

A Jewish woman needs to ensure that her home is a Jewish home, a *chassidishe* home. This is crucial not only in the most fundamental areas, but also in matters that are *hiddurim* and *minhagim* (since in reality, these are also fundamental). In the words of our Sages, "Do not sit and weigh up the *mitzvos* of the Torah. The lightest and the most severe should all be regarded as equal."[768] Through [such conduct], she will merit good and proper children...

Mother's *tznius* is most important factor in raising holy children

It[769] is explained in *Chassidus* that each and every person can בשעתא חדא וברגעא חדא ("in one hour and in one moment")[770] inspire in himself the ability to reach the level of the *Kohen Gadol* in the *Kodesh Hakadoshim* (Holy of Holies) on *Yom Kippur*.

What is the way to do this? With regard to this, the *Gemara* relates:[771]

> שבעה בנים היו לה לקמחית וכולן שמשו בכהונה גדולה, אמרו לה חכמים מה עשית שזכית לכך, אמרה להם מימי לא ראו קורות ביתי קלעי שערי.

> Kimchis had seven sons, and all served as *Kohen Gadol*. The Sages asked her, "What did you do to merit this?" She said to them, "All my days, the walls of my house never saw my hair."

Every woman of *Yisrael* must know this: The *chinuch* of the children and the way they are raised depends upon her, the Jewish mother, more than the father.

---

768 *Devarim, Rabba* 6:2.

769 *Toras Menachem* 5716, vol. 16, pp. 262-263.

770 Zohar, 1:129a.

771 *Yoma*, 47a.

What is demanded of her? Not that her house be meticulously well-kept, polished, and so forth ("אויסגעפוצט"); rather, what is demanded of her is the conduct of "All my days, the walls of my house never saw my hair" – the matter of *tznius*.

Tznius even while home alone affects children years later

Kimchis[772] conducted herself with the ultimate *tznius*[773] – to such an extent that even when she was at home alone, when no one was with her, the walls of her home did not see her hair. In this way, she influenced her sons to such an extent that they all merited to become *kohanim gedolim* (high priests). This means that her conduct affected her children even many years later, when her sons were well beyond *bar mitzvah* age, twenty years old, which is when they were fitting for the role of *kehunah gedolah* (high priesthood). This even affected their sons and grandsons, since *kehunah gedolah* is passed down from father to son.

Since the oral Torah tells us this story, it follows that this story is not merely describing a past event... because Torah is an "instruction for life" for every single *bas Yisrael*. She should know the importance of being careful in the matter of *tznius*, even when no one is home, and so on. The reason for this is that one's habits become one's nature. If she is not careful with the matter of *tznius* when she is alone at home, she may forget and behave in such a way even when someone is home. By behaving with the utmost *tznius*, the mother exerts a positive effect on her sons and grandsons, as is evident from the story above.

---

772 *Hisvaaduyos* 5742, vol. 4, p. 2190.

773 *Yoma*, 47a.

CHAPTER 12

The Responsibilities of the Father

"For I know him, that he will instruct his children and his household after him, so that they will keep the path of G-d, to do righteousness and justice."

Bereishis, 18:19

Chinuch – compared to the *mitzvah* of *tefillin*

There[774] is a well-known saying of my father-in-law, the Rebbe,[775] in the name of his father, that just as it is a *mitzvah* to don *tefillin* every day, so is it a *mitzvah* to devote time every day to influence one's wife and children.

The *mitzvah* of *tefillin* is a Biblical commandment, and moreover, "The entire Torah is equivalent to [the *mitzvah* of] *tefillin*."[776] Its intent is to subjugate the heart and mind to Hashem,[777] which then, in turn, rule over[778] the entire body and the entire soul of the person.

From this we understand just how important it is to make an effort to influence one's wife and children, for the Rebbe Rashab chose to compare it to a *mitzvah* that is not only Biblical, but also equivalent to all the other *mitzvos,* and is relevant to the entirety of the person through his mind and heart.

Some mistakenly believe that they are going above and beyond the requirement of *halacha* with even the minimal amount of time that they spend influencing their household members, explaining to them matters that seem to be simple, thinking that they don't have time for this, since they need time to devote to Torah study, *davening ba'arichus* (at length), and the like. First, they might be mistaken in thinking that this guidance one is imparting is a basic matter. And even if it is, in fact, a basic matter, for his family members it is *fundamental* knowledge, which has the potential to change their conduct in areas that are fundamental and essential.

When it comes the *mitzvah* of *tefillin,* which is equivalent to the entire Torah, no one will claim that something else is more important. He knows that *tefillin* is of the utmost importance, and the *avodah* of the heart and mind hinges upon this. Likewise, he should know that the same is true regarding his influence over his family members. The *Gemara* explains[779] the *pasuk,* כי ידעתיו

---

774 *Toras Menachem,* vol. 15, p. 271.

775 *Hayom Yom,* 22 Teves. Cf. *Igros Kodesh Admor HaRayatz*, vol. 13, p. 47.

776 *Kiddushin,* 35a.

777 *Shulchan Aruch, Orach Chaim,* 25:5. *Shulchan Aruch Admor HaZaken, Orach Chaim,* 25:11.

778 Cf. *Zohar,* 2:153b.

779 *Sanhedrin,* 57b.

אשר יצוה את בניו ואת ביתו אחריו ("For Hashem knew that he [Avraham] would command his sons and his home [referring to his wife] that they keep the way of Hashem"),[780] that in this merit, Avraham earned the love of *Hakadosh Baruch Hu*.

...No effort made in this area is sufficient in proportion to the demands of our times. The future of the younger generation depends upon this, for אם אין גדיים ("if there are no baby goats" [there are no adult goats])[781] ... The גדיים (baby goats) need to become תיישים (adult goats) in the coming years.

Ensuring that the *simchah* of *Shabbos* and *Yom Tov* is felt in the home

It[782] is exceedingly important that the *simchah* of *Shabbos* and *Yom Tov* be experienced not only at *shul* and during *farbrengens*, but also in the home of each and every member of *Anash* (the Chabad community).

Hence, *farbrengens* should be organized in such a way that there will be time during the auspicious days of *Shabbos* and *Yom Tov* [for the husband and father] to explain these matters to his family members in an appropriate way, using appropriate language. Surely there is enough time during those days to *farbreng* properly as well as to bring joy to one's wife and children properly. It is obviously not possible to give individual instructions about this to each and every person, for it all depends on one's personal nature. Surely, based on the above, each person can come to his own conclusions about the conduct that is appropriate for him and his home.

780 *Bereishis*, 18:19.

781 *Vayikra Rabbah*, 11:7.

782 *Igros Kodesh*, vol. 10, p. 61.

Father's dedication to Torah learning

When[783] a child is taught to recite morning *brachos* and he recites the *Mishnah,* תלמוד תורה כנגד כולם ("Torah study is equivalent to them all"),[784] it is crucial that his father's conduct be in harmony with this statement. Otherwise, the child will wonder. ... "My father is involved in many things throughout his workday, activities that are positive and constructive, but how is it that his Torah study is not in a manner of תלמוד תורה כנגד כולם – given attention in a manner equivalent to all those other activities?"

He should still have set times for Torah study. ... This impacts the *chinuch* of his children, for they see that their father studies Torah. If they have room to doubt [whether he is devoted to Torah study], one cannot invent baseless excuses, for the children will immediately detect that the excuse is nothing but an attempt to slip out of it.

This also affects the child's fulfillment of the *mitzvah* of *kibbud av* (honoring one's father). When a child sees that his father adds to the *kavod* of *Hakadosh Baruch Hu* by learning Torah, this increases the *kavod* of the child toward the father, and so too in the reverse...

Teaching one's child to be a *dugmah chayah*

Since[785] the father has a חלק אלוקה ממעל ממש ("a soul that is 'truly' a part of G-d above")[786] and he makes his soul primary,[787] he teaches his children the concept and practice of *mesirus nefesh.* He does this through his personal conduct in a manner of *mesirus nefesh*, and in such a way that the children will grow up to fulfill their *shlichus* in the world: to be a *dugmah chayah* in their personal conduct, demonstrating how a *Yiddishe* child should behave, even during childhood.

---

783 *Hisvaaduyos* 5747, vol. 2, pp. 674-675.

784 *Pe'ah,* 1:1.

785 *Hisvaaduyos* 5751, vol. 4, p. 156.

786 *Likkutei Amarim, Tanya* ch. 2, beg.

787 Cf. ibid., ch. 32.

When [parents] act as a *dugmah chayah* with true *chayus* (vitality), this has an effect, because "words that emanate from the heart, enter the heart"[788] and have their effect. How much more so is this true when they do so not only in their speech, but also by setting a living example.

Regarding the children of *Yisrael* in our times, the generation that will greet *Moshiach Tzidkeinu* very soon... children need to set a living example [through showing the world] how they are preparing for the future *geulah* and building of the third *Beis Hamikdash*, מקדש אדנ־י כוננו ידיך ("the sanctuary of Hashem, which Your hands founded").

The father's *yiras Shamayim*

One[789] must know that the *tznius* of a woman depends upon the *tznius* of her husband. It is not as some mistakenly believe, that there is no connection. This is a fundamental mistake, since if one wants to be *bishleimus* (complete and whole) in this matter, the other must also be *bishleimus*. Whoever initiates this [increase in *yiras Shamayim*] will be blessed, and both [husband and wife] will progress together at once [in their growth in this area].

It is important to know that if one partner is deficient in this area, it influences the other. If one increases in matters of *tznius*, this influences the other partner of the home, the children, and the home [life] in general.

The *tznius* of the husband is connected with sight and the like. [In order to improve in this area,] one need not look in *Kuntres Avodah*[790] to see what is written on the topic; rather, each person knows how sight and hearing, reading materials, and manner of dress affect him. There is no need to elaborate on this matter...

---

788 *Sefer HaYashar* of Rabeinu Tam. Quoted in *Shelah,* 69a.

789 *Hatzne'a Leches,* pp. 137-138 – *Sicha* of *Yom Beis* of *Chag HaShavuos,* 5728.

790 Ch. 2.

CHAPTER 13

The Jewish Home

"A person is not a person without a home."

Talmud, Yevamos 63a

The Importance of Shalom Bayis

One of the most lofty and important ideals

Shalom[791] *bayis* is one of the most lofty and important ideals, especially when the couple has been blessed with children. It is understandable how important it is for children to grow up in a home where there is peace, and to grow up in a complete household, a home where there is both a father and a mother. So it is obvious, as well, that if it is necessary to compromise on important matters – and certainly when we are speaking about compromising only on comfort – this should be done with desire and eagerness in order to create *shalom bayis*, especially since this is for the good of the children.

In addition, one should make the compromise *besimchah* and wholeheartedly, and not with a feeling that what one is doing is a great self-sacrifice, under pressure, and so forth. On the contrary, the feeling should be that they are doing [yet] another good thing for the home and for the welfare of the children, in addition to its being for the welfare of the parents themselves...

A vessel for *bracha*

Shalom[792] *bayis* is the vessel that *Hashem Yisborach* uses to bestow *bracha* and *hatzlacha*, good health, *parnassah,* and *nachas* from the children.

Ingrains in children the best possible *middos*

Family[793] life that is good and *frum*, and the refined manner in which husband and wife relate to each other – in addition to being one of the *mitzvos* that Hashem has given us the privilege to fulfill – is indirectly also the best *chinuch*, which influences the children and ingrains in them the best possible *middos* (character traits).

791 *Nitzutzei Or*, p. 98.

792 *Igros Kodesh,* vol. 5, p. 61.

793 *Igros Kodesh Admor HaRayatz*, vol. 7, pp. 53-54.

Hashem Yisborach blessed the Jewish woman with a special understanding regarding *chinuch* and the foundations of running a home. Therefore, the woman is called the *akeres habayis*, the foundation stone of the home. When the woman runs the home with *chochmah* according to Torah, she has the greatest possible influence over her husband and children. Everything that she sees fit to carry out, she does in a quiet and peaceful manner by influencing respectfully. This kind of conduct makes the whole family feel fulfilled, and the atmosphere in the home brings *simchah* and *hatzlacha*.

In addition, when the woman finds something lacking in the conduct of her husband, she is obligated to – and can – correct this only through speaking gently and maintaining a positive relationship. Under no circumstances should she use harsh words or an angry countenance, even when this is only in order to intimidate. This is the best way to succeed.

Children will wholeheartedly accept parents' instructions

The[794] *chinuch* of the children of *Yisrael* begins within family life. In order for the *chinuch* to be as it should be, the family must be united. This unity comes about through an atmosphere of following Torah and *mitzvos* in daily life, especially *mitzvos* that the entire family is involed in together, such as the observance of *Shabbos* and *Yom Tov*. …

When parents do all that is in their power to strengthen the *achdus* of the family, when they are attentive to and aware of what is going on with their children, both during the weekdays and the holy days of *Shabbos* and *Yom Tov*. Then they are able to give their children true guidance. The children will be permeated with true love, awe, and respect for their parents and will wholeheartedly accept their commands and instructions.

794 *Likkutei Sichos*, vol. 12, p. 209.

Don't emphasize your spouse's faults

Until[795] *Moshiach* arrives, no one exists in this world without faults. Thus, it is clear that just as one spouse has a fault, so does the other, and just as one would not want their own faults to be emphasized, so should one not emphasize and amplify the faults of the other. This is the way that all Jews should relate to one another; however, it applies all the more when relating to your husband, who is also the father of your children.

My intent is not to criticize, but merely to draw your attention to the fact that your situation is not as severe as you present it, nor is it unusual, as it appears to you to be.

Each of you should overlook certain things and instead find ways to bring peace in the home. Once this is attained, this is the vessel through which Hashem will provide *bracha* and *hatzlacha*, good health, *parnassah,* and *nachas* from the children.

Woman holds key to *achdus*

We[796] have emphasized on many occasions that there are matters of crucial importance to *klal Yisrael*, and especially with regard to Torah and *Yiddishkeit*, where the woman's role is of the greatest importance. One of them is the area of the *achdus* (unity) of the family. The key to *achdus* between parents and children, between husband and wife, and among the children, is in her hand.

In this area, we see clearly that most of the time, the wife and mother has a greater impact than the father, and for this reason she is called the *akeres habayis* (the foundation of the home). It is also clear that the matter of *achdus* among *Yidden* on a larger scale – *achdus* involving one family within society, and the *achdus* of the nation of *Yisrael* in general – depends upon the *achdus* of the family. When the *achdus* is (G-d forbid) lacking within a family, one can't expect *achdus* between that family and another family. Even when the *achdus* within the family has reached the ideal, the problem of a lack of *achdus* among the Jewish people in general still remains, for Torah and *mitzvos* are

---

795 *Igros Kodesh,* Vol. 5, p. 61.

796 *Igros Kodesh*, vol. 25, p. 150.

the foundation of true Jewish *achdus* [and large numbers of the Jewish people are still assimilated].

When parents do not agree on *chinuch* matters

The[797] importance of the matter of *shalom bayis* and [preventing] its opposite is understood from the teaching of our Sages:

1) *Hakadosh Baruch Hu* actually commands[798] that we blot out His ineffable (written) name in water in order to bring peace between a husband and his wife.
2) Regarding the opposite (the dissolution of a marriage), the *Mizbe'ach* sheds tears.[799] The *Mizbe'ach* is a spot where one atones for *the entire Jewish nation* and *davens* for their welfare. Divorce is not a personal matter relating to two people alone.

Our Sages say[800] that no two people think alike. Yet one can and *must* bring true peace between every single member of *Bnei Yisrael.* How much more so [does this apply] between husband and wife, for when they conduct themselves according to Torah and *mitzvos,* our Sages say[801] that the *Shechinah* dwells in their midst.

The concern [of the husband and wife] that they do not think alike on *chinuch* matters will be relevant after they are blessed with viable offspring and after the children reach the age of *chinuch* – i.e., only *years* later. Surely over such a length of time, every person's views change [including theirs]. It is also certain that having children leads parents to develop a far deeper emotional connection.

It is impossible to know ahead of time the exact nature of any change that may take place in the future, or the extent of the closeness that will develop.

---

797 *Likkutei Sichos*, vol. 24, p. 467.

798 *Likkutei Sichos*, vol. 35, p. 269

799 *Gittin*, 90a-b.

800 *Sanhedrin* 38a.

801 *Sotah*, 17a.

According to our faith, one should have a strong hope that all this will occur, and in an abundant measure. Even if in the future their differences of opinion remain, when it comes down to taking action, they will compromise with each another, and the *bracha* will be fulfilled between them that their home will be a *binyan adei ad* (an eternal edifice).

In conclusion, it is clear that they should strengthen and increase in *shalom bayis*, since every single *Yid* should make efforts to strengthen what is shared between him and the rest of *Bnei Yisrael*, and this is all the more true of husband and wife.

Also, do not seek out and reflect upon differences between you that may only be practically relevant in many years to come...

The great importance of *achdus* and *shalom*

Children[802] should be taught about the great importance of and need for *achdus* and *shalom,* to help and aid others, for the good of all humanity. [This should be done] by ingraining within them the belief in the Creator, Who runs the world.

...The right *chinuch* brings about closeness and *achdus* between the young generation being educated and the older generation that is giving the *chinuch*. [It unites] children, parents, and grandparents. This negates and nullifies the notion of a generation gap. On the contrary, it creates a closeness and unity between generations. The children, parents, and grandparents feel like one family and conduct themselves as one. They make use of the positive traits that Hashem endowed within each and every one of them – old, middle-aged, and young – for the benefit of the entire family. ...

Included in the role of *Bnei Yisrael* is to make efforts for the welfare of all the nations of the world. This is emphasized in [the duty to] give *tzedakah* to the poor of the nations of the world.[803] Similarly, we are to involve ourselves with influencing the nations of the world to fulfill the *mitzvos* incumbent on *Bnei No'ach*, as *Rambam* rules that Moshe *Rabeinu* commanded [the *Yidden*]

---

802 *Hisvaaduyos* 5750, vol. 3, p. 194.

803 *Mishneh Torah, Hilchos Matnos Aniyim,* 7:7.

what he heard from Hashem, to motivate all the inhabitants of the world to take upon themselves the *mitzvos* commanded of *Bnei No'ach*.[804]

The Home is a Place of Kedusha

The strength to overcome peer pressure

The *kedusha*[805] in the conduct of the home, and the *chinuch* of one's sons and daughters must be felt in a recognizable way. Not only is his home run in an entirely different way than a home of a non-Jew, *lehavdil*, but it should be on a higher level of *kedushah* than even other Torah-observant homes. In other homes, the norms of the world[806] have importance, but his home must be run only in accordance to Torah, *Yiddishkeit*, and *kedushah*.

This too we learn from the actions of our forefathers, particularly the conduct of the house of Yaakov. The Torah relates that "Reuven went out during the time of wheat-harvesting and found *dudaim* in the field". *Rashi* comments, "[This is] to tell the praise of the tribes. It was harvest time, and he did not stretch out his hand upon stolen property, to take wheat or barley, but only upon an ownerless thing, which no one cares about." From that which *Rashi* says, "[This is] to tell the praise of the [progenitors of] the tribes," is understood that around them there were no other people who conducted themselves in such a praiseworthy fashion. However, the tribes knew that their conduct must be different: that they needed to conduct themselves according to Torah and *kedushah* in every detail. This is how Yaakov ran his home, so that his home was different from every other person's.

One should not follow the spirit of the time. It should be so strikingly clear, that the children know that their father and mother are different from everyone else. Other women might not dress in a *tzniusdike* manner *be'hiddur*, but their mother dresses with the ultimate *tznius*. Other fathers are not careful not to deceive others in their business dealings, but their father is honest and does business with *emunah* and so forth.

---

804 *Mishneh Torah, Hilchos Melachim*, 8:10.

805 *Likkutei Sichos*, vol. 3, pp. 792-794.

806 Cf. *Choshen Mishpat* 3, *S'meh* 13.

Even when a child is small and not able yet to grasp the meaning of Torah and *kedushah*, he can already sense that his home is different from other homes, and thus he is automatically not influenced by other children. On the contrary, when he sees other children not behaving properly, and they are not being careful about taking things from foreign fields, this in itself makes it very clear to him that he will not behave this way and he knows that he should not become friends with them.

... When a Jewish child is taught while he is still young to know that he is different from all of the other children in the world, then also later, when he grows older, he will remain uninfluenced by others his age. But rather, he will go away just like his forefather, Yaakov, learning only Hashem's Torah. He will speak in a manner of ודברת בם ("You shall speak of them" [words of Torah) [807] until even his mundane speech includes only words of Torah. And just like Yaakov, when he matures and gets married, goes into the world, builds a family, and has the yoke of *parnassah* on his shoulders, then too he will establish set times to learn Torah every day, as did Yaakov *Avinu*. When he is involved in material matters, he will say *Shir Hamaalos* and have complete *bitachon* in Hashem, and automatically his whole business conduct will be only according to Torah.

Chassidishkeit should be felt in three areas

In[808] a *Chassidishe* home, every child needs to feel passion and inspiration for *Chassidishkeit*. This depends mainly on the woman, the *akeres habayis*. The *Chassidishkeit* should be felt in three areas:

Torah: The passion for Torah must be something the child experiences: that it is Hashem's Torah, Hashem's wisdom. While learning, the passion and *yirah* (awe of Hashem) must be as palpable as it was at *Matan Torah*.[809] This applies not only when saying a deep *pilpul*, but even when learning a simple *pasuk* with *Rashi*, and even without the *Rashi*, and even when learning *alef beis* – even then, it must be felt that this is Hashem's wisdom.

---

807 *Yoma*, 19b.

808 *Toras Menachem*, vol. 24, p. 276.

809 *Berachos*, 22a.

Gemilus chassadim: A child must feel that in his home a lot of *tzedakah* is given – not only *ma'aser*, not only *chomesh*, but without limits. When they find out that someone is in need, the family does not delay in giving to him. The family doesn't wait for him to ask. Rather, he is given immediately and without limitations.

Avodah: When the husband stays to continue *davening* after the *minyan* has concluded *davening*, even though the *minyan* finished hours ago, it should be known at home that he is arriving late because he *davened* with a *tzibur* (according the *chassidic* meaning of צ׳יבור: gathering all the *kochos* (energies) of the *neshamah* and refining [all the sparks of holiness]).

A palpable Torah atmosphere

Some[810] think that because their child is sent to a *frum* school, a school where the children learn only *limmudei kodesh*, they have fulfilled their obligation.

Parents must know that although a Torah institution is very important in order for the child to hold onto his *chinuch*, the Torah atmosphere in the home must be palpable. Even if the child comes home only to eat and sleep, he must sense the aura of Torah in the home.

This palpable aura in the home is created when his father, the businessman, grabs every free moment to say a *pasuk* from the Torah, or a *maamar* of our *chachomim;* when the child sees *sefarim* all around the home, and when in everyday conversations, the mother brings up points and ideas from *Tze'ena Ure'ena*, *Kitzur Shulchan Aruch,* and other Torah sources.

Conduct according to *Shulchan Aruch*

When[811] parents improve their conduct so that it is even more in keeping with *Shulchan Aruch* – which is the *ratzon* of *Hashem Yisborach* – this increases Hashem's *brachos* for the children as well.

---

810 *Shaarei Chinuch,* p. 127

811 *Likkutei Sichos*, vol. 36, p. 324.

Non-kosher music

Particularly[812] in the field of [popular] music, the current situation... is [that it is designed] to conquer the hearts [of listeners].

The approach is not only secular, but it also forms the listeners' attitude towards excitement of their evil inclination, [enticing them to] destroy the existing "boundaries" and "order" (including, to our greatest anguish, in the area of *tznius* in particular – and so on).

...Its slogan is: "Everything is permissible; it is *desirable* for you to try out everything yourself [and find out] what it is all about, and when the time comes, you will decide for yourself your attitude to everything without any preconceptions whatsoever".

Television

Television[813] is an unparalleled breach of standards. Even the non-Jews have now come out with a campaign against television, which is devastating for children. They are considering how to restore the situation as much as possible.

How shameful it is that in this case, Jews must learn from non-Jews. Moreover, we can see [how much of an effect it has had on the Jewish community] from the case of the four Jewish boys [who were recently involved in a murder], and other similar cases of killing and murder. Everyone admits that one of the causes of this is television and movies, where killings and shooting are viewed.

Moreover, even if one thinks that he will only view the "pious" programs on television that one is allowed to view, how can the parents guarantee that the children will not view other, forbidden programs as well? The children will argue that if the parents view television, they may also view whatever they want – and especially here in America, where children aren't so obedient to their parents.

And who can guarantee that the parents themselves will not fall into sin? Today they will view a permitted program, tomorrow they'll sneak a peek at another program, and little by little, everything will become permissible to them.

---

812 *Likkutei Sichos*, vol. 38, p. 179.

813 *Likkutei Sichos,* vol. 18, pp. 459-461.

An obvious argument: How could the world have existed ten years ago, before television was introduced? Didn't the world function just the same in all areas?

[Owning a television] will also result in another detrimental effect on others: When one knows that so-and-so, who has a full beard, has a television, and one doesn't know whether that Jew only views permissible programs, he will view all the programs, even those that are forbidden to view, relying on that person's conduct as permission.

One may ask, so why does so-and-so have a television? Are there not pious and even Chassidic Jews who have one? One should disregard them.

This is comparable to the 248 physical limbs. Not all of the person's limbs are healthy. One person's eyesight is weak, while another is weak in another limb, and so on. Would it be reasonable for one to say that since another is sick in his eyes, he also wants to be sick in his eyes? So too, with regard to spiritual matters: No one is perfect, and everyone does as much as he can in observance of Torah and *mitzvos*. Why should one learn a fault from someone else?

Of all those who have a television, none will say that he bought it to increase his fear of Heaven or fine character traits. Everyone has an excuse for it – it's a piece of furniture for his house, or for his wife. Or he says that he received it as a gift – should he throw it out?!

Once people were careful not to pass by a church; one would go around. A mother would not allow her child to go near a church or see a crucifix. Yet nowadays, through television they bring the church, the priest, and the crucifix into the house, *Rachmana litzlan* (may Hashem save us).

A young rabbi – in fact fine and G–d-fearing, from a pious yeshiva – related that he listens and watches television every day from twelve o'clock to one o'clock. At that time a priest speaks, and from the priest's sermon, he gathers material to speak about from the pulpit in his synagogue! He said this sincerely, and he thinks he's doing it for the sake of Heaven, so that he will have what to sermonize about in his synagogue. He is oblivious to the tremendous sin that this involves.

Once, people would give up their lives not to hear a priest speak, but now, through television, they bring the priest into their home, and they even vest this in holiness, as being for the sake of Heaven.

This was the way of the early followers of the Enlightenment movement, whose motto was: "Be a Jew at home, but a mensch outside" – and some of them were even qualified rabbis.

Really, what was wrong with this approach? The Code of Jewish Law does not forbid this. Indeed, one shouldn't go in the streets screaming, "I am pious!" So what was forbidden about their motto?

Did we not see from experience what happened to them? And among their children and grandchildren, no trace of Judaism remains.

We once related the story of a *shochet* (ritual slaughterer) in the village of Lubavitch who wore boots and was then fired from his position.

What was the prohibition? My father-in-law himself wore boots. Rather, in the time of this *shochet*, boots were a new thing, and only the Jews who dressed and acted like the *pritzim* [sing. *poritz* – the wealthy non-Jewish landowners], took part in their wild parties, and the like, would dress that way. If someone dressed like this, people knew that he had strayed from the proper path. In the end, it became known that this *shochet* and his family had indeed strayed from the proper path.

In Lubavitch, a Jew once came to his father and asked him: "Is it an accomplishment to sit in Lubavitch, closed in one's room, and be a fine Jew? If one walks on the street in Petersburg and doesn't sin there – that's an accomplishment." He continued: "Even that is no accomplishment. Being in Petersburg, going inside the theater, sitting with one's eyes shut, and not sinning – that's an accomplishment." Then the Jew went further: "Even that is not enough. Sitting inside a theater in Petersburg with one's eyes open, and not sinning – that's an accomplishment." He continued further: "Even that is not enough. Entering the theater, sitting near the stage where the performers perform, and then not sinning – that is a great accomplishment." In this way, he detailed an entire list of activities, and one can readily imagine how such a calculation can lead the person to fall to the lowest depths.

You should seek to correct this in your own city, and you can even start doing so in New York, because here the need to correct this is very great.

[From the time since the Rebbe said this, the situation has only deteriorated further.]

CHAPTER 14

Stories and Lessons from the Rebbe

"The Alter Rebbe would say: To hear Torah from the Rebbe... was Torah Shebe'al Peh, but to hear the Rebbe tell over a story, this was Torah Shebichsav."

Igros Kodesh Rebbe Rayatz, vol. 4, p. 65

Do not be satisfied with just "reading" a story

One[814] should not be satisfied with simply "reading" a story. We need to learn the story and take from it the proper instructions. We need to educate Jewish children in such a way that when they learn Torah, they will do so with passion and a desire to understand the matter. If they fail to understand something, they should seek out explanations for it.

A story is an instruction

The[815] fact that a story is passed down to us is an indication that there is a lesson for us to learn from it.

Chinuch applications

The[816] fact that the story has been publicized is an indication that it contains an instruction for every mother and father, and that it is within their ability that the *chinuch* of their children should reach such a level.

A story told by a *Nasi*

Every[817] story that has been related to us can and must be seen as a lesson to us in matters pertaining to us... In stories about *tzaddikim*, there is an intent and purpose: in particular the stories that a *tzaddik* has told, and even more so, those from a *Nasi*. [A *Nasi*'s] entire essence and purpose is to shepherd his flock. When a *Nasi* tells us a story, this is surely a matter that has relevance to us, from which we can and must learn.

814 *Sichos Kodesh* 5741, vol. 3, p. 1130 onwards.

815 *Sichos Kodesh* 5726, p. 50.

816 *Sichos Kodesh* 5741, vol. 4, p. 144.

817 *Toras Menachem*, vol. 4, p. 249.

How could it be that the best years of Yaakov's life were those he lived in *Mitzrayim*??

When[818] the Tzemach Tzedek was a child, his *melamed* taught him the *pasuk*, וַיְחִי יַעֲקֹב בְּאֶרֶץ מִצְרַיִם שְׁבַע עֶשְׂרֵה שָׁנָה and explained to him that Yaakov *Avinu* didn't simply reside in Egypt, but when he was in *Mitzrayim*, he lived. ...

When the Tzemach Tzedek returned home, he approached his grandfather, the Alter Rebbe, and asked him, "How can it be that the best years of Yaakov's life were those he lived... in Egypt, the most depraved of the nations?" The Alter Rebbe answered him, "Before Yaakov came to *Mitzrayim*, he sent Yehuda to make 'preparations in Goshen.' He sent him in order to set up a house of study so that he and his sons could study the Torah in Egypt. Goshen is from the root word גש, which means to approach, to become closer. When we study Torah, we become closer to Hashem, so in this way it is possible to live good years even in Egypt."

A new channel has been opened

My[819] father-in-law, the Rebbe, told in relation to the 20th of *MarCheshvan*, the birthday of the Rebbe Rashab *nishmaso eden*, a story that happened to the Rebbe Rashab when he was four or five years old, on *Shabbos Parshas Vayera:*

The Rebbe Rashab went to his grandfather, the Tzemach Tzedek, to receive a *bracha* for his birthday and he burst out into tears saying: "Why did Hashem reveal Himself to Avraham *Avinu* and to us (me), He does not reveal Himself?" The Tzemach Tzedek responded: "When a Jew who is a *tzaddik* decides at age ninety-nine that he needs to circumcise himself, he is deserving of Hashem revealing Himself to him."

Many instructions in one's *avodas* Hashem can be learned from this story, as with all stories of our *Rebbeim* which we have been informed of. Especially those that have been publicized have a special instruction for each and every person.

My father-in-law, the Rebbe, was precise when he told this story, and pointed out that the Rebbe Rashab was then *four* or *five* years old. Since each

818 *Sichos Kodesh* 5741, vol. 3, p. 1130 onwards

819 *Likkutei Sichos,* vol. 15, pp. 129-133.

word of a *Nasi* of *Yisrael* is calculated and precise, especially something that is said publically and which he instructs to have printed, it is probable to say that also *this* detail of the story does not come just to show us the greatness of the Rebbe *nishmaso eden*, that even in his young age he was so anguished, to the point of tears, that *Hakadosh Baruch Hu* does not reveal Himself to him. Rather, there is an instruction here for the *avodas* Hashem of each and every person.

From this, it is understood that despite the fact that this story has instructions for each and every person, there is a foundational instruction here for those who are four or five years old.

He too can demand with all of his strength (with a cry, which demonstrates such a degree of caring that is above and beyond his regular abilities) that *Hakadosh Baruch Hu* should reveal Himself to him, as He revealed Himself to Avraham *Avinu*.

[The reason that this demand is possible is that Avraham *Avinu* is one of the three patriarchs of each and every person of *Yisrael* in all generations; therefore these matters are inherited by all of *Yisrael*.]

Particularly a child, four or five years old *literally*, can be educated in such a way that he will demand with all of his strength, to the point of tears, that *Hakadosh Baruch Hu* should reveal Himself to him as he did to Avraham *Avinu*.

Seemingly, it is possible to ask: How is it possible to equate the Rebbe *nishmaso eden* to *every* Jewish child?

The Rebbe Rashab *nishmaso eden* was holy from the womb, a *Nasi* that was the child of a *Nasi*. The greatness that awaited him was recognizable already from his childhood. It is clear that even then he was far more knowledgeable than others, even adults. How is it possible to derive from him [conclusions] about the *chinuch* of every Jewish child, especially in light of the fact that the age of education for each child is as rules the Alter Rebbe in his *Shulchan Aruch* [343/3], בכל תינוק לפי חריפותו וידיעתו ("each child is to be taught according to his level of understanding and knowledge")?

This can be understood from the fact that even though it is written, שיעור החינוך... בכל תינוק לפי חריפותו וידיעתו ("the measure [of the amount one should be taught]... is according to the level of understanding and knowledge of each child"), as was mentioned above, nevertheless there are matters in *chinuch* that are connected to a certain age, including the general *halacha* stated in the Talmud that בציר מבר שית לא תקביל, בר שית קביל וספי ליה כתורא ("Do not accept [a pupil] under the age of six; a pupil of the age of six you shall accept and stuff him like an ox")- that learning Torah with a small child in a way of "stuffing him like an ox" which brings to a wholeness in *chinuch*, begins only when he is six years old.

However, the *Rambam* rules that this is dependent on כח הבן ובנין גופו ("the child's strength and constitution"). If one is כחוש ("weak"), one waits until he is כבן שבע ("like a seven year old"). Still, there is a limit here of "*do not* accept [a pupil] under the age of six", even if he is a strong and healthy child, more than a child that is already "like a seven year old".

This is to say, the age of בר שית (six) in relation to a complete *chinuch* –וספי ליה כתורא ("stuff him like an ox")- is not dependent on the knowledge of the child or his ability. This is similar to the measure of בן י"ג למצוות ("at age thirteen, one becomes obligated in *mitzvos*"). Even when a child is more knowledgeable than another child that is already older than him in years, he is still not obligated in *mitzvos* (according to Torah ruling, he is not counted in a *minyan)*.

...From this is understood also in our case, that since the Rebbe *nishmaso eden* was at that time בציר מבר שית ("younger than six years old"), his greatness and wisdom at this age is not of significance at this age, as despite everything he was on the level of בציר מבר שית, that still did not reach completion in *chinuch*.

Since when this story was publicized by the Rebbe Rayatz—hence demonstrating that it is not significant only to the *Nasi* of *Yisrael*—he was precise in giving over the detail that the Rebbe *nishmaso eden* was a four or five year old child, it is understood that the matters in this story apply to every Jewish child under the age of six, since according to *Toras Emes* it is catagorized on the same level of *chinuch*.

In publicizing this story, the Rebbe wanted to teach a certain instruction for the *chinuch* of a small child in the literal sense. From this it is understood that this story has an important *chiddush* about the way children should be educated. It is not simply an instruction for one's *avodas* Hashem, as will be explained.

The words of the *Rambam* are well-known regarding the method to be used in teaching a small child. He says that a child should be encouraged [using] בדברים שהם אהובים אצלו לקטנות שניו... קרא ואתן לך אגוזים ("things that are most dear to him in his young age ... 'read and I will give you nuts'"), since his young age and underdeveloped intellect do not understand the virtue of the goodness involved in learning.

We are expecting a small child to be remorseful to the point of tears over the lack of Hashem's revelation to him, and not over material treats. This is to say, we need to educate a child in such a way that G-dliness will be a significant factor in his life- דברים שהם אהובים אצלו ("things that are most dear to him"), to the point that the lack of Hashem's revelation to him the way He was revealed to Avraham will deeply affect his soul.

Had this event not occurred with the Rebbe *nishmaso eden*, it would not be possible to know if one can bring a Jewish child to such a feeling, for by nature he is drawn to material things, as the *Rambam* writes above, and he needs to be educated with the aid of things that "are beloved by him".

However after this event occurred, and especially after it was publicized by my father-in-law, the Rebbe, and printed, it is clear that a new channel, and a new path in *chinuch*, has been revealed and opened, such that in our time it is possible through correct *chinuch* to break through the limitations of a Jewish child's nature and accustom him to desire *ruchniyus*, to the point that this great desire for Hashem to reveal Himself to him will be permeated deeply into his heart.

When a Jewish child is not remorseful over the lack of Hashem's being revealed to him, this is because his educator is not speaking to him about this matter sincerely enough with words that come from the heart, and it is not due to the limitations of the child.

The sensitivity of the Rebbe Rashab as a child

Once[820], when the Rebbe Rashab was about four years old, a tailor delivered a garment he had sewn for Rebbetzin Rivkah. While the others were examining the tailor's work, the young Rebbe Rashab innocently pulled out a leftover fabric scrap from the tailor's pocket. The tailor became embarrassed and

820 *Likkutei Sichos,* vol. 15, pp. 134-136.

apologized that he had forgotten to return this leftover piece of material to Rebbetzin Rivkah.

When the tailor left, his mother, the Rebbetzin, reprimanded him that he had caused the tailor embarrassment. Hearing this, the child started to cry very bitterly.

A few weeks later, the Rebbe Rashab entered the office of his father, the Rebbe Rashab, and asked how one could correct the sin of embarrassing another person. His father asked him why he was asking about this, and the child responded that he simply wished to know, without telling his father what had happened. When his mother asked why he didn't want to tell his father the whole story he responded, "It's enough that I embarrassed someone; should I now go and say *lashon hara*?"

At first glance, no serious embarrassment was involved in this incident, because, as is told, the Rebbe *nishmaso eden* took out the garment "innocently," by accident. In addition, this was not done publicly – only his mother, the Rebbetzin, was there at the time. Despite this, when he heard that the tailor had been embarrassed, the child cared so much that it brought him to the point of shedding bitter tears.

That is to say, he didn't care so much that the embarrassment occurred through him, and that he would be punished; rather, he cared about the essence of the matter: that he had caused a Jew embarrassment.

Therefore, he did not tell the story to his father, despite the fact that his not responding to his father's question could have been considered a possible violation of *kibbud av* and the like. The only purpose of relating the story would have been to correct the sin, [but he could not bring himself to do it because] he could not tolerate retelling information about another *Yid* that was not positive.

Since the story is told to us with an emphasis on the Rebbe's having been four years old at the time, this is proof that it is now possible to raise every Jewish child of that age in the same way.

Mishnayos be'al peh for *gemilus chassadim*

The[821] following story occurred in the year 5651, when my father-in-law, the Rebbe, was eleven years old.

My father-in-law, the Rebbe, relates that at that time he had a fund for *gemilus chassadim*. When he would recite *mishnayos* by heart, he would receive money from his father. In this way he earned thirty rubles, which was a considerable amount of money even for an adult in those days. With this money, he would do acts of *chessed*. He performed the *chessed* with a warm countenance, which is the highest form of *gemilus chassadim*, so as not to embarrass the borrower *chas ve'shalom*. His pleasant and kind manner was expressed in the way he would seek out the *Yid* who needed a loan in order to do an act of kindness.

From this we can learn several lessons about the way to educate Jewish children.

Due to the *chinuch* of my father-in-law, the Rebbe, he was accustomed to make use of his free time by memorizing *mishnayos*, to the point where he knew two *sidrei mishnayos* by the age at eleven, which tells us that he started his memorization long before the age of eleven.

In addition, because of his *chinuch,* when he would acquire money through reciting *mishnayos* by heart, he understood on his own that he needed to do acts of kindness with the money, and he did so of his own good will.

From this we can derive a lesson for each and every person of *Yisrael* as to how he must raise his children.

In the continuation of the story about his involvement in *gemilus chassadim*, my father-in-law, the Rebbe, related his *mesirus nefesh* for the good of another. When he saw an officer hitting a Jew, he jumped on the officer, screamed at him, pushed him, and so forth.

The great intimidation that a Jew experienced in the presence of a police officer in Russia in those days is well-known. It was so great that when a Jew saw an officer at the end of the street, he would try to cross to the other side in order to avoid coming into contact with him. He knew that the officer

---

821 *Sichos Kodesh* 5741, vol. 4, p. 144.

might harass him for no reason whatsoever, so it was worthwhile to keep a distance from him.

Despite this, when my father-in-law, the Rebbe, was just eleven years old and he saw an officer hitting a Jew, he placed himself in danger for the good of another person by jumping on the officer, pushing him, and so forth. ...

Thus we see that when a Jewish child is taught to become involved in *gemilus chassadim*, his acts of kindness connect him with the other person, and this arouses within him the *mesirus nefesh* for the other person.

Since the *Baal Hageulah* (the Frierdiker Rebbe) told and publicized this story, we understand that this is a lesson for every father and mother: It is within their reach to give their child the same kind of *chinuch* as the [Frierdiker] Rebbe described in the story.

The difference between a *Yid* and a calf

My[822] father-in-law, the [Freirdiker] Rebbe was once in the market and saw a police officer hitting a *Yid.* Even though he was very young, before the age of *bar mitzvah*, without hesitation he screamed at the officer and pushed him in order to save the *Yid.* The furious officer arrested him and locked him up in a dark jail cell. The [Frierdiker] Rebbe suddenly heard groaning from the corner of the room and was alarmed. He immediately remembered that Hashem protects every *Yid*, and that he would now need to make proper use of his time in order to show that, even while in a dark jail cell, he acted like a Jewish child. Right away, he began to recite *mishnayos* that he knew by heart.

After a short while, the [Frierdiker] Rebbe was released from jail. At that point, it became known that the officer had stolen a calf from the *Yid* whom he had been beating when the young [Frierdiker] Rebbe jumped upon him in an effort to intervene. Moreover, the officer had falsely accused the *Yid* of stealing the calf, yet it was he himself who had hidden it in the jail cell, in the same dark room where the [Frierdiker] Rebbe had been incarcerated.

When the [Frierdiker] Rebbe returned home he told his father, the Rebbe Rashab, the entire story... His father praised him, saying that in his reciting

822 *Sichos Kodesh* 5741, vol. 4, p. 2.

mishnayos be'al peh in the jail cell with the calf, he had made apparent the difference between him and the calf: He had shown that he was a *Yid* who was connected with *Hakadosh Baruch Hu* through His Torah.

From this story, we can learn many instructions. A Jewish child needs to make efforts to learn Torah *be'al peh, pesukim, mishnayos,* and so forth, in order that in every place and in every situation it will be possible for him to be involved in Torah, even when the *sefer* is not within reach.

This conduct shows that the child is a true *Yiddishe* child and demonstrates the difference between him and the rest of the children in the world.

Even in the darkness of *galus*, like the jail cell, and even when confronted with the persecution of officers and the like, there is no need to be alarmed. A *Yid* should stand strong and take advantage of his time to learn Torah, from a *sefer* or *be'al peh.*

One must always hear the cry of a child

The Mitteler Rebbe, Rabbi Dov Ber, lived in the home of his father, the Alter Rebbe. The Mitteler Rebbe excelled in his ability to concentrate deeply, *bedveikus*, like no one else. While he was learning or *davening,* he had no awareness of anything going on around him.

One time when the Mitteler Rebbe was engrossed in his learning, the baby, who was in the corner of the same room, fell from his crib and burst into tears. The Mitteler Rebbe did not notice. His father, the Alter Rebbe—even though his room was on the top floor, and he too was immersed in his learning at the time—heard the cry of the child. He stopped his learning, went downstairs, entered the room of his son, picked up the baby, cared for him, calmed him, and returned him to his crib. He did not leave his place until he saw his baby grandson at peace. The Mitteler Rebbe never did notice his father or his son at all. Afterwards, and at an appropriate time, the Alter Rebbe rebuked his son, explaining to him that it is not the correct path to be so immersed in learning and so forth, to the extent that he does not hear the cry of a child.

This story has been passed down from generation to generation, and has been passed down to us from my father-in-law, the Rebbe, the *Nasi* of our generation. Surely it contains many practical instructions for our generation and for all of *Klal Yisrael.*

One of the instructions is that a person should not be so immersed in any matter – even the most lofty – to the point that he will not hear the cry of a child near him, in his surroundings, or even at a distance. The cry of a child needs to touch each and every person to the extent that they will stop what they are doing, take care of the crying child, and do everything possible to give the child what he is lacking.

In our time especially, there are many babies and children who for whatever reason "fell from the crib" and have become disconnected from "the crib" of true *Yiddishkeit*, or were never involved to begin with – and they are crying. They are crying either with a cry that can be heard, or else with an internal cry that is not heard, a cry that emanates from the depths of their souls, and each soul is a חלק אלוקה ממעל ממש ("a portion of *Hakadosh Baruch Hu*, literally"). They are hungry and thirsty for the words of Hashem and His Torah and *mitzvos*. There isn't anyone to care for them and fulfill their lack of a pure and holy *chinuch*.

So too, many of our Jewish brothers and sisters are grown in years, but small, or even babies, when it comes to the Torah which is our life, and the fulfillment of its *mitzvos*. Even if they do not see or notice, their *mazal* sees, and [causes them to] cry from the depths of their souls. Sometimes they don't recognize it. Sometimes they only feel the awful emptiness in their lives, a life without the meaning and purpose that it deserves.

It is forbidden to turn a deaf ear to the cry of these children of *Yisrael*, whether they are young in age or "children" in knowledge of Torah and *mitzvos*. Regarding each one, we have the instruction, command, and directive: Stop everything you are doing and care for this child. Return the child to his father, our Merciful Father, to learn the Torah of our Father and fulfill His *mitzvos*. The child will then live a true life, a full and good life.

Breaking the *kelipos* of our time

There[823] is a story that my father-in-law, the Rebbe, told (and it was later printed) about the Alter Rebbe, the *Baal haTanya*, who called in his grandson (son of the Mitteler Rebbe) for a conversation immediately after his wedding.

---

823 *Hisvaaduyos* 5715, vol. 1, pp. 244-245.

(In those times, it was customary to make weddings at a young age, shortly after the *chasson*'s *bar mitzvah.*) He had new clothes that he had received in honor of his wedding, including a fur winter jacket that was made partially of leather. This was considered a very nice garment in those times, and it was expensive as well. [The Alter Rebbe] told his grandson that if he would rip the main part which made the garment beautiful, then he promised him אתי עמי במחיצתי (he would be with him in *Olam Haba*).

The grandson asked him if he needed to do this sincerely, or whether it would be sufficient to do so only because his grandfather, the Alter Rebbe, had commanded him to do this. It seems that the young man had not yet reached the spiritual level of tearing the jacket based on his own wish to do so, and therefore the jacket remained as it was, intact.

Afterwards, at the end of his life, the grandson settled for a few years in Haditch, where the *Ohel* of the Alter Rebbe was located, in order to atone for the fact that to begin with he hadn't had the strength within him to rip the "קאטינקע".

When my-father-in-law told this story, he added an explanation for the reason that this matter was so important that for ripping the garment the Alter Rebbe had promised that the grandson would be with him in *Olam Haba,* which is one of the greatest promises and gifts that a Rebbe can give.

The explanation is that in the region where the Alter Rebbe lived, it was becoming customary for *Yidden* to adorn themselves in garments similar to those of the nations of the world.

When the Alter Rebbe saw that this was a new *kelipah* of a *taivah* (lust), and this lust was now standing at its very peek, he decided that it needed to be broken and nullified at its beginning, before it could increase and spread.

The breaking of a *taivah* has to be done by those who have a connection to the *taivah*. This is most applicable to those of a young age, especially right after marriage when there is a desire to אויספּיינען זיך, outfit oneself with fine clothing... and according to Torah, there is a place for the matter of jewelry and the like.

Since this was a matter of breaking a *taivah* when it is at its strength... the Rebbe was willing to promise his grandson a place with him in *Olam Haba*!

From this we understand that when we see that at a certain place or time there is a powerful trend toward a matter that is not according to Torah, if one causes a breaking away from and evasion of the matter, this can have a powerful impact on it for years to come.

In regard to this country, one of the matters that is not as it should be is that before a child even knows how to read and write... his parents already begin to think about and worry about the child's future career. They do this by preparing the child according to what is acceptable through the calculations of the physical mind. To them it seems that a significant portion of the child's time needs to be devoted to external matters, secular learning, and conduct in ways that separate him from Torah and ingrain in him "the norms of the world." According to the calculations of the *nefesh habehamis*, especially as she is misguided as a result of her being invested in physical and material matters, it seems that this is *the only way* to ensure that a child will have a career when the time comes, when he will need to stand on his own two feet.

Clearly, according to Torah this has no place, since the *Mishnah* rules that בן עשרים לרדוף ("At twenty years of age one pursues [a livelihood]"), meaning that the time to pursue *parnassah* is "age twenty." In any case, the fitting time to prepare for this needs only be a short period beforehand.

When the child begins to speak, he needs to be taught תורה צוה לנו משה מורשה קהלת יעקב. This is an inheritance that is constant without interruption, so it continues for all generations to come until the arrival of *Moshiach*. Even after [the coming of *Moshiach*], the matter of receiving the Torah as an inheritance will continue to exist. After this comes the stage of בן חמש שנים למקרא ("At five years of age to textual learning"), and after this the child proceeds to *Mishnah* and *Gemara*.

Despite this, the custom in this country is that from the most tender age a significant portion of school hours is deducted from *limmudei kodesh*. From that point on, this attitude toward the predominance of secular subjects becomes habitual for the boy or girl. Nevertheless, even when they mature and begin to understand and think about *parnassah,* the fact remains, as it states in the *Gemara,* אין אדם יודע במה משתכר ("a person does not know from where he will gain sustenance"). More than this, as the Alter Rebbe emphasizes, the matter of *parnassah* is mentioned in the *Gemara* as one of the seven things a person does not know for certain, together with the time of the coming of *Moshiach*... both with the same amount of concealment... We can have no certain knowledge of these, and there is no possibility to make calculations.

From this approach, we understand that there is no place for starting to prepare for a career from childhood through secular learning. It is clear that this time is being stolen from *limmudei kodesh*, about which is said כי הם חיינו ואורך ימינו, ("They are our life and the length of our days"). There is great doubt as to whether there is any gain from this at all...

Thus we understand that if it is possible to break the *kelipos* connected to this matter, specifically in this country where people are so invested in this area—in a way that is utterly incomparable to protocol in other countries in the past or at present—it would constitute the shattering of a most undesirable matter in its full force and strength.

The Greatest Pidyon Shevuyim

Reb Berl Futerfas relates:

"My father, the Mashpia Reb Mendel, would spend a few weeks every winter fundraising for Russian Jewry. This was a continuation of his work there: to help Yidden begashmius. One year he was also asked to collect funds for Oholei Torah Cheder. Not knowing what to do, he asked the Rebbe in a yechidus, and was encouraged by the Rebbe to fundraise for the cheder as well."

"My father was still troubled. He said to the Rebbe, 'But someone who gave a thousand dollars last year will give the same again, to be split between the two causes. This will mean that it is on the account of pidyon shevuyim (redemption of captives) funds?'

"The Rebbe looked at my father and said, 'Saving children from learning limudei chol is the greatest pidyon shvuyim!'"

(Lma'an Yishmeu, vol. 410)

Torah is acquired through *mesirus nefesh!*

One[824] of the details in the *chinuch* of the Tzemach Tzedek that is accompanied by an anecdote is the story that my father-in-law, the Rebbe, told during one of the days of *Sukkos* thirty years ago, in the year 5696.

By way of introduction to the story, my father-in-law, the Rebbe, described the layout of the Alter Rebbe's house:

There was one particular room where the Alter Rebbe would deliver *Chassidic maamarim*. That room contained a furnace which heated up the room. The furnace was built in such a way that in order to fuel it with firewood, it was not necessary to enter the Alter Rebbe's room (as this would be a disturbance); instead, it was possible to do this from an external room, and the wall between the two was not thick...The wall next to the furnace was not very thick because its purpose was to heat the room on the other side of the wall, and the desire was that most of the heat would enter that room.

In those days, it was customary that not everyone was permitted to enter to hear every *maamar.* There were certain *maamarim* which everyone was allowed to hear, but there were also *maamarim* that were delivered only before select individuals.

The Tzemach Tzedek was then a child of eight years old, and not only did he have the desire to learn *nigleh*; he also wanted to learn every bit of *Chassidus* that was within his ability to learn. This was the case even though the Alter Rebbe began to learn *Chassidus* with him regularly and in a *seder* only in later years.

When the Alter Rebbe would deliver *maamarim* publicly, the door was open, and the boy would enter as well. However, when the Alter Rebbe would deliver *maamarim* to exclusive individuals, according to the instructions of the Alter Rebbe, the Tzemach Tzedek could not enter the room. What did the Tzemach Tzedek do? He crawled inside the furnace in the adjacent room and put his ear to the wall. Because the Alter Rebbe delivered the *maamar* in a loud sing-song voice, the boy was thus able to hear the *maamar,* or at least catch parts of it.

---

824 *Sichos Kodesh* 5726, p. 50 onwards.

Since it was then winter-time and the furnace was large, the non-Jewish servant came to prepare the furnace to be heated. In those days, coal was expensive, so they would heat the furnace with wood which was much cheaper. To the logs they would add small woodchips and pieces of paper, and they would light this kindling material in order to enable the furnace to begin to give heat. However, since the Tzemach Tzedek filled a large portion of the furnace pit, the smoke began to swirl back out.

The servant thought that he had not put in enough fuel and started to push in more wood, but this did not help. He began to remove the logs one by one in order to see what was happening inside – when suddenly he saw that there was a child inside... He pulled the boy out and barely revived him before he *chas ve'shalom* choked from the smoke.

After this, the grandmother, *Rebbetzin* of the Alter Rebbe, approached the Alter Rebbe and complained, "You allow the students to enter into your room; but your grandson who wants to hear the *maamar* needs to hide and risk his life, *Rachmana litzlan*?"

The Alter Rebbe replied, "Torah is acquired through *mesirus nefesh!"*

...The Tzemach Tzedek could have remained in his room during that time and learned Torah on his own. But since he heard that right at that moment his grandfather the Rebbe would be teaching a new Torah that could not be found in any *sefer*, he placed himself in danger. Even as he realized the servant was pushing more wood into the furnace, he did not reveal the fact that he was there, since if people would know this, they would remove him from his hiding place immediately, and then he would not hear the *maamar*. Through his not revealing himself he gained the opportunity to hear yet a few more words, and for this he risked his life.

This type of conduct is not uniquely exclusive to special people like the Tzemach Tzedek, but rather, כך היא דרכה של תורה ("This is the way of Torah"). If one wants to educate the children of *Yisrael* to live Jewish lives according to Torah, it is through training them at the age of seven or eight to have *mesirus nefesh* for additional Torah learning. The purpose of this is not that as a result he will become the *ga'on hador,* and so forth, as an adult. Rather, what hangs in the balance is the entire question of whether the child will grow to be a Jew who lives according to Torah or *chas ve'shalom* the opposite.

CHAPTER 15

Challenges and Solutions

"If a person tells you, 'I have toiled but I have not found,' do not believe him."

Talmud, *Megillah* 6b

Parents should *daven* for their children

In[825] order for one to be truly certain that after ten or twenty years their sons and daughters will be connected to *Yiddishkeit* ... it is necessary for both the mother and the father to request of *Hakadosh Baruch Hu* that despite all of the tests that the children face, they will remain *Yidden*, and good *Yidden*, in their relationships with Hashem, with their parents, and with others.

A *segulah* for children not to go off the derech

I heard from the elder *chassidim* that in their time there was a custom that every day each person would say the *kepital* of *Tehillim* that corresponds to the years of his life [his age]. For example, if a person was 20 years old, he would say *kepital* 21 of *Tehillim*. Similarly, they would say also the *Tehillim* that corresponded to the the age of their sons and daughters, saying that this is a *segulah* that they should not go off to [take part in] a bad culture ["go off the *derech*"].

(*Igros Kodesh of the Freirdiker Rebbe*, vol. 1, *Iggeres* 16)

Hashem grants the ability to overcome all obstacles

In[826] this week's *parshah* and the following *parshiyos,* the holy Torah relates what happened to our patriarchs and matriarchs. Our Sages, of blessed memory, say מעשה אבות סימן לבנים ("The experiences of the patriarchs are a sign [and a lesson] for the children").[827] Naturally, this aphorism also applies to the events in the lives of our matriarchs – Sarah, Rivkah, Rochel, and Leah. The tests they faced and their devotion to establishing generations of faithful Jewish children, sons and daughters of Avraham, Yitzchak, Yaakov, Sarah, Rivkah, Rochel, and Leah – serve as a demonstration and a lesson for all Jewish women, and for the women of our generation in particular.

---

825 *Igros Kodesh*, vol. 3, p. 435.

826 *Igros Kodesh,* vol. 18, pp. 53-54.

827 Cf. *Bereishis,* 12:6, *Ramban*; *Bereishis Rabbah,* 40:6.

The practical lesson is that when difficulties seem to arise, or even mere disruptions, it is certain that these are nothing but *tests* that *Hakadosh Baruch Hu* puts before a *Yid*. He does so in order to elicit within him or her great and even concealed inner powers necessary to overcome these challenges – challenges that Hashem meant to be overcome. In order to accomplish this, all one needs is strong willpower, since *Hakadosh Baruch Hu* has already granted the strength necessary for each and every man and woman to fulfill their role. Of course, fulfilling this role is the greatest possible merit and true good fortune for every person individually, as well as for their families. Hashem will bless them from His full hand, materially and spiritually, in everything that they need.

An increase in observance of one family member benefits entire family

Inasmuch[828] as all members of a Jewish family constitute one body, it is clear that an additional effort by one member of the family in matters of Torah and Mitzvos is of benefit to all the family.

This is particularly true in the case of parents who, in any case, have to set an example of high standards. Needless to say, there is always room for improvement in all matters of Torah and Mitzvos which are infinite, being derived from the infinite. And although these should be observed for their own sake, they are at the same time also the channels and vessels to receive and enjoy G-d's blessings in all needs.

The Rebbe's pilot program: *Tzivos Hashem*

As[829] an educator, you know that children need motivation, but that is only one aspect of the problem. The most important aspect, in my opinion, in this day and age, is the lack of

---

828 Letter of the Rebbe from 3rd of Iyar 5732, reprinted with permission from Chabad.org.

829 Letter of the Rebbe from 26th of *Teves*, 5742, reprinted with permission from Chabad.org and reproduced exactly as in the original letter.

Kabolas Ol [acceptance of the yoke], not only of *Ol Malchus Shomayim* [the yoke of the sovereignty of Heaven], but also general insubmission to authority, including the authority of parents at home and of teachers in school, and the authority of law and order in the street. There remains only the fear of punishment as a deterrent, but that fear has been reduced to a minimum because there has in recent years been what amounts to a breakdown of law enforcement, for reasons which need not be discussed here.

On the other hand, American children have been brought up on the spirit of independence and freedom, and on the glorification of personal prowess and smartness. It has cultivated a sense of cockiness and self-assurance to the extent that one who is bent on mischief or anti-social activity feels that one can outsmart a cop on the beat, and even a judge on the bench; and, in any event, there is little to fear in the way of punishment.

As with every health problem, physical, mental or spiritual, the cure lies not in treating the symptoms, but in attacking the cause, although the former may sometimes be necessary for relief in acute cases.

Since, as mentioned, the root of the problem is the lack of *Kabolas Ol,* I thought long and hard about finding a way of inducing an American child to get used to the idea of subordination to a higher authority, despite all the influence to the contrary—in the school, in the street, and even at home, where parents—not wishing to be bothered by their children—have all too often abdicated their authority, and left it to others to deal with truancy, juvenile delinquency, etc.

I came to the conclusion that there was no other way than trying to effect a basic change in the nature, through a system of discipline and obedience to rules which she/he can be induced to get accustomed to. Moreover, for this method to be effective, it would be necessary that it should be freely and readily accepted without coercion.

The idea itself is, of course, not a novel one. It has already been emphasized by the Rambam in the Introduction to his Commentary on Mishnayot, where he points out that although ideally good things should be done for their own sake *(lishmoh)*, it is necessary to use inducements with young children until they are old enough to know better.

Thus, a "pilot" Tzivos Hashem was instituted. It immediately proved a great success in getting the children to do good things in keeping with the motto V'Ohavto L'Reacho Komocho (Thou shalt love thy neighbor as thyself), coupled with love and obedience to the "Commander-in-Chief" of Tzivos Hashem, namely Hashem Elokei Tzivo'os (the G-d of Hosts).

The Tzivos Hashem Campaign has a further reward, though not widely applicable to Jewish children attending Hebrew schools. This, too, has already been alluded to by our Sages, in their customary succinct way, by saying that a person born with a violent nature should become a (blood-letting) physician, or a *Shochet* [ritual slaughterer], or a *Mohel* [circumciser]—in order to give a positive outlet to his strong natural propensity (T.B. Shabbos 156a). Thus, children that might be inclined to aggressiveness, and hence easy candidates for street gangs, and the like, would have a positive outlet by diverting their energy in the right direction.

This brings us to the point that although the ideal of peace is so prominent in the Torah, as mentioned, the fact is that G-d designed and created the world in a way that leaves man subject to an almost constant inner strife, having to wage relentless battle with the *Yetzer Hora* [evil inclination]. Indeed, the Zohar points out that the Hebrew term for bread—*lechem*—is derived from the same root that denotes "war," symbolizing the concept of the continuous struggle between the base and sublime natures in man, whether he eats his bread as a glutton, in a way an animal eats its food, or on a higher level—to keep the body healthy in order to be able to do what is good and right in accordance with the Will of the Creator.

This is the only kind of "battle" the Tzivos Hashem are called upon to wage. By the same token, the only "secret weapon" they are encouraged to use is strict Shabbos observance and other Mitzvoth which have been the secrets of Jewish strength throughout the ages.

Our experience with Tzivos Hashem—wherever the idea has been implemented, in the U.S.A. and Canada, Eretz Yisroel [Israel], and in many parts of the world—has completely convinced us of its most successful positive results, with no negative side-effects whatever. I can only hope that it would be adopted in other sectors, outside of Lubavitch, in growing numbers.

I trust that the above lines will not only put to rest all your apprehensions concerning Tzivos Hashem, but will also place you in the company of the many prominent educators and spiritual leaders who have enthusiastically acclaimed the Tzivos Hashem operation as uniquely successful in attaining its desirable goal.

Pleasant methods are always more successful

I[830] received your letter in which you write about problems with your eldest son, and [you ask] how you should influence him.

Clearly, there are no fixed rules for dealing with such a situation, since people are different from one another, "their temperaments are not the same"[831], and the characteristics of their souls are not the same. It also depends on how far the situation has gone in the interaction between the two people involved. However, what can be applied to every situation is that דרכי נועם (peaceful methods) are usually more successful than the opposite methods.

---

[830] *Igros Kodesh*, vol. 20, p. 191.

[831] *Sanhedrin,* 38a.

Influence through friends

We[832] see tangibly how it is often possible to exert a greater influence on one's children through friends than is possible through direct influence, even from the closest family members. The friend should speak to the child about the matter once, twice, or multiple times, and with words that emanate from the heart. It should not be recognizable that the friend is acting as the parent's agent.

Influence through others

Regarding[833] what you write about your son and daughter, you surely do not suffice with speaking to them yourself, but you make efforts to bring them to meet with others who may be able to influence them in matters of Torah and *Yiddishkeit.* We see tangibly how very often, children are receptive to influence from others more easily than from their own parents, because other people do not detract from their sense of independence. Another reason is that a non-relative can speak without becoming overly emotional, which can sometimes be destructive, unlike parents and close family, who are not always able to muster that self-control.

In[834] the present day and age, when it is desired to influence children, experience has shown that it is more effective if it comes from friends or acquaintances, rather than directly from parents.

Children are less inclined to accept advice, guidance or suggestions from parents because they think that their parents still consider them immature, or wish to impose their authority on them, etc. Therefore, it would be well that you should find

832 *Igros Kodesh*, vol. 24, p. 201.

833 *Igros Kodesh*, vol. 15, p. 88.

834 Letter of the Rebbe from 3rd of Iyar 5732, reprinted with permission from Chabad.org.

friends that would speak to your son, but of course, they should do so in a way that would not arouse his suspicion that they have been asked by his parents to speak to him.

Parents can influence their children more than they think

In[835] my opinion, you should exercise more of your influence over your sons to strengthen them in Torah and *mitzvos*. ...

Many parents do not properly estimate their influence over their children, and they think that their toil is in vain, so they forfeit much of their ability to influence their children. They are mistaken, because parents can influence their children much more than they estimate. When they make efforts in this area, surely they will have a great impact. Even if their impact is not [to effect a change] one hundred percent, they will certainly have an influence to a great degree.

Keep trying and eventually they will be affected

Regarding[836] your letter in which you write that your daughter is embittered over the fact that her children do not conduct themselves according to the path of *Yiddishkeit*,

Pass on the message to her that bitterness alone does not help, and she must involve herself and influence the situation. She can only do this through using pleasant means, speaking and requesting in a nice way. She should not tire of speaking about it, once, twice, and three times, until finally they are affected. At first they will only be affected a little bit, and later, more and more.

Maintain a strong *bitachon*

I[837] received your request for a *bracha* for your son and for his conduct. At an auspicious time, I will mention him at the *tzion* (gravesite) of my father-in-law, the Rebbe... for *yiras Shamayim* (fear of Heaven) and for proper conduct, and that he build a home in *Yisrael* on the foundations of Torah and *mitzvos*.

---

835 *Igros Kodesh*, vol. 4, p. 344.

836 *Igros Kodesh*, vol. 5, p. 80.

837 *Igros Kodesh*, vol. 10, p. 325.

However, it is self-understood that:

1) Regarding what you write, that you have fulfilled all the advice you received until now, and [it made no difference], in areas such as these it is necessary to take action, and then to take action once again, since each and every time you act, you bring closer the results that you are requesting, especially since your words emanate from the heart.
2) It is necessary for you to maintain complete and strong *bitachon* (trust) in Hashem *Yisborach,* Who works wonders, that ultimately the heart of your son will be transformed to serve Hashem *Yisborach*, since no other way is possible, and Torah promises us[838] that nobody will be left out (from the final redemption). Your strong *bitachon* and service of Hashem *Yisborach* with *simchah* even in this matter, despite the fact that [the *simchah*] is mixed with bitterness, will hasten the change...

Elevate the child

Regarding[839]... [person's name], it would be worthwhile to try to influence him by elevating him. There is a well-known story about one of the great *chassidim* of the Alter Rebbe, of whom it was said that it was difficult for him to commit a sin, regardless which one, because of his [high measure of the] character trait of pride. He would say to himself, "Is it fitting for me, one of the great *chassidim* of such a great Rebbe, to give in to the *yetzer hara,* which would jeopardize my standing among the Jewish people and among the community of *chassidim* in particular?!"

It is unwise to hover over a child's every move

It[840] is unwise, especially in our times, to follow children's every move and to direct them in how they should conduct themselves in every detail, even when the parents are sure that they are one-hundred percent correct [in their instruction].

838 Cf. *II Shmuel,* 14:14. Or, in the vernacular, "no Jew will be left behind."

839 *Igros Kodesh*, vol. 8, p. 310.

840 *Igros Kodesh*, vol. 28, p. 82.

Supporting those who study Torah

The[841] greatest guaranteed assurance (of Divine assistance) for all Jewish parents in need of special help and deliverance for their children is through their support of those who study Torah.

Child prefers to play than to learn

[In[842] response to a woman's question about her younger brother, who preferred to play rather than to learn, especially regarding *limmudei chol.*]

It is quite common and normal for children to prefer games over learning, even when they are older than your brother. Hence, there is no need to be alarmed by this, although there is certainly a need to influence him *be'darkei noam* (in ways of pleasantness). The main thing is to utilize competition and comparison with his peers who are more studious. It is also worthwhile to minimize the hours that he learns *limmudei chol*, if it is not possible to eliminate this study entirely. This is because it is possible that this [reluctance] is a sign that he doesn't want to pursue *limmudei chol*, even if at the moment he doesn't understand the deeper reason behind this, and [eliminating *limmudei chol*] will automatically have a positive effect on his diligence in *limmudei kodesh*.

Child with an abundance of energy/exaggerated demands

...When[843] difficulties arise in the *chinuch* of a child – for example, in the case of a child who has an overabundance of energy and acts wildly – one should not be intimidated or alarmed about this. On the contrary, this *zerizus* (eagerness) and energy should be channeled in a good direction, טוב לשמים ("good for the Heavens," i.e., in his relationship with Hashem) – enabling the child to increase in energy and enthusiasm for Torah study and fulfillment of *mitzvos*, and טוב לבריות ("good for the creations") – enabling him to increase in his energy and enthusiasm for bestowing goodness upon his peers.

Similarly, when a child comes with exaggerated demands or complaints against his teacher or counselor, and the like, he should be told a story –as

841 *Hayom Yom*, 9 Tammuz.

842 *Igros Kodesh*, vol. 10, p. 293.

843 *Hisvaaduyos* 5745, vol. 4, p. 2303.

there is a special advantage in teaching through stories – about the events that transpired from generation to generation with *Bnei Yisrael,* or even with an individual *Yid,* in which we see how even matters that at first seemed undesirable were revealed in the end to have been for the good, to the point that they *thanked* Hashem for this – יודו לה׳ חסדו ונפלאותיו לבני אדם ("they thanked Hashem for His kindness and His wonders with people").[844]

The main point here is that the true, underlying reason for this trait and nature – excessive energy, exaggerated demands, and the like – is that the youngsters are בנים ... לה׳ אלקיכם ("children ... to Hashem your G-d").[845] Nevertheless, one should strive to bring the *nefesh Elokis* and the *yetzer ha'tov* to utilize these energies. This task lies in the hands of the teachers and counselors.

Mischievous behavior

Regarding[846] a child who exhibits mischievous behavior [שובב], this is quite normal, especially for a firstborn son. Hence, there is no reason to be alarmed. As for how to improve that which needs improvement in this area, consult with educators who are experienced with this, and they should instruct you based on their experience.

Child has an aggressive nature

The[847] way to educate children who are born with a tendency toward aggression is to redirect this inclination in a positive way.

Obedience and concentration difficulties

Regarding[848] your son... [of whom you say] that it is difficult for him to be under supervision all day and to follow a set schedule... and you write about treating him with medications: Since this is a new treatment, I hope you will undertake this with the utmost caution. The boy should be checked [by a

---

844 *Tehillim,* 107:8.

845 *Devarim,* 14:1.

846 *Igros Kodesh*, vol. 20, p. 296.

847 Adapted from a letter of the Rebbe from 26th of *Teves*, 5742.

848 *Igros Kodesh*, vol. 17, p. 287.

professional] every few days, and he should be given the minimum dosage, not the maximum.

Dyslexia

Regarding[849] what you write regarding [name], whom you say does not know how to combine letters and so forth:

You should consult with a doctor who specializes in this area. You should investigate whether, as is very often the case when this occurs, the person is developed enough in some areas that when one encourages him to use the skills that he has already developed, then in some cases, the skills that until now have not been sufficiently developed will also develop.

A child who has begun to "go off the *derech*"

[In[850] response to a woman whose son had begun to go off the *derech*, who inquired about the correct way to influence him to return to the good path:]

You should endeavor to engage others to try to influence your son, and it would be even better if some of these people were the same age as your son.

However, the parents' refraining from discussing this matter with him should be done in a manner that cannot be interpreted as approval of his conduct. This message is particularly necessary since they must prevent, as much as is in their power, his behavior from having a negative influence on the other children.

The parents should conduct themselves more in accordance with Hashem's will – i.e., according to *Shulchan Aruch* – and this will increase Hashem's *bracha.*

Know how to answer questions from a secular perspective

[Regarding[851] a son who is living the same life as his father, a life of Torah and *mitzvos*]: One must make efforts to respond to his questions, in order that he will be able to serve Hashem with *simchah* (joy) and liveliness. ...

---

849 *Igros Kodesh*, vol. 16, p. 3.

850 *Shaarei Chinuch,* pp. 162-163.

851 *Likkutei Sichos,* vol. 31, pp. 67-68.

However, there is another son who has no connection to the lifestyle of his father, from "a new period," a generation אשר לא ידע את יוסף ("that did not know Yosef").[852] It is clear that his questions do not come only from a lack of knowledge, but that a way of life according to Torah and *mitzvos* is something new and foreign to him, and not according to his spirit.

Yet the Torah instructs that even this kind of son, since he is "*your* son," it is your responsibility and privilege to respond to his questions and to bring him under the wings of the *Shechina*.

By being involved with all kinds of Jewish sons, we establish *Tzivos Hashem* (the army of Hashem),[853] and we will merit the true and complete redemption with *Moshiach Tzidkeinu* very soon. ...

Sending children away for school

I[854] write regarding [your letter in which you write] that it is difficult to provide a *frum chinuch* for your children in your current place of residence, and so you have two options before you: 1. You and the children live in Gateshead while your husband remains in your current location, where he earns *parnassah*. 2. The two older children are sent to learn in Gateshead, even though this will be difficult for them at their relatively tender age.

My opinion is inclined to going with the second option, because it is not a [desirable] way of life for the husband to be in one place and the wife and children in another. However, for the children to travel to a place where they will receive a good *chinuch* is a very common practice, and especially in recent years. Surely you will be able to find a trustworthy family in Gateshead to supervise the children as much as is necessary. Although at first they will miss home, the Torah says הוי גולה למקום תורה ("Exile yourself to a place of Torah"),[855] and especially in our generation, when [Torah study] is not merely a matter of knowing Torah, but also of directing one's [future] life in the way of Torah and *mitzvos*.

---

852 *Shemos* 1:6.

853 Cf. ibid. 12:41.

854 *Igros Kodesh*, vol. 10, p. 229.

855 *Avos*, 4:18.

Another reason is that when you are together with your husband, you will surely be able to find ways to influence your environment in order to make it more *frum*.

Child who is spoiled and lacking motivation

... I[856] stated that in my opinion, [the son] should not be sent away from home, since in another location, there will certainly not be the same quality of supervision over him as is possible at home. However, along with this, in order to prevent him from being overindulged at home and – which is of primary importance – to strengthen his motivation, it would be a good idea to find him, in addition to his learning, a position of communal activity where he will be a leader, such as with a group of children younger than himself, whom he will teach *limmudei kodesh* and the like. We see tangibly that success in this area contributes vigor and independence to a young person. When his parents supervise his involvement in this from nearby, from time to time they will surely also be able to find ways to add to his role in a manner that will develop him further and further.

Lack of passion in learning

[I[857] am writing] in response to your letter, in which you write that you do not feel a passion and an inner desire in your studies, and so forth.

I wrote previously about this to some of your peers, and I added that all of the *yeshivah* students are included in that letter, [pointing out that] our holy Torah, *Toras Chayim,* rules that יגעתי ולא מצאתי, אל תאמין ("If someone says, 'I have worked hard, but I have not been successful,' don't believe him").[858] Hence, it is in your hands to endeavor with diligence, to internalize your learning and to establish a fixed time to learn. This means keeping to the times and *seder* of learning, being involved in Hashem's Torah, Torah *temimah,* with true devotion and without external thoughts, calculations [about one's future *parnassah*], and the like. [If you do so,] you are assured that you will succeed.

---

856 *Igros Kodesh*, vol. 19, p. 373.

857 *Igros Kodesh*, vol. 10, p. 17.

858 *Megillah,* 6b.

You need only purify "the vessel" for receiving the Torah, which is the body, and especially [by refining your] thought and speech.

Therefore, it is necessary to be careful with *tevilas Ezra* [the custom to go to the *mikvah* every morning], to be careful in the *mitzvah* of *ahavas Yisrael* to a very great degree, to conduct yourselves with good *middos* in general, and to be involved with *pnimiyus haTorah* (the Torah's inner, mystical dimension), which is the *neshamah* and *chayus* (vitality) of Torah. Through such efforts, the *chayus* in *nigleh de'Torah* (the Torah's "revealed," *halachic* dimension) is revealed as well. ...

Child dating a non-Jew

In[859] response to your letter in which you write about your son who has a relationship with a non-Jew...

You add in your letter that you don't know what you did to deserve this, and so forth. Many situations such as this are a result of the mother's not keeping *taharas hamishpachah* (*mikvah, hefsek taharah,* and the like) properly when this child was conceived. If this is the case in your situation *chas ve'shalom*, in order to correct the matter to a certain extent, you need to make sure to influence other Jewish women to keep the laws of *taharas hamishpachah*. When you influence at least two or three women, it will be an atonement to a certain extent for what was said above.

The power of *teshuva*

Despite[860] the fact that the following is not pleasant to write, I find it is my obligation not to ignore this. Many times, situations like these occur with children as a result of the parents' not properly keeping the laws of *taharas hamishpachah* when the child was conceived. If in this situation this was the case *chas ve'shalom*, it is self-understood that when one wants to undo this event, one needs to first correct that which caused the event. Even though seemingly this is something of the past, the instruction of our Torah is known, that nothing stands in the way of *teshuvah*. Also regarding [*teshuvah*], Torah

---

859 *Igros Kodesh*, vol. 17, p. 49-50.

860 *Igros Kodesh*, vol. 16, p. 261.

provides advice that the *teshuvah* needs to be greater, it needs to be twofold: the parents themselves from now on should keep the laws of *taharas hamishpachah* strictly, and they should influence others, as much as they are able, to keep *taharas hamishpachah*. Then it will be according to the well-known words of the *Midrash*, "You saved a soul..." And when Hashem *Yisborach* sees that through you many children were saved (because their parents kept *taharas hamishpachah*), this will heal all of the consequences to your own children.

CHAPTER 16

The Importance of Involvement in *Chinuch*

"And you shall teach them to your children, and you shall speak of them when you sit in your house and when you go on the way; when you lie down and when you rise."

Devarim, 11:19

In a time of crisis

We[861] are living … in a period of crisis, particularly in regard to traditional *chinuch* and especially *Chassidishe chinuch.* Every moment in which we can save the character of the young generation is precious.

In this state of emergency, work on *chinuch* that will bear immediate fruit takes priority over work which will not bear fruit until a later point in time, because in the meantime we are losing (*chas ve'shalom*) tens and maybe even hundreds of Jewish youth.

From this standpoint, it surely follows that all the means and energy that we can muster should be prioritized to focus with the maximum effort on immediate *chinuch* … and mainly to allow the *chinuch mosdos* to be able to absorb a greater number of young students.

Self-evaluation

I[862] call upon and request of each and every member of *Anash*, and especially the young, to evaluate him/herself as to whether he/she is able to [be involved in] the *chinuch* of *bnei* and *bnos Yisrael.* Since a person is biased regarding him/herself and can make a mistake in his/her own judgment of this, he/she should seek the advice of experts in this field.

Hastens the *geulah*

The[863] rectification for the destruction of the *Beis Hamikdash* and the *galus* is accomplished by being involved, and intensively so, with teaching [Torah to] Jewish children both in *Eretz Yisrael* and in the Diaspora, … and with all types of Jewish children, including those currently enrolled in public schools. They especially need a Jewish, Torah *chinuch.*

---

861 *Likkutei Sichos*, vol. 22, p. 340.

862 *Igros Kodesh*, vol. 17, p. 174.

863 *Hisvaaduyos* 5750, vol. 4, p. 232.

Chinuch is Heavenly work

It[864] is known that work in *chinuch* is מלאכת שמים ("Heavenly work"). ושננתם לבניך ("And you shall teach them [the *mitzvos*] thoroughly to your children")[865] is one of the foundations of the existence of *Bnei Yisrael*.

Educating Hashem's dear children

It[866] would be preferable [for you to work] in the field of *chinuch*... It is a good and holy task to educate the children of *Yisrael*. Of each *Yid* it is said, בנים אתם לה' אלוקיכם ("You are children to Hashem your G-d").[867] Even more precisely, we can point to the well-known saying of the Baal Shem Tov that the love of Hashem toward every *Yid* is incomparably greater than the love of elderly parents to whom their only child is born in their old age.

Spiritual *pru u'rvu*

...[The[868] *mitzvah* of] פרו ורבו ("Be fruitful and multiply") also applies in the spiritual sense. Thus, it applies even to those unable to bear physical children through natural means, on account of their advanced age. As our Sages teach, כל המלמד בן חבירו תורה מעלה עליו הכתוב כאילו ילדו ("Every one who teaches Torah to his fellow's child is considered as though he gave birth to him"). [869]

The Baal Shem Tov's example

The[870] Baal Shem Tov introduced a new relationship between Jew and Jew, based on the inner meaning of "Have we not all one father" (As interpreted by the Alter Rebbe). By the example of his own dedicated word, he showed us what should be our attitude and approach to our fellow Jews. For, the Baal Shem

864 *Likkutei Sichos*, vol. 28, p. 346.
865 *Devarim*, 11:19.
866 *Likkutei Sichos*, vol. 22, p. 366.
867 *Devarim*, 14:1.
868 *Hisvaaduyos* 5742, vol. 4, p. 2292.
869 *Sanhedrin*, 19b.
870 *Letters from the Rebbe*, vol. 6, p. 20.

Tov began his work as an assistant "Melamed", taking tender care of little children, and teaching them the Shema, Berachos, and so on. At the same time he revealed to the mature minds some of the profoundest teachings of the Inner Torah, the Kabbala and the true way to serve Hashem with heart and mind together, a profound philosophy which founds its systematic expression and exposition in Chabad.

Nowadays... it is the duty and privilege of every Jew to help educate Jewish children; "children" in the literal sense, in age; and "children" in knowledge in Yiddishkeit. In a true sense, a man's education is not confined to the school-bench; it should continue throughout his life; getting wiser and better every day. One must be a student and teacher at the same time, and in both cases success depends on mutual affection, on true Ahavas Yisroel.

The Baal Shem Tov's devotion to the *chinuch* of small children

Before[871] the Baal Shem Tov revealed himself, he was an assistant to a *melamed* [teacher] of small children. He would take them to and from *cheder*, and he would recite with them אמן יהא שמי רבא *("Amen, y'hei shmei rabba")*, and so on. ...

The Baal Shem Tov could have spent all his time occupied with the loftiest of matters, yet instead he was involved with children. This surely prevented him from being involved with more lofty matters, as is known that when a *pnimi* (a person of depth and profundity) does something, he is entirely immersed in that with which he is involved.[872] This is especially true when speaking of the *chinuch* of children, for children can sense whether we are truly focused upon them, or whether while we are with them we are preoccupied with other matters.

871 *Likkutei Sichos*, vol. 8, p. 251.

872 *Toras Sholom*, p. 39 ff.

Teaching Hashem's Torah

During one of the farbrengens of 5718 (1958), the Rebbe announced that all those who were involved in *chinuch* should say *lechaim*. Reb Elya Chayim Roitblat, the founding *melamed* of Oholei Torah Cheder, was also present at the *farbrengen*, but he did not say *lechaim*. Even as others encouraged him to do so, he refused, saying that he had his reasons.

The Rebbe noticed that Reb Elya Chaim had not said *lechaim*, and turned to him: "When a *rosh yeshiva* says a *pilpul*, there is reason to doubt the accuracy of the *pilpul*. We could therefore never be sure that he is actually teaching the true Torah of Hashem. But when one teaches a child '*Kometz-Alef-OH*,' we could be certain that he is indeed teaching Hashem's Torah.

"Therefore," the Rebbe concluded with a smile, "say *lechaim*!"

(Lmaan Yishmeu, issue 321)– Reprinted with permission from Merkaz Anash

The Tzemach Tzedek tested students

The[873] Tzemach Tzedek had a custom that once a month he would test the students in the *cheder* where the Rebbe Maharash, who was seven years old, was learning. After testing them, he would give them money as a gift. He could have relied on a *shaliach* to do this for him, and to send him the results, yet each month he did this himself.

It is known how precious the time of the Tzemach Tzedek was, as he was involved in communal work for *Klal Yisrael* and matters that could not be taken care of by others. He was a giant among the giants of Torah in his generation, and he was the leader of his generation. Still, he would detach himself from his own learning and work in order to personally fulfill ושננתם לבניך ("And you shall teach them thoroughly to your children").

The fact that these stories have been repeated to us is a sign that they contain an instruction for every one of us. We learn to what extent we need to have *mesirus nefesh* for *chinuch al taharas hakodesh*. This activity is vital even

873 *Sichos Kodesh* 5726, p. 88, *Likkutei Sichos*, vol. 11, p. 197.

when it is difficult and involves detaching oneself from one's personal learning and other matters; as important as they are, *chinuch al taharas hakodesh* is even more important.

The Frierdiker Rebbe risked his life for the *chinuch* of children

The[874] *Baal HaGeulah* [the Frierdiker Rebbe] displayed self-sacrifice for the education of little Jewish children and for the youth. He toiled to establish and maintain educational institutions for them, *chadarim* and *yeshivos*, even though it was this activity that provoked the anger of the hostile [Soviet] regime and was one of the main reasons for his imprisonment.

What is striking is the way in which he devoted himself to the *chinuch* of children and youth. He did this knowing that in so doing he was endangering his own life and by extension, all his work to support *shuls, mikvahs,* and all the other services vital for adult Jews, which also depended upon him.

This shows the degree of importance he placed on the *chinuch* of children and youth, both for themselves and for our entire nation, for the future of the Jewish people depends upon them.

The Frierdiker Rebbe's *mesirus nefesh* for a kosher *chinuch*

My[875] father-in-law, the Rebbe, had *mesirus nefesh* for kosher *chinuch* and strengthening *Yiddishkeit* even in the most "simple" areas, even though he could have used his time to study the deepest secrets of Torah.

This is a lesson for us all, since a person can be tricked by the *yetzer,* which sometimes comes disguised as a *tzaddik tomim* [righteous, pure person] and claims, "Why should you be involved in teaching *alef beis* to others and saying *Modeh Ani* [with children]? In these areas your impact is uncertain. At the same time you could be involved in *Toras haChassidus* and thus be connected with the Rebbe, and in this way the learning will without a doubt influence you, since you are a *chossid* and connected to the Rebbe; if so, the learning will certainly affect you."

---

874 *Likkutei Sichos*, vol. 13, p. 248.

875 *Likkutei Sichos*, vol. 11, p. 212.

Chinuch when seemingly there will be no continuation

[I[876] write] in response to your letter... in which you write about your work in the field of *chinuch* of girls *al taharas hakodesh*, and about the bitter situation that there is no continuation of the *chinuch* of the students in your institution. Some of the girls get swept away in the tide [of the surrounding secular culture] and so forth. You question whether it is permissible for you to be involved as an educator in such a situation, since you are taking such responsibility for the students.

It is shocking that you even harbor a doubt about this, since according to your assessment a great number of the students remain in *frum* institutions, and even one Jew is an entire world. This is especially the case since there is no doubt that even those who go out to a foreign institution remain deeply impacted by the years of traditional *chinuch* that they received. This impact affects not only their thinking but also their actions, as we can see with our own eyes. Yet it is also clearly crucial to find ways to impact the students so that they will continue in a *frum* environment, and the greatness of this cannot be overstated.

Teachers should be paid respectfully

[When[877] a *Yid* is blessed with wealth,] it should be given ... to be used to make garments לכבוד ולתפארת ("for honor and for glory")[878] for the *kohanim,* the servants of Hashem, such as a *rav, rosh yeshiva, melamed, shochet,* and the like. They should be given not only according to what they need, but also in a manner of לכבוד ולתפארת. The *melamed* simply should not need to plead for a raise in his salary, and how much more so he should not need to make efforts in order to be paid on time!

Even a child who is בן חמש למקרא (five years of age, when a child is brought into the study of *Chumash*) can understand this lesson. Not only that, but he can explain to his parents that Hashem blessed them and gave them an abundance of gold so that they would be able to give to his *melamed* and the like, because when the needs of the *melamed* are provided for in a way of לכבוד ולתפארת, he can devote himself even more to *avodas hakodesh.*

---

876 *Igros Kodesh*, vol. 14, pp. 58-59.

877 *Hisvaaduyos* 5748, vol. 2, p. 456.

878 *Shemos,* 28:2.

Segulah for having children

I[879] received your letter in which you write about your work in providing a *kosher chinuch* as a teacher in a *frum* school... You express your request and desire that Hashem bless you with healthy children. You add that a specialist doctor suggested that you stop your work because you are damaging your health.

In my opinion, since your *avodah* is in drawing close the hearts of children of *Yisrael* to their Father in *Shamayim*, and arouses them to feel that they are children to Hashem *Elokeinu*, it is not worthwhile to stop entirely in order to be blessed with children, since this is a contradiction. Drawing close the Jewish sons and daughters of Hashem *Yisborach* to Him is a *segulah* for giving birth to sons and daughters *begashmiyus*. Therefore, my suggestion is that you should continue your involvement in *chinuch*, but in a way that would not strain your health, as much as this is possible. Surely with proper efforts, you will be able to obtain this type of work near your place of residence, and also improve your working conditions, even if doing so will reduce your income... May Hashem *Yisborach* help you and your husband to have good tidings in the near future in which the requests of your heart are answered in the positive, בזרעא חייא וקיימא (with healthy children).

It is understood that all the above must have a basis in nature, and you and your husband should follow the instructions of doctors specializing in this area.

A person's mind and heart become refined a thousandfold

[The[880] following was written regarding providing a kosher *chinuch* and drawing *Yidden* close to their Father in Heaven:]

The Alter Rebbe—the *Baal haTanya* and author of the *Shulchan Aruch*—writes in the beginning of his *sefer, Torah Or*, that through acts of *tzedakah* one's mind and heart become a thousand times more refined. If this is the truth in reference to physical *tzedakah*, how much more does this apply to spiritual *tzedakah*.

---

879 *Igros Kodesh*, vol. 5, pp. 304-305.

880 *Likkutei Sichos*, vol. 22, p. 368.

CHAPTER 17

Educational Institutions

"Whoever teaches his friend's child Torah is considered as though he gave birth to him."

Sanhedrin, 19b2

Imparting good middos

The[881] most important aspect of *chinuch* is not expressed in acquiring a vast amount of knowledge (good knowledge and so forth). Rather, the main essence of *chinuch* is in relation to [the students'] *middos*. This means that the one being taught should be an *adam* fitting of that title, being good-natured in day-to-day life. Consequently, it is understood that the one being taught makes use of all of his knowledge for righteous, honest, and peaceful purposes.

To say this in other words: First of all, the student needs to be molded to be an *adam* fitting that title, having a good and moral nature. Only afterwards does there come the secondary stage of *chinuch*, acquiring knowledge in order to know how to make use of the abilities and opportunities that he was given in practice [in the first stage].

In the acquisition of the student's knowledge, care must be taken that there won't be the matter of יוסף דעת יוסף מכאוב ("An increase in knowledge brings an increase in [causing others] pain") *chas ve'shalom*, i.e., that he will not utilize his acquired knowledge in a negative manner. Furthermore, even when he is not making any use of these abilities at all [neither for positive or negative], it is also undesirable. The knowledge [that is imparted to the student] is part of the creation of *Hakadosh Baruch Hu*, and if there is part of *Hakadosh Baruch Hu*'s creation which is not utilized, this causes disorder in all of creation.

Therefore, in order that the general matter of "increasing in knowledge" will take place in the appropriate way, it is necessary to preface it with the main aspect of *chinuch*, which is to cause the student to have a good nature. [Having a good nature] expresses itself in conduct in a manner of שלי שלך ושלך שלך ("What's mine is yours and what's yours is yours"). It goes without saying that he does not take something that belongs to his friend and that his general conduct is pleasant and peaceful.

This matter needs to be especially emphasized to educators and the general directors of all *chinuch* institutions: The purpose and goal of *chinuch* is that all male and female students grow to be people who behave in a humane and moral way. To reach this goal, the students are taught information of different

881 *Hisvaaduyos* 5742, vol. 3, p. 1197.

subjects in order that they should be able to [eventually] fulfill their purpose and *shlichus* in this world in the best way possible.

Focus on beauty of *Yiddishkeit* and on *asseh tov*, not *sur me'ra*

The[882] students should always be spoken to about the greatness of Hashem, the greatness of the creation, and the preciousness of man.

There should be more emphasis on the beauty of *Yiddishkeit* and the pleasantness of *mitzvos,* than on criticizing *Olam Hazeh.* This is to say, focus more on *asseh tov*, and not on *sur me'ra.*

Do not be embarrassed by scoffers; *Kabbalas Ol*

There[883] are two foundations that need to be emphasized more in the *chinuch* of American youth, and in the *chinuch* of girls in particular:

1. The first *halacha* of the first section of the *Shulchan Aruch*: "One should not be embarrassed by those people who scoff at one's service of G-d..."
2. *Kabbalas ol*: Obedience to parents and teachers, as well as the yoke of Torah and *mitzvos.*

Fundamental obligation of a teacher

Certainly[884] it is unnecessary to make mention of the fundamental and underlying obligation of each teacher and educator: to immunize children so that they will be able to stand up to the tests of life and the winds that blow in the world without wavering from the path of life, which is the path of our Torah, the Torah of life.

---

882 *Hosafos Le'Sichos Kodesh* 5728, vol. 1 p. 506

883 Ibid.

884 *Igros Kodesh*, vol. 13, pp. 332-333.

... [It is necessary] to implant in the students a deep *emuna* in the Creator and Conductor of the world, and [the knowledge] that He is the essence of goodness and in His great goodness He showed us the way of life which leads to a life of fulfillment. With suitable contemplation of this matter, one will find the correct words to explain this matter in a way that is appropriate for their age and level of understanding.

Find a way to connect all learning to *yiras Shamayim*

The[885] educator should seek out a way to integrate in all of the learning a saying that will arouse *Yiras Shamayim* and conclude regarding the performance of *mitzvos*.

A fund for *gemilus chassadim*

In[886] every school [or in every class], the students should establish a fund for *gemilus chassadim* to which each individual will donate from his own money from time to time.

It is worthwhile for various reasons that each student have his own charity box and give [of his own money] occasionally towards charity (and even better if this is done every weekday morning).

In order to ingrain in the hearts of children to not only be נדיבים בממונם (generous with their money) but also נדיבים בגופם (generous with their actions), the children themselves should manage the fund. The students of the school (or class) should choose a manager, treasurer, and so forth of the fund from among themselves. This will increase the feeling of responsibility of each student (and also the enthusiasm) and connection to *gemilus chassadim*.

The division of jobs (manager, treasurer, bookkeeper, and the like) should change occasionally in order to allow each child (or the majority, at least) the opportunity to volunteer not only their money, but also their time, energy, and capabilities.

---

885 *Igros Kodesh*, vol. 15, p.132.
886 *Likkutei Sichos*, vol. 16, p. 625.

Reveal the child's G-dly soul

...The[887] underlying content [of *chinuch*] should be to reveal in the students their *chelek Eloka mi'maal mamash* in a way that it should penetrate their entire essence. This means that all of their actions, speech, and even thoughts will be permeated with G-dliness. ...

...In all of their affairs there needs to be a common, unchanging point, לא שניתי, that fits with the will of the *neshamah, the chelek Eloka mi'maal mamash.* Although due to their young age this needs to be revealed to them, nevertheless, it is not necessary to create something new; one need only reveal what they already possess. One needs to bring it from a state of concealment to revelation.

...The role of a true educator is to find the right words to explain these matters to children. Even though they are still young and their intellect is not well-developed, the fact remains that they possess a *chelek Eloka mi'maal mamash*, and therefore their conduct needs to be befitting of this. All of their actions need to be permeated with G-dliness, Torah, and its *mitzvos.*

Releasing the student from the coercion of the *yetzer hara*

In[888] truth each and every person to a certain extent, and perhaps even a great degree, is coerced against his will. He does certain things because of the direct or indirect pressures of his environment. Our great teacher (*Rambam, Hilchos Gerushin*, end of chapter 2) phrased it thus: "A person is compelled by his *yetzer hara*, but in reality he wants to be part of *Yisrael* and desires to fulfill all of the *mitzvos* and distance himself from sin." One of the roles of the educator is to release his student and *mushpa* from all external coercion, and especially from the internal coercion of the *yetzer hara* and *nefesh habehamis*, and to connect him internally and externally to the *yetzer hatov*. Only then will the child (whether he is young in years or in knowledge) grow to live a fulfilling life without rifts and wars between the *yetzer hatov* and the *yetzer hara*; or, in the words of *Chassidus*, between the *nefesh haElokis* and the *nefesh habehamis*. Hashem responds measure for measure: through this effort [on

---

887 *Hisvaaduyos* 5745, vol. 4, p. 2301-2302.

888 *Igros Kodesh*, vol. 10, p. 100.

the part of the educator], it becomes easier for the educator to win his own personal battle as well.

Chinuch of children from non-observant homes

It[889] is apparent from the curriculum that the number of hours devoted to *chinuch* is rather limited, yet it is also clear from the general memorandum that it is at the school that the children must receive their essential *chinuch*, since, for various reasons, the home is not, as yet, a very strong factor in *chinuch*, and the street is certainly not conductive to it. These circumstances place a special responsibility on the school, and make it imperative that the curriculum should be used to the fullest advantage and effectiveness.

Consequently, the maximum time and maximum emphasis should be dedicated to the practical aspects of *chinuch* and the deepening of the Jewish faith, so that the children should grow up to be faithful and loyal Jews in the utmost possible degree.

...I would suggest that the curriculum could be improved by allotting more time to the practical aspects of *Yiddishkeit*, in the knowledge and observance of the practical *mitzvos*, imbued with the true spirit of Torah, even if this would mean curtailing other subjects.

In the same vein, with regard to the study of Hebrew, considering the limitations of time, I believe it would be more useful to devote less time to *dikduk*, especially as Hebrew grammar is quite complicated, and more time to the practical knowledge of the language through a better acquaintance with the *nusach* of *Tefillah*, translation of the prayers, the study of *Chumash*, *Nevi'im* etc.

Finally, I would like to be more explicit on a point alluded to earlier, but which is most important and effective in *chinuch* and beneficial influence, namely, to involve the children in actual projects. These can be related every week to the weekly *Sidrah*, and to *Shabbos* in general, such as candle-lighting, *Kiddush*, etc., and to the special days in our *luach*, particularly to the festivals, etc., of timely relevance...

---

889 Letter written to Shaliach in Madrid, dated 15th of Elul 5733.

True *chinuch*: When the one being taught will be able to stand on his own

Chinuch[890] [should be] in a manner of בהעלותך את הנרות ("When you light the lamps"), 'שתהא שלהבת עולה מאלי' ("the flame rises by itself"). True *chinuch* is given in such a fashion that the one being taught is not dependent on the encouragement of the educator to ask him questions and so forth, for each and every step of the way, because he is able to continue on his own, in a manner of 'שלהבת עולה מאלי'.

Making children into leaders

I[891] would lke to know if efforts are being made to train students of the higher grades to be *madrichim* (counselors) and *mechanchim* (educators) to the younger grades. To be sure, my intention in this is not to give them a job or the like, but rather to accustom them to the area of *hadracha* (leadership, guidance) and *chinuch*.

Another great advantage to this is that it motivates them to be more diligent in increasing their knowledge and scrupulous in their good conduct.

There are various ways of bringing this about, such as through the appointment of a *mashgiach* (supervisor) that changes each week. The appointed student serves as the *mashgiach* over his friends in his class, or *madrich* and *mashgiach* during breaks between *shiurim* and so forth.

We[892] see clearly that showing trust in students of the higher grades and elevating them to the level of teacher and *mashpia,* even for a few hours, increases their motivation to be diligent and studious in their learning, and connects them to the institution and its goals and purpose.

...It is understood that not all the students in the higher grades are suitable for this, because in addition to demonstrating good conduct and a sense of responsibility, there needs to be some talent and so forth in this area. ...

---

890 *Hisvaaduyos* 5746, vol. 3, p. 519.

891 *Igros Kodesh*, vol. 11, p. 206.

892 *Igros Kodesh*, vol. 15, p. 371.

Fear of "bad influence" in school

You[893] write that among the students there are girls who are having an undesirable influence over their friends, and there are parents who for this reason are not enrolling their daughters into the school. On the other hand, there is a concern that if these girls are removed from the school, there is the possibility that they may go into a culture that is not good.

It is understood that in such scenarios there cannot be a general rule made applicable to all [the students of bad influence], since one person's nature is not similar to another. Therefore, the teachers who know the girls well should be consulted about each individual girl, and should weigh the pros and cons. In accordance with this, the course of action should be decided. Although in general, the good of the majority takes precedence over the good of an individual, nevertheless oftentimes increasing supervision over students that are of negative influence, improves their conduct in a short period of time. In addition, the increased supervision alone diminishes the fear of harm [of the negative influence].

Another suggestion, when a girl is given a position of responsibility, usually this arouses additional *yiras Shamayim*, good conduct, etc., since she feels that she needs to be a *dugmah chayah* to her friends.

In general, there is no need to be alarmed by the above, since this situation exists in every *chinuch* institution that caters to many students. ...

Contact with parents

Establishing[894] a regular and increasing connection with the mothers of the students in the schools, specifically *Chabad* schools, is most vital. They should be strengthened and encouraged to make the environment in their home a continuation of the environment in the school, and not *chas ve'shalom* a contradiction to this atmosphere, which is an obstacle of untold proportions in the *chinuch* of the students.

... It is necessary to have meetings with them from time to time in order to explain to them the great value of *chinuch* in the spirit of our Torah, *Toras*

893 *Heichal Menachem*, vol. 1, p. 125.

894 *Likkutei Sichos*, p. 398, printed in *Shaarei Chinuch*, p. 239.

Chayim, and to encourage them to ask questions and reveal any deep problems that are troubling their hearts, so that it is possible to solve the problems in a desirable way and remove some of the obstacles in the life of the child and in the lives of the parents.

Maintaining a connection with past students

I[895] was very pleased with what he writes that his wife keeps in touch with her past students. This will surely have a positive effect on the students in many ways. According to what our Sages say, יותר ממה שבעל הבית עושה עם העני העני עושה עם בעל הבית ("the poor person does more for the *baal habayis* (the wealthy man) than the *baal habayis* does for the poor person").[896] Surely this will also benefit his wife, may she live, and her entire home.

The[897] connection between a teacher and past students should be full of enthusiasm, as it was when they were together [in the class]. One should also build on this connection, since in the meantime, the students have matured and their knowledge has increased, so one cannot continue to connect with them as in the past, but should develop the relationship in such a way that is appropriate to the maturity level of the students.

For example: Even when a teacher has taught her students the laws of *kashrus,* the lighting of the *Shabbos* and *Yom Tov* candles, or Family Purity, if she later gains a deeper understanding of these matters, or of their importance, she must impart this deeper understanding to her students, even if the students themselves are already teaching their own classes.

Distribution of prizes

It[898] is very good that a contest was made and prizes distributed. The *psak* of our *Toras Chayim* is known that קנאת סופרים תרבה חכמה ("competition between scholars increases wisdom").

---

895 *Igros Kodesh,* vol. 7, p. 324.

896 *Midrash Rabbah, Rus* 5:9.

897 *Hisvaaduyos* 5749, vol. 3, p. 207.

898 *Igros Kodesh,* vol. 18, p. 225.

I[899] said a few times that the prize for a lottery, or prizes handed out to children, should be *sifrei kodesh* and the like. ...

How is it that it did not occur to even ONE out of ALL of those in charge that a prize connected to a *mivtzah Chabad* and the Alter Rebbe can be... candies etc., but not a soccer ball.

Classroom bullying

In[900] response to a teacher's question on how to avoid undesirable phrases that are heard in the class:

They need to be explained that each and every person from *Bnei Yisrael* is loved by *Hashem Yisborach* even more than parents who give birth to their only child towards their old age. The Baal Shem Tov taught that about *Hashem Yisborach* it is said הנוטע אזן הלא ישמע, אם יוצר עין הלא יביט ("He who implants the ear surely hears, He who formed the eye surely sees"), and when one speaks good about Hashem's son He sees, looks, and listens to the words said, as well as their content and tone. A person would not dare to speak in a negative manner about the son of a king of flesh and blood while in the presence of the king, how much more so must a person be cautious not to insult the King of kings, *Hakadosh Baruch Hu*. Surely it is possible to elaborate and emphasize what was said [above]. What would have even more of an impact is if a slogan would be hung on the wall where the learning takes place with the message: Think about what you say, because there is an Eye that sees and an Ear that hears, etc.

Teacher who keeps Torah and *mitzvos*

Chinuch[901] of children is a matter of life [and the opposite of life]. A teacher who keeps Torah and *mitzvos* and instructs his students in the way of Torah and *mitzvos* brings them life in *Olam Haba* and *Olam Hazeh*. Parents who hand over their child to be taught by a "קרקפתא דלא מנח תפילין" (head that has

---

899 *Tzeirei Aggados Chabad*, p. 134, *Shaarei Chinuch*, p. 238

900 *Igros Kodesh*, vol. 20, p. 142.

901 *Reshimos Choveres* 52, p. 14.

not had *tefillin* placed on it), or an apostate, are spilling the blood of their sons and daughters, G-d forbid.

Best for teachers to be married

In[902] regards to teachers... efforts should be made, as much as possible, that they should fulfill the *Mishnahaic* criteria to be married. Even those that are accepted into the position before they are married should be obligated, and duly motivated after being hired, to marry as soon as possible, especially being that this demand is based on a *psak din* of the *Mishnah*.

Female teacher for female students is preferable

A[903] female teacher should be chosen [for female students] over a male teacher because her *yiras Shamayim* is stronger and her influence will be more recognized by the students.

Tznius of female teachers very important

The[904] mode of dress of female teachers is obviously very important, not only in the higher grades, but even in the lower grades. One must place extensive attention to this matter, especially based on that which is told that in one city in the times of the Tzemach Tzedek, a *shochet* was fired because he wore galoshes. Obviously, this is not because it is prohibited to wear galoshes, but rather because this is an external sign of what is going on internally, and this suffices for the wise.

In[905] regards to choosing (female) teachers, it is foremost necessary to consider that they should not be a negative influence over the (female) students *chas ve'shalom* regarding *yiras Shamayim, Yiddishkeit*, and its *inyanim*. Students are influenced not only by what the teacher says, but even more so by

---

902 *Mikdash Melech*, vol. 3, p. 57.

903 *Hosafos Le'Sichos Kodesh* 5728, p. 1.

904 *Shaarei Chinuch*, p. 284.

905 *Igros Kodesh*, vol. 13, p. 352.

the teachers conduct. Our Sages teach that one must be similar to [an angel] regarding Torah learning, and how much more so in our case.

The teacher-student relationship

The[906] best way for a teacher to succeed in permeating in children a love of Hashem and a love of Torah and *mitzvos* is through the children feeling a special connection with the teacher.

Expelling a child from school

About[907] what you write that a single individual [from amongst the faculty] forced [the administration] to expel a certain student from the *yeshiva Tomchei Temimim*, it is understood that this is alarming; especially to a person that has a correct understanding of Torah and *Chassidus* and its path and customs, and thus understands the meaning of expulsion *chas ve'shalom*, from being attached to the camp of Hashem. Elaborating on this matter is unnecessary and the time being wasted on corresponding on such saddening matters, matters that are obvious on their own, is unfortunate... The time could have been used for matters of an entirely different sort.

What is good for the many

I[908] wrote previously a few times what is of benefit to the public takes precedence over what is good for an individual. From this it is obvious that not every person that wants to be accepted into the *yeshivah* needs to be accepted. This is especially so when it is mentioned in your letter that the potential student learned in a few *yeshivos* and was expelled from all of them because of undisciplined behavior. [Accepting such a student] is the opposite of benefit to the public, and I am shocked that this matter is even being questioned.

---

906 *Igros Kodesh*, vol. 13, p. 424.

907 *Igros Kodesh*, vol. 21, p. 333.

908 *Igros Kodesh*, vol. 14, p. 302.

Rarely is it not possible to influence the student not to be destructive

[Regarding][909] what should be done with a student when there is concern that he may have a bad influence over his friends, if he should be distanced from the *yeshiva*, even though this will be harmful to him:

It is obvious that when there is [potential] harm to an individual versus [potential] harm to the public, prevention of harm to the public precedes. However, in situations in which it is possible to influence the student to no longer be destructive (and only very rarely is this not possible), *bedarchei kiruv* (through ways that draw him close), most of the time the conduct of the student improves. First the student is not destructive towards others, and eventually the student corrects himself.

Do everything possible to keep the student in the fold

Regarding [910] what you write that you have students who are breaking the boundaries [in *Yiddishkeit*], it is known that the good of the public overrides the good of an individual; however, one must [also] do everything in his power to see to it that no individual is pushed away [i.e. stays within the fold]. *Chazal* say that our right arm [the more dominant one] should be dedicated to being *mekarev*. It is therefore my fervent hope that if you talk with them at a *farbrengen*, and also influence them through their friends, they will change their ways…

Supervision during mealtimes

Regarding[911] what you write that the teachers will supervise the students during mealtimes, this is correct and very necessary, as there are *minhagei Yisrael* and also *dinei Yisrael* which are applicable during the time of eating, in addition to the *halachos* of *derech eretz*.

---

909 *Igros Kodesh*, vol. 7, p. 310.

910 *Igros Kodesh*, vol. 10 page 173, Reaching In, Merkaz Anash, p. 15

911 *Igros Kodesh*, vol. 12, p. 66.

Summer "vacation"

There[912] is a sly scheme of the *yetzer hara* that is called "ימי החופש" (vacation days), and to our sorrow and regret it has become acceptable even by some people who are careful to do Hashem's will throughout the year. They say that vacation days are different [and exempt from certain aspects of religiosity], and they don't need to place as much effort [in their service of G-d]. They do not feel that this is the opposite of Torah, which says that man was born to toil, לא יגעת ומצאת אל תאמין ("if someone says,] 'I have not toiled and I have been successful' don't believe him"). ימים יוצרו ולו אחד בהם ("[Hashem] creates days, and to Him they are like one"). This means that not even one day or even one hour is extraneous, as they have been rationed and given no less and also no more than the amount a person needs to fill his inner mission which is, as it says in the *Mishnah,* אני נבארתי לשמש את קוני ("I was created to serve my Maker"). Therefore, every moment that is not taken advantage of... is a loss that does not return. ...

From learning Torah a person cannot be "free"

From[913] learning Torah, a person cannot be "free", G-d forbid. ... On the contrary, אין לך בן חורין אלא מי שעוסק בת"ת ("the only free people are those involved in Talmud Torah")[914]. Furthermore [the verse states], היא חייך ואורך[915] ימיך ("For that is your life and the length of your days"). In the life force of a person, there cannot be a pause even momentarily. ... Just as fish cannot live without water, so too people when they leave Torah and *mitzvos*, they immediately..."

Summer "vacation" should not be "empty" time

On[916] summer days, when many children have an abundance of free time, as the school in which they learned during the winter and beginning of the

---

912 *Igros Kodesh*, vol. 13, p. 302.

913 *Likkutei Sichos*, vol. 8, p. 363.

914 *Pirkei Avos*, 6:42.

915 *Netzavim*, 30:20.

916 *Hisvaaduyos* 5746, vol. 3, p. 618.

spring is closed (for whatever reason), and especially on *Shabbos kodesh* and *erev Shabbos*, the child has a few extra hours free each day. A child should not be left in a state of time that is "empty of substance" (זמן ריק מכל תוכן), even if the child is not aware of it. The truth is that if [his time] doesn't have substance, it is "empty" time (as is emphasized in many places in our Torah, called *Toras chayim*). It is therefore necessary to fill this time with true content.

Even though this is not the school year, when time is filled by being in a *yeshivah* or school and learning through *sefarim*, there are other ways for the time to be filled with true content. In in many aspects it is possible to have even a greater impact on the child. For example:

[A child learns] when externally it seems that the child is being told a story, but the content of the story is a lesson, and even more, of *chassidishe* content.

Another way [to make the time meaningful] is to show a child that his playing can involve toys that emphasize the importance of *tzedakah,* or helping another, etc.

For example, one can play a game of searching for "treasure", which emphasizes how each *Yid* needs to search for the "treasure" hidden within the world and in each *Yid*. The Baal Shem Tov teaches on the *pasuk*, כי תהיו אתם ארץ חפץ- that Hashem tells each and every person of *Yisrael*, and to the whole nation of *Yisrael*, that each one of them is a whole world "ארץ" that has אבנים טובות ומרגליות ("precious stones and pearls") spiritually - the most precious thing that there could be, true preciousness and importance, spiritually and literally. Each *Yid* is given a holy *shlichus* to reveal this "treasure" within himself, and all *Yidden* around him.

When the mind is freed from secular studies

...During[917] "vacation days", it is easier to ingrain in children matters of Torah and *mitzvos* because they have a break from secular studies which confuse them. ... A person's mind and heart become a thousand times more refined.

---

[917] *Likkutei Sichos*, vol. 23, p. 407.

Keeping the school open throughout the year

If[918] the teachers feel it is necessary for health reasons, or other reasons, to have a break for a few weeks, it should be organized in such a way that not all teachers [are off] at the same time, and the school will remain open at all times.

All schools require segregation

I[919] emphasized that my firm request to keep the principle of separation in *Chabad* institutions is not [applicable only] when they are *Chabad* institutions. Rather, my view is clear that this is how it must be in all schools and *chinuch* institutions. In our orphaned generation, this is not only a matter of religiosity, but also a matter of ethics and modesty according to the most simple terms. We see the results in institutions where this principal is not followed. It has become so common that even though efforts are made to conceal these things and avoid unpleasant publicity, despite this, from time to time it gets out and reaches the ears of the public.

"Contagious Disease"

Surely[920], it is not necessary to explain that a majority vote is not relevant when there is a ruling on the matter in *Shulchan Aruch*. It is also not relevant to say that times and conditions have changed, as one of the Thirteen Principles of Faith is that the Torah will not be altered. A change in the ruling can only occur for the sake of making a fence or [making] a greater stringency than the ruling, whenever there is a need. This is then in the realm of עשו סייג לתורה "make a fence for the Torah." Also, regarding this, the deciding factor is the ruling of a Rav and so forth.

If this is said regarding all matters of Torah, how much more so in regard to the suspicion of a lack of separation [between boys and girls], the opposite of *tznius*, etc. It is apparent that if one boy or one girl in the class or group stumbles in this area, it is like a "contagious disease." Since corruption of this sort tends to take place discreetly, the danger is even greater, as it takes some

918 *Igros Kodesh*, vol. 11, p. 293.

919 *Igros Kodesh*, vol. 14, p. 433.

920 *Likkutei Sichos*, vol. 38, p. 177.

time before it becomes known. It is then difficult to piece together what happened, who was involved, and so forth.

Regarding difficulties in the matter, it has been spoken about a number of times that since the Torah was given by the Creator of the world, who rules the world in every place and at all times, including now in our times, surely He gives the strength needed to overcome the obstacles and the concealment. Hashem wanted each and every person of Yisrael to recognize that he is a descendent of a wise nation, and therefore he has been given free will. The desire of the Creator, however, is clear: ובחרת בחיים ("and you shall choose life").

From the above, it is understood that in the matter of separation one must not make any compromises. And regarding what was written that there is a mixed event, but only once every three weeks, I am astounded as to how one can explain to those who take part, that once every three weeks, it is permissible, but more often it is not.

Avoid coeducation no matter the financial cost

The[921] purpose of Chinuch (Jewish education) is to bring up the Jewish child, boy or girl, to a life of the utmost possible degree of perfection, religiously as well as morally and ethically. Coeducation is **not** conductive to the attainment of this end; on the contrary, it is a sure step in the opposite direction. The state of morality of present-day youth is too painful a subject to dwell upon. Even non-Jewish educators have largely come to realize the harmful effects of coeducation. Statistics, by no means complete, since for obvious reasons they are not fully reported or even recorded, reveal the state of moral depravity to which coeducation leads.

It has therefore been one of the cardinal and basic principles of our educational institutions not to permit co-education at all costs, and it grieves me very much to hear that the Yeshivah in ... has not abided by this principle. It has thus taken upon itself the responsibility for a breach in

[921] *Letters from the Rebbe*, vol. 2, p. 44-45.

the fortress of chastity and morality of young children, a terrible mistake which if not quickly rectified is likely to bring to irreparable harm, G-d forbid.

Needless to say, the financial argument that it is more expensive to run separate classes for boys and girls, is no argument at all, since the matter vitally concerns the future of many children. And even if the future of a single child were involved, money could be no consideration, as our Sages say, "He who saves one life is deemed to have saved a whole world."

I am also aware of the argument that other institutions permit coeducation, or that some Rabbinical authorities have not openly objected to it, etc. These arguments are not convincing even to those who offer it, and certainly will be of no avail years hence, when some young man or woman, products of this system, come forward with an accusing finger and soul-stirring cry, "Why did you ruin my life?" Even if this would be an isolated case, there would be no justification or excuse but the chances are that such would not be an isolated case, judging by present-day statistics.

Segregation is equally necessary for non-Jews

... This[922] is not a matter exclusive to the Jewish religion, (although that alone should be more than enough) for in recent years gentiles have also begun to see the harm of mixed schooling. The alarming situation is well-known to the teachers of these schools, but for understandable (though unacceptable) reasons, it is hushed up. In any case, since ultimately the main thing is to correct the situation, [in your case] this matter could be approached differently [in order that those opposing segregation could be pacified]. By increasing the number of students, there will be a need [for a division of classes and] a new teacher, or at least an assistant teacher. It is possible that they [those who are objecting the segregation] may sense that your ultimate goal is for the students to be

922 *Igros Kodesh*, vol. 16, p. 284.

segregated, but because of the above reason [i.e. the need for a division of classes due to the increase of students], they will turn a blind eye.

Segregation should begin from the youngest age

... Anyone[923] with knowledge of education certainly needs no explanation concerning the most serious importance of the segregation [of boys and girls], beginning from the youngest age. For this [segregation] is not only relevant with regard to the obligation of the male and female students to observe *mitzvos*, which is related to the ages of *Bar Mitzvah* and *Bas Mitzvah*. Rather, it is relevant many, many years beforehand, for the habit of the little boy and girl then becomes their nature in the following years, and so on. This is easy to understand.

Draw attention to the separation

In[924] regard to the separation [between boys and girls], if at all possible, it is worthwhile to make one *kinus* for boys and girls at the same time, [with a separation] in order to draw attention to the separation. However, it is simply understood that, if it is not possible to ensure separation [within the one *kinus*], or, if there is even a doubt, especially with regard to singing, then, there will be no other choice, as this is an un-negotiable condition [for having a single *kinus*], and therefore there should be two *kinuses*.

Segregation is an ethical and educational imperative

In[925] reality, segregation is not merely a question of religion, but also an ethical and even an educational one to which the heart readily consents. The staggering devastation caused by co-education is well-known from an ethical and even a basic educational standpoint. The student's attention is distracted from his studies, impinging on his academic progress. ... With the appropriate and persistent explanation, those who have the ability to correct this matter can surely be convinced to do so. ...

---

923 *Igros Kodesh*, vol. 25, p. 2.

924 *Igros Kodesh*, vol. 19, p. 261.

925 *Igros Kodesh*, vol. 17, p. 29.

A man is compared to a tree, and in his childhood he is compared to a soft sapling. Just as even a tiny scratch in a soft sapling can cause a deformation in a large tree, so is it with a child. Thus alacrity is particularly needed in matters of education.

Great caution in gender segregation is praiseworthy

Concerning[926] your question whether to establish a girls school in [the city of] Michnaz, this is certainly proper, and not just in Michnaz, but also in other places. However, one must be particular that they not be together with the boys. This means that not only should the boys and girls not learn in the same classroom, but the school should be built such that each gender enters and leaves from a separate entrance. Furthermore, if possible, it is preferable that the two schools be housed in separate buildings and streets, for the greater the caution in such matters, the more praiseworthy.

Halachos needed for day-to day-life

The[927] vast majority [of people] lack knowledge in the *halachos* needed in everyday life, such as *birkas hanenin*, interruptions in *davening, Muktzeh* on *Shabbos*, etc. To our great regret, and between me and you, the more the Torah knowledge of the *bachur* or *yeshivah* student increases, his knowledge of the above decreases. The *psak Mishnah* is known, that learning is not the main thing, but rather, the action. This is especially [true] regarding actions that occur on a day-to-day basis. Usually there is no time to look in the *sefer* and one must make decisions on the spot. Despite all of this, we don't find that efforts are being made to learn these *halachos*. Not only that efforts are not being made, but it is taken for granted that it is common knowledge and not worthy of study, that this is a part of Torah that is relevant to the ignorant and to women. This is so even though it is known and publicized that one of the first *takanos* of Moshe *Rabeinu* was to learn the *halachos* of a festival during the festival and before the festival for the above reasons. See also the *Shulchan Aruch* of the Alter Rebbe at the beginning of section 429, and in the *halachos* of Talmud Torah at the end of Chapter 1, and in the wording of the Alter Rebbe at the end of *Igeres Hakodesh*.

926 *Igros Kodesh*, vol. 6, p. 33.
927 *Igros Kodesh*, vol. 10, p. 130.

...It[928] is surprising that among the classes there is no class for learning the *halachos* that are necessary in day-to-day life. The lack of knowledge in this area is alarming, despite the fact that knowledge specifically in this area is most necessary. ...

May it be Hashem's will that he will merit his surroundings through the learning said above, beginning with knowledge of the laws, even without the sources and reasons behind it. My intention is in [the studying of] *birkas hanenin* (*brachos* over food), laws of *davening*, *Muktzeh* on *Shabbos* etc. ... If I had the power, I would establish the learning of these subjects in all *chinuch* institutions beginning in kindergarten and concluding in *yeshivos* and *kollel*. To our deep sorrow and regret the common denominator in all the above institutions is the lack of proper attention given to these subjects. Especially as in this generation people do not attain knowledge in the above subjects through seeing the conduct at home and on the street, and on the contrary... this is enough for those who understand.

...The[929] youth of the United States, of all ages and in all grades, need to be taught the *halachos* that are practically needed in everyday life. Furthermore, if only there would be a set learning in these subjects even for the adults... in *birkas hanenin*, *davening*, guarding *Shabbos*, etc. The lack of knowledge in these areas is most alarming, and the non-desirable outcomes from this are visibly apparent. ... It is necessary to inform and to motivate the students that in their free time as well, they should review these laws and increase their learning of them, especially as the *Kitzur Shulchan Aruch* is translated also into the language of the country, the English language.

Davening in *yeshiva*

Regarding[930] your question as to whether students should be forced to come to *daven* specifically at the *yeshiva*:

Understandably, force is not the correct way to go about this. It should be spoken about when an appropriate time presents itself, and in a *farbrengen*.

---

928 *Igros Kodesh*, vol. 10, p. 270.
929 *Igros Kodesh*, vol. 17, p. 210.
930 *Igros Kodesh*, vol. 10, p. 132.

It will be good if it would come not only from the *yeshiva's* faculty, but also from people of *Anash* who are not in the faculty. However, students should not be forced ([to *daven* at the *yeshivah*, by giving consequences], etc. On the contrary, conduct in a way of "the right hand draws near" will be effective, much more than with "the left hand pushes away" [*gevurah*].

The sensitivity of the student

A[931] student is sensitive and responds not only to revealed matters, but also to the inner feelings of the teacher and educator, his mood, his relationship with him, etc.

"I Cannot Sleep at Night..."

During the month of Tishrei 5721, Harav Shmuel Chefer, the dean of Beis Rivka of Kfar Chabad, had a lengthy *yechidus* with the Rebbe. During the *yechidus*, the Rebbe began to discuss the location of the girls' school and seminary. The Rebbe raised his voice and said, "I cannot sleep at night due to the close proximity of the girls' and boys' schools!"

This view was echoed in a letter written to President Shazar (*Igros Kodesh*, vol. 24, page 126), where the Rebbe writes that only due to technical difficulties was the Kfar originally set up as one village. But now that it has been made possible, the educational institutions "should be situated in separate locations, the boys in Kfar Chabad, and the girls in Kfar Chabad II."

The letter continues to say that while the villages should be separate, they should be close enough that the residents may be able to visit each other on *Shabbosos*. The Rebbe's vision was indeed realized, with the completion of Kfar Chabad II in 5735.

(*Lmaan Yishmeu* issue 121) – reprinted with permission of Merkaz Anash

931 *Igros Kodesh*, vol. 23, p. 282.

The right priorities

For[932] various reasons, the vast majority of *yeshivos* in this country learn *limmudei kodesh* and also—*lehavdil ben kodesh le'chol*—secular studies. ...

It is necessary that the child will see very clearly that though both are taught in the *yeshivah,* the learning of our holy Torah, the Torah of life, is most important and that the secular learning is only secondary and not of comparable importance.

Indirectly and sometimes also directly the emphasis is the opposite. This is to say, not only that both are [depicted as being] of equal value, but more importance is given to the secular studies. This extra "importance" is expressed in different ways during the learning - in the careful monitoring of the progress being made, homework, frequent examinations, etc. Success in the tests is praised and glorified with prizes and badges of excellence, etc. All of this is even within the *yeshiva,* and it is unnecessary to add, also at home. In external matters as well - in the form of the textbooks, the way the classroom is decorated, etc. [there is greater emphasis placed in *limmudei chol*]. [Also in] the personal relationship with the *limmudei kodesh* teachers compared to the secular studies teachers [there is greater emphasis placed on the latter]. There is even favoritism expressed towards the secular teachers in certain matters [that relate to the administration], including that they have an increase in salary, etc. [over the teachers of *limmudei kodesh*].

Jewish subjects in the morning

... It[933] has been a basic principle in all institutions founded by my father-in-law of saintly memory, and in others to which his influence extended, to set up a system whereby the sacred Jewish subjects are taught is the morning, and the English department in the afternoon. Apart from the fact that the child's mind is more receptive and retentive in the morning, there is the basic principle of impressing upon the child the

---

932 *Igros Kodesh*, vol. 22, p. 221-222.

933 Letter of the Rebbe from 4th Day of Chanukah 5715 26th, reprinted with permission from Chabad.org.

order of importance of these two departments, namely that the Torah and Jewish way of life come first and foremost. Only in this way could he be brought up to properly appreciate his great Jewish Heritage, and with pride and fortitude face any challenge he may encounter as a Jew.

'Ivris b'Ivris'

It[934] is unnecessary to emphasize how limited, and therefore how precious, the time is during which the child can devote himself to the Jewish studies. This makes it imperative that every moment that the child is at the yeshiva be utilized to the fullest capacity and efficiency, and anything, that causes less of teaching time should have no place in the Yeshiva. Were it only a loss of time which could perhaps be somehow made up at a later age, it would be regrettable enough. Unfortunately, it is more than that, for the loss of this precious time will leave a gap in the child's knowledge and upbringing, not likely ever to be filled.

I refer to the method of 'Ivris b'Ivris,' i.e. using Hebrew as the medium of instruction, and the consequent loss of time and energy.

The method of 'Ivris b'Ivris' has its origin in the anti-religious drive inaugurated by the so-called Haskalah ('Enlightenment') movement, many years ago, which paved the way to mass assimilation. The original ambitions and motivations of this method have long been discredited. Even non-orthodox educators recognize the great loss of time involved in this method, which is prepared to sacrifice the child's time and education for the sake of teaching him a few phrases in Hebrew, or a Hebrew speech, which the child will anyway forget eventually. Yet, blinded by considerations which are certainly

934 Letter of the Rebbe from 4th Day of Chanukah 5715 26th, reprinted with permission from Chabad.org.

not in the interests of the child's Jewish education, some circles still cling to this method.

In[935] regard to learning *Ivris b'Ivris*:[936] It is known just how much the Rebbeim fought against this (despite the "arguments" of the "educators" who supposedly sought the "benefit" of the students, which are the reasons cited in your letter).

It would be better and easier for the candidates for teachers to learn the Yiddish language.

Learning the language is secondary

To[937] the honorable representatives of the parents of the students of the Talmud Torah in Kfar Chabad: ...

I acknowledge the receipt of your letters and their point ... the question about the language of instruction with the students of the Talmud Torah. ...

My opinion is that the main purpose of the Talmud Torah is to educate the students to have fear of Hashem and love for Him, and to teach them the Torah of Hashem and His *mitzvos*, whose "measure is longer than the earth and wider than the ocean."[938] Our Sages have warned us[939] not to interrupt the learning of *tinokos shel beis rabban* (schoolchildren), to the extent that we are even forbidden from doing so for the purpose of building the *Beis Hamikdash*.

Based on this, it is obviously clear that the language used to teach the students is not the main thing, rather the points that were mentioned – the effectiveness [of the language] and increasing in quantity and quality in knowledge of Torah and *mitzvos*.

---

935 Ibid., p. 146.

936 A pedagogical technique of language immersion by which Ivrit is used as the classroom language for all subjects.

937 Ibid., vol. 25, pp. 142-143.

938 *Iyov*, 11:9.

939 *Shabbos*, 119b; *Hilchos Talmud Torah Admur HaZakein* 1:10.

Obviously, in a locale where the language of instruction influences the fear of Heaven and the like, this must be taken into account when determining the language of instruction. …

As for the special qualities of the Yiddish language that you mention, it bears looking into whether acquiring these advantages is the task of the school or the obligation of the parents and the atmosphere in the home.

You[940] write asking what the language of instruction should be for the *bachurim* and *talmidim*.

We need to inform them of Hashem's *mitzvos* and what things we may not do in actual practice, and so, obviously there is no time to wait until they understand a language other than the one they are accustomed to. Therefore you should teach them in the language that they understand now and use the entire time at your disposal to influence them, not by teaching a language, but by imbuing them with a spirit of fear of Heaven, love of Hashem, and love of Torah – and this should be easy to understand.

You[941] write asking whether you should be particular that the [Torah] study with your son be done specifically in Yiddish and not in English.

Both you and your wife know Yiddish, and the number of hours your son spends in school are exceedingly limited, as is the practice in this country. Therefore it would be proper for accustoming your son in speaking in Yiddish and understanding it to be something that you and your wife are involved in. However, in school, until he is used to Yiddish, he should learn in the language in which he is more accustomed, so that he will acquire greater knowledge.

Regarding[942] the question about the language of instruction.

As you describe the situation, our advice is to teach the children entirely in English, and at the same time to make an effort over the course of time for

940 *Igros Kodesh,* vol. 15, p. 84.

941 Ibid., p. 128.

942 Ibid. vol. 21, pp. 38-39.

them to learn Yiddish as well, and then later you can switch the language of instruction to Yiddish. According to your judgment, you can accustom the students to Yiddish, or do it in a way that the review of the studies is done in Yiddish (which will also arouse more interest in review on the part of the students who already know their studies well from the first time). You could also allocate a period to study of the Yiddish language (or you could combine two of these methods).

Dealing with students who arrive late to class

[Regarding[943] how to deal with students arriving late to class:]

This of course depends on the nature of the students; not all are equal in this regard. There are those that come late through no fault of their own, and those who do it by choice, and also those who are somewhere in between.

There are two general points [to be taken into consideration]: Discipline and order must be maintained, and on the other hand, one must make efforts not to distance students from the *yeshivah*. Therefore, under certain circumstances, such as when students live farther away and so on, and the late arrival is unavoidable, a class should be made comprising of those students and the school day should formally begin later for those students.

Varying skill levels

Regarding[944] your predicament that there are students at different skill levels in the class, but that because of the small number of students it is difficult to divide the class:

This problem exists in every *chinuch* institution because it is not possible to equalize the skills of the students in each class. The staff need to find a balance so the classes wont be too small, and the students also won't lose out. It is not possible to set rules in the matter, since this changes from time to time, and also depends on the circumstances of each place.

943 *Igros Kodesh*, vol. 12, p. 238.
944 *Igros Kodesh*, vol. 12, p. 239.

Every institution should appoint an external committee for oversight

Appointing[945] a committee that consists of three members is extremely important for institutions. An institution is responsible not only for an individual, but for multitudes of people. This is especially true regarding institutions dedicated to the teaching of Torah, Judaism, and the like.

As is readily apparent, especially in our times, once the members of the committee have been appointed, and have worked enthusiastically at the outset of their service, their motivation may decline and they may not give their full attention and devotion to carrying out their task in a complete manner. In reality, they should be increasing their activity further. Therefore, it is sometimes necessary for individuals outside the institution [to get involved, for they will bestow] "fear of mortals," and encourage them [to increase their activity].

Therefore, it is most worthy and appropriate for the institutions in every location to designate a committee of three who are *not* part of the institution's management so that they may periodically – and as often as possible – examine whether the institution is fulfilling its role and increasing in holiness; to inspire and demand from them, but in a respectful and pleasant manner, to accomplish more and more.

The more they demand, the better, for when it is apparent that the demand is sincere, given in a pleasant manner, and heartfelt, they inspire the institution's management to increase their activities. As their activities increase, so shall the demand increase, since "He who has one hundred desires two hundred, and he who has two hundred desires four hundred."[946]

Maintaining high standards

In[947] response to some points that you brought in your letter. ...

You write that Chabad institutions place high demands on their students' level of learning, on their conduct, and so on, and some [prospective students] might be afraid to take this yoke upon themselves. There is then a danger that

945 *Sefer Hasichos* 5748, vol. 2, p. 597.

946 *Koheles Rabba,* 1:13.

947 *Likkutei Sichos,* vol. 22, pp. 424-425.

they will leave and instead receive a *chinuch* that is undesirable, or at least not as desirable.

Now you yourself write that lowering the demands [academically and in the conduct of students] will adversely affect the good and average students as well, so the benefits will be outweighed by the losses. However, there is another very important point: Chabad institutions have a special character and reputation for being institutions that maintain a certain standard. This is true regarding Chabad institutions all over the world. This means that lowering the standards in one place will definitely adversely affect other Chabad institutions, and not only in this country, but also in other countries.

[I wish to make] another point based on a story[948] that I heard from my father-in-law, the Rebbe: People's actions have a chain-reaction affect on others. When at a certain stage, the spiritual level falls one step down, this is prone to cause a descent from level to level on all levels below it. Therefore, even if the descent on the first level was from *kadshei kedoshim* (Holy of Holies) to *kodesh* (Holy), this causes an immediate descent on all the other levels from *kodesh* (Holy) to *chol* (mundane), and even lower, from permissible to forbidden. My father-in-law, the Rebbe, explained how each person on his own level should grow in *kedusha,* and he should surely not decline, even if he remains on a higher level than all those around him after the descent. The lesson with regard to the *chinuch* institutions above is understood.

All of the above applies even if this [standard] was not customary for a number of years, and how much more so when this special conduct continued for many years. In such a case, it is not at all worthwhile to lower [the standard]. This is especially true in light of the fact that doing so would likely be interpreted as a statement that times have changed, customs are changing, and therefore expectations [of the younger generation] too [are changing].

This is especially true in *Eretz Hakodesh,* where for various reasons, several worthy *chinuch* institutions are not demanding from students those matters that you mention. Therefore, there is no danger, *chas ve'shalom*, that applicants not accepted into Chabad institutions will be forced to attend entirely different

---

948 Cf. *Sefer Hasichos* 5684, p. 53 ff.

institutions, since they could be accepted into a school whose program doesn't include these particular expectations [but which are still G-d-fearing].

Some time ago, I had a similar discussion [with someone], and I responded to the questioner that here too, there is an explicit instruction from the words of our Sages, of blessed memory, on this matter. As is their way of speaking, the saying is short but straight to the point. The saying is: רב בקעה מצא וגדר בה גדר ("Rav found a wide-open field and built a fence within it").[949] This means that when Rav saw an area [of Torah observance] being treated lightly, he acted stringently and added a fence, creating edicts specifically in this area. This means that when one sees that in a certain group a breach exists in a particular area, and there is seemingly room to fear the above – that if one will be stringent in this area, one will be distancing them in general or pushing them into worse matters – [Torah's] instruction is to do the exact opposite: to urge them and to impose strictures on them specifically in this neglected area. This is easy to understand.

Beautiful facilities for learning institutions

But[950] of course, in order that the message should have a lasting impact, it is not sufficient to give it to them now and then, but they must be provided with the facilities where they could dedicate themselves to the study of the Torah and daily religious experience, in an institution and surroundings which are permeated with the true spirit of *Yiddishkeit* and *Ahavas Yisroel*.

Moreover, it is nowadays equally important to have the proper physical facilities, since the distraction of external aspects is so strong. This is why I am particularly gratified to see from photographs, as well as from the reports that I have received, that the new buildings and campus of the college are truly magnificent.

---

949 *Eruvin*, 6a.

950 *Letters from the Rebbe*, vol. 2, p. 42.

School plays

Regarding[951] plays that are staged from time to time, in general, this is a very appropriate thing to do. However, it is important to be cautious about matters that people sometimes take lightly, even though they are prohibitions from the Torah. For example, "a woman should not wear the garments of a man, etc.", women singing in public, the separation of men and women, and the like.

Advice for parents: Choosing a school

Choosing a day care option

[Advice[952] to a person in regards to choosing a kindergarten for his child:]

The main thing in connection to the *chinuch* of children in general, and the beginning of *chinuch* in particular, is the matter of *yiras Shamayim*.

> It[953] is well-known that in a kindergarten the teachers permeate more into the soul of a child than in school.

Only *Chabad* institutions

In[954] response to his letter... regarding the place of the *chinuch* of children of *Anash*, may they live:

It is clear that our holy *Nasis*, the *Nasis* of *Chabad* are the one's running the *chinuch* institutions of Chabad of all types: *Yeshivos, Talmud Torahs*, schools for acquiring a trade, schools for girls, etc.. How fortunate is each and every person from *Anash* (and all of our brothers in *Bnei Yisrael* are in the category of *Anash*), that the *chinuch* of their sons and daughters is in these institutions. It is good for them materially and spiritually, and in a revealed way.

---

951 *Igros Kodesh*, vol. 10, p. 238.

952 *Igros Kodesh*, vol. 4, p. 447.

953 *Igros Kodesh*, vol. 5, pp. 95-96.

954 *Igros Kodesh*, vol. 13, p. 96.

It obvious that you have my permission, and the merit, to inform all others who want to know my clear view and opinion on this matter.

According[955] to what we heard a few times from my father-in-law, the Rebbe, the *Nasi* of *Yisrael*- it is clear that the *chinuch* of the sons and daughters of *Anash* must be in *Chabad* institutions. This applies throughout **all** ages [of education].

Of course, I have heard of a number of *Anash,* may they live, conducting themselves differently, and not only this, but they garment it in the cloak of "*yiras Shamayim*"- I am sorry for them and even more for their offspring, may they live - since ואלה הצאן מה חטאו ("These sheep, what have they done?" [Meaning: it is beyond their control, of no fault of their own]). May it be Hashem's will that also those failing in this have a spirit from above descend upon them, etc. [and make them retract from this method of conduct].

Regarding[956] what he writes about continuing the *chinuch* of his daughter, may she live, it is understood and obvious that she has to be educated in *Chabad* institutions. Since your family lives in *Kfar Chabad*, it should be in a *chinuch* institution in *Kfar Chabad.* This matter relates also to the public [i.e. it is not just a private instruction].

In regards to what you write about deficiencies in the institution... if there are matters requiring correction, everyone should come together to discuss how to correct these shortcomings, as everyone is interested in the good of the institution and the *chinuch* it provides, and nothing stands in the way of one's will. The way to do this is in pleasant and peaceful means, as is the instruction of our *Nasis*, especially my father-in-law, the Rebbe, the founder of the community and its leader.

---

955 *Igros Kodesh*, vol. 23, p. 189.

956 *Igros Kodesh*, vol. 21, p. 367-368.

Homeschooling

[In[957] response to a question about homeschooling a child when there is no *chassidishe* institution in the area:]

It is understood that it is good for children to be taught with other (suitable) children and not alone at home.

Open a new class

Regarding[958] your question about the *chinuch* of your daughter and if she should be sent to school. It would be best to try to create a class with a few girls and take for them qualified teachers so they can be spared from going to another school. Then it will be certain that the supervision is as it should be in matters of Torah and *yiras Shamayim*.

A good *chinuch* should not be postponed

In[959] general, it is obvious that her education needs to be in an institution that teaches *Yiddishkeit,* Torah and its *mitzvos*, etc., and in an environment of *yiras Shamayim*, etc. There is no room to ponder delaying all this for the next year.

In particular, all of the above should be told to a practicing *rav, halachic* authority, and he will tell you the opinion of the Torah.

Should not consider sending child to school with non-Jews

"...Request[960] of more women or men to speak with the above and explain to her that if *chas ve'shalom* she sends her daughter to a school mixed with non-Jews, she is taking upon herself the full liability towards *Hakadosh Baruch Hu* for all which may possibly occur, may Hashem spare us, as a result of this. That is sufficient for the wise.

This may be said also in my name."

---

957 *Igeres Hachinuch* p. 254.
958 *Igros Kodesh*, vol. 3, pp. 455-456.
959 *Igeres Hachinuch,* p. 256.
960 *Shaarei Chinuch,* p. 71.

CHAPTER 18

Instructions Regarding Children's Publications

"Without wisdom, there is no awe; without awe, there is no wisdom."

Pirkei Avos, 3:17

Only *tahor* animals

When[961] the child gets older and begins to learn the shapes of letters, and is shown different shapes to make it easier to grasp the shape of the letters, efforts should be made that only *tahor* animals are shown. If any magazines, advertisements, and the like contain pictures of animals, especially those meant for children of *chinuch* age, these should be in the form of *tahor* animals.

When the animals come to aid in Torah study, to illustrate the story in *Tanach* and *Midrashim*, and so forth, the above does not apply.

Care in this area is especially important now since we are in the time of עקבתא דמשיחא when את רוח הטומאה אעביר מן הארץ ("I will remove the spirit of impurity from the land"). Therefore, we need to prepare for the coming of *Moshiach* by "tasting" from what will occur in the future by influencing those around us to use only images that are *tahor* and holy.

There[962] is no need at all to have pictures in the form of impure animals.

Boys and girls separate, distinct clothes, *tzitzis* out, *tznius*

In[963] publications that are printed (from time to time) for *Tzivos Hashem*, there are pictures of a boy and girl who are members of *Tzivos Hashem*.

In addition to the fact that the boy and girl are separate from one another, כרוב אחד מקצה מזה וכרוב אחד מקצה מזה[964] ("One cherub on one end, and one cherub on the other end") – (This matter has been as it should be up until now) – it should also be emphasized and stand out noticeably that there is a distinct difference in all of their garments: different garments for the boy and for the girl.

Regarding their hats, this too should be emphasized: a special hat for the boy and another special hat for the girl.

Up until now the publication has been printed in a kosher way, but it would be worthwhile to emphasize this distinction between the boy and girl

---

961 *Hisvaaduyos* 5744, vol.1, p. 487.

962 Response to Moshiach Times Magazine, *Igeres Hachinuch,* p. 278.

963 *Sichos Kodesh* 5741, vol. 2, p. 418.

964 *Shemos,* 25:19

even more (by having the artist design a hat that is only for the boys, and for the girl a hat that is especially for girls).

It should be emphasized in the picture of the boy that his *tzitzis* are visible and out.

In the picture of the girl, her clothes should be suitable, in the ultimate *tznius*: sleeves that are as long as they should be, and so forth. ... The matter of *tznius* according to most *poskim* begins when a girl is three years old and a day[965].

Luchos not rounded at the top

...The[966] drawing of the *luchos* in the form of semi-circles on the top is a custom of the nations of the world, and *lehavdil* the opposite of the words of our Sages of blessed memory. [Our Sages tell us] that their length was six [measures], their width was six [measures], and they were 3 [measures] thick (ב"ב יד, א). This should be publicized, especially to children, and they should be told that we are careful about this.

Menorah should be depicted with straight branches

...All[967] who draw the *menorah* should learn how it looked from the *menorah* in the *Mishkan* and in the *Mikdash*. The *menorah* should be drawn with straight branches, as is the opinion of *Rashi*, who interprets literally, and as is according to the drawing of the *Rambam*. There is no dissenting opinion regarding the above.

Since the purpose of the drawing a *menorah* is to remember the *menorah* in the *Mishkan* and *Mikdash*, it is worthwhile for *chinuch* institutions and the like that print the form of the *menorah* on their publications and signs depicting the branches as bow-shaped to change the image and draw the branches [straight and] on a diagonal.

...The famous image of the *menorah*, in which the six branches appear as half-bows [rounded], is copied, it seems, from a drawing of the *menorah*

---

965 See *Kevuda Bas Melech*, Rabbi Moshe Wiener, p. 101 onwards

966 *Igros Kodesh*, vol. 24, p. 288.

967 *Likkutei Sichos*, vol. 21, pp. 169-171.

which non-Jews in Rome drew on the Arch of Titus, may his name be blotted out forever.

When the evil Titus destroyed the *Beis Hamikdash*, he instructed his soldiers to take all of the vessels to bring them to Rome. To "honor" that *rasha*, they built the "victory gate" in Rome bearing his name, the Arch of Titus. On the gate, they sculpted a procession depicting the way they transported the stolen vessels from the *Mikdash*, including the *menorah*. In the drawing of the *Menorah* on the Arch of Titus, the branches appear rounded.

In addition to this, the drawing of the *menorah* on the gate of Titus is not accurate at all. Clearly, it was created in order to express the rulership and victory of Rome over *Yisrael, rachmana litzlan*. ...

Depicting the rounded branches of the *menorah* as they appear on the gate of Titus needs to arouse a cry and a protest. In addition—and this is essential—this depiction is the opposite of the words of *Rashi* and *Rambam*, and so forth. Accepting this depiction is agreeing to some extent *chas ve'shalom* with the depiction on the Arch of Titus which was created in order to sadden and humiliate *Yisrael*!

Instead of the drawing of the *menorah* reminding and arousing *Yisrael* about their role to be a "light unto the nations"[968]... the form of the *menorah* commemorates the exact opposite: the victory of Rome over *Yisrael, rachmana litzlan*!

Exaggerated features in comics

It[969] is not advisable that people should be drawn in an intentionally non-realistic manner—very fat, with an overly enlarged nose, and the like—although they [the people who draw comics] have become accustomed to doing so. In my opinion, this is a great educational mistake, for with regard to children, the more simple and normal, the better.

---

968 *Isaiah*, 42:6

969 Response to Moshiach Times magazine, *Igeres Hachinuch*, p. 278.

Three *Shabbos* candles

[Regarding[970] a picture which included, among other things, two *Shabbos* candlesticks:]

As has been spoken about a number of times previously, it is worthwhile to add a third candle between or next to the two candles.

Don't use Biblical figures in allegorical interpretations

... I[971] find it my duty, as difficult as it may be, to express my negative stand toward using the characters and events of our Holy Books [*Tanach*] in allegorical interpretations, especially in the direction that darkens their illumination and chosenness, even when this was not the intent of the poet.

In poetry, one is accustomed to allowing oneself various kinds of license. However, in my opinion, this should not be applied to the characters and stories of *Tanach*, whose lives and events have to this day an influence upon Jews of all ages, and even upon non-Jews. This demands that we take care not to employ poetic license even for the sake of elevating them [Biblical personalities] to a higher level than the way they're portrayed in *Tanach*, for this can bring the reader to conclude that since some of the description is exaggerated, the entire original story might be overdone. This will certainly be the case [that the reader will think less of the *Tanach* personalities] if this license is used in the opposite direction [by portraying the Biblical personalities as even more flawed than in the original].

Talks and Tales

I[972] would like to take this opportunity to request that you make efforts to publicize *Talks and Tales* in your institution, because it has a great and valuable impact on the young people who read it, as you surely have recognized.

---

970 Ibid.

971 *Igros Kodesh*, vol. 24, pp. 131-132.

972 *Igros Kodesh*, vol. 1, p. 36

Books that are inappropriate

Forbidden books similar to forbidden foods

Books[973] that are against our Torah and its *mitzvos*… in the opinion of some of the great *halachic* authorities… are similar to forbidden food. It is forbidden to eat even if one has in mind to make efforts to regurgitate the food afterwards.

The Rebbe Rashab's disapproval of secular *sefarim*

During a search conducted in *Yeshivas* Tomchei Temimim, secular books were found among the possessions of some *bochurim*. The Rebbe Rashab was extremely disturbed, and he was very upset at all of the *bochurim* for allowing such a thing to happen.

The *mashpia* Reb Groinem and the *chozer* Reb Moshe traveled to the Rebbe's summer residence in order to bring about reconciliation between the *bochurim* and the Rebbe. Speaking to the Rebbe, they said, "Being that only a few *bochurim* had the books, why is the Rebbe upset at all the *talmidim*?" "What do you mean?" exclaimed the Rebbe. "They are being showered with *Chassidus*!"

Reshimos Devarim, new edition, p. 175., Merkaz Anash, "Raising the *Kedushah*")

Books should be reformatted and given a new title page

… One[974] should not use reading books that are from secular authors. A suggestion: take the good stories and organize them in a new format with a new title page. (Twenty-five years after their publication, this ceases to involve a legal issue.)

[973] *Igros Kodesh, vol. 14, p. 86.*

[974] *Hosafos Le'Sichos Kodesh* 5728, vol. 1.

Judge a questionable *sefer* on the side of stringency

In[975] general, regarding books for study that one doubts, one should judge on the side of stringency. This is because what is spoken of is the ***chinuch*** of children, in which one needs to be extremely careful even when there is one small shortcoming. [Allow me to remind you of] the known example of a small scratch on a seed which can damage the growth of the tree *chas ve'shalom*. ...

For the above, one cannot bring a proof that it is permissible based on the fact that we sometimes use a book that has a number of authors, without mentioning the name of the authors, and only include a small segment of what is written. On the other hand, if one uses an entire book written by a certain author, this gives a *hechsher* to all of his content.

Reading materials that negate Torah and *mitzvos*

I[976] am responding to your letter in which you write that you may be required to teach your class using books whose views are against our Torah and its *mitzvos*. However, you say that there are those who claim that if this information is taught by others, the negativity in the writings will be affirmed and not denounced, but if she teaches it, the gains will outweigh the losses.

What we see from experience is that when young people are introduced to new matters in order for these to be refuted later on, it is certain that they will grasp the new matter, but a big question remains as to whether they will accept the refutation and negation. They will accept it in its totality, especially when they see how great the other side is. [They will reason:] If these ideas and these books should be negated, why are they being taught in school, and by a *frum* teacher?

The above arguments have always existed, and whoever accepted them ended up losing out. There is great doubt as to whether there have ever been even slightly positive results from teaching this material in order to refute it. There is an additional problem: others will see what is being done and not ask questions in order to get the entire picture regarding the way the matter is taught and the conclusions the teacher is presenting. They will only ask about

---

975 *Igros Kodesh*, vol. 18, p. 484.

976 *Igros Kodesh*, vol. 14, p. 86.

the curriculum and will find out that such-and-such book was taught by a *frum* person, and then they will take this as if a total *hechsher* was given to the *sefer*. ...

Ensuring that students do not have inappropriate *sefarim*

Surely[977] [the staff] can see to it in a suitable manner that such *sefarim* do not enter the *daled amos* of the students. However, this has to be done in such a way that it does not arouse in them a desire for such books, as it is written, "Stolen waters are sweet."[978] Therefore, you should consult with the other teachers, as it is written, "Help comes with a lot of advice."

Encouraging better reading materials

Given[979] that reading secular *sefarim* is destructive and so forth, it is [nevertheless] known that one must go from the easier-to-accept to the more difficult, especially regarding publicizing the matter among women. After all, as our Sages have said in terms of this as well as regarding *Matan* Torah, women must be spoken to in a gentle way, as is explained in *Rashi*'s commentary on the *pasuk* כה תאמר לבית יעקב[980] ("So you shall say to the house of Yaakov). So too regarding the above, greater emphasis needs to be on *aseh tov*, reading *sichos* and the like. Then over time the *psak din* will be fulfilled: that a bit of light dispels a lot of darkness (and how much more so when it is a lot of light!). It is understood that my intention is not to give consent to their reading the secular books, but rather that slowly and gradually there will be a shift, with an emphasis on the matter of *aseh tov*.

---

977 *Igros Kodesh*, vol. 18, p. 333.

978 *Mishlei*, 9:17.

979 *Igros Kodesh*, vol. 9, p. 96.

980 *Shemos*, 19:3.

CHAPTER 19

Chinuch Around the Year

"And you shall rejoice in your festivals... and you shall be happy."

Devarim, 16:14-15

Elul

Children bless Kesivah VaChasimah Tovah

Minhag[981] *Yisrael* is that children before their *bar mitzvah* and *bas mitzvah* also bless *Kesivah VaChasimah Tovah, LeShanah Tovah U'Mesukah.* Children have also been given the ability to draw down Hashem's bracha, as in certain matters children have the same ability as adults.

True, it is not generally considered *derech eretz* for a small child to bless an older person, and more than this, it is the child who requests a blessing from the older person[982]. Still, since in our times there are children who do not conduct themselves with the proper respect [toward those older than they are] and so forth, it is good for them to utilize this [shortcoming in respecting elders] for positive and good matters, *brachos*, and the like, particularly on auspicious days.

Ensuring all children are given a holy *chinuch*

Particularly[983] in our times when the school year begins in the month of Elul in these countries, this time period should be utilized to bring children to learn in kosher schools, and more than this, schools that teach *al taharas hakodesh*, to the point of a holy *chinuch*. ...

It is especially necessary to take advantage of these days when children return home from camp and are preparing to begin the new school year. People should make efforts immediately when these children return home, even before they start school, that their *chinuch* will be *al taharas hakodesh.* It is necessary to make special efforts that these children (and all Jewish children) apply to and be accepted at **kosher** schools, schools that teach *al taharas hakodesh.*

---

981 *Hisvaaduyos* 5748, vol. 4, p. 339.

982 *Sotah,* 49b

983 *Likkutei Sichos*, vol. 14, p. 261.

The King is in the field

There[984] is a special connection between the matter of *chinuch* and the month of *Elul.*

Likkutei Torah[985] explains a parable (in connection with the month of *Elul*) that during these days *Hakadosh Baruch Hu* is a King who is in the field, and each person can (and must) approach Him. The King shows each person a friendly countenance and welcomes him or her.

Surely this parable is connected to small children as well, since they too can also understand this parable if it is explained to them properly. They have an added advantage when the King is in the field (in comparison to when He is in His palace) beyond what adults have, since a child cannot come before the King when He is in His palace as an adult can... but when the King is in the field, even a child can approach Him.

Another difference between a child and an adult is that an adult possesses an awe and fear of the King, which can prevent him from approaching the King. A small child, on the other hand, will not be prevented by his fear from approaching the King to speak with Him. (We see this from the fact that when he sees something expensive and shiny and the like, the child rushes to take it, as is understood as well from the story of Moshe *Rabeinu.*) However, children must be given an explanation about the greatness of the King. We must educate each child in such a way that the King should be precious in his eyes, and then when the King is in the field, he will run toward Him.

Thirteenth of Elul

The[986] thirteenth of Elul is the wedding day of my father-in-law, the Rebbe, the *Nasi* of our generation. Special days including this day are remembered and repeat themselves each year [spiritually there is the same energy in the world as the first year that the event occurred]. ...

Clearly, the marriage of the *Nasi* (leader) of the generation has significance for all of *Bnei Yisrael* in the generation including men, women, and children,

---

984 *Likkutei Sichos*, vol. 14, p. 261.

985 *Re'eh,* 32B.

986 *Hisvaaduyos* 5749, vol. 4, p. 289

because הנשיא הוא הכל (*Rashi, Parshas Chukkas 21:21:* "The leader of the generation is equal to the entire generation, because the leader is everything").

Rosh HaShanah

Erev Rosh HaShanah

Every[987] man, woman, and child should utilize this day (*erev Rosh HaShanah*) to add to the merit of the Tzemach Tzedek in matters that express his main *avodah*. Included in this are: spreading Torah, *pnimiyus haTorah* in particular; the *avodah* of *tefillah*; and doing all *mitzvos be'hiddur, including* and especially the *mitzvah* of *tzedakah*.

A year permeated with light

Through[988] lighting candles on *erev Rosh HaShanah* one causes the ushering in of the new year to be accompanied **with light**. As a result of this, the entire year becomes one permeated with light – because of the action of a small girl. Through this *mitzvah*, it is openly recognizable how she brings light into all of her surroundings.

...The candle light exists before the husband returns from *shul*, before he, as head of the household makes *Kiddush*, and even before the first prayer of *Rosh HaShanah,* the *tefillah of ma'ariv.* It is the custom of a woman or girl that the *Yom Tov* is ushered in through her lighting of a candle (or candles) before the time that the *chag* actually enters according to the clock. (This is in accordance with the ruling, and as is the Jewish custom, to light candles, including *Rosh HaShanah* candles, before the time that it is possible to make *kiddush* or *daven.*)

Even small children are brought to hear the *shofar*

It[989] is customary that everyone – men, women, and children – assemble to hear the blowing of the *shofar.* This includes even very small children. Although

987 *Hisvaaduyos* 5749, vol. 4, p. 388.
988 *Hisvaaduyos* 5746, vol. 4, p. 464.
989 *Hisvaaduyos* 5750, vol. 1, p. 257.

they cannot understand the *bracha* recited by the person sounding the *shofar*, they also respond "*amen*" out loud along with everyone else.

Make a *kinus*

These[990] *Selichos* days are auspicious days of mercy. Furthermore, our Sages of blessed memory have advised us of the greatness of *hevel shel beis rabban* (the breath of small children that sustains the world). In light of all this, I request and suggest that during one of the *Selichos* days (the first day, if possible), a children's *kinus* be organized.

At this event, boys and girls prior to the age of *bar* (and *bas*) *mitzvah* should be gathered. The organizers should make every effort that the number of participants be as great as possible.

Teachers should explain to the children, according to their level of understanding, that this is the beginning of the week of *Rosh HaShanah* and the time to prepare for *Rosh HaShanah*.

Rosh HaShanah is the time when each and every person accepts upon himself Hashem's *Malchus* for the entire year, to keep His *mitzvos* and so forth, and Hashem blesses all of *Bnei Yisrael* with a *Kesivah VaChasimah Tovah U'Mesukah*.

This time is particularly auspicious as the Alter Rebbe explains that on these days *Hakadosh Baruch Hu* is, so to speak, like a King in the field. It is then permissible for all who wish to greet him to be accepted before the King, and he welcomes everyone with a friendly countenance.

Therefore, everyone involved in the *kinus* is asked to say in unison:

> "*Torah tziva lanu* Moshe *morasha kehilas* Yaakov."
> "*Shema Yisrael Hashem Elokeinu Hashem Echad.*"
> "*Baruch Shem kevod Malchuso leolam va'ed.*"
> "*Avinu Malkeinu Avinu Ata. Avinu Malkeinu Ein Lanu Melech ela Ata. Avinu Malkeinu racheim aleinu. Avinu Malkeinu chaneinu va'aneinu ki ein banu maasim asseh imanu tzedakah va'chessed le'maan Shimecha hagadol vehoshiainu.*"

---

990 *Likkutei Sichos*, vol. 14, p. 265.

Afterwards, one of the speakers should explain how the Baal Shem Tov said that every *Yid* comes into this physical world with a certain *shlichus* of Torah, the Torah of light. He goes with this *shlichus* of Torah and *mitzvos* in every place he may be – in his city and every other place where he may find himself and whenever the opportunity presents itself.

We bless each and every person to be able to fulfill this *shlichus* in its proper time and with success; and may all be blessed to be written and sealed for a good and sweet year.

I request that afterwards each person should be given two coins. One coin will be a gift from me, with my suggestion (but it is not a precondition) that they give it to *tzedakah;* and the second coin, I request that they be my *shluchim* in giving it to *tzedakah.*

In addition, it would be good and correct to do all of the above once again during one of the Ten Days of Repentance. At that time, however, instead of imparting the message of "the King being in the field," the children should receive an explanation that regarding these days it is said, "Seek out Hashem when He can be found, and call out to Him when He is near."[991] According to the explanation of the Alter Rebbe, the parable is of the spark – referring to the G-dly soul that exists inside each and every Jew – being close to the Luminary – G-d Himself.

Yom Kippur

Kapparos when pregnant

In[992] regard to the *minhag* of *kapparos* on the eve of *Yom Kippur*, the *Shulchan Aruch*[993] states that in addition to the chicken she takes to atone for herself, a pregnant woman takes a chicken to atone for her baby. In this matter, there are two opinions as to whether or not it is sufficient to use one chicken. This is because if the fetus is female, it is enough to have the one chicken for the mother and the baby together. After all, two men can be atoned for by using

991 *Isaiah,* 55:6

992 *Likkutei Sichos*, vol. 22, pp. 58-60.

993 *Shulchan Aruch Admor HaZaken, Orach Chaim* 605/3

one chicken, and two women can be atoned for by using one chicken. The other opinion is that it is necessary to use three chickens: one for the mother, and an additional chicken and rooster because of the uncertainty as to whether the fetus is male or female. The latter opinion, that a pregnant woman uses three chickens, is the view of the *Arizal.*

...Why[994] does a fetus need a *kapparah* when it is the mother's uterus?

...When a pregnant woman eats something that is forbidden, it becomes her flesh and blood, and she needs a *kapparah.* Her food becomes her blood and her heart, and the heart of the fetus.

Sukkos

Visiting in a *sukkah*

I[995] hope that you made a *farbrengen* for the students in your school in honor of *Simchas Beis HaSho'evah* and that they visited a *sukkah.* Very often sights such as these become engraved in their hearts, and surely some of the students live not far from *shul.*

Spreading the wellsprings

During[996] the festival of *Sukkos,* one is encouraged to travel out of the city in order to bring *Simchas Beis HaSho'evah* to the Jews there amid joy and good heartedness, ... to spread the wellsprings [of *Chassidus*], ... and to strive to provide them with the merit of fulfilling the *mitzvah* of the Four Species. ...

It would be even better for one's spouse and children to accompany him in his travels in order to educate them as well on the importance of "spreading the wellsprings [of *Chassidus*]," and of being concerned about all of the Jewish people, even those who are distant spiritually and physically.

Most of all, it is important to ensure that in every place where Jewish people are found, *Simchas Beis HaSho'evah* is held. For, inasmuch as all Jewish people should be together as one, either others will come to join you or if they

---

994 See *Siddur Alter Rebbe Seder Kapparos*

995 *Igros Kodesh,* vol. 12, p. 37.

996 *Sichos Kodesh,* 13 Tishrei 5752 p. 98.

don't go to you, you will go to them. Celebrate *Simchas Beis HaSho'evah* along with them, and bring along joy, a happy tune, happy activities, and joyful news.

Simchas Torah

Children brought to *hakafos*

[The[997] *simchah* connected with concluding the entire Torah] is the greatest *simchah* that envelopes and unites all of *bnei Yisrael*, the men, women and children, and thus there is the custom to bring infants, as well, to the *hakafos*.

Simchas Beis HaSho'evah

[Children][998] also take part in *Simchas Beis HaSho'evah*.

Many[999] Jews should be gathered in accordance with the verse, "Gather the nation; the men, women, and children"[1000] – to take part in the celebration of *Simchas Beis HaSho'evah*. This applies to the men and to the women as well. [As was discussed a few times[1001], even in the *Beis Hamikdash* women would come only to "see and hear[1002]." In the time of *galus*, an advantage has been added (*yeridah letzorech aliyah* – the descent of *galus* occurred in order that there be an ascent): that women celebrate their own *Simchas Beis HaSho'evah*. This applies to children as well; everyone is united in celebrating *Simchas Beis HaSho'evah*.

---

997 *Hisvaaduyos* 5749, vol. 1, p. 87.
998 *Hisvaaduyos* 5749, vol. 1, p. 130, footnote 77.
999 *Hisvaaduyos* 5748, vol. 1, p. 178.
1000 *Devarim* 31:12.
1001 See *Maayanei Hayeshua*, p. 44.
1002 See *Rambam*, Laws of Lulav, Chapter 8, law 14.

Chanukah

Children light at the entrance to their room

In[1003] addition to lighting Chanukah candles in all Jewish homes, and lighting Chanukah candles in public places to emphasize the matter of *pirsumei nisah* (publicizing the miracle)... it would be correct and worthwhile to inspire others regarding lighting Chanukah candles at the entrance of children's rooms.

...Each Jew, big and small, should make his home a *Mikdash me'at*, a house of Torah, *tefillah*, and *gemilus chassadim*. This includes—and is particularly applicable to—Jewish children: they should do so in their own rooms through having a *Siddur* (*tefillah*), *Chumash* (Torah), and *tzedakah pushka* (*gemilus chassadim*) in the room. Each day, they should learn from the *Siddur*, learn from the *Chumash*, and give *tzedakah* (on weekdays and *erev Shabbos* double the amount, in order to include *Shabbos* as well).

In addition, it would be worthwhile and correct that at the entrance to the children's room there should be a Chanukah *menorah* (and it should be lit there as well). Surely the children will also receive an explanation about the meaning of the lighting of Chanukah candles in a way that they can understand... When they see the candles at the entrance to their own rooms, it leaves a strong impression on their souls. Their room, their *Mikdash me'at*, is similar to and hints to the dedication of the *Beis Hamikdash* during Chanukah.

Even[1004] though in order to publicize the miracle, one *menorah* is lit in each home... since there has been an increase in undesirable matters (which have already occurred or that can still occur *chas ve'shalom*), it is best and most fitting for more light to be added to the world. In addition to the *menorah* normally lit, a *menorah* should be lit in the children's rooms as well: the rooms of the boys and the rooms of the girls. This will add to the *chinuch* and good feelings of the children, parents and of all who enter the home.

1003 *Hisvaaduyos* 5748, vol. 2, p. 64.

1004 *Hisvaaduyos* 5748, vol. 2, p. 91

Regarding this, there are a few questions: 1) Must every child light [a *menorah*]? 2) Is it necessary to light in each [child's] room or, because of the expense, is lighting in one room sufficient? 3) Should girls also light?[1005]

In general, since this is done for *chinuch* purposes and so forth, in each situation, one should examine what the practical outcome could be, and do whatever will have the most positive effect on the *chinuch* of the children.

Since each *mitzvah* has a practical consequence... the giving of the *mitzvos* is in order to involve human beings in *avodas* Hashem, and to illuminate each and every Yid... The lighting of the *menorah* in the children's rooms serves a purpose: to further the publicizing of the miracle and to have a positive impact on the *chinuch* of the children. That being the case, one should determine in what way this goal can be best achieved.

Giving children Chanukah gelt

Since[1006] the custom [of giving Chanukah *gelt*] is meant to educate children, the reason it has not been customary to give [Chanukah *gelt*] each night is that by repeating it every single night, it loses its novelty and no longer elicits such a great reaction.

However, because of the increased darkness of *galus*, and especially regarding the decreased state of *chinuch*, it is necessary to increase in light and *kedusha*. It is possible to say that there is a need to add to this custom of giving Chanukah *gelt* as well: not only once, as is the main custom, but also each day [of Chanukah].

1005 The Chabad custom: According to *Sefer Haminhagim* (p. 157 [English]), the Chabad custom is for girls not to light candles. Nonetheless, in the year 1988 the Rebbe stated that even girls are to light candles if it will add to their education in a positive light. [*Hisvaaduyos* 5748, vol. 2, p. 91] However, the next year the Rebbe was asked by N'shei U'bnos Chabad if this instruction applies for the coming year as well, and the Rebbe answered that this question belongs to a Rav. The widespread custom today amongst daughters of Anash is not to light candles, as is the custom mentioned in *Sefer Haminhagim*.

1006 *Hisvaaduyos* 5748, vol. 2, pp. 64-66.

So as to fulfill the instruction of our Rebbe, our *Nasi*, to give Chanukah *gelt* on *yom revi'i* and *yom chamishi*[1007], and in order that it should not come to feel ordinary [i.e. unexciting], my suggestion is to give double or three times the amount on these days.

Matters of *kedusha* should be carried out in the most *mehudar* way

The[1008] miracle of Chanukah was that a jug of oil was found with the seal of the *Kohen Gadol*[1009] intact. According to *halacha*, it is possible to light the *menorah* with impure oil since for congregational use this is allowed only in the case of communal contamination[1010]. Despite this, in order to show His affection for the Jews, *Hakadosh Baruch Hu* made a miracle making it possible to fulfill not only the beginning of the *mitzvah*, but the entire *mitzvah* in the most beautiful way, without any compromises, even those permissible according to *Shulchan Aruch*.

From this we can learn a lesson applicable to all matters of *kedusha*. Immediately from the beginning of the *chinuch* of the child, the matters of *kedusha* should be carried out in a way that is totally complete and in the most *mehudar* way possible.

Using only "pure oil" in *chinuch*

Throughout[1011] the ages, the Jewish nation has endured the unyielding persecutions of their gentile neighbors. Each nation posed its own unique threat to the survival of Jewish life. Some engaged in open battle, while others implemented subtler means of oppression.

A classic example of the latter is exhibited in the story of Chanukah. The Greek oppression (essentially) sought to eliminate the inherent division between the Jewish people and society at large.

[1007] *Hayom Yom*, 28th of Kislev

[1008] *Likkutei Sichos*, vol. 1, p. 81.

[1009] *Talmud Bavli*, *Shabbos*, 21B

[1010] *Pesachim*, 80A

[1011] *Likkutei Sichos*, vol. 20, p. 439, Issue 9 of The Rebbe's Holy Care

They said, "*K'chol hagoyim beis Yehuda*"— "The Jewish people ought to adapt to the modes and cultures of society rather than remain a unique identity, independent of and indifferent to the rest of civilization."

The approach of the Greek oppression – to dissolve the division between the Jewish and gentile nations – manifests itself in a similar outlook toward Jewish education, i.e., raising a child to pursue and aspire to the lifestyle of the gentile society.

In truth, the Greek method of oppression poses a far greater threat to the continuity of the Jewish nation than a decree forbidding Torah study and the fulfillment of *mitzvos*.

For a decree prohibiting religious observance is temporary and short-lived. Thus, the moment the decree is annulled, Jews subsequently return to studying Torah and observing the *mitzvos*.

Yet, a greater threat to Jewish survival exists when the oppression is such that Jews are persuaded by society to assimilate and raise their children to pursue *goyishkeit* – secularism, sensuality, etc., as this yields consequences long after the oppression has abated. For children retain the lessons they were taught in their youth, even after growing old.

The catalyst to such a condition is neglecting a *klaynikeit* – a minute deviation from the traditional Torah path.

Oftentimes, in the attempt to illuminate a child's life, one may consider using *goyishe* "oil" that promises to yield benefit for the child. Why, does it really make a difference what oil one uses? As long as the flame is bright and luminous, what harm can this cause?

Chanukah therefore teaches that when seeking to illuminate a Jewish home or the education of a Jewish child, one must use the glow of pure light from holy, undefiled oil.

The division between the Jewish people and the gentile nations must remain intact. For if a child is raised with principles gleaned from "Greek oils," its effect is twofold: Not only does such oil fail to illuminate the appropriate course in life, but it actually encourages the child to depart from the Jewish tradition and embrace a Hellenistic life instead, to "become a Hellenist."

Of course, a Jew remains a Jew under all circumstances, as he has no freedom to choose otherwise. Yet in the realm where one is granted freedom of choice, he can of course adopt a new Hellenistic lifestyle.

In light of the above, one can begin to understand the importance of maintaining a firm division between the Jewish people and the gentile nations, especially with regard to the education of Jewish children.

Twentieth of Teves, Yohrtzeit of the Rambam

The[1012] *avodah* of *Bnei Yisrael* nowadays should be geared toward "bringing to the days of *Moshiach*". ...

More specifically, this includes – in connection with the *Rambam*'s *Yohrtzeit* – increasing in the study of the *Mishneh Torah* of the *Rambam*, as well as taking part in (or strengthening one's involvement if one is already involved in) the learning of a cycle of *Rambam* of which many Jews are involved, whether it is three chapters, or one etc., or *Sefer Hamitzvos*.

Especially, people should learn the *halachos* of *Melech HaMoshiach* in the last two chapters of *Halachos Melachim* at the conclusion of the *Rambam*'s *Mishneh Torah*.

In addition to one's personal study, one should also influence other *Yidden* around him – men, women, and children – in a manner of "establishing many students[1013]," and then those we influence will in turn influence others to learn from them as well.

15 BeShvat

Customs

Parents[1014] and educators should arouse children's enthusiasm to fulfill the custom of eating different types of fruit, specifically fruit for which *Eretz Yisrael* is praised. Someone should explain to them, in a way that they will understand,

---

1012 *Hisvaaduyos* 5752, vol. 2, p. 107.

1013 *Pirkei Avos, 1:1*

1014 *Hisvaaduyos* 5749 vol. 2, p. 270.

the meaning of *Rosh HaShanah Leilanos,* the New Year for the trees, planting and growing in all matters of *Yiddishkeit,* Torah, and its *mitzvos,* to be a tree that bears good fruit.

Planting trees should not be added to *minhagim*

Regarding[1015] planting trees on the 15th of Shvat, this should not be mixed with the *minhagim* of the *Shulchan Aruch* and so forth. It should be removed from a book that is meant to apply to everyone.

Adar

Increasing *simchah*

Every[1016] Jew should increase in all matters of *simchah*, both in his own life and in his efforts to make another Jew happy, since we know that a complete state of joy necessarily includes others.

First of all, *simchah* comes about through adding in פקודי ה׳ ישרים משמחי[1017] לב, ("The commandments of Hashem are upright, they gladden the heart"): learning Torah, *nigleh*, and *Chassidus,* in accordance with the words of our Sages, "Great is learning that brings to action[1018]": fulfillment of *mitzvos behiddur.*

Furthermore, and this is the main thing, increasing one's *simchah* in Torah and *mitzvos* adds to one's general level of joy. This applies as well to using material objects as a means to bring joy in accordance with the instruction of the *Shulchan Aruch* [regarding *Yom Tov*]. A person brings happiness to himself as well as others, beginning with family members: a husband brings cheer to his wife, and parents bring extra joy to their children by giving them the things that make them happy according to their nature, as is the *psak din* of the *Shulchan Aruch*[1019].

1015 *Igros Kodesh*, vol. 9, p. 66.

1016 *Hisvaaduyos* 5752, vol. 2, p. 297

1017 *Tehillim,* 19:30.

1018 *Megillah,* 27A, *Kiddushin,* 40:2.

1019 *Shulchan Aruch Admor HaZaken, Orach Chaim* 529:7.

Purim

Living with Torah

When[1020] Mordechai heard the *pesukim* from the children when they were returning from school, he was struck with the full awareness that their *chinuch* was so potent that not only during school hours were they inspired and infused with *emuna* and *mesirus nefesh*—as evidenced by אל תירא, "Have no fear[1021]," a *pasuk* one of the children recited to Mordechai—but they were so empowered while on their way home from school as well. ...

...From this we learn a lesson for all generations, especially the generation of *Ikvesa DeMeshicha*, when we are still "the servants of Achashverosh[1022]": When a person wants to know the present and future state of the Jewish people, one should look at the spiritual condition of the children, especially while they are returning home from school.

...When the Jewish children are living with the *pesukim*, outside as well as inside of school, and are bringing this with them into their homes, then, as it was in the days of Mordechai and Esther, so will it be in our times: this will ensure the existence and the continuity of Torah among the Jews, and there is no need to fear a thing in the world in accordance with the verse, מפי עוללים ויונקים יסדת עוז...להשבית אויב ומתנקם ("From the mouths of babies and suckling infants You have established strength... to silence the enemy and avenger").

The *mitzvos* of Purim

Even[1023] though these *mitzvos* [*Mishloach Manos* and *Matanos L'Evyonim*] are easier to fulfill than other *mitzvos*... the *yetzer hara* tries all types of tricks to prevent people from keeping them. Therefore, even among those who keep other *mitzvos* of Purim with *hiddurim*, these *mitzvos* are neglected...

Therefore, it is an obligation and a merit to make more efforts, especially for those who have an influence over their surroundings, to publicize the great

---

1020 *Likkutei Sichos*, vol. 21, pp. 211-213.

1021 *Mishlei*, 3:25.

1022 *Megillah*, 14:1

1023 *Likkutei Sichos*, vol. 4, p. 1285

advantage of these *mitzvos* in all places that they can possibly reach, and the ease with which they can be fulfilled and the obligation on each person to do them. Each and every person over *bar* and *bas mitzvah* age – also small children who reached the age of *chinuch* – should fulfill these *mitzvos* themselves. Surely these efforts to influence the multitudes to fulfill these *mitzvos* will be successful.

Salvation of the Jewish people

When[1024] Haman rose and made his request to wipe out the Jewish nation, in addition to Mordechai's request of Esther that she plead before Achashverosh, Mordechai gathered Jewish children and learned Torah with them. His specific choice of subject matter was the *halachos* pertaining to the time when the *Beis Hamikdash* will be built. *Chazal* say that this is what annulled the decree of Haman.

This means that during a time of trouble, one of the main things that saves the entire Jewish nation is the *chinuch* of children in the spirit of Torah and *Yiddishkeit*, and implanting in their hearts the hope of redemption. And then ונהפוך הוא אשר ישלטו היהודים ("the situation will be transformed into one in which the Jews will rule[1025]") וליהודים היתה אורה ושמחה וששון ויקר, ("The Jews had light and joy and gladness and honor."[1026]).

Each person must take part in *chinuch*

I[1027] would like to know if you take part in *frum* life in your city, and specifically if you are involved in *chinuch*, which is one of the important matters of our time during the days between Purim and *Chag HaPesach*. The decree of Purim was annulled through Mordechai himself, the *Gadol* in his generation in Torah, *Yiras Shamayim*, and *chochmah*, who learned with *tinokos shel Beis Rabban* (children), as our Sages tell us[1028]. This point is also applicable to *Chag HaPesach*. At the beginning of the *Seder*, we use all kinds of strategies in order

1024 *Likkutei Sichos*, vol. 26, p. 446.

1025 *Esther*, 9:1.

1026 *Esther*, 8:16.

1027 *Likkutei Sichos*, vol. 31, p. 281.

1028 End of *Midrash Esther Rabba*.

to pique the interest of the small children so that they won't sleep (physically and certainly spiritually). We begin the *Seder* with the questions of small children. At the conclusion of *Chag HaPesach*, we recall the matters of *Kriyas Yam Suf* (as is told in *Shemos Rabba*[1029]), and we recall how the babies that were born and raised in *Mitzrayim* were the first to recognize *Hakadosh Baruch Hu.*

The lesson from this is that the *geulah* of *Yisrael*, materially and spiritually, is dependent on the *chinuch* of the young generation. Each and every Jew, even someone as great as Mordechai, about whom it is said[1030] that Mordechai in his generation was like Moshe in his generation, is obligated to take part in this *chinuch*.

Hashem should grant each and every one of us the merit to illuminate their portion in the world, and through this we hasten and bring the *geulah hashleima ve'haamitis* of *Klal Yisrael.*

Playing the part of Haman

In[1031] many places, it is customary to stage "Purim plays" in which children act out the entire story of the *Megillah.* Just as people are needed to play the parts of Mordechai and Esther... someone is needed to play the part of "Haman," to recite his words, and so forth.

...When the child plays his role as "Haman" with *chayus* (enthusiasm), with a nice, loud, lively voice, he will "merit" receiving the *kavod* of his teachers and friends. All will see that he is a very good actor, because he played his role as "Haman" in the best possible way, to the point where he was able to scare the listening audience. Since he spoke the words of Haman (which are the opposite of *brachos* and so on) with the greatest enthusiasm and passion, everyone was able to imagine to themselves that Haman the *rasha* himself spoke precisely in this way, G-d forbid!

...From this we understand to what extent one needs to be careful and pay close attention to the *chinuch* of children. Specifically, we must instill in them the principle that even if someone speaks to their hearts, telling them that for

---

1029 See *Sotah,* 11B.

1030 *Midrash Esther Rabba.*

1031 *Likkutei Sichos*, vol. 31, pp. 279-280.

honor and for money and even if he says that you will be able to give *tzedakah* with the money (because the *yetzer hara* can trick the child into thinking this is a good thing), and therefore it is worthwhile for them to behave (even for a short time) in a way that is not fitting for a *Yid* – they should know that they should not be convinced by this suggestion! What's more—and this is the main thing—these words should not have any impression upon him at all.

When one makes efforts to teach a child in this way while he is still young, *chanoch lanaar* (educate the child), then one can be confident that *ki yazkin lo yasur mimenah*[1032] (when he ages, he will not depart from this path).

Directives for *N'shei U'bnos Yisrael*

... [*N'shei*[1033] *u'bnos Yisrael*] especially should learn from Queen Esther and should increase their efforts in a manner of *mesirus nefesh*, in a way of דלא ידע[1034], beyond intellect – arousing all of *Yisrael* to fulfill the directive, לך כנוס את כל היהודים[1035] *("Gather all of the Yidden"): achdus Yisrael,* unity of the Jewish people.

Similarly, women should strengthen in their main *shlichus*: the *chinuch* of *bnei* and *bnos Yisrael.* This *shlichus* is placed especially in the hands of women. In addition, there should be an emphasis on educating small children in the matters connected with the days of Purim,[1036]וזכרם לא יסוף מזרעם ("Nor shall their memory [of Purim] depart from their descendents"), since the decree was nullified through small children[1037]...

The[1038] *minhag Yisrael* is to take advantage of the days of Purim to increase in the *chinuch* of small children. Efforts are also made to include the children in the *mitzvos* of Purim. *Mishloach Manos* are sent through children. At the time of the reading of the *Megillah*, the custom is for small children to take

---

1032 *Mishlei, 22:9*
1033 *Hisvaaduyos* 5748, vol. 2, p. 410.
1034 *Megillah,* 7B
1035 *Esther,* 4:16.
1036 *Esther,* 9:28.
1037 *Midrash Raba Esther* 29:4, *Yaakov Shimoni 1057.*
1038 Ibid. Footnote 114

smooth stones and write on them the name "Haman," and when the reader of the *Megillah* reads the name "Haman," they strike the two stones together to erase his name.[1039]

Directives for children

I[1040] hope that you received my suggestion and request—connected with the days of Purim—for all students in *chinuch* institutions, in each and every country and city, especially those who have not yet reached *bar mitzvah* and *bas mitzvah* age: to spur them to go in the ways of the Jewish children in the times of Mordechai and Esther. As our Sages of blessed memory teach us[1041], in the merit of *tinokos shel beis rabban* (small children), the decree of the evil Haman was nullified, and the *Yidden* had *orah, vesimchah, vesasson v'yikar*[1042] (light and joy, gladness and honor).

Even more important, I appeal to you to follow this two-fold suggestion and request:

1. All should add in Torah learning in two ways: 1) In quantity, by setting additional times for learning Torah, in addition to their school studies; and 2) In quality: adding in the diligence, passion, and depth of their study. They should learn a topic that their hearts desire, be it *parshas hashavua* or one of the other 24 books of *Tanach*, or *Mishnah* and *Gemara*, and so forth – whatever they choose.
2. They should increase in an area of *tzedakah*.

Shabbos Hagadol

On[1043] the days between *Shabbos HaGadol* and Pesach, one should increase in, and complete, everything connected with Pesach preparations. This should begin with preparations that are permissible to do on *Shabbos*, during *Shabbos*

1039 *Avudraham, Tefillas Purim.*

1040 *Likkutei Sichos*, vol. 16, pp. 621-622.

1041 *Midrash Raba Esther* 29:4, *Yaakov Shimoni 1057.*

1042 *Esther,* 8:16.

1043 *Hisvaaduyos*, 5749, vol. 3 p. 15

HaGadol itself, such as preparing our children for the *Seder* night, ensuring that they know the Four Questions and the rest of the *Seder* procedure. This is a preparation for the fulfillment of the Torah's command, "You shall tell your child [the story of the Exodus][1044]" on the night of Pesach.

Pesach

The importance of customs

The[1045] order of the Four Questions according to *Minhag* Chabad is: *Matbilin* (dipping), *matzah*, *maror*, and *mesubin* (leaning).

It seems hard to understand: Isn't this the incorrect order regarding the importance of the matters? After all, *matzah* is a Biblical obligation[1046], *maror* is a Rabbinic obligation, and dipping is only a *minhag*.

There are those who say that Biblical *mitzvos* need to be fulfilled with diligence to the point of *mesirus nefesh*. Rabbinical *mitzvos* need to be fulfilled as well, being that they are included in the *mitzvah* of לא תסור (and as *Rambam*[1047] explains at length in the matter of fences, Rabbinical *mitzvos* in particular are included in לא תסור[1048]). However, *minhagim*, if possible to fulfill with ease they should be kept, but one is not obligated to have *mesirus nefesh* for them.

More than this, they claim: During the time while children are receiving a Torah education, it is very difficult to succeed in every area. Sometimes, it is worthwhile to compromise the *minhagim* and to devote oneself only to ingraining within them the most important matters.

Here we learn a lesson from the order of the questions on the *Seder* night: The first thing the child asks about, the first thing that he notices and that leaves an impression on him, is not a Biblical or a Rabbinic matter, but rather, *minhag Yisrael*. This is what catches his eye and leaves the greatest impact.

1044 *Shemos*, 11:8.

1045 *Toras Menachem*, vol. 16, p. 198, *Likkutei Sichos*, vol. 1, p. 244.

1046 *Pesachim*, 120, *Shulchan Aruch Admor HaZaken*, *Orach Chaim*, 475:15.

1047 Beginning of *Hilchos Mamrim*

1048 *Devarim*, 17:11.

If a child's conduct and the conduct surrounding him is similar to that of the the non-Jewish environment, then – even if he sets aside times to learn Torah, *daven*, and do *mitzvos* – because his conduct is similar to the behavior in his surroundings, and it is not clearly recognizable that he is Jewish, and the matter of המבדיל...בין ישראל לעמים, ("You distinguish between holy and mundane" [1049]) and אתה בחרתנו מכל העמים ("You chose us from all of the nations"[1050]) is not felt by the child, this brings about that eventually he himself will not experience the *kedusha* in the *mitzvos* he does and the Torah he learns.

When there is a lack in the foundation – the *kedusha* of Torah and the *kedusha* of *mitzvos* – then over time it is possible that *chas ve'shalom*, the lacking will be even in their fulfillment.

Should not sleep

...Regarding[1051] the *chinuch* of children (those who are young in years and those who have but a small amount of knowledge), in order that they should stay awake[1052], physically as well as spiritually, throughout the *seder*: This begins with the תינוקות [the underdeveloped part] within a person himself not sleeping. On the contrary, they should accomplish their mission, beginning with the asking of the Four Questions, until the conclusion [of the questions] כולנו מסובין ("we all recline"), the matter of freedom.

The[1053] asking of the Four Questions includes the action of את פתח[1054] לו, ("you open for him" [his mouth], regarding the child who "does not know how to ask"), until he too will be able to understand and ask the question of the "wise son".

1049 *Havdalah* liturgy

1050 *Yom Tov* liturgy

1051 *Hisvaaduyos* 5748, vol. 2, p. 444.

1052 *Shulchan Aruch Admor HaZaken, Orach Chaim* 472:1, 472:23.

1053 Ibid. Footnote 120

1054 *Pesach Haggada*

Children and *Gebrachts*

Being[1055] extremely cautious to stay away from *Matzah shruya* (*gebrachts*: *matzah* that has become wet) is also applicable to children, since for *chinuch* purposes they too need to take care to stay away from *gebrachts*. The *tikkun* [for deficiencies in one's *avodah*] and *shlaimus* in this matter applies to them as well.

Each child should have their own *Haggadah*

It[1056] is worthwhile for each person, and especially children, to have their own *Siddur*, *Chumash*, and *tzedakah pushka*, as well as other *sefarim*, and – what is relevant to our time now – a *Pesach Haggadah*... This will add to the child's enthusiasm and motivate the child to use them.

Each [1057] child should have their own...Pesach *Hagaddah* (with pictures).

Stealing the *Afikoman*: A taste of stealing

There[1058] is a custom that small children "steal" the *Afikoman* (and it is ransomed from them through some gift). They say that it is hinted to in the wording of our Sages: חוטפין מצה בלילי פסחים בשביל התינוקות שלא יישנו[1059]. My father-in-law, the Rebbe, related how one time the eldest daughter of the Rebbe Maharash "stole" his *Afikoman*, and she did this at a young age. This was an exceptional case, as such was not the custom in *Beis Harav*. To comment, [according to the] teaching of our Sages, בָּתַר גַּנָּבָא גְּנוֹב וְטַעְמָא טְעֵים ("Steal from a thief and feel the taste [of stealing][1060]")!

Baking *shemurah matzah*

Regarding[1061] what you write about the *mivtzah* of *shemurah matzah* and what I wrote about this in my previous letter... it is understood from the saying of our

---

[1055] *Hisvaaduyos* 5748, vol. 3, p. 111, footnote 258

[1056] *Hisvaaduyos* 5748, vol. 2, p. 480

[1057] *Likkutei Sichos*, vol. 32, p. 26

[1058] *Haggadah Shel Pesach Im Likkutei Taamim, Minhagim U'Biurim*, end of section on יחץ.

[1059] *Pesachim*, 109a; *Chok Yaakov*, 482:2.

[1060] *Gemara Brachos,* 5b.

[1061] *Igros Kodesh*, vol. 19, p. 319.

Sages that more than what the *baal habayis* gives[1062] [he gains through giving]. Specifically regarding *shemurah matzah*, as you surely know as well, my father-in-law, the Rebbe, related[1063] that a number of students underwent an obvious change in essence through being involved in the baking of *shemurah matzah*.

Distributing *shemurah matzah*

I[1064] was very pleased to read what you wrote about the distribution of *shemurah matzah*, and that this was at a school and kindergarten.

Asking the four questions

Surely[1065] you already learned commentaries on the *Pesach Haggadah* and will also ask the Four Questions of *Mah Nishtanah.* Through learning and conducting yourself as said above, you will put yourself into the category of the wise son.

Acharon Shel Pesach

On[1066] *Acheron Shel Pesach*, we are not only lenient in tolerating *gebrachts*, we are scrupulous to eat *gebrachts*! As my father-in-law, the Rebbe, related[1067] about his father, he would display both extreme caution in avoiding *gebrachts* throughout the first seven days of Pesach, and extreme scrupulousness in eating *gebrachts* on *Acheron Shel Pesach*.

We saw this conduct of my father-in-law at his own table. He was scrupulous to eat *gebrachts* during all of the meals on *Acheron Shel Pesach,* beginning with the night meal. He did not do this only once during the meal, or three times, but with each and every food: fish, meat, and especially soup... even foods that during the entire year it is not customary to eat with bread. From this we understand how great an emphasis there is on this matter.

1062 *Midrash Raba Vayikra, 34, Midrash Raba Rus, 5:9.*

1063 *Likkutei Dibburim*, vol. 1, p. 183A.

1064 *Igros Kodesh*, vol. 12, p. 450.

1065 *Igros Kodesh*, vol. 23, p. 155.

1066 *Hisvaaduyos* 5748, vol. 3, p. 171.

1067 *Sefer Hasichos* of the Freirdiker Rebbe 5702, p. 105.

This conduct has become a directive for the general public. It is not reserved for special people, how much more so not only for *Nesi'im* alone. My father-in-law, the Rebbe, instructed all those present at his table to follow his example. They acquiesced not only in his presence, but also outside of his presence. Thus, this has become a directive for the general public, for men, women, and children.

Pesach Sheni

Opportunity for *teshuvah*

On[1068] *Pesach Sheni*, one is given an increased ability to correct and complete one's past conduct (in addition to the recent past, days, weeks, months, and the past year, and so forth). *Pesach Sheni* also has the ability to affect one's entire past, from *bar mitzvah* age and even before this. As the Alter Rebbe writes in his *Shulchan Aruch*[1069] regarding sins one committed as a child: even though he doesn't need to do *teshuvah* when he's older, it is still good for him to take upon himself to do something as a *teshuvah* and *kapparah* (atonement). We find[1070] in some stories of *Gedolei Yisrael* that they corrected matters that had occurred even before they reached an age of comprehension, matters that occurred when they were of nursing age, and even before that, from the moment they entered into the world.

This does not apply only to an inadequacy according to the simple meaning of the word, but even an insufficiency on a higher level: [that the *mitzvah* could have been performed in a better way.] With a bit of contemplation on this matter, each person will come to the conclusion that they could have done certain matters in a better way. Therefore, it is necessary to correct this "inadequacy" too. This applies to one's personal conduct, as well as one's conduct toward others, beginning with his household members and including and especially one's teachers, educators, *mashpi'im, rabbanim*, and so forth. ...

1068 *Hisvaaduyos* 5749, vol. 3, p. 159.

1069 *Shulchan Aruch Admor HaZaken, Orach Chaim,* end of 343.

1070 *Maamarim Haktzarim* of the Alter Rebbe top of p. 409.

It is important to add and emphasize that all of the above applies to each and every Jewish person: men, women, and also children. It is easy to explain to children that certain matters could have been carried out on a higher level. Then they will be motivated to correct and complete things on a higher level. ...

Lag Ba'omer

Judging favorably

There[1071] is a well-known story in the *Gemara*[1072] connected to *Lag Ba'omer*, that the students of Rabbi Akiva died because they did not treat each other respectfully, and on *Lag Ba'omer* they stopped dying.

As with all stories in the Torah, they are Torah and their purpose is to give us an instruction. This story about the students of Rabbi Akiva holds a lesson for each Jewish person, especially students. ... The story of the *Gemara* teaches us how we must conduct ourselves toward each person. ...

It is necessary for each person to look at all those who keep Torah and *mitzvos* with a positive eye, even if his path is a different one; since he is also an *oved Hashem*, the only difference between them is that this one serves with *ahavas Hashem*, and that one serves with *Yiras Hashem*, and so forth. ...

Another lesson in the above story applies even when we meet a person who has not yet reached the level of serving Hashem as he should. He should also be treated respectfully, in accordance with the instruction of our Sages of blessed memory in the *Mishnah*[1073] הוי דן את כל אדם לכף זכות ("Judge each person favorably"), especially when it is possible that the insufficiency [in his service] is not his fault, but that he did not have the opportunity to be educated in the ways of Torah and *mitzvos* for reasons entirely beyond his control. ... As a matter of fact, one should have even greater compassion toward him and make a greater effort to help him to grow in *Yiddishkeit*. The help must be in the best possible manner, out of love and respect, and in a peaceful manner.

1071 *Likkutei Sichos*, vol. 7, pp. 341-343.

1072 *Yevamos*, 62:2.

1073 *Pirkei Avos*, 1:6.

Day of rejoicing

One[1074] needs to make efforts that *Lag Ba'omer,* the *Rashbi's* day of *simchah*, will be *yom simchaseinu,* the day of our rejoicing. This applies to all of *Bnei Yisrael,* wherever they are (in *chutz la'Aretz*, and how much more so in *Eretz Yisrael)* through organizing celebrations and parades and the like, which involve men and women (separately, with the ultimate *tznius* of course) and children.

Especially regarding the children, in accordance with *minhag Yisrael* (which is Torah) going back many generations, on *Lag Ba'omer* the teaching of children is reduced for half or a third of a day, and people go out to (seemingly) celebrate with children in permissible matters (*inyanei reshus*). However, since it is *tinokos shel beis rabban* that we are speaking of (who are getting a proper education), this is done sincerely as a *minhag Yisrael Torah hi*, to the point that this adds to their desire to learn Torah (after *Lag Ba'omer*), and as a preparation beforehand, in their knowing that *Rashbi's* life and essence was all about *Toraso Omanaso*[1075] (his Torah was his main occupation).

Customs for children

[On[1076] *Lag Ba'omer*] there are also special customs for children, including mentioning Rabbi Shimon bar Yochai and his good actions, learning from his instructions in Torah, and making a strong *hachlatah* (resolution) to fulfill it properly and *besimchah*.

[One must also] influence others to do the same. ...

On *Lag Ba'omer*, the day of "his *simchah,*" (as Rabbi Shimon ben Yochai called this day), there should be a gathering in his honor, and one should ensure the organization of parades in one's community, in order to further publicize a Jew's connection with Torah through Rabbi Shimon ben Yochai, who's Torah was "*Toraso Omanaso*" (his main occupation).

[1074] *Hisvaaduyos* 5748, vol. 3, p. 269.

[1075] *Shabbos,* 11:1.

[1076] *Likkutei Sichos*, vol. 32, p. 252.

Kinusim for children

Efforts[1077] should be made to make special *kinusim* for children, with boys and girls separate of course. ...

At these *kinusim*, the great preciousness of Torah should be spoken about in order to implant within the children a love for learning Torah. This matter is especially connected to *Lag Ba'omer*, the *yom hahilulah* of the *Rashbi*, because the *Rashbi* was on a level and in a state of "his Torah is his trade."

Similarly in these *kinusim* the general matter of *ahavas Yisrael* should be spoken about... as was explained by our Rebbeim, our *Nesi'im*, that love of Hashem and love of Torah are one matter.

According to the story in the *Gemara*[1078], after Rashbi and Rabbi Elazar his son went out of the cave... *Rashbi* did not suffice with only learning Torah: he also was involved with improving the world – making efforts to influence others, which fits in with the entire matter of *ahavas Yisrael.*

More than this, *Rashbi* did not wait for others to come and ask him to help them do a certain matter; he himself went out and took an interest to see if all was as it should be... [When it was not] he fixed it. ...

In addition to saying words of Torah at these *kinusim*, the events should be connected as well with the matters of *tefillah* and giving *tzedakah*; these are practical actions in keeping with the matter of *ahavas Yisrael.*

Shavuos

The mother prepares the home spiritually and physically

Since[1079] each and every [woman] is an *akeres habayis*, the entire atmosphere of the home is dependent on her, so clearly it is the case as well with the matter of preparation for the receiving of the Torah anew.

As it is now a few days before the 6th of Sivan, *zman Matan Toraseinu* (the time we receive the Torah), each *akeres habayis* has a special *shlichus* placed

---

1077 *Hisvaaduyos* 5742, vol. 3, p. 146.

1078 *Shabbos*, 33b.

1079 *Hisvaaduyos* 5748, vol. 3, pp. 366-367.

upon her: to establish the way her home will prepare for the receiving of the Torah anew, with a fresh *simchah* and vitality.

Just as the preparation for *Matan Torah* began with the women[1080] (and since this is written in the Torah, it is an eternal lesson for each and every year), so too when we prepare to receive the Torah from Hashem each year, the preparation begins through the women. Each woman succeeds in influencing her family in this path, to such an extent that a few days before *Matan Torah* the entire home becomes permeated with matters of Torah.

The preparations increase with each coming day, just as with the physical preparations for the festival. Beginning a few days before the festival, and as the day approaches, more is added, more vitality, *zerizus* (haste) and *simchah*... until the *Yom Tov* itself arrives and we merit the moment that we bless *Shehecheyanu*.

Bringing all family members to *shul*

The[1081] Torah was given to *Yisrael* in the merit of Jewish children: בנינו עורבים אותנו[1082] ("Our children will be our guarantors"). In each and every place, people should be aroused to make efforts to bring all of the children of *Yisrael* to *shul* during *zman Matan Toraseinu* in order to hear the *Aseres HaDibros*, including the smallest children as well. ...

In order to ease the burden of bringing the entire family to *shul* at once, especially when it is necessary for someone to stay at home, it is possible to divide the shul-going for the purpose of hearing the *Aseres HaDibros* into separate times, either by attending two *shuls* that read the *Aseres HaDibros* at different times, or hearing it at two separate times at the same *shul* as is done in some congregations.

What's more—and this is the main thing—is to explain to children the great importance of receiving the Torah and the need to prepare to receive the Torah in the appropriate way. Even though the giving of the Torah is by *Hakadosh Baruch Hu*... Hashem desires that *Bnei Yisrael* make preparations

---

[1080] *Shemos*, 19, 3, *Rashi*

[1081] *Hisvaaduyos* 5750, vol. 3, p. 252

[1082] *Shir HaShirim Raba parsha* 1:4.

to receive the Torah, so that the receiving of the Torah will take place in the most complete way possible.

Children brought to shul for the reading of the Ten Commandments

All[1083] of *Bnei Yisrael*, including children, should be in *shul* (at least) for the time of the reading of the *Aseres HaDibros*.

To note, the reason *Matan Torah* was able to take place was because the adults promised בנינו עורבים אותנו ("Our children will be our guarantors").

"Our children will be our guarantors"

It[1084] is known that Torah was given on the foundation of "our children will be our guarantors." From this is understood the great abilities that have been given to students in learning Torah and doing *mitzvos*, together with the greatest responsibility of keeping them and passing Torah and *mitzvos* along from generation to generation. As great as is the responsibility, so is the great merit, as we can easily comprehend.

Bein Hameitzarim - *the Three Weeks*

Learning *Hilchos Beis Habechirah*

During[1085] the three weeks, *Bein Hameitzarim*, one needs to add in learning Torah in matters relevant to the time and topics connected to the building of the *Beis Hamikdash*.

First of all, we learn the *halachos* of *Beis Habechirah* in *Rambam*, including *pesukim* in the written Torah. ... As the *Rambam* writes at the beginning of the *halachos* of *Beis Habechirah*: "It is a positive *mitzvah* to make a home for Hashem... as is written, 'Make for Me a *Mikdash*[1086]'"...

[1083] *Likkutei Sichos*, vol. 28, p. 315.

[1084] *Likkutei Sichos*, vol. 13, p. 173.

[1085] *Hisvaaduyos* 5748, vol. 4, p. 50.

[1086] *Shemos*, 25:8.

Children in summer camps should also learn Torah matters connected to this time period, including *Hilchos Beis Habechirah.*

The cure is in the children

There[1087] is a special connection between the *chinuch* of even the smallest children and the days of *Bein Hameitzarim*... As our Sages say[1088], the cure is given before the plague, since this is the way to stop the enemy from striking.

In addition to this, every day the world only exists for הבל תינוקות של בית רבן ("the learning (literally: breath) of little children")[1089].

Likewise, regarding the *chinuch* of *mitzvos* (in addition to learning Torah), the main and essential thing applicable to all of the days of the life of the child is to educate the child... in such a way that even when he grows old he will not depart from it.[1090]

This includes as well (and mainly) the *chinuch* of giving *tzedakah* and *gemilus chassadim.*

...All this is in keeping with the words of the verse: ציון במשפט (עסק התורה) תפדה ושבי' בצדקה ("*Tzion* will be redeemed through justice (involvement in Torah), and those who return to her through *tzedakah*")[1091].

1087 *Likkutei Sichos,* vol. 13, p. 267.

1088 *Megillah,* 13:2.

1089 *Shabbos,* 119b; *Hilchos Talmud Torah Admur HaZakein,* 1:10.

1090 *Mishlei,* 22:6.

1091 *Isaiah,* 15:27, and see *Likkutei Torah* beginning of *Parshas Devarim.*

CHAPTER 20

The Greatest Blessing

"Be fruitful and multiply"

Bereishis, 1:28

The first *mitzvah*

The[1092] order of the Torah itself also contains within it a lesson[1093]. The first *mitzvah* in the Torah is *pru u'rvu*[1094] ("Be fruitful and multiply"). When *Hakadosh Baruch Hu* blesses a couple with a good *shidduch*, good and healthy lives, and a life according to Torah (keeping *taharas hamishpachah*, etc.), it is necessary to do everything possible to fulfill the *mitzvah* of *pru u'rvu.* Each and every child that is born draws down Hashem's *Shechinah* – *veshachanti besocham* – into the heart of the child!

One should make every effort to bring more children into this world

Chana[1095], the mother of Shmuel, was a Jewish prophetess. Some of her prophecies even contained novel matters of prophecy, such as the name צבא-ות and so forth. She wanted to give birth to a child and had *mesirus nefesh* to this end. After he was born, she had *mesirus nefesh* for his *chinuch.* She gave up her custom of going each year to the *Mishkan Shiloh* in order to be able to raise him properly. She named him Shmuel because כי מה' שאלתיו, ("From Hashem I requested him"[1096]).

...From this story we learn, first of all, the extent to which one should make great efforts to turn over worlds in order to give birth to children!

As was previously discussed, it's tremendously important to make efforts to fulfill the *mitzvah* of פרו ורבו ומלאו את הארץ וכבשוה in the most *mehudar* way.

This means that it is not enough even if twelve *shevatim* and a daughter were already born, as we find in the case of Yaakov *Avinu*. This certainly appears to be enough children according to the *Shulchan Aruch*[1097]. Nevertheless, the *pasuk* says, פרו ורבו ומלאו את הארץ וכבשוה, which means to be fruitful and multiply in the manner of כבשוה, (conquering)!

1092 *Hisvaaduyos* 5747, vol. 2, p. 650.

1093 *Likutei Dibburim,* vol. 4, p. 746:1, *Sefer HaSichos* 5701 p. 46.

1094 *Bereishis,* 1:28.

1095 *Hisvaaduyos* 5744, vol. 1, p. 157.

1096 See *Shmuel* 1, Chapter 1.

1097 *Shulchan Aruch Even Hoezer*, 1:5-6.

Therefore, as long as one has not yet fulfilled the *mitzvah kepshuta* (as explained above) – even though one has the excuse that he already fulfilled his obligation according to the *Shulchan Aruch* and so forth – when he engages in a true and honest accounting of his soul (and the woman, of her soul), there is no doubt what conclusion he will reach...

Women do not need to be commanded *pru u'rvu*

A[1098] man needs to be commanded regarding the *mitzvah* of *pru u'rvu* ("Be fruitful and multiply"), because without the command of the Torah he cannot be relied upon that he will be involved in *pru u'rvu* due to his nature. On the other hand, a woman does not need this command, because she senses that her *shlichus* in this world is to be an *akeres habayis* and to establish generations of *Yidden*, and because of these feelings, even without the *mitzvah* she would do this naturally from within herself.

Hashem will provide for the needs of this child

... A[1099] newborn baby is considered an עולם מלא (a whole world). It is not a "big world," "medium world," or "small world," but a "**whole** world," as the world was at the time of the creation of Adam *harishon* in *Gan Eden Mikedem* (in the Garden of Eden before the sin). We learn that each person is an עולם מלא from the fact that Adam was created יחידי (as a single individual on his own) before Chava was created.

...In this vein, even after giving birth to a son and daughter, and even after giving birth to a number of sons and daughters, one should make efforts to give birth to more children, because when one Jewish child is added (even when one already has a number of sons and daughters), the *Mishnah* says that this child is an עולם מלא... Great is the merit of parents who have the privilege to bring into the world another Jewish child, an עולם מלא, in the state of *Gan Eden* before the sin. All of *seder hishtalshelus* is included in this, because its creation was בשביל ישראל שנקראו ראשית ("For *Yisrael* which is called 'first'").

1098 *Hisvaaduyos* 5751, vol. 1, p. 243.

1099 *Hisvaaduyos* 5742 vol. 4, pp. 2291-2292.

From this is understood that parents simply have no reason at all to worry about how they will be able to fulfill all of the child's needs (food, drink, clothing, and so on). A child is like Adam *harishon* in *Gan Eden* before the sin, and it is obvious that no person would think for a moment (even in a very confused world) to ask, "Who will take care of all of Adam *harishon*'s needs in בגן עדן מקדם (*Gan Eden* before the sin)?"

This applies to the spiritual needs of a child as well: his education and upbringing to Torah, *chuppah*, and *ma'asim tovim.* Even when parents have already made efforts to raise a number of sons and daughters involved in Torah and *mitzvos*, they need to toil and make efforts with all of the tumult, commotion, and excitement with this child that was just born. They should not be satisfied that they have already raised a number of sons and daughters involved in Torah, because this child is a "whole world," and not only an ordinary "whole world," but a "whole world" in the state of "*Gan Eden* before the sin"!

When Hashem blesses parents and adds to their holy *shlichus* by depositing in their hands another Jewish child, they need to know that this child is a "whole world" and as such is very dear to *Hakadosh Baruch Hu*, as the Baal Shem Tov teaches that *Hakadosh Baruch Hu* loves each child of *Yisrael* as older parents love their only child who was born to them toward their old age.

According to this, surely Hashem gives parents all of the necessary strength and ability to raise this child: both materially, to satisfy all of the child's physical needs, and so too spiritually, to educate and raise him to Torah, *chuppah*, and *ma'asim tovim.*

It[1100] has been explained a number of times that the purpose of keeping *taharas hamishpachah* is פרו ורבו גו' ("Be fruitful and multiply" and so forth), to raise sons and daughters without making any calculations, but rather out of total reliance on *Hakadosh Baruch Hu*, knowing that when Hashem decides to give His *bracha* in having children, this is the greatest *bracha* and joy that Hashem grants parents.

Clearly, there is no reason at all to worry about the state of *parnassah* when an additional child will be born, because since Hashem has the ability

---

1100 *Hisvaaduyos* 5742, vol. 4, p. 2026.

to provide for an entire world full of four billion people, certainly it is within His ability to provide for an additional child, and many additional children!

It has been discussed a number of times that when an additional child is born, together with him is born the channel and the vessel to draw down his *parnassah*, and therefore this does not diminish the slightest bit *chas ve'shalom* the *parnassah* of all of the other household members. On the contrary, through this is drawn additional *bracha* and *hatzlacha* to all of the family members – the parents, brothers, sisters, and grandparents.

The strength for more children

There[1101] are those who claim that they do not have the needed strength, physically or spiritually, in order to raise many sons and daughters. To do this requires great efforts, both spiritually and physically.

It is necessary to know that since *Hakadosh Baruch Hu* commands in this regard[1102], and "He does not request more than a person is able to do"[1103], it is clear that He gives the necessary abilities to fulfill the command. One should not involve personal calculations, but should rely totally, and with *simchah*, as with everything connected with *avodas Hashem*, on *Hakadosh Baruch Hu*.

It is self-evident that there are situations where, according to Torah, one does not need to be involved in *pru u'rvu* because of health reasons and the like. It is also obvious that this needs to be established through a *rav*, and not just by a person's own calculations.

If it is truly the case that the person does not have the strength [to have another child], *Hakadosh Baruch Hu* will worry about it for them.

The vessel for Hashem's *bracha*

With[1104] regard to the command *pru u'rvu* ("Be fruitful and multiply"), [one should] not [be satisfied with fulfilling it] as *Rashi* interprets, that *pru* ("Be fruitful") can be fulfilled through having only one [child]. One should

---

1101 *Likkutei Sichos*, vol. 25, p. 34.

1102 See *Rambam Ishus,* 15:16.

1103 *Bamidbar Rabbah,* 12:3.

1104 *Sicha* said 1st of Shevat 5741, according to recorded footage.

urvu, ("multiply"), having many children until one "fills the Earth." In order to fulfill this *mitzvah,* two partners are necessary: the mother and father. However, whether the *mitzvah* comes to fulfillment in actuality through the birth of sons and daughters depends on the third Partner: the Creator. Hashem knows when the best time is, not only spiritually, but even physically, for the child, for the mother, and for the father. When one begins to calculate, saying, "I will put this off until tomorrow"... [then] a wondrous story that the *Gemara* tells about Moshe *Rabeinu* [can provide a lesson to be applied in this situation].

In the beginning of *Maseches Brachos*, the *Gemara* says that Moshe *Rabeinu* implored Hashem, "Please inform me of Your ways." Hashem responded, "When I wanted, you didn't want," meaning, "When **I** called upon **you**, and I wanted to make you My *shliach*, you didn't want [to do this]." [The end result] was that Moshe was allowed to see Hashem's "back," but His Face could not be seen. One should not G-d forbid say that Hashem was angry at Moshe *Rabeinu* and that is why He punished him and didn't fulfill his request. Even a person of flesh and blood would not behave in such [an uncharitable] way. Rather, there is a lesson that Hashem wants to teach us here. Hashem wants an individual to feel that he is an active participant in every area, not that we receive the blessings of *Hakadosh Baruch Hu* as a gift from above, as "bread of shame..." When we rely on Hashem and trust that He knows the future as well as the current circumstances in all of their details, then He chooses the best and most auspicious time, the time that is most perfect for the child, the mother, and the father.

However, if one says, "When You want, I don't want...", making calculations, choosing to follow one's own wishes as opposed to relying on the time Hashem chooses, *chas ve'shalom*... Every person, even the greatest person, is limited as to how much he can calculate, know, and predict. The person himself knows just how limited he is.

When one imposes [his own] limitations by saying, in effect, "I don't rely on the time frame You want," not trusting in the will of Hashem, and he waits until his calculations fall into place at a certain time, on a certain day, he may then lack the appropriate vessel to receive "the blessing of Hashem which brings riches." Hashem's blessings are absolute and include spiritual riches as well.

In our context, surely Hashem extends His patience, especially since the person had good intentions in postponing having another child. The person thinks that in order to have a healthy body, failure to interfere with Hashem's plan will lead to harm. This individual believes that whether through the pain of pregnancy or labor or child-rearing, having another child would harm the mother, father, and/or the upbringing of the existing children. The person reasons that having one child after another results in the parents' not tending to them with the proper care.

However, when one examines the reality more carefully, one fact remains: Both parents recite in *Birkas Hamazon* that Hashem "sustains and provides livelihood for all, with goodness, kindness, and mercy." Practically speaking, we see that Hashem has the power to sustain four billion people, because when we say that Hashem "sustains and provides livelihood for all," this refers not only to Jews, but to all of mankind, to all people on earth. Furthermore, this also includes all creatures and the specific food that each and every one of them requires.

Yet, a person can choose to deprive himself of the great privilege that we are granted: that of being a true partner with Hashem. A true partner doesn't make a decision on his own and then insists that the other partners must obey him. Likewise, since the father and mother are partners with Hashem, they may think and even express an opinion, but their decision should follow the opinion of all three of the partners. This is especially true when the third partner is Hashem, Who has expressed His opinion in His Torah, the Torah of life, which provides an instruction for life. It is all explained in the *Shulchan Aruch* which delivers clear *halachic* rulings on this matter.

"Family Planning"

As[1105] has been discussed a number of times regarding the subject of family planning: בהדי כבשי דרחמנא למה לך ("What concern of yours are the mysteries of Hashem?"[1106]). Why should you make calculations on your own as to whether having a child is something worthwhile? And once you yourselves come to a

1105 *Hisvaaduyos* 5744, vol. 1, p. 157-158.

1106 *Berachos*, 10a.

certain conclusion, He may very well do things to prevent and delay it from happening and the like. Even though a person has a *heter* for it... he knows that this is nothing other than an "artificial" means and that this is not the most honest and truthful way to approach the matter!

When people don't get involved with the calculations of *Hakadosh Baruch Hu* – since *Hakadosh Baruch Hu* is the Source of goodness and the Essence of goodness, and the nature of goodness is to do good unto others – in any case, surely Hashem will bring all matters to fruition in the most proper, suitable time and way. If a certain amount of time needs to pass, Hashem will search for the ways to cause this to happen, in ways of pleasantness, without their needing these methods that people use based on their own calculations, practices that have well-known effects materially and spiritually, affecting both the couple and the people surrounding them who look at them...

Difficulties conceiving

At[1107] times, there is a delay in the *bracha* of Hashem for healthy, viable children that comes from a lack of scrupulous and meticulous observance of the laws and regulations of *taharas hamishpachah* (*niddah, hefsek taharah*, immersion in a kosher *mikvah*, and so forth). Since a shortfall in knowledge leads to an inadequacy in the fulfillment, they should clarify all of the details with a *Rav*, with the intention to observe these laws from now on.

It would be proper to check the *tefillin* and *mezuzos* in their home to ensure that they are all kosher according to Jewish law.

Male offspring

... In[1108] response to your letter... to be blessed with healthy, viable sons:

It would be correct for you to increase your efforts in *ahavas Yisrael, ahavas haTorah,* and *ahavas* Hashem *Yisborach.* It is brought down in books of *Kabbalah* and *Chassidus* that "giving birth" to "love" spiritually is a *segulah* for giving birth to actual physical male offspring. One accomplishes the establishment and strengthening of the love spiritually through the contemplating of the

---

[1107] *Likkutei Sichos*, vol. 12, p. 178.

[1108] *Likkutei Sichos*, vol. 12, p. 179.

greatness of Hashem as the *Rambam* states[1109], and this draws down many long, goodly years and a production of physical male offspring. Therefore, until your wife gives birth to a male child, you should resolve *bli neder* to give a franc or two to *tzedakah* every weekday before *davening Shacharis*. It would be appropriate for this *tzedakah* to be associated with feeding poor students. When the child is born, he should be named after my father-in-law, the Rebbe, that name being Yosef Yitzchak. May Hashem *Yisborach* grant you the merit of good tidings in all of the above. …

[1109] *Hilchos Yesodei HaTorah*, beginning of chapter 2

ADDENDUM

More on Teaching Kriya

(Continued from page 128)

Excerpts from Perspective Magazine, by Rabbi Shimon Hellinger

A ladder downward

[*When the book Reishis Daas Sfas Ever (The Beginning of Knowing the Hebrew Language) was published, it became widely popular and became a standard reading curriculum in many undiscerning frum schools. Wherever he went, the Frierdiker Rebbe made people aware of the danger in using those new methods.*]

In[1110] the year 5688 (1928), when I arrived in Riga, Latvia, I spoke at the *yeshiva* called "Torah and Derech Eretz (worldliness)." I told them that the objective must be "Torah with *yiras Shomayim.*"

A child must be taught "*komatz alef uh, komatz beis buh.*" Not like in the curriculum *Reishis Daas*, which is actually void of understanding *(bli daas)* and was initiated by people with inadequate understanding *(kalei hadaas)*.

The most corrupt and immoral among the kings of Israel was Achaz. Our Sages say that he seized (achaz) the *shuls* and *batei midrash* so that there wouldn't be any schoolchildren. His true intent was that the study should follow the "new teaching methods," and omit the study of the nekudos by their names. Learning the nekudos with a child instills holiness in him. The nedukos were given to Moshe Rabbeinu together with "*Anochi Hashem Elokecha*," and they bequest the child the power for *mesiras nefesh*. It is this holiness that Achaz wished to take away.

Yeshaya Hanavi realized that this was the first rung of a ladder of descent which would eventually lead to actual *kefira* (heresy). When he managed to acquire two students and teach them in the correct manner, he no longer feared Achaz, for he knew there would be a future for pure education.

A question of life and death

[Many Yidden were unaware or indifferent to how Alef-Beis was being taught to their young children in cheder or Hebrew school. The Frierdiker Rebbe made it clear that this was a serious matter that required their urgent attention.]

The[1111] letters and *nekudos* of Torah are holy. Komatz contains the spiritual light of *Kesser*, *patach* contains the light of *Chochma*. The holiness of these

---

[1110] *Sefer Hasichos 5704*, p. 156-7.

[1111] *Sefer Hasichos* 5691, p. 159

letters and *nekudos* radiate into the *neshamos* of the children who learn them, so that they will always remain loyal Jews.

This must be publicized amongst *Yidden* everywhere, so that parents know that their child must learn *"komatz alef, patach alef."* Life itself hinges on this matter.

There has risen a new generation of teachers who seek to uproot the kedusha of the letters and nekudos from these children. They present themselves as good and loving people ("*baalei tovah'nikes, ohavei Yisroel*"), who have the children's best interests in mind. I am telling you, *Yidden*, they are your biggest enemies! They are turning these children into *apikorsim*!

Yidden! Remember this well, that it is the *cheder* and the *chinuch* of your child that will determine the future of your entire life, namely, that your child should remain a faithful *Yid*.

Haste makes waste

[Reading experts had challenged the traditional method of learning alef beis, and argued that it held children back and delayed the reading process. At the Purim farbrengen of 5716 (1956), the Rebbe countered that even if it were true, it is irrelevant, for it is learning in the traditional way that fulfills Hashem's desire:]

We [1112] must begin children's education in the correct order – that is, by teaching them Hashem's Torah, according to Hashem's ways. For example, how *alef beis* should be taught…

Do not think that it would be preferable for Hashem's sake to save time by trying to get the child to read sooner by not telling him about the holiness of the letters and the nekudos, so long as he can repeat the words like a parrot...

Time is in Hashem's hands. If we take the time to teach children in line with the holiness of the letters and the *nekudos*, Hashem will compensate the child with longevity and good years, so that he can make up for what he missed, and add even more.

1112 *Toras Menachem*, vol. 16, p. 142; *Sichos Kodesh* 5716, p. 184

Truth Prevails

[When the Frierdiker Rebbe insisted that the alef beis should be taught in the traditional style, it seemed to be a sacrifice of good methodology for the sake of pure chinuch. Only years later did the experts discover that, in the long term, the traditional manner actually brings better results:]

Now[1110] that we are on the threshold of *Moshiach*, when everything becomes much clearer, the methodology experts too have realized the truth, that specifically through teaching the child in the traditional manner will the child succeed, though it may seem that another method is quicker."

[Thirteen years later, in Elul 5742 (1982), the Rebbe reemphasized this point:]

Our[1111] *Rebbeim* instructed to teach children to read, by first teaching them the letters, then the *nekudos*, and only then to blend them together. This is in contrast to the erroneous claim that the traditional method slows the child's development and reading progress. It is not true; in fact the opposite is true!"

[Thus, the Rebbe reveals the underlying reason for the long-term effectiveness of the traditional method: It bequeaths the child with the spiritual potential to understand Torah. While it may take a little longer to read, it will ultimately pay off in years of Torah study.]

Primary and Secondary

[In response to someone who argued that the traditional method was too burdensome, especially for children who are accustomed to the English alphabet, the Frierdiker Rebbe wrote a sharp and lengthy letter:]

The[1112] worst moral offence is to exchange that which is primary for that which is secondary, thereby disgracing the primary function and uprooting it from its place. Especially when they do so with brazenness and pride saying, "I am an expert of education, and I know how to teach Jewish children and to give the proper knowledge of the language."

1110 *Sichos Kodesh* 5729, p. 48

1111 *Toras Menachem 5742. vol, 4m p. 2123.*

1112 *Igros Kodesh Rayatz*, Vol. 7, p. 142

[The Frierdiker Rebbe continues to explain the difference between the dikduk studied by the earlier generations, which began with the correct pronunciation of the holy words, and the dikduk propagated by the maskilim, which approached it as any ordinary language. The Frierdiker Rebbe concludes by writing that although some rabbonim were excited by the maskilim's revival of dikduk, our Rebbeim sensed their unholy motivation and opposed them, and the unfortunate end of that study is widely known today.]

Are you doing it right?

[A common challenge to this notion is the sense that the facts seem to prove otherwise. When looking around we find "products" of the traditional system who have failed. If the traditional system is really superior, what explains all these failures?
This letter of the Rebbe, signed by the Rabbi Chadakov, clarifies that the success of traditional methods is naturally dependent on being implemented correctly.]

On[1113] the subject of teaching *alef beis* the traditional way, or as you put it, "the approach that was the convention in the 'cheder,'" we must really divide this issue into two:

1. The approach itself, which is teaching children the *alef beis* using the proper names, "*alef beis*," etc. in sequential order, and the same for the nekudos, using their names and combining them with the letters in the proper order
2. The means of teaching this approach, namely the methodology, which is a science of its own, since it is necessary to know how to use even the best system, as it's possible for two to employ the same method, and one succeeds while the other doesn't, or worse. So when we witness a lack of success in a particular system, we can't extrapolate to the approach in its entirety, because we have to assess whether the person administering it is aware of the means of using it and whether he is in fact doing so.

Now, on the first count, teaching the *alef beis* in order and so on is based on holy foundations as is well-known, and while this is not the place to do so, you

---

1113 *Igros Kodesh*, vol. 26, p. 234

can certainly locate all the relevant sources. Not only may this approach not be abandoned, but whoever tampers with it is tampering greatly with implanting a sense of holiness in a child's soul.

Even if one could argue (although realistically it isn't true) that learning this way isn't as interesting etc. in comparison with the new systems, it would still not justify retreating from our sanctified approach and employing a new system whose losses outweigh its benefits.

But in truth, when we think into *Chazal's* statements that "Hashem consulted the Torah and created the world," and "Its ways are pleasant ways," it becomes clear that if only the method of teaching *alef beis* according to Torah's instructions was used properly, there would be success not only in matters of holiness, but simply in the very learning and progress of the child. We have seen from experience, that the teachers who became adept in the knowledge of the means and methods of teaching beginner's *kriyah* realized that specifically this approach is the most successful.

For example, I'm aware of a number of teacher training programs in Europe and in the Unites States, which elected for teaching the *alef beis* the traditional way over all the other approaches.

In light of the above, not only should the method not be switched, but the teachers using it should be encouraged, and those who are struggling with it for whatever reason should be directed to experts who, in addition to being G-d-fearing, should be well-versed in how to train these teachers on how to teach their pupils in the best possible way according to this system.

And we're confident that your honor, as an educational counselor on behalf of the [Israeli] Ministry of Education in the religious schools, will investigate and learn more about everything discussed above, and will yourself assist as much as possible in this area, and you'll be from those bringing virtue to the public, the merit of which is great and eternal.

Index

A

B

M

N

O

T

Glossary

Achdus - unity

Adam - rises over his natural inclinations

Adar - twelfth month in the Jewish calendar; the month in which Purim is celebrated

Ahavas Hashem - love of Hashem

Alef: the first letter of the Hebrew alphabet, a silent letter, with a numerical value of 1

Alef Beis, The - the Hebrew alphabet

Aggadah/(Aggados): (lit. "lore or narrative"); the portions of the Talmud and Midrash which contain homiletic expositions of the Bible, parables, stories, maxims, etc., in contradistinction to Halacha

Ahavas Yisrael - love for a fellow Jew

Aidelkeit - refinement

Akeidas Yitzchak - (lit. "the binding"); Avraham's preparation of Yitzchak as a sacrifice

Akeres habayis - the foundation of the home

Aliyah - to ascend, immigration to the Land of Yisrael, The honor of being called up to recite one of the blessings over the Torah.

Alter Rebbe - Rabbi Schneur Zalman of Liadi, 1745-1812, founder and first Rebbe of the Chabad branch of chassidism, known also as "the Rav," and as Baal HaTanya; lived in Li'ozna and Liadi, White Russia; author of Tanya, a classic text of the chassidic tradition, and Shulchan Aruch Harav, a code of Jewish law.

Amen - (lit. "so be it"); response given after hearing a prayer or blessing; expresses concurrence with what has just been said

Amidah, The - (lit. "standing"); also referred to as Shemonah Esrei (Eighteen Benedictions); the main section of prayer, recited standing

Anash - (acronym for anshei shlomeinu, lit., "men of our peace"); the chassidic fraternity; usually refers to the fellowship of the chassidim who follow a specific Rebbe

Arizal: Rabbi Isaac Luria (1534-1572), also known by the acronym "Ari" or "Arizal." Born in Jerusalem, died in Safed. One of the greatest kabbalists of all times, he founded a new school in Kabbalah – the so-called "Lurianic Kabbalah" – which is the basis of almost all mystical works that followed him. He studied with Rabbi Moshe Cordovero, whom he succeeded as the leading mystic of Safed.

Aron hakodesh - holy ark

Asseres HaDibros - the Ten Commandments

Assur - forbidden

Av, month of - the fifth month of the Jewish year, corresponding to July-August; the month in which both Temples were destroyed; also called Menachem Av

Aveirah - (lit. "transgression"); a transgression of one of the laws of the Torah

Avodah (Service of Hashem) - Service; striving; prayer.

Avodas Hashem - service of G-d

Avodah zara - idolatry

Avos - our forefathers

Baal habayis - owner of the home/ one in charge

B"H - Abbreviation of "Baruch HaShem" (lit. "blessed be G-d")

Baal Shem Tov - (lit. "Master of the Good Name"); Rabbi Yisrael ben Eliezer (1698-1760), founder of Chassidism

Bar mitzvah - a Jewish boy who reaches the age of thirteen, the age of adulthood in Jewish life, thus becoming religiously responsible for his own conduct; also refers to the event marking this milestone

Bas mitzvah - a Jewish girl who reaches the age of twelve, the age of adulthood in Jewish life, thus becoming religiously responsible for her own conduct; also refers to the event marking this milestone

Bas Yisrael - Jewish girl

Bayis be'Yisrael - a Jewish home

Be'al peh - by heart

Behiddur (see hiddur)

Bein HaMetzarim: (lit. "between the straits"); refers to the Three Weeks of mourning from the Seventeenth of Tammuz through the Ninth of Av

Beis midrash - place of learning Torah

Beis Hamikdash - the Holy Temple in Jerusalem

Ben - son

Ben chamesh lemikreh - five years old, learns text

Besimchah - in a state of joy

Bencher -

Bitachon - trust in Hashem

Bittul (Self Abnegation; Selflessness) - (lit. "self-nullification"); a commitment to G-d and divine service that transcends self-concern

Binah - Sefirah of understanding

Birkas Hamazon - grace after meals

Bli Neder - lit. "without a promise"; a term used when expressing our intent to do something. Bli Neder is said since it's proper to avoid making a promise or commitment as we may not always (be able to) follow through with it.

Bracha/brachos - (a) ritual blessing recited before eating, the performance of certain mitzvos, and at certain other occasions; (b) a blessing shared with another for good health, etc

Bris milah - circumcision

Chachomim - our Sages

Cholov Yisrael - (lit., "Jewish milk"); a Torah-observant Jew must be present throughout the production of milk products, from milking through processing, to ensure that only milk from kosher animals is used

Chas ve'shalom - G-d forbid

Chayus - (a) liveliness; (b) life-force

Chazal - our Sages

Cheder - (lit. "room"); Torah school for young children

Cheleck Eloka mi'mal mamesh - the soul is a portion of Hashem, literally

Chessed - act of kindness; the sefirah

Chomesh - one fifth

Chiddush - novelty

Chinuch - education, raising a child

Chochmah - Sefirah of wisdom

Chuppah - wedding canopy

Daas - Sefirah of knowledge

Darchei noam - ways of pleasantness

Daven - to pray

Deoraysa - derived from the Torah

De'Rabanan - derived from our Rabbonim

Derech eretz - conducting oneself in a respectful way towards others, halacha, law etc.

Din - Halachic ruling

Dirah betachtonim - Hashem desired to have a "dwelling place in the lower worlds"; the purpose of Creation

Dugmah chayah - living example

Echad Ve'Yachid - Hashem, the One and United One

Ein Sof: (lit. "the Infinite"); used to refer to the infinite dimension of G-dliness

Elokus - G-dliness

Emes - truth

Emuna - faith

Erev - (lit. "evening" or "eve of"); the day or evening preceding Shabbos or the festivals; Friday is often referred to as "Erev Shabbos"

Family Purity - The system of laws which govern Jewish marital life.

Farbrengen - a chassidic gathering

Farbreng: (*Yiddish*) to gather in the chassidic spirit

Fleishik - (*Yiddish*, lit. "of meat"); pertaining to meat or poultry; a category of the kashrus laws

Frum - (*Yiddish*) (a) devout; (b) one who is fully observant of the Torah laws.

Galus (Exile) - exile; diaspora.

Gashmiyus: (lit. "materiality"); material reality (in contradistinction to ruchniyus—spirituality)

Gemach - Acronym for the Hebrew words gemilut chesed--"deed of kindness," a term used for an interest-free loan, or for a fund which distributes such loans

Gemara - (lit. "learning") A reference to the Babylonian Talmud.

Gemilus chassadim - acts of kindness

Geonim - brilliant scholars

Gevurah - the sfirah of strength; severity/restraint

Geulah - redemption

Goy kadosh - holy nation

Hachlata/ hachlatos tovos - resolution

Haftorah - (lit. "concluding portion"); reading from the Prophets at the conclusion of the weekly Torah reading.

Halacha –(lit. "the pathway"); (a) the body of Jewish law; (b) a single law

Haggadah - (lit. "the telling") book that retells the story of the exodus, from which the Passover seder is conducted

HaMelech - The king

HaMotzi - (lit. "Who brings forth"); blessing recited over bread

Hamshachah - the drawing down (of Divine light) from Above

Hashem - (lit. "The Name") G-d

Hashgachah pratis - Divine providence

Hatzlacha - success

Hefsek - an unwarranted interruption (during prayer)

Helem - concealment

Heter - leniency

Hiddur mitzvah - the beautification or enhancement of a mitzvah or meticulous observance of a mitzvah

Hiskashrus - (lit. "connection"); the bond between a chassid and his Rebbe

Horaah - directive

Ikkar - of primary importance

Ikvesa DeMeshicha - (Aramaic) our generation, the time immediately before the coming of Moshiach

Inyan - matter

Imahos - our matriarchs

Issur - prohibition

Kabbalas ol malchus shamayim - accepting the yoke of Heaven, total submission and subordination to the will of G-d

Kadosh - holy

kappara/kapparos - attonement

Kapitel(s) - chapter(s) of Tehillim

Kashrus - The laws of kosher

Kavanos - (lit. "intentions, concentration"); mystical themes for devout meditation during prayer and the observance of the mitzvos

Kavod - honor

Kedusha - holiness

Keilim - (a) (lit. "vessels") the powers which enclothe Divine light and express it in a limited form; the relationship between the keilim and the orot ("lights", the Divine energy) is compared to that between the body and the soul (b) the name of a tractate of the Mishnah

Keli - a vessel or utensil

Kelipah/Kelipos - (lit. "shell") the outer covering which conceals the G-dly light within all creation; hence, the unholy side of the universe

Kelipat Nogah - (lit. "illuminating shell")—Kelipah* that can be utilized for good

Kinus- gathering

Klal Yisrael - the Jewish nation
Kriyas Shema - (See Shema)
Kriyas Yam Suf - splitting of the sea
Koach - a source of energy or force as it exists in a potential state
Kohen - priest, descendant of Aaron, responsible for the service in the Holy Temple
Kohen - the "high priest," or chief of the Kohanim; only he may enter the Holy of Holies
Komatz - one of the Hebrew vowel signs
Kosher - (lit. "fit"); (a) complying with the dietary laws; (b) fit to be used for ritual purpose
L'chatchila - At the outset; a halachic term for the initially recommended or appropriate course of action, as opposed to b'dieved
Lashon hakodesh - Hebrew, the Jewish language
Lashon Hara - forbidden speech
LeChaim! - (lit. "To life!"); A toast or blessing, often exchanged over wine or other strong drink.
Lehavdil - to distinguish, make a separation
Licht - candles
Lishmah - (lit. "for its own sake") an action done for its own sake, and not for the promise of reward; often used in reference to Torah study
Limmud - learning
Maamar - lit. "word" or "essay." Often a reference to a formal discourse of Chassidic teachings delivered by a chassidic Rebbe.
Maariv (evening prayer) - The evening prayer services
Ma'aser - ten percent
Ma'asim tovim - good deeds
Malachim - heavenly hosts, angels
Malcha Meshicha - the king Moshiach
Mashpia (Spiritual Mentor) - (lit. "source of influence"); a spiritual chassidic mentor
Mazal - a) A medium that conveys spiritual influence to worldly beings; in its Talmudic usage, the celestial constellations that serve this purpose. b) The root or main part of the soul, which is not experienced consciously.
Mehudar - (see *Hiddur mitzvah*)
Melamed/melamdim - teacher(s)
Melaveh Malkah - "Escorting the Shabbos Queen"
Mesirus nefesh - lit. "giving of the soul"); self sacrifice
Mesiras ratzon - sacrificing one's personal desires
Mesorah - tradition

Mezuzah - parchment scroll attached to doorpost

Middos - emotional attributes. charachteristics

Midrashei Chazal - teachings of our Sages

Mikvah - ritual pool of water for ritual immersion

Minchah - (lit. "the offering"); afternoon prayer service

Minhag - Jewish custom or tradition

Minhag hamakom - the custom of that community

Mikdash - holy temple

Mishkan - Tabernacle, dwelling place

Mishnah - Oral Law of the Torah compiled by Tannaim under the leadership of Rabbi Yehudah Hanassi

Mitzrayim - the biblical name for Egypt

(Mitteler Rebbe) - (Yiddish, lit. "the Middle Rebbe"); Rabbi Dov Ber of Lubavitch (1773-1827), the second Chabad Rebbe, son and successor of the Alter Rebbe, and uncle and father-in-law of the Tzemach Tzedek

Mitzvah (pl. Mitzvos) - Divine commandment(s) derived from the Torah

Mitzvas asseh - positive commandment

Mitzvas lo taseh – negative commandment

Mitzvos - commandment, means of connecting to Hashem

Mivtzah - mitzvah campaign initiated by the Rebbe

Modeh Ani - first words of the following prayer said immediately upon awakening: "I offer thanks to You, living and eternal King, for you have restored my soul within me; Your faithfulness is abundant."

Moshiach - (lit. "anointed one")—the Messiah

Muktzeh - (Aramaic, lit. "set aside"); an object that may not be moved or handled on Shabbos or the festivals

Mushpa - person who is advised, trained or counsled by a mentor (mashpia)

Mussar - (a) rebuke; (b) Jewish philosophic works dealing with personal conduct and character, and methods for self-improvement in these areas

Nachas - satisfaction, pleasure, usually from children

Nashim tzidkaniyos - righteous women

Nashim z'keinos be'Yisrael - the elder women of Yisrael

Nasi - lit. Prince, leader of the generation

Nefesh - Hebrew for "soul of vitality"; lowest of five levels of the soul

Nefesh Elokis - G-dly soul

Nefesh hakedosha - G-dly soul

Nefesh HaBehamis - Animalistic Soul of a person

Negel Vasser - (Yiddish), or netilat yadayim in Hebrew, a ritual handwashing to remove spiritual impurity from the hands upon rising in the morning, before eating bread, etc.

Nekudos - vowels

Neshamah/Neshamos (plural) - Hebrew for "breath of life"; third-highest of five general souls

Nigleh - revealed dimension of Torah; in contrast to nistar (e.g., Kabbalah and Chassidus)

Niggunim - melody

Nisayon/nisyonos (pl.) - test

Nistar - inner dimension of Torah* (lit. "hidden"); the mystical levels of the Torah (e.g., Kabbalah and Chassidut); in contrast to nigleh

N'shei Yisrael - Jewish women

Olam - world

Olam Habah - the world to come

Olam Hazeh - this world

Opsherenish - when a boy turns three, ritual hair cutting and begins to be careful regarding certain mitzvos

Or - Light, metaphor for Divine energy

Or Ein Sof - Hebrew for "Light of the Infinite"; metaphor for Divine energy used in Creation

Parnassah - livelihood

Parshah - weekly Torah portion

Pasuk/pesukim - verse(s)

Pas akum - bread that is forbidden for a Jew to be eaten

Pasken - halachic ruling

Pas Yisrael - (lit., "Jewish bread") It is preferable to use grain-based products that were cooked or baked with the participation of a Torah-observant Jew

Patach - one of the Hebrew vowel signs

Peyos - sidelocks

Pilpul - sharp analysis

Posek - Rav that makes halachic rulings

Pnimiyus - internal

Pshat - "simple" interpretation of the Torah

Pushka - tzedakah box

Rabbonim - rabbis

Rachamana litzlan - G-d forbid

Ratzon - desire

Rebbe - leader of Chassidim

Rebbetzin - (*Yid*dish) (a) wife of a rabbi or Rebbe; (b) a pious woman of great spiritual achievements

Rosh Yeshivah - academic leader of a yeshivah

Ru'ach - spirit

Ru'ach Hakodesh - (lit. "holy spirit") Divine inspiration

Shechina - Divine presence

Seder, the - (lit. "order"); the order of service observed at home on the first night (first two nights in the Diaspora) of Passover. Plural: Sedarim.

Seder Hishtalshelus - (Chassidic term; lit. "order of evolution"); the chainlike progression of spiritual worlds; the spiritual cosmos

Seudah - meal

Shaar - title page

Shabbos licht - Shabbos candles

Shalom bayis - peace in the home

Sheliach - emissary

Shema - (lit. "hear"); the daily declaration of faith, recited in the morning and evening prayers and before retiring for the night

Shmurah Matzah - (lit. "matzah that has been watched"); matzah prepared under exacting supervision from the time the wheat is harvested through the end of the baking to guard against the minutest moisture

Shlichus - emissaries

Shochet - (lit. "ritual slaughterer"); One who slaughters and inspects cattle and fowl in the ritually-prescribed manner, for kosher consumption

Shofar - Ram's horn sounded during the month of Elul, on Rosh HaShanahh and at the close of Yom Kippur; reminiscent of the ram "tangled in the bush by its horns" during the Binding of Isaac (Genesis 22), the shofar sounded at Sinai (Exodus 19) and the shofar of Moshiach (Isaiah 27:13, etc.)

Shulchan Aruch- code of Jewish Law

Seder Hishtalshelus - the chain of spiritual worlds

Sefer/ sefarim - book(s), sacred book(s)

Segulah - spiritually propitious act

Sifrei kodesh - sacred books

Siddur - prayer book

Simchah - happiness

Siyum - (lit. "completion"); the celebration held upon completing the study of a tractate of Mishnah or Talmud.

Shechinah - Divine Presence

Shemita - Sabbatical year

Shidduch - match
Shir Hamaalos - Psalms
Shlita - (acronym for: ShYichiya L'Aruch Yomim Tovim Amen) "May he live a good and long life"
Shvatim - tribes
Taharas hamishpachah - family purity
Tahor/ tehorah/ taharah - pure/ purity
Tamei - spiritually impure
Tallis katan - (literally: small cloak) four-cornered poncho-like fringed cloak worn by Jewish men and boys beneath their shirts.
Tanach - acronym for Torah (i.e., the Five Books of Moses), Nevi'im (Prophets), and Ketuvim (the "Writings"; i.e., the Hagiographa).
Tehillim - Psalms
Tefillah - Prayer
Tikkun - correction
Toras Emes - the Torah of truth
Teshuvah - repentance
Tumah - spiritual impurity
Twelve Psukim - A campaign begun by the Lubavitcher Rebbe in 1976, children the world over have been urged to learn these 12 Torah verses and sayings of our Sages by heart, with children leading each other in their recitation at youth events and gatherings. Many of Judaism's fundamentals are encompassed in these selections.
Tzaddik/tzaddikim - righteous person
Tzedakah - charity
Tefillah - prayer
Tzivos Hashem - the "army of Hashem", organization for children initiated by the Rebbe to motivate children
Tznius - modesty
Upsherin - (Yiddish, lit. "to cut off"); traditional first haircut of a little boy when he turns three
Yarmulka - kippah, head covering for males
Yechida - Highest aspect of the soul
Yesh - (lit. "there is"); an entity which enjoys seemingly self-sufficient existence, as if independent of its Creator; in the mortal realm, yesh describes a person who is egocentric
Yetzer hara - evil inclination
Yetzer tov - good inclination
Yid/ Yidden - Jews
Yiddishe - Jewish
Yiddishkeit - Judaism
Yiras Shamayim - fear/awe of Heaven
Yisborach - blessed be He

Yom Tov - festival day

Yohrtzeit - (Yiddish lit., "time of year"); the anniversary of someone's passing, observed by the recitation of Kaddish, the study of mishnayos, etc.

Zchus - merit

Zohar - the classic text of the Kabbalah; compiled by 2nd century mishnahic sage Rabbi Shimon ben Yochai

Dedicated in the merit of

Chana bas Keren,
Shalom DovBer ben Keren,
Sarah bas Keren

May you give *Hakadosh Baruch Hu* and the Rebbe *nachas* always, and may you merit to grow up in the *Geulah.*

May we always be blessed with the wisdom and strength to care for you the way *Hakadosh Baruch Hu* wants for His precious *kinderlach*.

Lovingly dedicated in the merit of

Shlomo Nissan ben Shoshana

May he grow to Torah, *chuppa* and *maasim tovim*. May he be a *chossid*, *yirei shomayim* and *lamdan*.

Dedicated in the merit of

Menucha bas Leah

In honor of the

Rebbe and Rebbetzin,

who have revolutionized Chinuch in our generation,
and my dear Parents,

Count & Countess Elkaim,

sheyichyu,
to whom I will be forever grateful
for having dedicated themselves
unreservedly to always giving me the
best Chinuch al taharas hakodesh, and
for being examples of true Chassidim.

Esther Rochel Elkaim

With immense gratitude to Hashem,
we dedicate this to

Shneur Zalman ben Chaya-Bracha,

in whose merit the Anash Chinuch project began.

May he grow to be a *chassid*, a *lamdan* and *yirei shemayim*; May he merit good health and happiness all of his days; May he grow to Torah, *chuppah*, and *maasim tovim*; may he have *arichas yamim* and raise his own *doros* with *simcha* and *tuv leivav*; may he give *Yiddishe* and *Chassidishe* nachas to Hashem and to the Rebbe, and may he be a true shining light and inspiration to all, wherever he goes.

We would also like to thank the Anash Chinuch director and staff for their incredible friendship and *mesiras nefesh*. May you and your families know only goodness, kindness and revealed good all the days of your life and get tremendous, enduring *nachas* from your physical and spiritual children.

This is also in the *zchus* of *Baila bas Feiga* for her highest *zivug b'karov mamash*, for good health and *parnassa tova b'shefa v'l'kavod.*

Dedicated in the merit of

Bracha Chayah bas Refael, a"h

May her *neshamah* have an *aliyah*.

She devoted herself to *chinuch al taharas hakodesh*.

Dedicated in the merit of all of

Klal Yisrael

May we merit the true and complete redemption through our righteous Moshiach speedily in our days.

To our dear

Sarah Mushka,
Naftali Aharon and
Yehuda Menachem
Mendel,

May you have a meaningful life, full
of happiness and revealed *brachot.*
From your loving parents,
Ariel and Chaya Director

Dedicated by

Varda Rivka Solewicz

In honor of her granchildren:

Chana Ester, Shmuel Meir, Levy Yitzchak, Sheina Braina, Chaya Mushka and Isroel Dovid.

May they live be'darkei chassidus with hiskashrus to the Rebbe.

Dedicated in the merit of

Chana bat Avraham

and

Nechama Dina bat Chana

May they grow in the way of
chassidut, in their hitkashrut
to the Rebbe and have a strong
bitachon in Hashem.

Dedicated in the merit of

Chaya-Bracha bas Baila &
Yehoshua Moshe Ben Michla

May they be blessed with *zera chai vekayam* and only revealed *brachos*

Dedicated in the merit of

Chanana Shalom ben

Kasriel David Levine, a"h

May his neshamah have an aliyah.

L'ilui Nishmat

Yosef ben Menachem Mendel
Shimon Baruch ben Shmuel
Rachel Yeshka bas Zeev Wolf
Sara bas Menachem Mendel

In the *zechus* of:

Yehoshua Shneur Zalmen ben Chana, Yitzchak ben Chaya Yitta, Nuchum Meir ben Chaya Yitta, Dovid Yehonoson ben Rifka, Shalom Yehoshua ben Rifka, Chana bas Miriam Yehudis, Chaim Yosef Yitzchak ben Chana, Yaacov ben Chana, and Menachem Mendel ben Chana.

May we all, and for all *doros*, give the Rebbe *Chassidishe Nachas*!

לע"נ

הרה"ת ר' יצחק בן ר' אליהו

נפטר ה' אלול תשל"ט

ולע"נ

מרס בלומא בת ר' יהודה ליב

נפטרה ד' אייר תשס"ו

To my son,

Yosef Shlomo

May you always follow the ways of the Torah and build a beautiful life based on the teachings of our Rebbe.
I love you, Your Mommy

Liluy nishmat my grandparents who have merited to have grandchildren and great grandchildren oskim bTorah ubmitzvos, kein yirbu!
Frajda bas Avrohom Mendel
Yaakov Yisroel ben Shamai
Rayzl bas Pinchos
Yeshaya Yaakov ben Boruch

In honor of our parents
Yisroel Yosef ben Faiga
Sora Pearl bas Malka
Yosef David ben Sara
Yehudit Shulamit bas Tuba Feiga
in appreciation for the Chinuch we received.
May you enjoy much Yiddishe Chassidishe Nachas from all of your descendants.

Dedicated L'ilui Nishmat

Moishe ben a Rab Chayim Klein Z'L

by your grandson and great-grandchildren.

לזכות
מנחם מענדל בן חנה
שמואל דוד בן חנה
מרדכי דובער בן חנה
מנוחה רחל בת חנה
חיה מושקא בת חנה
שניאור זלמן בן חנה
משה בן חנה
שטערנא שרה בת חנה
שיגדלו לתורה לחופה ולמעשים טובים

In memory of

Yisrael Peretz Barton

- Teach each child with love and according to their way

Dedicated to our son, *Nossen Menachem*

and his wife *Ella Jochewed,*

may they be *zoiche* to bring up their children in the Rebbe's *derech*

In memory of

Chana bas Sholom Azimov

by her children and grandchildren

שיגדלו לתורה לחופה ולמעשים טובים

In honor of our grandchildren

Chana, Shalom DovBer & Sarah

Love, Grandmom and Grandpop

לזכות הילד **יוסף שלום** שיחי'

לאריכות ימים ושנים טובות

Dedicated to all the Yiddishe mommies who put in their *koichos* to raise children who will go in the path of Torah and *mitzvos*, in a *chassidishe* way. May Hashem gift us with infinite Yiddishe & *chassidishe naches* from our *kinderlach*.

In honor of our dear children
Sara Debora Bracha & Moshe Tzvi Avraham

L'ilui Nishmas Menachem Mendel ben Shmiel HaKohen

In the *zechus* of
Chaya Mushkah bas Miriam Yehudis

L'illui Nishmat Esir ben Avraham Benjamin and Feigel bat Tuvia Nisan (my beloved parents) Tobolowsky, Hakarat Hatov to the Rebbe

Dedicated in *zechus* of Reuven Yehuda Ben Chaya Mushka. May he grow to be a *chayal* of the Rebbe, a *chossid*, *yarei Shamayim*, and a *lamdan*.

In honor of Shprintza Goldberg, who personifies the teachings in this *seifer* in her work as a *mechaneches* and mother. Dedicated by her husband and children.

וַיִּרְעֵם כְּתֹם לְבָבוֹ וּבִתְבוּנוֹת כַּפָּיו יַנְחֵם
Thank You, Rebbe.

In merit of our children Mushkale, Shalom Ber, Mendel, Menucha Rochel and Avremel Shor. May they bring nachas to the Rebbe.

L'Ilui Nishmas Chaya Mushka Bas Arye Leib
L'Rfuah shleima U'miyadis shel Nechama Leah bas Zelda

In honour of our dear children,
Miriam Bracha, Shaina Rivka, and Menachem Mendel Shulman.

Dedicated with love to one of this generation's true *nashim tzidkanios*,

Shoshana bas Menucha

and her husband,

Daniel Ben Galia

May they be blessed with זרע חי וקיים and only revealed good materially and spiritually